HTML

By

EXAMPLE

que

Todd Stauffer

HTML By Example

© 1996 by Que® Corporation

Library of Congress Catalog Card Number: 96-68582

ISBN: 0-7897-0812-4

98 97 96   6   5   4   3   2   1

Interpretation of the printing code: the rightmost double-digit number is the year of the book's printing; the rightmost single-digit number, the number of the book's printing. For example, a printing code of 96-1 shows that the first printing of the book occurred in 1996.

All terms mentioned in this book that are known to be trademarks or service marks have been appropriately capitalized. Que cannot attest to the accuracy of this information. Use of a term in this book should not be regarded as affecting the validity of any trademark or service mark.

Screen reproductions in this book were created using Capture from Mainstay, Camarillo, CA.

President: *Roland Elgey*

Publisher: *Joseph B. Wikert*

Publishing Manager: *Jim Minatel*

Editorial Services Director
Elizabeth Keaffaber

Managing Editor
Sandy Doell

Acquisitions Manager
Cheryl D. Willoughby

Product Director
Mark Cierzniak

Production Editor
Maureen A. Schneeberger

Editors
Gill Kent
Kathy Simpson
Patrick Kanouse
Elizabeth A. Bruns

Product Marketing Manager
Kim Margolius

Assistant Product Marketing Manager
Christy M. Miller

Strategic Marketing Manager
Barry Pruett

Technical Editors
Jim Minatel
Tobin Anthony

Technical Support Specialist
Nadeem Muhammed

Acquisitions Coordinator
Jane K. Brownlow

Software Relations Coordinator
Patricia J. Brooks

Editorial Assistant
Andrea Duvall

Book Designer
Kim Scott

Cover Designer
Ruth Harvey

Production Team
Marcia Brizendine
Jenny Earhart
Bryan Flores
Trey Frank
Amy Gornik
Daniel Harris
Damon Jordan
Bob LaRoche
Michelle Lee
Casey Price
Kaylene Riemen
Laura Robbins
Kelly Warner
Paul Wilson

Indexer
Brad Herriman

Composed in *Palatino* and *MCPdigital* by Que Corporation.

Dedication

To Mom: In addition to everything else you've given me over the years, thanks for the time, support, help, concern, cash, and, perhaps most of all, your technical writing gene.

About the Author

Todd Stauffer has been writing nonstop about computers since his graduation from Texas A&M University, where he studied English, Management Information Systems, and entirely too much golf. Since that time, he has worked as an advertising writer, freelance magazine writer, and magazine editor—all in the computer industry.

Todd is currently the Internet-issues columnist for *Peak Computing Magazine* and host of the weekly Peak Computing Hour Radio Show in Colorado. He has written a number of other books published by Que including *Using Your Mac, Using the Internet with Your Mac, Easy AOL, Special Edition Using Netscape,* and *Special Edition Using the Internet with Your Mac.*

He does other, non-computer-related things, too—just in case you were concerned.

Acknowledgments

As is generally the case, this book was only brought to fruition by the dedication and hard word of a big chunk of the staff at Que, without whom this project would just be a bunch of random, poorly edited text characters in generic-looking Courier. Thanks especially to Cheryl Willoughby, Mark Cierzniak, Maureen Schneeberger, Jim Minatel, and all the copy editors who worked on this book.

I'd also like to thank the folks at *Peak Computing Magazine* for being so understanding about deadlines, helping me make the transition to Colorado living, and giving me enough money to keep buying Campbell's soup for the duration of writing this book. Editor-in-Chief Laura Austin-Eurich was especially helpful in talking me down out of trees, and I appreciate General Manager Dean Jacobus' willingness to let me sleep through his meetings.

Big thanks to Dad (Chris Stauffer) for buying me dinner and a game of golf every once in a while to keep me sane. (Not to mention helping me through the trauma of tax session.) And, finally, thanks to all my friends back in Texas for calling every once in a while, just to make sure I wasn't dead.

We'd Like to Hear from You!

As part of our continuing effort to produce books of the highest possible quality, Que would like to hear your comments. To stay competitive, we *really* want you, as a computer book reader and user, to let us know what you like or dislike most about this book or other Que products.

You can mail comments, ideas, or suggestions for improving future editions to the address below, or send us a fax at (317) 581-4663. For the online inclined, Macmillan Computer Publishing has a forum on CompuServe (type **GO QUEBOOKS** at any prompt) through which our staff and authors are available for questions and comments. The address of our Internet site is **http://www.mcp.com** (World Wide Web).

In addition to exploring our forum, please feel free to contact me personally to discuss your opinions of this book: I'm **mcierzniak@que.mcp.com** on the Internet, and **76245,476** on CompuServe.

Thanks in advance—your comments will help us to continue publishing the best books available on computer topics in today's market.

Mark Cierzniak
Product Director
Que Corporation
201 W. 103rd Street
Indianapolis, Indiana 46290
USA

Overview

Contents

Contents

Contents

Contents

Part III Interactive HTML

12 Clickable Image Maps and Graphical Interfaces
183

13 HTML Forms
199

Contents

Contents

Contents

Part VI HTML Editors and Tools

Contents

Part VII HTML Examples

30 HTML Examples   481

Appendix

A Answers to Review Questions   513

Index   529

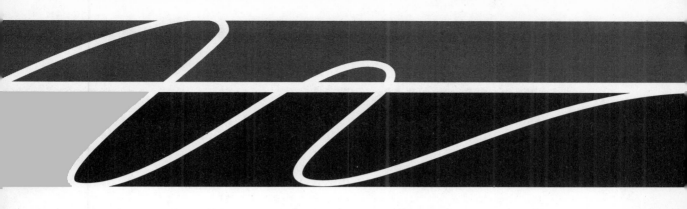

Introduction

If you're ready to jump into the world of creating HTML pages, you've found the right book—regardless of your previous experience with programming or the World Wide Web. That's because *HTML by Example* uses a "hands-on" approach to creating Web pages that will make learning HTML a pleasure. Forget about tired reference manuals or overly technical treatises that make HTML actually seem difficult. It's not! If you've got a text editor in DOS, Windows, OS/2, Mac, or a UNIX variant, the only other tool you need is this book. Now you're ready to create your presence on the Web.

What's the *by Example* Advantage?

There are two major reasons why learning HTML is easier when it's *by Example*. First, HTML isn't a typical programming language—in fact, it isn't a programming language at all. It's a "mark-up" language that builds on very basic concepts that are all somewhat related to one another. Learning by example, then, allows you to start with the initial concepts and learn to build to make complex Web pages come to life easily.

Second, with the included CD-ROM, *HTML by Example* gives you a major headstart in Web creation. Why? Because if you see an example that's similar to what you want to create, just copy the example from the CD and alter it to suit your needs. It's possible to have a Web page created within minutes of finding a suitable example! Just copy and paste.

Who Should Use This Book?

Before you get to the point of actually creating HTML documents (Web pages), you'll go through a little refresher course on the Internet and the World Wide Web. So, even if you're not terribly familiar with the Web, I'll try to get you there before throwing any strange codes or address at you.

Essentially, all you need to use this book is a rudimentary grasp of the Internet and Web, and a desire to create your own presence. If you've just "heard" of the Web, or even if you've been surfing for a while and want to know more about Web page creation, you've found the right book.

Programmers and graphic artists will also find this book useful for making the transition to the Web—although I should make the point that Web design is not in any way as complicated or cerebral as programming. For the basics (and even for the best looking Web pages), no programming expertise is required. Later in this book, you'll learn how to make your pages "cutting-edge" with emerging tools like JavaScript. But even for that, programming is not a prerequisite.

Why Should I Learn HTML?

The World Wide Web is easily the fastest growing part of the Internet, and thousands of new sites are added daily. As business and commerce begin to embrace the Web more fully, HTML skills are a wonderful enhancement to any résumé.

Creatives like writers, designers, and artists should also be learning more about the Web. The commercial art and advertising worlds are already making this transition to the new medium, and you should be getting yourself ready for it as well. A solid understanding of HTML will take you a long way into the future of your craft.

By the same token, nearly any computer professional should have some notion of how HTML works and why the Web is based on it. But that doesn't mean it takes a scientist to create Web pages. Office workers, editors, public relations specialists, salespeople, real estate agents, financial advisors, and consultants of all flavors should all have a Web presence, and can benefit from doing it themselves.

And the Web is so diverse that it's impossible to categorize all the reasons to learn HTML page creation. Home office pages, small businesses online, family photo sessions, and even hobbyists are all hanging their shingle on the Web—and finding new contacts, comrades, and cohorts in the process. And perhaps the most important reason to learn about HTML is to find out that it simply isn't that difficult to master. This book will give you a wonderful reason not to pay $150 an hour for Web services.

What Tools Do I Need?

For the approach you're taking to Web creation, all y(
program like Windows 95 Notepad, WordPad, the Ma
Emacs on UNIX platforms. Any basic ASCII text editor will wo

There are a number of HTML editing programs that are beginning to a
both in shareware and commercial versions, but you're not going to start with them.
(Some of the more popular of these are discussed in the final chapters of this book.)
The reasoning is simple—even the most advanced HTML editors require an
understanding of HTML if you're going to create anything more than the most
rudimentary of pages. It's still an industry in its infancy, and you're much better off
if you know what you're doing.

Once you're through with this book (which shouldn't take long!) and you've got
a solid grasp of HTML, feel free to try out some of the graphical HTML editing
programs. They'll make creating basic pages much easier—although you still have
to fire up your text editor to get some of the sophisticated design accomplished.

You'll also need a stand-alone (i.e., not part of an online service) Web browser
program or two for viewing and critiquing your documents. If you don't have a
Web browser program (like Netscape Navigator or Microsoft Internet Explorer),
some popular versions are available on the included CD-ROM. You don't necessarily need an Internet connection for most of this book, since you'll be dealing with
files that you create or copy from the CD-ROM.

How This Book Works

Each chapter starts by explaining a particular concept, giving examples in "snip-
pets" of HTML markup as you go along. Once you've got that concept under your
belt, you'll be ready to work with a full-blown example. You can either type in the
example or copy it from the CD—some of the examples will also suggest that you
modify the text to make it more suitable for you personally. When you're done, you
can simply view the document in your Web browser, if appropriate.

The key to the organization of this book is simple: it builds. You'll start out very
simply, by going over Web concepts and creating basic pages. From there, you'll
learn the various "standards" of HTML and how to decide which one is right for
you. Then, you'll work from that foundation to learn the latest in HTML and Web
developments, including all of the current codes for Netscape, Internet Explorer,
and HTML 3.0 level development. Finally, you'll end with a look at virtual reality
on the Web and do a little programming in JavaScript.

You'll also notice that nearly every chapter includes review questions and exercises to help you reinforce what you've learned. If you gave up review questions in grammar school, that's fine. Just skip to the next chapter. If you'd like to make sure you've covered all the material, though, the "Summary" section will help you know for sure that you're ready to move on.

Overview of Chapters

This books is divided into logical parts and chapters to help you find the lessons that are most appropriate for your knowledge level. What follows is a description of each part of the book, including a look at each chapter.

Part I: Internet, Web, and HTML Fundamentals

Chapter 1, "What is HTML?," introduces you to the fundamentals of creating documents for the Web. Chapter 2, "The World Wide Web and Web Servers," discusses the different conventions used to addressing computers, servers, and services on the Internet. Chapter 3, "How Web Browsers Work," takes a look at how the typical Web browser program reads HTML documents that you create, and what you need to consider to create better pages.

Chapter 4, "HTML's Role on the Web," is concerned with the different standards for HTML, and it helps you decide what's best to use on your pages. Chapter 5, "What You Need for a Web Site," rounds out this introduction with a discussion of the arrangements you need to make to make your Web pages visible to the online world.

Part II: Creating Basic Pages with HTML 2.0

This section discusses creating the basic Web page with HTML 2.0 standard commands. Chapter 6, "Creating a Web Page and Entering Text," and Chapter 7, "Changing and Customizing HTML Text," show you how to get started with your Web document and emphasize regular text. In Chapter 8, "Displaying Text in Lists," you learn the various types of HTML list that can be used to organize text in a more readable way.

Chapter 9, "Adding Graphics to Your Web Pages," is your first look at adding basic images to enhance your Web page presentation. Chapter 10, "Hypertext and Creating Links," and Chapter 11, "Using Links with Other HTML Tags," show you how to get serious about your Web pages by adding clickable hypertext links.

Part III: Interactive HTML

Here's where things really start to get fun. Still using only HTML 2.0 elements (although these are not all supported by every Web browser anymore), we take three chapters to discuss making your Web site truly interactive. In Chapter 12, "Clickable Image Maps and Graphical Interfaces," we discuss creating images that move your user around the Web site. Chapter 13, "HTML Forms," and Chapter 14, "Form Design and Data Gathering with CGI Scripts," shows you how to gather information from your users, whether it's for statistical data, online ordering, or just for fun.

Part IV: Page Layout and Formatting

These chapters move you out of the HTML 2.0 standard and into some of the more recent additions to HTML. Coverage includes HTML 3.0 level standards and HTML elements added by the popular browsers Netscape Navigator and Microsoft Internet Explorer.

In the HTML 3.0 discussion, you get Chapter 15, "Adding Tables to Your Documents," Chapter 16, "Images, Multimedia Objects, and Background Graphics," and the exciting new standard for adding clickable images to any Web page in Chapter 17, "Client-Side Image Maps." Chapter 18, "Other HTML 3.0 Proposals," is a catch-all chapter for some of the HTML 3.0 commands you may be seeing in the near future.

Next up are the Netscape-specific commands. Although some of these are slowly being adapted by other browsers, at the time of this writing they aren't "official" standards, so we set them off on their own. In Chapter 19, "Netscape HTML," you learn about the appearance-oriented additions that make Netscape pages standout from HTML 2.0. Chapter 20, "Netscape Frames," shows you exactly how to use the exciting new frames interface that's sweeping the Web.

Chapter 21, "Internet Explorer Extensions," takes a quick look at some of the additions offered by Microsoft's entry in the browser wars. These commands are specific to Microsoft and have yet to be incorporated into an official standard.

Part V: Internet Programming and Advanced Web Technologies

In this section of the book, you delve into some of the most cutting-edge and exciting technologies to be introduced to the World Wide Web. Chapter 22, "Using Java and JavaScript," and Chapter 23, "JavaScript Objects and Functions," are an easy-to-follow look at the world of JavaScript, showing you how to do your own programming in one of the most advanced scripting languages available for Web developers.

Chapter 24, "Understanding VRML and Creating VRML Objects," and Chapter 25, "Creating VRML Worlds," show you how to use a standard text editor to create 3D virtual reality worlds for use on your Web pages. Chapter 26, "Adding Portable Documents to Web Sites," introduces you to the concept of portable documents and offers advice for creating your own "nearly-free" portable documents for distributing on the Web.

Part VI: HTML Editors and Tools

In this section, we discuss some of the more popular applications for creating Web pages quickly and easily. As Web development becomes more popular, the tools become more advanced. Chapter 27, "Creating HTML Documents with Netscape Gold," introduces you to the all-in-one solution to Web browsing and editing from Netscape Corp. Chapter 28, "Using Microsoft Internet Assistant," discusses Microsoft's powerful (and free) HTML add-on for Microsoft Word. Chapter 29, "HTML with Adobe PageMill for Macintosh," takes a look at the tool that many feel may soon change the way you look at HTML and the Web.

Part VII: HTML Examples

This last part of the book has only one chapter, Chapter 30, "HTML Examples," but it's a long one. Here, you'll take a look at two completely different reasons to create a Web site: personal and business. In each, you'll review some of the basic and advanced Web concepts you've encountered throughout the book. The best part is that all of these pages are on the included CD-ROM. If you find a page that does something you want to add to your Web site, then just copy it from the CD and alter it to suit your needs!

Conventions Used in this Book

This books uses the following typeface conventions:

Typeface	Meaning
Italic	Variables in "pseudocode" examples and HTML terms used the first time
Bold	Text you type in, as well as URLs and addresses of Internet sites, newsgroups, mailing lists, and Web sites
`Computer type`	Commands, filenames, and HTML tags

> **Note:** Notes provide additional information related to a particular topic.

> **Tip:** Tips provide quick and helpful information to assist you along the way.

Icons Used in this Book

 Pseudocode is a special way of explaining a section of code by using placeholders, set in italic. In this book, pseudocode usually precedes a code example and is indicated by this icon.

The Other Advantage

In my experience writing computer-oriented books, I've found that one advantage I can offer might be more valuable to many readers than nearly any other. That advantage is my personal e-mail address. I will take any question, concern, praise, or complaint you have about this book, and its examples, errors, or anything else that comes up. Write me at **tstauffer@aol.com** via the Internet or **TStauffer** on the America Online service.

It is very important to me that you are satisfied with everything you come across in this book. If you get through a chapter and review questions and still have trouble with a concept, do not hesitate to send me an e-mail and ask about it. I'll return your e-mail as quickly as possible. I don't want you wasting time on a concept that I've explained poorly or on an error (however impossible) that I've made. So write before you lose too much time hitting yourself over the head.

Also, I'll continue to post updates, errata, and anything else that might be of interest on my personal Web site, currently located at **http://members.aol.com/ tstauffer/**. That address may change in the future, but I'll do my best to leave a link to the new address, if and when it changes. For now, at least, that page on the Web will be a great place to stop by and check on *HTML by Example* developments.

Part I

Internet, Web, and HTML
Fundamentals

## CHAPTER 1

What is HTML?

The explosive growth of the World Wide Web is relatively unprecedented, although it resembles the desktop publishing revolution of the early and mid-1980s. As personal computers became more common in homes and offices, people began to learn to use them for document creation and page layout. Although early word processing programs were not terribly intuitive and often required memorizing bizarre codes, people still picked them up fairly easily and managed to create their own in-house publications.

Suddenly, the same kind of growth is being seen as folks rush to create and publish pages of a different sort. To do this, they need to learn to use something called the *Hypertext Mark-up Language* (*HTML*).

HTML at a Crossroads

HTML and the World Wide Web in general are currently in a stage of development similar to that of the desktop publishing revolution. Still working to reach maturity as a standard, HTML is feeling the same growing pains that early word processing programs did—as more users flock to HTML, there is a growing need to standardize it and make it less complex to implement.

These days, word processors are much more intuitive than they were 15 years ago. There are fewer codes and special keystrokes required to get something done. The applications have matured to the point where most of the low-level formatting is kept hidden from the user of the application. At the same time, the printed page is now more completely mirrored on the computer screen, with accurately represented fonts, emphasis, line breaks, margins, and paragraph breaks.

Although programs are quickly being developed to offer similar features for HTML development, these tend to be less than ideal solutions. Currently then, anyone who decides to learn HTML is going to have to know some codes, memorize some syntax, and develop pages for the World Wide Web without the benefit of seeing all the fonts, emphasis, and paragraph breaks beforehand.

But anyone who has had any success with word processing programs of ten or 15 years ago (or desktop publishing programs as recently as five years ago) will have little or no trouble learning HTML. Ultimately, you'll see that HTML's basic structure makes a lot of sense for this emerging medium—the World Wide Web. And, as with most things computer-oriented, you'll find that once you've spent a few moments with it, HTML isn't nearly as difficult as you might have originally imagined.

HTML is not a Programming Language

There's nothing I'd like more than to say: "Yes, HTML is a very difficult programming language that has taken me years to master. So I'll have to charge $75 an hour to develop your Web pages for you." Unfortunately, it's simply not the case. As I've already hinted, creating an HTML document is not much more difficult than using a ten-year-old copy of WordPerfect with the Reveal Codes setting engaged.

> **Tip:** Remember the definition of HTML: Hypertext Mark-up Language. In HTML itself, there is no programming—just the "marking up" of regular text for emphasis and organization.

In fact, I prefer to call people who work with HTML "designers" or "developers," and not programmers. Actually, there's only limited design work that can be accomplished with HTML (especially the most basic standards of HTML), and anyone used to working with FrameMaker, QuarkXPress, or Adobe PageMaker will be more than a little frustrated. But the best pages are still those created by professional artists, writers, and others with a strong sense of design.

As Web page development matures, we are starting to see more concessions to the professional designers, as well as an expansion into realms that do require a certain level of computer programming expertise. Creating scripts or applets (small programs) in the Java language, for instance, is an area where Web page development meets computer programming. It's also a relatively distinct arena from HTML, and you can easily be an expert in HTML without ever programming much of anything.

The basics of HTML are not programming, and, for the uninitiated in both realms, HTML is much more easily grasped than are most programming languages. If you're familiar with the World Wide Web, you've used a Web browser like Netscape, Mosaic, or Lynx; and if you have any experience with a word processor or text editor like WordPad, Notepad, SimpleText, or Emacs, then you're familiar with the basic tools required for learning HTML.

A Short HTML History

HTML developed a few years ago as a subset of *SGML* (*Standard Generalized Mark-up Language*) which is a higher-level mark-up language that has long been a favorite of the Department of Defense. Like HTML, it describes formatting and hypertext links, and it defines different components of a document. HTML is definitely the simpler of the two, and although they are related, there are few browsers that support both.

Because HTML was conceived for transmission over the Internet (in the form of Web pages), it is much simpler than SGML, which is more of an application-oriented document format. While it's true that many programs can load, edit, create, and save files in the SGML format (just as many programs can create and save programs in the Microsoft Word format), SGML is not exactly ideal for transmission across the Internet to many different types of computers, users, and browser applications.

HTML is more suited to this task. Designed with these considerations in mind, HTML lets you, the designer, create pages that you are reasonably sure can be read by the entire population of the Web. Even users who are unable to view your graphics, for instance, can experience the bulk of what you're communicating if you design your HTML pages properly.

At the same time, HTML is a simple enough format (at least currently) that typical computer users can generate HTML documents without the benefit of a special application. Creating a WordPerfect-format document would be rather difficult by hand (including all of the required text size, fonts, page breaks, columns, margins, and other information), even if it weren't a "proprietary"—that is, nonpublic—document format.

HTML is a public standard, and simple enough that you can get through a book like this one and have a very strong ability to create HTML documents from scratch. This simplicity is part of a trade-off, as HTML-format documents don't offer nearly the precision of control or depth of formatting options that a WordPerfect- or Adobe PageMaker-formatted document would.

Marking Up Text

The most basic element of any HTML page (and, therefore, any page on the Web) is ASCII text. In fact, although it's slightly bad form, a single paragraph of regular text—generated in a text editor and saved as a text file—can be displayed in a Web browser with no additional codes or markings (see fig. 1.1). An example of this might simply be:

```
Welcome to my home on the World Wide Web. As you can see, my page isn't
completely developed yet, but there were some things I simply had to say
before I could get anything else done. My name is Emmanuel Richards, and
I'm a real estate developer located in the San Fernando Valley. If you'd
like, you can reach my office at 555-4675.
```

Note: Although possible, you would never want to display plain text on the Web without conforming to certain HTML conventions, which are explained in Chapter 6, "Creating a Web Page and Entering Text."

Figure 1.1

Text is so basic to HTML that it can be displayed in a Web browser with no additional commands or codes.

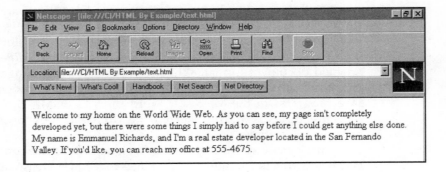

Remember that HTML-formatted documents aren't that far removed from documents created by a word processing program, which are also basically text. Marking up text, then, simply means you add certain commands, or *tags*, to your document in order to tell a Web browser how you want the document displayed.

One of the most basic uses for HTML tags is to tell a browser that you want certain text to be emphasized on the page. The HTML document standard allows for a couple of different types of emphasis including explicit formatting, where you choose to make something italic as opposed to bold, or implicit formatting, where it's up to the browser to decide how to format the emphasized text.

Using part of the example above, then, an HTML tag used for emphasis might look something like this:

```
Welcome to <EM>my home</EM> on the World Wide Web.
```

In this example, <EM> and </EM> are HTML tags that tell the Web browser which text (in this example, my home) is to be emphasized when displayed (see fig. 1.2).

Figure 1.2

HTML tags can be used to mark certain text for emphasis.

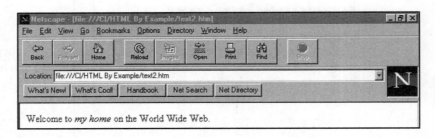

The browser isn't just displaying regular text; it has also taken into account the way you want the text to be displayed according to the HTML tags you've added. Tags are a lot like margin notes you might make with a red pen when editing or correcting term papers or corporate reports. After you've entered the basic text in a Web document, you add HTML mark-up elements to tell the browser how you want things organized and displayed on the page.

You'll learn more about the specific types of tags in Chapter 6, "Creating a Web Page and Entering Text," but for now, the most important distinction is between text and HTML tags. All HTML documents will be basically text, as are all word processing documents and most desktop publishing documents. The only difference, then, is how the text is described for display on the screen (or, in many cases, for a hard copy printout).

In most word processing documents, the "mark up" that describes the emphasis and organization of text is hidden from the user. HTML, however, is a little more primitive than that, as it allows you to manually enter your text mark-up tags to determine how the text will appear. You can't do this with an MS Word document, but, then again, MS Word documents aren't the standard for all Web pages and browsers on the Internet!

Who Decides What HTML Is?

It's difficult to pin down exactly who is responsible for the HTML standard and its continued evolution. While what may be the most important question is who uses HTML, and how they use it, a number of groups exist to monitor, brainstorm, and try to pin down the standards as they evolve.

The HTML Working Group

The HTML standard is maintained and debated by a group called the HTML Working Group, which, in turn, is a creation of the Internet Engineering Task Force. The Working Group was charged in 1994 with the task of defining the HTML standard that was in widespread use on the Web at the time (known as HTML 2.0), and then submitting proposals for future standards, including the HTML 3.0 standard.

Up until the spring of 1996, the Working Group seemed to be the bearer of the basic standard for HTML around the world, while others work to agree on standards for other Web-oriented technologies that have a cursory relationship— like graphics formats, digital movies, sounds, and emerging Web languages such as Java and VRML (Virtual Reality Modeling Language). Now, nearly all responsibility for future Web development will most likely fall to an industry cooperative called the W3 Consortium.

The World Wide Web Consortium

HTML was originated by Tim Berners-Lee, with revisions and editing by Dan Connolly and Karen Muldrow. Up until the time when the Working Group took over responsibility for the standard, it was largely an informal effort.

Still very much involved in the evolution of the standard is Tim Berners-Lee, who now serves as director of the World Wide Web Consortium (W3C)—a group of corporations and other organizations with an interest in the World Wide Web. The group is run by the Laboratory for Computer Science at MIT, and includes members such as AT&T, America Online, CompuServe, Netscape Communications Corp., Microsoft Corp., Hewlett Packard, IBM, and many others.

Here, member organizations get together to iron out differences over Web-related standards and practices while working to maintain some level of standardization between their products. Corporate self-interest can sometimes get in the way, but it is definitely of utmost importance to most of these organizations that their products stay abreast of the most popular standards, and that their customers are fully able to take advantage of the Web.

Individual Companies and HTML

In the meantime, HTML continues to evolve, sometimes in spite of standard-bearing organizations. As more and more commercial companies take an interest in the HTML standard, it has become increasingly difficult to know who, exactly, decides what HTML will become in the future.

Some notable deviations from the standard are the *extensions*, or additional commands, that Netscape Communications Corp. has added to HTML 2.0 (see fig. 1.3). Only Netscape's browsers (and those written to be compatible with Netscape's products) can view all of these extensions, and some of them have yet to be recognized by the HTML Working Group. Netscape can get away with this, though, since it controls somewhere around 60 percent of the World Wide Web browser market.

With that sort of influence, Netscape can sway the hearts and minds of members of the W3 Consortium to some degree—plans for future HTML specifications often take into account the additions made by companies such as Netscape.

Other companies, notably Microsoft, have also distributed Web browsers—in Microsoft's case, the Internet Explorer—that offer enhancements over the agreed-upon HTML standards, and acceptance of those extensions by a majority of Web designers may further sway groups like the HTML Working Group.

Figure 1.3

Aside from being able to view most of the HTML standard tags recognized by the HTML Working Group, Netscape Navigator can also display text in special ways.

Centered text

Text wrap around graphics

Right-justified graphics

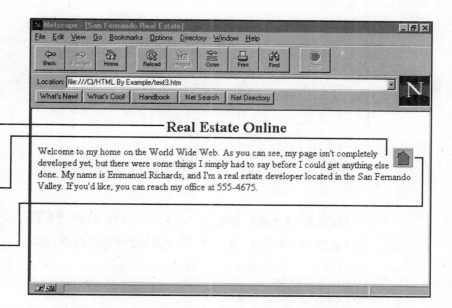

What is the IETF?

The Internet Engineering Task Force (IETF) is a fairly loose organization of people interested in affecting the growth and infrastructure of the Internet. It is the main group engaged in the creation of new Internet standards and specifications.

The first IETF meeting was held in January 1986 in San Diego, and drew 15 attendees. The IETF now meets in a variety of locations, including meetings held occasionally in Europe and elsewhere around the world. Meetings and participation are completely voluntary, and anyone can attend meetings, which are held three times a year.

Although there is no formal or legal power behind the specifications created by the IETF, they are often reasonable and useful enough that they are adopted by the Internet community as a whole. The Internet, perhaps more so than many other computing communities, relies on useful and widely available standards in order to reach the greatest number of people.

The IETF's role in the future of HTML is a little vague, since it seems that most Web-related development efforts have been shifted to the W3 Consortium, with the emphasis seemingly on cooperation between the competing corporate standards emerging on the Web.

Anyone can also join the IETF announcement mailing list or the IETF discussion list (**ietf@cnri.reston.va.us**). This is where the broadest Internet discussions are held (most working groups have their own mailing lists for discussions related to their work). To join the IETF announcement list, send an e-mail with the word *subscribe* in the body to **ietf-announce-request@cnri.reston.va.us**.

To join the IETF discussion list, send an e-mail with the word *subscribe* in the body to **ietf-request@cnri.reston.va.us**.

To join the discussion list for the HTML Working Group, send a blank e-mail message to **www-html-request@w3.org**.

Additional Information on HTML Standards and Organizations

Most of the HTML standard bodies and organizations maintain an active presence on the World Wide Web, and information about these groups and their work can be found in many places.

For more on the World Wide Web Consortium, consult the W3C Web site at **http://www.w3.org/**. This site will probably be the most useful as you continue to learn more about HTML and emerging new standards.

For more information on the IETF, point your Web browser to the URL **http://www.ietf.cnri.reston.va.us/home.html**. This is the IETF's home on the Web, offering tons of links to related projects as well as information about meetings and other Internet-related groups.

To learn about the HTML Working Group, take a look at **http://www.ics.uci.edu/pub/ietf/html/**. Here, you'll find a little about the history of HTML, who the current members and officers of the Working Group are, and how to contact the group.

Information about Netscape and Netscape's additions to HTML can be found at **http://www.netscape.com/**.

Summary

HTML is a document format, somewhat like word processing or desktop publishing formats, but considerably less complicated and based on more open standards. Creating HTML programs isn't really programming—although some programming can be necessary in other aspects of Web page creation. There are a few different organizations that make it their business to oversee the HTML standard, but the standard can just as easily be affected by the software companies that write Web browsers. The standard is also influenced very much by what commands and layout features Web designers implement, and what commands they ignore.

Review Questions

1. Is HTML a programming language?

2. True or false. HTML documents can be created with nothing more than a text editing program.

3. What other mark-up language is HTML based on?

4. What's the difference between explicit formatting and implicit formatting?

5. True or false. You can directly edit a WordPerfect-format document.

6. Is the HTML Working Group a subsidiary of the World Wide Web Consortium?

7. Why is it important that HTML be a public standard?

8. How can individual Web designers affect the HTML standard?

## CHAPTER 2

The World Wide Web and Web Servers

Probably the most important thing to remember about the World Wide Web and the Internet in general is that they are global in scale and often a very cooperative venture. Information on the Web tends to be distributed around the world, and it's just as easy for you to access a site in New Zealand or Japan as it is to access Web information in your own state.

The basic reason for learning HTML is to create pages for the World Wide Web. Before you start, though, you'll want to know a little about how this whole process works. We'll begin by taking a look at Web browsing programs, then we'll talk about how the World Wide Web works, and we'll discuss some of the terms associated with surfing the Web. Finally, we'll round out the discussion by talking about the Internet in general and the different services available on the Internet and how they interact with the Web.

What's the World Wide Web?

The World Wide Web is an Internet service, based on a common set of protocols, which allows a particularly configured server computer to distribute documents across the Internet in a standard way. This Web standard allows programs on many different computer platforms (such as UNIX, Windows 95, and the Mac OS) to properly format and display the information served. These programs are called Web browsers.

Note: Notice that the Web is composed of different *sites* around the world. A site is basically just a collection of HTML documents that you can access with your Web browser. HTML documents offered for viewing by Que Corporation (**http://www.mcp.com/que**), for instance, are organized in a site. I personally have created a Web site that people can visit to read about me, my books, and writing services.

The Web is fairly unique among Internet services (which include Internet e-mail, Gopher, and FTP) in that its protocols allow for the Web server to send information of many different types (text, sound, graphics), as well as offer access to those other Internet services. Most Web browsers are just as capable of displaying UseNet newsgroup messages and Gopher sites as they are able to display Web pages written in HTML (see fig. 2.1).

Figure 2.1

Here's a Gopher site as displayed through Netscape Navigator.

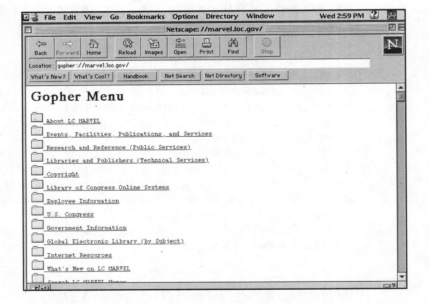

This flexibility is part of what has fueled the success and popularity of the Web. Not only do the Web protocols allow more interactive, multimedia presentations of information, but the typical Web browser can also offer its user access to other Internet resources, making a Web browser perhaps a user's most valuable Internet application.

How the World Wide Web Began

The Web protocols were first created by Tim Berners-Lee when he was with the European Laboratory for Particle Physics (also know as CERN). His initial goal was to allow other physics groups and labs to collaborate over the Internet, but others soon began implementing the protocols for their own uses.

Mosaic, the first graphical browser for the Web, appeared in 1993, at a time when there were not many more than 50 HTTP (Web) server computers running in the world.

The arrival of Mosaic and similar browsers caused an explosion in the popularity of the Web (and arguably, of the entire Internet) because of their ability to display graphics and other multimedia elements. Within nine months, the number of Web servers had jumped to over 300.

In 1994, the World Wide Web Consortium (W3C) was formed by interested corporate and educational entities to combine their resources and continue creating standards for the Web. The W3C continues to be largely responsible for negotiating standards and creating technology to enhance data transfer on the Web.

The Hypertext Concept: Web Links

Unlike any other Internet service or protocol, the World Wide Web is based on a concept of information retrieval called *hypertext*. In a hypertext document, certain words within the text are marked as *links* to other areas of the current document or to other documents (see fig. 2.2). The basic Windows help engine (and many other online help programs) uses this same hypertext concept to distribute information.

As you can see in the figure, links can be text or graphics. The user moves to a related area by moving his or her mouse pointer to the link and clicking once with the mouse button. This generally causes the current Web document to be erased from the browser's window, and a new document is loaded in its place.

Note: Links can point to another part of the same document, in which case clicking the link will cause the browser to move to a new part of the currently displayed document.

Consider then, that this hypertext concept will affect the way that information is presented and read on the Web. A normal printed book (like this one) presents its information in a very linear way. Hypertext, on the other hand, is a little more synergistic.

Figure 2.2

Typical hypertext links in a Web document.

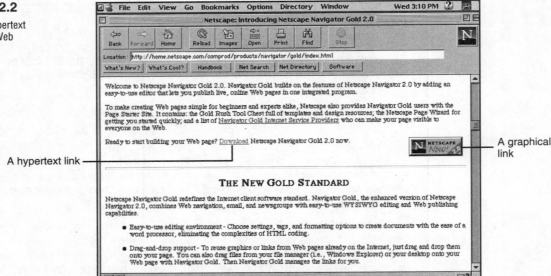

A hypertext link ——

A graphical link

On the World Wide Web, this synergy can be taken to an extreme. For instance, you might use hypertext to define a word within a sentence. If I see the following example on a Web page:

```
The majority of dinosaurs found in this region were herbivores, and
surprisingly docile.
```

then I can assume that the word *herbivores* is a hypertext link. That link might take me to a definition of the word herbivore that this particular author has provided for his readers. This link might also take me to a completely different Web site, written by another person or group altogether. It might take me to a recent university study about herbivores in general, for instance, or a drawing of a plant-eating dinosaur done by a ten-year-old student in Australia.

Example: Thinking in Hypertext

For just a moment, imagine you're reading a hypertext document instead of a printed page.

If, for instance you were reading a Web page about my personal hobbies, you'd find that one of the things that interests me most is **private airplanes**. Clicking that link might take you to a new Web site dedicated to the discussion of personal aircraft, including a link to **Cessna Aircraft**'s Web site. Once there, you could read about Cessna's particular offerings, prices, and perhaps a **testimonial** offered by a recent satisfied customer. Clicking this link whisks you away to that customer's personal Web site, where you read his accolades for Cessna, and then notice he's a professor at **Yale**, and has provided a link for more information. Clicking the Yale link takes you to the university's Web site, where you can see different sorts of information about registration, classes, research projects, alumni, faculty, and other interesting tidbits.

This offers important implications for HTML writers. For one, you've got to take into consideration this particular style of presenting information. Also, building a good Web site often means being aware of other offerings on the Web, and creating links to other people's pages that coincide with or expand upon the information you're presenting.

The Web Page

The World Wide Web is composed of millions of Web *pages*, each of which is served to a browser (when requested) one page at a time. A Web page is generally a single HTML document, which might include text, graphics, sound files, and hypertext links. Each HTML document you create is a single Web page, regardless of the length of the document or the amount of information included (see fig. 2.3).

Figure 2.3

A typical Web page as viewed through Netscape Navigator.

The name of the HTML document

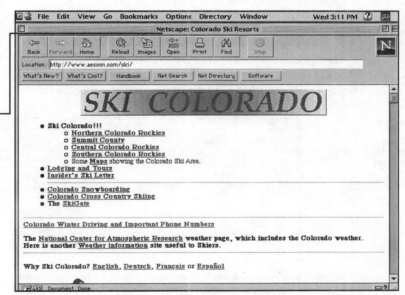

The Web page in figure 2.3, for example, contains more information than can be shown on the screen at one time, but *scrolling down* the page (by clicking the scroll bar to the right of the browser window) reveals the rest of that particular Web document—note, though, that scrolling doesn't present you with a new Web page.

> **Tip:** Most browser programs have a text box at the top of the screen that tells you the name of the HTML document being displayed. HTML document names will end with the extension .HTM or .HTML.

The Web Site

A Web site, then, is a collection of Web pages under the control of a particular person or group. Generally, a Web site offers a certain amount of organization of its internal information. You might start with an *index* or *default* page for a Web site, and then use hypertext links to access more detailed information. Another page within the Web site may offer links to other interesting sites on the Web, information about the organization, or just about anything else.

Web site organization is an important consideration for any HTML designer, including those designing and building corporate Web sites. The typical corporate Web site needs to offer a number of different types of information, each of which might merit its own Web page or pages.

Example: A Corporate Web Site

The typical corporate Web site will start with an index page that quickly introduces users to the information the site has to offer. Perhaps *index* is a misnomer, as this page will usually act as a sort of table of contents for the Web site (see fig. 2.4).

Figure 2.4

This corporate index page offers links to different parts of the Web site.

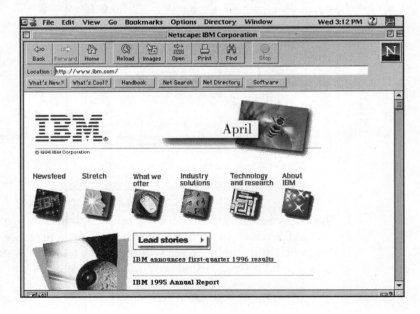

The rest of the pages within a hypothetical corporate Web site will be accessed from a similar index page, allowing users to move directly to the information they want. If users are interested in getting phone numbers and addresses for a company, for instance, they might click a link that takes them to an *About the Company* page. If they're interested in the company's products, they'd click another link that would take them to a product demo page (see fig. 2.5).

Figure 2.5

Organizational chart for a basic corporate Web site.

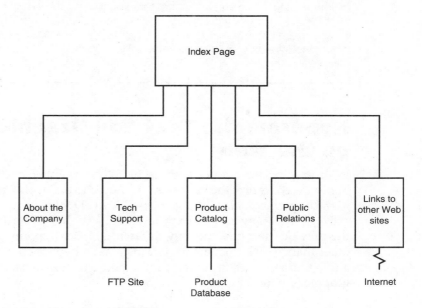

By organizing the site in this way, the designer makes sure that users can get to every Web page that's part of the site, while allowing them to go directly to the pages that interest them most.

Intranets vs. the Internet

Another use of HTML and Web technology worth talking about is the growing popularity of *intranets*, or Internet-like networks within companies. In the Web organizational chart discussed in this section, notice that most of the information presented is geared toward the external users.

This same technology can be applied to Web sites for internal uses, allowing employees to access often used forms, company news, announcements, and clarifications. For instance, the Human Resources department might make available job listings and addresses on the Internet, but would discuss changes to the company's health insurance policies on their intranet.

In fact, many companies are even using HTML to create "front ends" to corporate databases and other shared resources. Using a Web browser application, employees can access data stored on the company's internal network. This takes some programming expertise (usually using CGI-BIN scripts, discussed in this book), but the majority of the work is done in HTML.

Fortunately, designing intranet sites and Internet sites isn't overwhelmingly different. The skills you'll gain in this text will be equally applicable to both. The only real difference is a question of organization and the type of information you'll want to offer on your intranet—generally, it's the sort of thing that's not for public consumption.

Hypermedia: Text and Graphics on the Web

With graphical browsers such as NCSA Mosaic and Netscape Navigator, the hypertext concept of the Web was introduced to the world of multimedia, resulting in the hypermedia links that are possible in HTML.

Now, this really isn't much different from the hypertext links we talked about in the previous section—the only difference is that hypermedia links point to files other than HTML documents. For instance, a hypermedia link might point to an audio file, a QuickTime movie file, or a graphic file such as a GIF- or JPEG-format graphic (see fig. 2.6).

Figure 2.6

Hypermedia links are simply hypertext links that lead to non-HTML documents.

A link to a sound file ——

A link to a graphics file ——

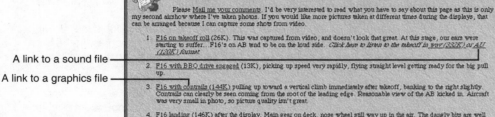
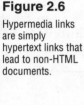

> **Tip:** A hypermedia link can be identified by the fact that the associated file has something other than an `.HTM` or `.HTML` extension.

Because of the flexibility of the Web protocol, these files can be sent by a Web server just as easily as can an HTML document. All you need to do is create the link to a multimedia file. When users click that link, the multimedia file will be sent over the Web to their browser programs.

Helper Applications

Once the multimedia file is received by the user's Web browser, it's up to the browser to decide how to display or use that multimedia file. Some browsers have certain abilities built in—especially the basics, such as displaying graphics files or plain ASCII text files. At other times, browsers will employ the services of a helper application (see fig. 2.7).

Figure 2.7

Examples of Web browser helper applications.

Audio helper application

Video-player helper

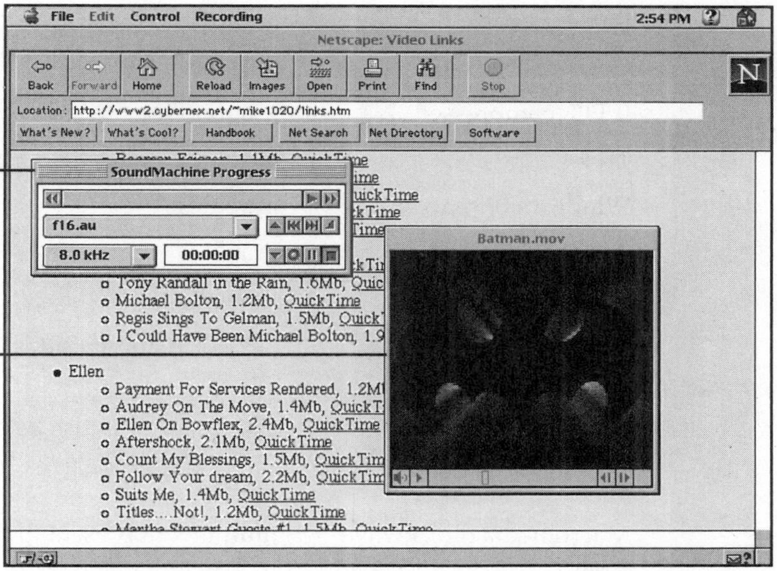

Most of these helper applications will be add-on programs that are available as commercial or shareware applications. The browser will generally need to be configured to recognize particular types of multimedia files, which, in turn, will cause the browser to load the appropriate helper application. Once loaded, the downloaded multimedia file will be fed to the helper applications, which can then play or display the multimedia file.

Common Multimedia Formats

Although it seems that multimedia formats are constantly being added and improved for the Web, some of the more common types of multimedia files are listed in Table 2.1 with their associated file extensions. This list isn't exhaustive, but it should give you an idea of the types of files that can be distributed on the Web.

Table 2.1 Multimedia Formats Common to the Web

File Format	Type of File	Extension
Sun Systems sound	audio	.au
Windows sound	audio	.wav
Audio Interchange	audio	.aiff, .aifc
MPEG audio	audio	.mpg, .mpeg
SoundBlaster VOiCe	audio	.voc
RealAudio	audio	.ra, .ram
CompuServe GIF	graphics	.gif
JPEG (compressed)	graphics	.jpg, .jpeg
TIFF	graphics	.tif, .tiff
Windows Bitmap	graphics	.bmp
Apple Picture	graphics	.pict
Fractal Animations	animation	.fli, .flc
VRML	3D world animation	.wrl
MPEG video	video	.mpg, .mpeg
QuickTime	video	.mov, .moov, .qt
Video For Windows	video	.avi
Macromedia Shockwave	multimedia presentation	.dcr
ASCII text	plain text	.txt, .text
Postscript	formatted text	.ps
Adobe Acrobat	formatted text	.pdf

Not all of these different file formats necessarily require a special helper application. Many sound helpers will play the majority of different sound files, for instance, and some graphics programs can handle multiple file types. For the most part, you will need different helper applications for the various video, animation, and formatted text file types.

Internet Services and Addresses

Aside from being hypertext-based and capable of transferring a number of multimedia file formats, the Web is unique in its ability to access other Internet services. Being the youngest of the Internet services, the Web can access all of its older siblings, including Internet e-mail, UseNet newsgroups, Gopher servers, and FTP servers. Before we can access these services, though, we need to know what they do and how their addressing schemes work.

Internet E-mail

Internet e-mail is designed for the transmission of ASCII text messages from one Internet user to another, specified user. Like mail delivered by the U.S. Post Office, Internet e-mail allows you to address your messages to a particular person. When sent, it eventually arrives in that person's e-mail box (generally an Internet-connected computer where he or she has an account) and your recipient can read, forward, or reply to the message.

Internet e-mail addresses follow a certain convention, as follows:

username@host.sub-domain.domain.first-level domain

where *username* is the name of the account with the computer, *host* is the name of the computer that provides the Internet account, *sub-domain* is an optional internal designation, *domain* is the name assigned to the host organization's Internet presence, and *first-level domain* is the two- or three-letter code that identifies the type of organization that controls the host computer.

An example of a simple e-mail address (mine) is **tstauffer@aol.com,** where **tstauffer** is the username, **aol** is the domain, and **com** is the first-level-domain. *com* is the three-letter code representing a *commercial* entity. This e-mail address describes my account on the America Online service, which is a commercial Internet site. (See Table 2.2 for some of the more common first-level domain names.)

Table 2.2 Common First-Level Domain Names

First-level domain	Organization Type
.com	Commercial
.edu	Educational
.org	Organization/Association
.net	Computer Network
.gov	Government
.mil	Military Installation
.ca	Canadian
.fr	French
.au	Austrailian
.uk	United Kingdom
.jp	Japanese

You may have also noticed that my address doesn't include a host name or a sub-domain. For this particular address, it is unnecessary because America Online handles all incoming Internet e-mail through a gateway. Once it receives the e-mail, it may indeed send it to another computer within its online service, but this is an internal operation that doesn't require a specified host in the Internet address.

Consider **todd@lechery.isc.tamu.edu**. This is an address I had a few years ago when I worked at Texas A&M University. (I no longer receive e-mail at this address.) Notice how it uses all of the possible parts of an Internet address. **todd** is the username, **lechery** is a host computer (in this case, an actual, physical computer named "lechery"), **isc** is a sub-domain name that represents the computers in the Institute for Scientific Computation, **tamu** is the domain name for all Internet-connected computers at Texas A&M University, and **edu** is the three-letter code for *educational*, which is the type of organization that Texas A&M is considered to be on the Internet.

When is a Host a Server?

The Internet community uses the words *host* and *server* when talking about the type of computers you'll encounter. But what do these names mean?

I like to use the analogy of a party. At a party, a host or hostess will welcome you into his or her home and point you to the various things you can do at the party. He or she will show you where to put your coat, point you to the refreshments, and tell you about their home.

Now, depending on how large or lavish the party is, you may also have servers. Servers will perform more specific tasks, like bringing you beverages or food, opening the door, taking your coat, or moving furniture around. At a small party, the host may act as a server. At a larger party, the host will coordinate the servers.

That's how hosts and servers work on the Internet. A host computer is generally a computer that allows its local users to gain access to Internet services. It may also allow other users to gain access to information in its organization.

Depending on the size of the organization's Internet site, however, the host often doesn't *serve* that information itself. Instead, it relies on server computers that have more specific functions, like serving HTML documents, serving shareware programs, or serving UseNet news. These servers will be accessed through the host, though, so it's really only important to know the host's address on the Internet—just like in the real world.

UseNet Newsgroups

The next Internet service we'll talk about is UseNet newsgroups. These are the discussion groups on the Internet, where people gather to post messages and replies on thousands of topics ranging from computing to popular entertainers, sports, dating, politics, and classified advertising. UseNet is a very popular Internet service, and most Web browsers have some built-in ability to read UseNet discussion groups.

Note: Although you'll hear the word "news" a lot when you talk about UseNet, there isn't an overwhelming number of newsgroups that offer the kind of news you expect from a newspaper or CNN. In general, UseNet is comprised of discussion groups like the forums on CompuServe or the message areas on America Online.

Like Internet e-mail, UseNet discussion groups have their own system of organization to help you find things. This system uses ideas and syntax that are similar to e-mail addresses, but you'll notice that UseNet doesn't require that you find specific hosts and servers on the Internet—just a particular group. UseNet newsgroup names use the following format:

first-level name.second-level.third.forth...

The *first-level name* indicates the type of UseNet group this is, the second narrows the subject a bit, and the address continues on until it more or less completely describes the group. For instance, the following are both examples of UseNet newsgroup addresses:

co.general

comp.sys.ibm.pc.misc

The first-level name **co** means this is a local UseNet group for the Colorado area, and **general** shows that it's for discussion of general topics. **comp** is a common first-level name that suggests this is an internationally available newsgroup about some sort of computing issue (see Table 2.3). The other levels of the name tell you more about the group.

Table 2.3 Common UseNet First-Level Newsgroup Names

First-Level Name	Description
alt	Alternative groups
biz	Business issues
clari	Clarinet news stories
comp	Computing topics
misc	Other general discussions
news	General news and help about UseNet
rec	Recreational topics
sci	Scientific discussions
soc	Social issues
talk	Debate-oriented groups

Gopher and WAIS

Gopher has been described as the poor man's Web, and it's definitely true that Gopher is a precursor to some of the Web's capabilities. Gopher is a system of menu items that link sites around the world for the purpose of information retrieval. This isn't a hypertext system like the Web, but it is similar to the Web in that it's designed for document retrieval (see fig. 2.8).

Figure 2.8

Accessing Gopher
menus with
TurboGopher for
Mac.

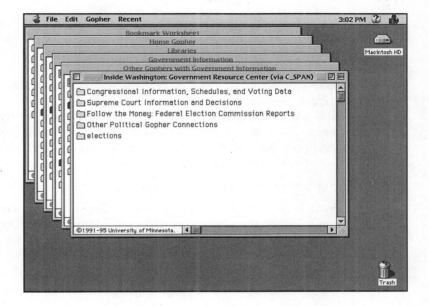

While Gopher can only offer access to text files and allow you to download files using the FTP protocol, it is still used occasionally by academic, government, and similar sites. Fortunately, your Web browser can easily offer Gopher access too, so there's no need to have a separate application.

WAIS, or *Wide Area Information Servers*, are basically database servers that allow you to search databases that are attached to Gopher menus. Library databases, academic phonebooks, and similar information are kept in WAIS systems.

Gopher and WAIS both generally require that you have the exact address of the Gopher server available to you. These addresses are in the following form:

host.sub-domain.domain.first-level domain

This works essentially like an e-mail address without a username. All the Gopher application needs to know is the exact Internet location of the Gopher server computer you'd like to talk to. An example might be **marvel.loc.gov.** This takes you to a Gopher menu for the Library of Congress.

FTP

The File Transfer Protocol (FTP) is the Internet service that allows computers to transfer binary files (programs and documents) across the Internet. This is the *uploading/downloading* protocol that you might use to obtain copies of shareware or freeware programs, or that might be useful for downloading new software drivers from a particular computer hardware company.

Using a model identical to the Gopher system, FTP addresses use the following format:

host.sub-domain.domain.first-level domain

Like Gopher addresses, an FTP address is simply the Internet address of a particular host computer. In fact, the same host address can be used to serve you both Gopher documents and FTP file directories, based on the type of protocol your access software requests. The following example is the FTP address for downloading support and driver files for Apple Macintosh computers and Apple-created Mac and Windows software:

ftp.support.apple.com

In most cases, FTP connections also require some sort of *login* procedure, which means you'll need a username and password from the system administrator to gain access. The majority of public FTP sites, however, are anonymous sites, which allow anyone access to their files. For these sites, the username is generally **anonymous**, and you're asked to enter your e-mail address for the system's password.

> **Note:** Many Web browsers can access only anonymous FTP sites. You may still need a dedicated FTP program to access FTP sites that require an account username and password.

Summary

The World Wide Web is the youngest and most unique of the Internet services. Its protocols allow it to transmit both text and multimedia file formats to users, while also enabling Web browsers to access other Internet services. The Web is based on a concept called hypertext, which means that text within the paragraphs on a Web page is designed to act as links to other Web pages. There is no hierarchy on the Web, which is only loosely organized by this system of links.

Other services that can be accessed via the Web include Gopher, WAIS, UseNet, e-mail, and FTP. Each of these older Internet services has its own scheme for formulating addresses. Most of these services require a server computer of some sort to allow Internet applications to access their information. These server computers have specific addresses on the Web which you need to know in order to contact them.

Review Questions

1. The Web protocols are considered flexible by Internet standards. Why?

2. What does *hypertext* mean? Where else might the typical computer user encounter hypertext?

3. True or false. Hypermedia links are hypertext links to newswire stories.

4. What makes a Web site different from a Web page?

5. What is the purpose of having helper applications?

6. Why are file extensions important to Web browsers?

7. Among UseNet, Internet e-mail, Gopher, and FTP, what two Internet services use similar addressing schemes?

8. What should you enter as the password to an anonymous FTP Site?

Review Exercises

1. If you have an Internet account or an account with an online service, use your e-mail address to determine your service's domain name and first-level domain.

2. If you have an FTP application, see if your ISP offers an FTP site. Try the address: **ftp.*ispdomain.first-level domain***. An example might be **ftp.service.net**.

3. Using your Web browser, attempt to connect to a Gopher address like **marvel.loc.gov**. What happens?

## CHAPTER 3

How Web Browsers Work

HTML codes are written specifically for display in browser applications designed for the World Wide Web. Unlike some other document formats or specifications, this is the only application for HTML coding. So it's important to get to know these browsers.

In this chapter, you'll be learning about some popular Web browser applications, how Web browsers interact with Web servers, and how browsers interact with the other Internet services that are available to them.

Web Browser Applications

All Web browsers are capable of certain basic tasks, like finding and loading new Web pages, and displaying them following HTML standards and conventions. There's enough freedom in HTML and the Web standards in general, though, that each Web browser ends up being slightly unique.

As you look at these browsers, I'd like to make one point clear: although most of them display HTML documents in a particular way, each browser application actually has quirks or features that you should keep in mind while you're creating your documents.

> **Note:** This book cannot provide an exhaustive survey of the Web browsers available. It is fair to say that I'm covering about 90 percent of the current market, but you should recognize that there are other browsers being used to access HTML pages.

NCSA Mosaic

Originally released by the National Center for Supercomputing Applications (NCSA) in 1993, Mosaic was the first widely available graphical browser for Web users (see fig. 3.1). It is currently written for Windows, Windows 95, Macintosh, and various UNIX platforms. It is also the basis of a number of other browsers on the market—most notably those created and licensed by SpyGlass Corp.

Figure 3.1

NCSA Mosaic for Windows 95.

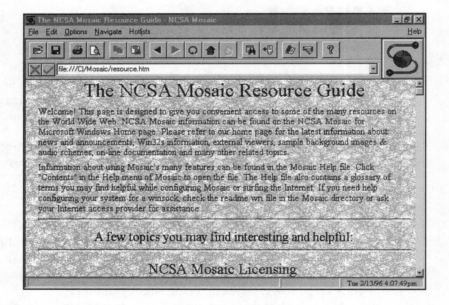

Although definitely in widespread use, the Mosaic family of browsers is nowhere near the most popular of Web browsers, losing by a significant share of the market to Netscape Navigator. Mosaic has its merits, though, especially as a straight HTML standards-based Web browser known for being relatively well-programmed and effective.

One of the most compelling reasons to use NCSA Mosaic might just be that some versions are free to academic and nonprofit organizations and individuals. It can be downloaded from **http://www.ncsa.uiuc.edu/SDG/Software/SDGSoftDir.html** or by FTP at **ftp://ftp.ncsa.uiuc.edu/**.

Netscape Navigator

Easily the most popular Web broswer currently available, Netscape Navigator (often simply referred to as Netscape) made a splash on the Internet in 1995 with its totally free first version of the application. Created in part by programmers who had worked on the original NCSA project, Netscape became quickly known as the finest second-generation Web browser, noted for both its flexibility and speed gains over Mosaic—especially for modem connections.

Another reason for Netscape's popularity is its ability to accept *plug-ins*, or helper applications, that actually extend the abilities of the Netscape Navigator browser window. Netscape users who have the Macromedia Shockwave plug-in, for instance, can view Macromedia presentation files that are embedded within HTML documents in Navigator's window (instead of loading a separate helper application).

Netscape is also available for Windows, Mac, and UNIX users and is available free to certain qualifying (nonprofit and academic) users (see fig. 3.2). It can be downloaded on the Web from **http://home.netscape.com/comprod/mirror/client_download.html** or by FTP at **ftp.netscape.com**.

Figure 3.2

Netscape
Navigator for
Macintosh.

When introduced, Netscape's main advantages were speed and the ability to display more graphics formats than Mosaic. Since that time, however, Netscape has introduced security features and other technologies (like a built-in e-mail program and built-in UseNet newsreader) that continue to set it apart from other browsers.

Another advantage is the support of Java applets and JavaScript authoring within Netscape itself. Again, Java applets can be embedded in the Netscape browser window, allowing the user access to truly dynamic pages that can be an interface for anything from simple games to stock quotes to bank-by-computer information. JavaScript gives Web designers programmatic control over their pages, allowing them to check HTML form entries, load different pages based on user input, and much more.

Perhaps most significant to HTML writers, however, is yet another addition that Netscape offers beyond Mosaic—Netscape HTML extensions. These are extra HTML-like elements that Netscape can recognize in Web pages. Although a good deal of debate has raged about whether or not this is ultimately a good thing for the Web (see sidebar), it remains a fact that a Web site can be designed in such a way that although most browsers can display the page's basic text and graphics, it is best viewed in Netscape Navigator.

Why is this? Netscape adds many HTML elements that offer more control over the layout of a page than the HTML standard allows. This includes such features as centering text and graphics, wrapping text around figures, and adding tables to Web pages. These elements are not found in HTML 2.0, although their popularity on the Web has caused many of them to be incorporated into HTML 3.0 level standards.

Are Netscape HTML Commands Good for the Web?

When Netscape first introduced its extensions to HTML, two strong reactions came from opposite sides of the playing field. Experienced HTML designers—especially those interested in more control over the pages—said, "Cool." Defenders of the original HTML, however, were not as pleased.

Why would you be against HTML extensions? Because using them leaves a large percentage of Web users out in the cold. If people begin to write their Web pages using Netscape HTML extensions, suddenly at least 40 percent of the Web's users will see a less-than-ideal version of the site.

Clearly, adding the extensions was shrewd marketing on Netscape's part. After all, if you want to see the best layouts on the Web, all you have to do is get a copy of Netscape.

But for some users, like those using NCSA Mosaic, the America Online Web browser, or some other popular Web application, they're just out of luck. The extension won't display correctly in their browsers and, in some cases, will cause errors.

Purists will point to the Netscape HTML extension as going against the spirit of HTML. HTML is supposed to offer less control over a page, so that it can be platform- and application-independent. Netscape HTML, by definition, flies in the face of this spirit.

Fortunately for everyone, new HTML 3.0 level standards are emerging that support many of the Netscape HTML commands in a more "official" way. That means the best of both worlds—layout features and total compatibility—as more browsers come to support HTML 3.0 level additions.

In the meantime, will Netscape strike again with some other innovation? Don't be too surprised if it does.

Microsoft Internet Explorer

Recently released for free to the general public is the Internet Explorer, a Web browser created by Microsoft Corp (see fig. 3.3). Loosely based on the Mosaic technology, Internet Explorer is a reasonably well-featured browser with decent speed for modem users. Microsoft's browser is available for Windows 95, Windows 3.1, and Macintosh platforms. It can be found on the Web at **http://www.microsoft.com/IE/** or by FTP at **ftp.microsoft.com**.

Figure 3.3

Microsoft Internet Explorer for Windows 95.

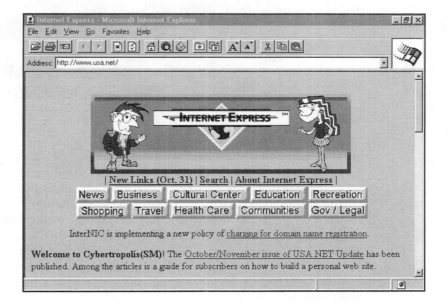

Like Netscape, Internet Explorer also incorporates elements that are not compliant with the generally accepted HTML standard. Again, these codes are geared more toward page layout than is the HTML standard. More and more often, sites on the Web are recommending that you use Internet Explorer to view the site because it uses the nonstandard HTML elements recognized by Internet Explorer.

Lynx

Lynx and similar browsers are a little different from the others discussed so far, because they lack the ability to display graphics. It may be surprising that people still rely on text-based browsers to access the Web, but it remains true that not everyone has a high-speed connection to the Internet. In fact, many users don't even have a graphical operating system (such as Windows, Mac OS, or OS/2) for their computer.

Lynx was originally written for the UNIX platform. In fact, it is the browser used by most service providers for text-based accounts. There is also an MS-DOS version that offers users browsing capabilities in a text-only format (see fig. 3.4).

Figure 3.4

The Lynx browser through a text-only UNIX account.

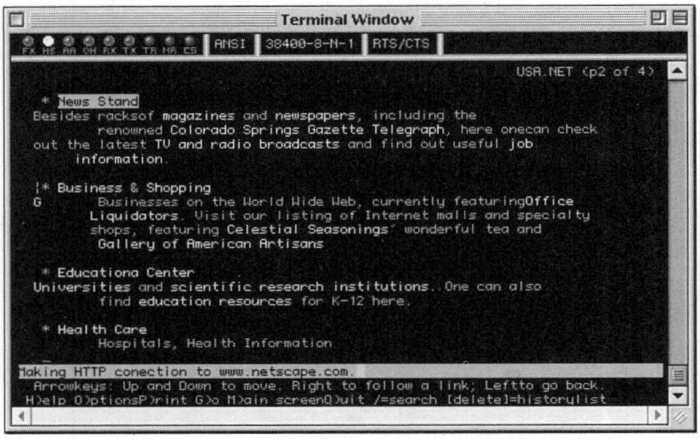

Special considerations must go into your HTML documents if they're going to support text-based browsers like Lynx. Fortunately, as you'll see in the HTML formatting chapters, the HTML 2.0 and 3.0 standards are heavily in favor of text-based browsers—in the spirit of not leaving anyone out.

The individual HTML designer must be wary, though, especially when designing highly graphical Web sites and interfaces. Something that you should constantly ask yourself while creating a Web site is: Am I leaving out my text-based viewers? Is there anyone out there who can't get the full effect of what I'm communicating because they can't see the graphics?

Inevitably, that will indeed be the case—but a good HTML designer works to minimize that possibility.

> **Tip:** Many considerate Web designers go so far as to create two or more versions of their Web site—one for graphical browsers, and one that offers only text.

Uniform Resource Locators

Now that you've looked at the various different Web browsers that might be accessing your Web site, let's talk about something they all have in common: the use of *Uniform Resource Locators* (*URLs*). What's an URL? If you remember our discussion from the last chapter, you may recall that I mentioned that most Internet services have "addresses" for accessing information within that service.

> **Tip:** Not everyone follows this convention, but this book is written in such a way that it will be easier to read if you pronounce "URL" as you would the name "Earl."

Each of these addresses is a bit different. For instance, you would send an e-mail message to my America Online account using **tstauffer@aol.com** in an e-mail application.

To acccess the AOL public FTP site, on the other hand, you would enter **ftp.aol.com** in the FTP application you are using.

The World Wide Web also has its own addressing scheme, but it's slightly more advanced than the schemes of its predecessors. Not only is the Web newer, but its addresses have to be more sophisticated because of the Web's unique ability to access all of the different Internet services.

URLs are these special addresses. They follow a format like this:

protocol://host.domain.first-level domain/path/filename.ext

or

protocol:host.domain.first-level domain

An example of an URL to access a Web document would be **http:// www.microsoft.com/windows/index.html**.

Let's look at that address carefully. According to the format for an URL, then, **http://** would be the protocol, **www** is the host you're accessing, **microsoft** is the domain, and **com** is the first-level domain type for this system. That's followed by / to suggest that a path statement is coming next.

The path statement tells you that you're looking at the document **index.html**, located in the directory **windows**.

> **Note:** Those of you familiar with DOS, Windows, or UNIX will probably recognize path statements right away. Mac OS users and others simply need to realize that a path statement offers a "path" to a specific file on the server computer's hard drive. A Web browser needs to know in exactly which directories and subdirectories (folders and subfolders) a file can be found, so a path statement is a standard part of any URL.

There are two basic advantages of the URL. First, it allows you to explicitly indicate the type of Internet service involved. HTTP, for instance, indicates the HyperText Transfer Protocol—the basic protocol for transferring Web documents. You'll look at this part of the URL in a moment.

Secondly, the URL system of addressing makes every single document, program, and file on the Internet a separately addressable entity. Why is this useful?

Example: The URL Advantage

For this example, all you need to do is load your Web browser (whichever you happen to use) and find the text box or similar interface element that allows you to enter an URL manually to access Web pages (see fig. 3.5). The point of this example is to show the benefits of using URLs for the Web. With Gopher and FTP, you really only need to know a host address. But, on the Web, knowing just the host address often isn't enough.

Figure 3.5

The Go To/ Location text box in Netscape for Windows allows you to enter an URL manually.

Once you've located the appropriate entry box, enter **www.mcp.com**. Depending on the browser you're using, you'll more than likely need to hit the Enter or Return key after typing this address.

What happens then depends on your Web browser. Some browsers will give an error, which isn't exactly perfect for this example, but it does prove the point that you need more than just a server address to get around on the Web. Others will take you directly to the Macmillan Computer Publishing Web site.

> **Tip:** If your browser gives you an error, enter **http://www.mcp.com**. Some browsers require at least a partial URL. Others guess the protocol from the type of server address entered.

Notice that **www.mcp.com** follows the addressing conventions established for Internet services like FTP and Gopher. The problem is that, if the Web used this method for addresses, you'd have to begin at the first page of the Web site every time you wanted to access one of the hundreds of pages available from Macmillan.

To get around that, an URL provides your Web browser with more information. Try giving **http://www.mcp.com/que/index.html** to your Web browser, followed by Enter or Return (as appropriate).

All Web browsers should easily handle this address. With an URL, you're able to be much more specific about the document you want to see, since every document on the Internet has an individual address. In this case, you've instructed your Web browser to go directly to the **que** directory on Macmillan's Web site and load the HTML document called **index.html**.

The Different Protocols for URLs

You've already looked at Internet addresses such as **www.mcp.com** in depth, and you should be familiar with the concept of a path statement. That just leaves one part of an URL that's new to you: the protocol.

I've already mentioned that HTTP is the protocol most often used by Web browsers to access HTML pages. Table 3.1 shows some of the other protocols that can be part of an URL.

Table 3.1   Possible Protocols for an URL

Protocol	*Accesses…*
http://	HTML documents
https://	Some "secure" HTML documents
file://	HTML documents on your hard drive
ftp://	FTP sites and files
gopher://	Gopher menus and documents
news://	UseNet newsgroups on a particular news server
news:	UseNet newsgroups
mailto:	E-mail messages
telnet:	Remote Telnet (login) session

By entering one of these protocols, followed by an Internet server address and a path statement, you can access nearly any document, directory, file, or program available on the Internet or on your own hard drive.

> **Note:** The **mailto:**, **news:**, and **telnet:** protocols have slightly different require-ments to create an URL. **mailto:** is followed by a simple e-mail address, **news:** is followed by just the newsgroup name, and **telnet:** is followed by just a server address. Also notice that **file://** is often slightly different for different browsers.

Example: Accessing Other Internet Services with URLs

Over time, applications designed to access non-Web Internet services (like FTP or Gopher programs) will begin to use the URL system more and more. For now though, as a rule, basically only Web browsers use URLs.

Fortunately, by simply changing the protocol of a particular URL, you can access most Internet services directly from your browser. For this example, you'll need to load your Web browser once more and enter **ftp://ftp.cdrom.com/pub/win95/demos/**.

This should result in a listing of the subdirectory **demos** located on the FTP server **ftp.cdrom.com**. Notice that you didn't enter a document name, because, if you're using the FTP protocol, the document or file will be automatically downloaded.

> **Tip:** If your browser tells you that there are too many users presently connected for you to connect to this FTP site, wait a moment or two, then click your Reload button or otherwise reload this URL with your browser.

Not all browsers support the **mailto:** command—let's see if yours does. In your browser's URL window, type **mailto:tstauffer@aol.com** and hit Enter or Return if necessary.

If your browser supports the **mailto:** protocol command, you should be presented with a new window, complete with my e-mail address in the Mail To field (see fig. 3.6).

Figure 3.6

A **mailto:** protocol URL in action.

Enter a **mailto:** URL here...

...and the address shows up here in an e-mail messsage

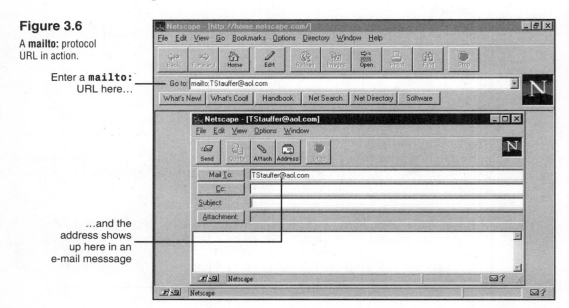

How Web Browsers Access HTML Documents

When you enter an URL in the URL field on your browser, the browser goes through the following three basic steps:

♦ The browser determines what protocol to use.

♦ It looks up and contacts the server at the address specified.

♦ The browser requests the specific document (including its path statement) from the server computer.

Using all of this information, your browser was able to access the variety of Internet services discussed previously in Table 3.1 and in the subsequent example. But what does this have to do with HTML design? Just about everything.

In HTML, a hypertext link is simply a clickable URL. Every time you create a link in a Web document, you assign an URL to that link. When that link is clicked by a user, the URL is fed to the browser, which then goes through the procedure outlined above to try and retrieve it.

Example: Watching the Link

If you've used your Web browser much, then you've watched this happen countless times, even if you didn't realize it. If you're using Netscape, Mosaic, or a similar browser, start by pointing your mouse pointer at just about any link you can find. You may notice that when your mouse pointer is touching the link, an URL appears in the *status bar*—probably at the bottom of the page (see fig. 3.7).

That's the URL associated with the link to which you're pointing. Clicking that link will cause the browser to accept that URL as its next command, in much the same way that you manually entered URLs in the earlier example. To see it happen, click the link once. Now check the URL field that you used before to enter URLs (see fig. 3.8). You should see the same URL that was associated with the link to which your mouse was pointing. Then, after a few seconds, you should be at the new page.

Figure 3.7

An URL in the status bar of Netscape Navigator.

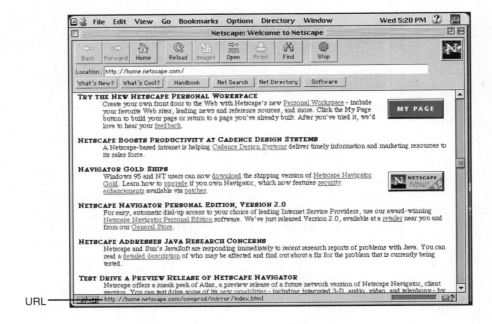

URL ——

Figure 3.8

The link's URL now appears in the URL field (which is Location in Netscape).

URL field ——

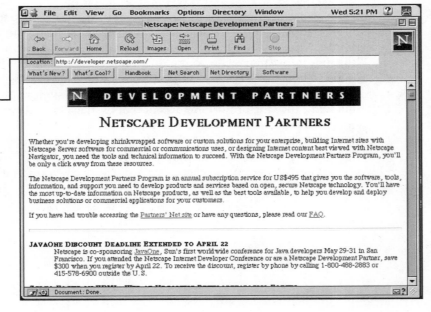

What Can Be Sent on the Web?

Part of the magic of the HTTP protocol is that it is fairly unlimited (by Internet standards) in the sort of files that it can send and receive. For instance, like Internet e-mail, much of what is sent on the Web (via the HTTP protocol) is ASCII text. But, unlike Internet e-mail, HTTP isn't limited to ASCII text.

> **Note:** There are two different types of files that can be sent over various Internet services. These are ASCII text files (plain text) and binary files. Binary files are any documents created by applications (such as word processing or graphics applications) or even the applications themselves. It's easiest to think of binary files as anything that isn't an ASCII file.

In fact, HTTP can send both of the major types of files—ASCII and binary—using the same protocol. This means that both plain text files (such as UseNet messages and HTML documents) and binaries (such as downloadable programs or graphics files) can be sent via the Web without any major effort on the part of the user. In certain cases, the HTML author will have to make a distinction (for instance, as to whether or not a graphics file should be displayed or downloaded to the user's machine), but, for the most part, HTTP figures this stuff out by itself.

How exactly does it figure these things out? Usually by a combination of the protocol selected and the *extension* to the filename in question. For instance, a file called INDEX.HTML that's accessed using an URL that starts with the **http://** protocol will be displayed in a browser as an HTML file, complete with formatting and hypertext links.

The same file, however, if it is renamed to be INDEX.TXT, even if it's loaded with an **http://** protocol URL, will be displayed in the browser as a simple ASCII file, just as if it were being displayed in WordPad, SimpleText, or Emacs. Why is this? Because the extension tells the Web browser how to display the file (see figs. 3.9 and 3.10).

Figure 3.9

INDEX_TEST.HTM is loaded as an HTML document by the browser.

Welcome to My Home on the Web

In the interest of Web developers everywhere, I've put together this *great* collection of Web tools for Windows 95. You'll notice that, like most things on the Web, I've started with Netscape. From there, it's on to a great deal of useful resources for refining your own Web pages, working with advanced Web topics like VRML and Java, and integrating other Internet services into your Web sites.

Figure 3.10

INDEX_TEST.TXT is displayed simply as an ASCII text file.

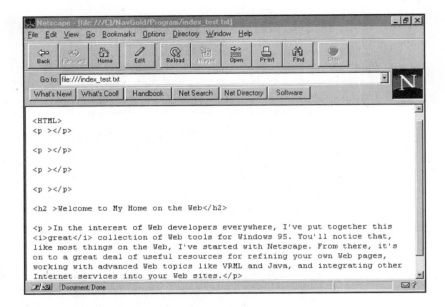

You may recall from Chapter 1 that much of an HTML document is "text" (the rest being HTML codes). In fact, all of an HTML document is *ASCII text*, as is demonstrated in figure 3.9. It is only the extension .HTML (or .HTM on DOS-based Web servers) that tells a Web browser that it needs to interpret some of the text as HTML commands within a particular ASCII text document.

> **Tip:** Because HTML documents are ASCII text, it's possible to create them in simple *text editor* programs. A Microsoft Word document, on the other hand, is not ASCII text—it's saved in a binary format. So, if you use a word processor to create HTML documents, remember to use the Save As command to save the HTML page in an ASCII format.

Binaries on the Web

When a binary document such as a graphics file is sent over the Web, it's important that it have the appropriate extension. That's how Web browsers know whether a document should be viewed in the browser window (like a JPEG- or GIF-format graphic) or whether it should be saved to the hard drive (like a ZIP or StuffIt archive file).

To the HTML designer, this means two things. First of all, you should recognize that your HTML pages can offer just about any other type of file for transport across the Web. If you want to send graphics, games, WordPerfect documents, or just about anything else, just put a hypertext link to that file on your Web page.

Second, you need to remember that the most important part of a filename is its extension. If you fail to put the correct extension on a filename, your user's browser won't know what to do with it. If you're trying to display a graphic on your Web page, for instance, but put a .TXT extension on it, it won't display.

Everything is Downloaded

There's one other thing you should realize about the Web and Web browsers before you begin to develop Web pages. Very simply, everything you view in a Web browser has to be downloaded from the Web site first. What do I mean by this?

Whenever you enter an URL or click a hypertext link, the HTML document (or binary file) that you're accessing is sent, in its entirety, from the Web server computer to your computer's hard drive. That's why, for instance, Web pages with a lot of graphics files take longer to display than Web pages with just text.

For the Web user, this is both good and bad. It's good because once a page is downloaded, it can be placed in the *cache,* so that the next time you access the page, it will take much less time to display. It's also good because anything that's currently displayed in your browser window, including the HTML document and any graphics files, can be instantly renamed and filed on your hard drive for your personal use.

> **Tip:** If you use Netscape Navigator, click and hold the mouse button (on a Mac) or click the right mouse button (in Win95) while pointing to a Web page graphic. Notice that, after a few seconds, you can rename that graphic and save it to your hard drive.

The bad side of downloading, though, is that every graphic and all of the text you include in an HTML page has to be transmitted over the Internet to your user's computer. If your user is accessing the Web over a modem, then downloading and displaying your page can take a long time—especially if your Web page includes a lot of graphics. This means that HTML designers have to be constantly aware of the size of their HTML documents and their Web page graphics in order to avoid causing their users unnecessary irritation and wasted time.

> **Note:** It takes 15 to 30 seconds (on average) for a 25 kilobyte graphic to be transmitted over a 28.8 Kbps modem connection. So a 100 kilobyte Web page could take around two minutes to transfer—the length of four television commercials.

Summary

There are a number of popular Web browser applications that Web designers should take into consideration when designing their Web pages. Each browser displays HTML codes in slightly different ways and some—like Netscape and MS Internet Explorer—even add their own HTML-style commands.

The Web uses a particular style of Internet address, called an URL, which allows it to address individually any document on the Internet. This offers an advantage over other Internet address schemes because it specifies the Internet service protocols desired and points directly at documents.

It's important for the Web designer to remember that everything on a Web page is downloaded, including text and graphics. The larger the graphics on a Web page, the longer it will take to display. This is also an advantage, though, since pages can be cached for future use.

Review Questions

1. Which browser was the first graphical browser on the market? Which is currently most popular?

2. Most Netscape HTML extensions are designed to help with what aspect of Web pages?

3. What makes the Lynx browser different from the others discussed?

4. Is the following an URL, a server address, or a path statement?

   www.mcp.com

5. What makes the **mailto:** command different from a standard URL?

6. What ASCII character comes between each folder or directory in a path statement?

7. If I entered the following in my browser's URL field (and hit Return, if necessary), would it download a file?

   http://ftp.cdrom.com/pub/win95/games/four.zip

8. True or false. Graphics displayed on a Web page are downloaded to the user's computer, which is why they often take extra time to display.

9. Are the following files ASCII files or binary files? A CorelDRAW! picture, an HTML page, a Microsoft Word document, and a WordPad document.

Review Exercises

1. Use your current Web browser to access one of the FTP sites mentioned in the "Web Browser Applications" section of this chapter. Notice how browsers handle FTP connections.

2. Use an **ftp://** URL to download one of those other Web browsers (or another file) directly. Hint: you'll need to figure out the path to the file first.

3. If your ISP allows it, use a modem communications program to dial up your account, and then use Lynx or a similar text browser through your ISP's connection. Notice how different the Web is without graphics and a mouse!

## CHAPTER 4

HTML's Role on the Web

You've already seen how HTML is used to emphasize and organize text in Web documents. And you've seen how hypertext and hypermedia links can be used to maneuver on the Web, access information, and download different file formats. You've also seen that extensions to HTML from Netscape and Microsoft have added certain abilities to HTML.

Now let's discuss where HTML is today and where it's going in the future. In this chapter, you'll learn about the advantages of Web pages compared to other Internet services, how HTML has changed with the Web, how to recognize and understand the different flavors of HTML, and how to decide what types of HTML you're going to use.

Why Create Web Pages?

Having discussed how exactly the Web works, you can move on to why you might want to create Web pages. There are a number of reasons you may want to do this—more than likely, you've already got some ideas. But consider the following possible examples:

♦ **Small Businesses**—Not only is the Web an inexpensive place to advertise your business, but it's also a relatively interactive and convenient way to communicate with customers and potential customers. If you haven't already, it's a good idea to put up some Web pages that explain the services you provide from your small business or home office. Then put your URL on your business cards, your brochures, and other advertising so that customers know where to go for detailed information about you.

♦ **Large Businesses**—Large businesses should be on the Web too, especially technical and customer-service-oriented businesses. The Web is a wonderfully unique way to provide customer service, technical support, and informational services at relatively low cost to the business. A good Web designer and a creative Information Systems (IS) staff can put together some very unique services that might save a business tons of customer support dollars (see fig. 4.1).

Figure 4.1

Federal Express has come up with a great reason to use the Web—customers can track packages without calling their 800 numbers.

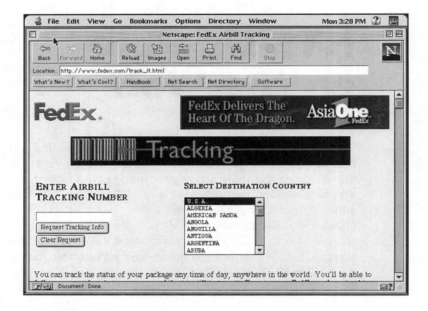

♦ **Community Groups**—Do you lead or participate in a group in your neighborhood, church, school, or community? If you do, then a Web page is a great way to offer information about the group, present a meeting schedule, post announcements, and recruit new members. A Web page can even be a great way to inform members of changes to the club or the schedule, or to praise special members for accomplishments.

♦ **Hobbies**—Even if your major hobbies aren't computer-related, you can create a Web page and put it up on the World Wide Web. Eventually, people with the same interests as you will be visiting your page, sending you e-mail, and helping you find more information about your hobby. You may even find others who've put up similar Web pages, and you'll be able to add links to their information on your page.

♦ **Personal or Family Pages**—What else can you put on a Web page? Your résumé, samples of your work, samples of your kids' work, pictures of the house, the car or the kittens you're selling, and even clips from home movies. Is there a better way to make up-to-the-minute photos available to your family than on the Web? Maybe not. It's also a great place to post writing samples and old articles about yourself or your family from the local paper.

Web Applications

Another emerging use for HTML on the Web is as a basis for something called a *Web application*. In essence, a Web application is a Web site designed to do more than simply present pages and hypermedia links to its users—it actually acts as a front end for data processing.

For instance, consider the notion of a Web site designed to give a company's salespeople the ability to access product information and confirm orders while on the road. Using HTML, the basic interface for this sales database can be made available on the Web. With the appropriate browser software and an Internet connection (perhaps even over a cellular modem), a salesperson for your company has nearly instant access to the information she needs.

Once the data are entered on the page, they are passed by the Web server to programs (often referred to as CGI-BIN scripts or applications, as discussed in Chapter 15) that process the information—looking up the product in the database or taking the order. The results of these programs can be generated complete with HTML codes, so that the answers can be viewed by the salesperson in her Web browser.

Example: Searching on the Web

Not all Web applications are necessarily business-related—and even the applications that are don't necessarily have to be limited to employee use. Consider one of the most popular Web applications available: the Web-based search engine.

These Web applications use HTML pages to offer an interface to a database of Web sites around the world. You begin by accessing the page and entering keywords, which the Web application passes to a CGI-BIN program. The program uses your keywords to check the database of Web pages, and then generates an HTML page with the results.

The URL for that results page is returned to the Web server, which treats it as a standard link. Your browser is fed the link, and it loads the newly created page, complete with hypertext links to the possible database matches.

Let's take a look at the popular Infoseek search application. Start out by entering **http://guide.infoseek.com/** in your browser and hitting Enter or Return.

Once the page is loaded, it should look something like figure 4.2. In the field on the Web page that allows you to enter text, enter a few keywords that might suggest a hobby that interests you. One of my hobbies is acting, so I might try entering **acting plays musicals** or something similar.

Figure 4.2

The Infoseek Web search application.

Enter keywords here ——

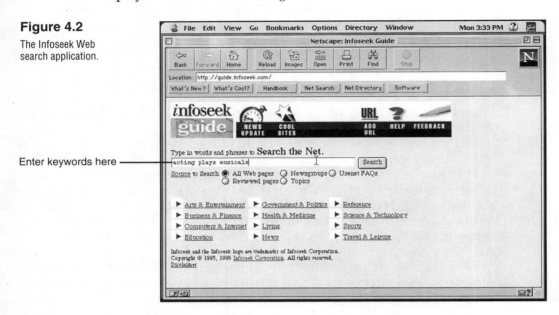

Click the Search button on the Web page, and the Infoseek engine will begin searching for related Web pages. When it's finished, you're presented with a list of hypertext links. Click any link to view the related page and see if it offers the information you're seeking.

Advantages and Disadvantages of the Web

Most small or large businesses have a compelling reason to create a presence on the World Wide Web. It's an important new medium for communication that is relatively inexpensive to implement, it's a boon for dealing with customer service issues, and it's gaining popularity in leaps and bounds. But any good HTML designer should realize that there are also certain disadvantages to the Web.

Advantages

There are many good reasons to commit to creating a presence on the World Wide Web. I've already hinted at some of these in this chapter, but let's look at them in detail. Most of these are geared toward businesses, but you'll notice that these advantages are available to any Web site:

♦ **Multimedia presentation**—A Web site allows you to do things that are simply not possible in any other medium. With some of the visual impact of television, the informational utility of print, and the personal appeal of radio, the Web is an effective tool for taking marketing information to another level. Products can be explained and offered in depth, along with pictures, video, sound, and even animation.

♦ **Interactivity**—There are a number of different areas where the fact that your user can interactively determine what to view or hear can really make the difference for a business. Especially important is the added value the Web gives you for customer service, technical or product support, and immediate feedback. While most of any Web site is automated, it gives you an opportunity to answer frequently asked questions and point customers to resources that may help them solve problems on their own. While this may seem like an advantage reserved for computer companies, consider the implications for service-oriented industries like travel, consulting, catalog sales, and business-to-business sales.

♦ **Flexibility**—If your business relies on printing or publishing as a medium, you may immediately see the advantage of the Web. Changes on the Web are relatively instantaneous, and the speed with which an update can be made is measured in minutes, not weeks. Consider the financial planner's or real estate agent's sales newsletter. Instant changes on the World Wide Web give their Net-savvy clients a time-based edge. Incorporating the Web into the services you offer a client gives you an added value in their eyes, especially in time-sensitive industries.

♦ **Easy High-Tech**—Whether you're a small or large business, it's important to keep up with technology in order to satisfy customers and be up on the "latest." Web pages are moving toward a point where they'll be expected of large businesses and not unusual from small ones. Like e-mail a couple years ago, and fax machines before that, it's become important to keep up with the Web. Fortunately, it's also rather easy to get started with HTML and quickly develop a Web site.

Example: Travel Agent Web Site

Let's roll all of these advantages into a hypothetical Web site for a travel agency to show exactly what I mean.

All-Rite Travel has decided that it needs a Web site and is trying to determine the ways in which the site will help win and keep customers. The agency relies on professionally designed and printed brochures that are updated annually for general information about the agency and its services. It has a quarterly newsletter for repeat customers and generates laser-printer flyers and mailers for special deals. How can the Web help All-Rite Travel (see fig. 4.3)?

Figure 4.3

Here's what our fictious travel agent's index page might look like.

Multimedia and Interactivity

First of all, the agency's presentations can be multimedia-oriented. Taking advantage of the Web protocols allows sending sounds, graphics, and even video of travel destinations across the Web. If the agency has pictures of accommodations in a vacation resort, for instance, it can put those on its site. Sounds, video, or text generated by a travel writer or photographer can also be added. A map to its offices, links for customers to send e-mail, and information about its affiliations can all be online.

And using hypertext, All-Rite can pick from relatively unlimited resources for more information. It would take only a few hours to build links to all of the Chambers of Commerce in major U.S. metro areas. Links to airlines, major hotel chains, limousine services, car rentals, and credit card companies could all be added.

Flexibility

While All-Rite would probably want to continue with its print advertising and brochures, the possibilities for offering information over the Web are enticing. Since customers can take on as little or as much information as they want, the Web can house all sorts of extras. Special employee pages could tell customers which agent is most specialized in their area of interest. Editorial writing by agents and other specialists could give tips on travel safety, saving money in restaurants, or tracking expenses on corporate trips.

And the Web page could be instantly updated with the best deals the agency comes across or packages—as they happen. The moment you're ready to make a sale notice or offer a special price, you can do it on the Web. Once All-Rite's customers are used to its Web presence, those with a special interest in traveling can easily check the Web site every few days for the latest offerings.

Easy High-Tech

Once the agents have learned a little HTML, they can add pages or edit them on their own. Make the Web site known on business cards, brochures, and elsewhere, and customers will see it as an extra value—All-Rite is "plugged in" to the Web, and its Internet-savvy customers can learn a lot of what they need to know without bothering to phone or come by the agency's office.

Disadvantages

It's difficult to say that there are disadvantages in having a Web site, since most people and companies will use a Web site to enhance their marketing and customer service efforts, not supplant them. That said, there are a few hurdles to leap, and they should definitely be considered before your Web project takes off:

♦ **Learning Curve**—It will take a while for folks to learn HTML, figure out how to upload pages, create appropriate graphics, and design effective Web sites. You'll also need to find an effective and helpful Internet service provider (or a similar in-house IS employee at a larger corporation) who can help you get online.

♦ **Appearance**—To be truly effective, a Web site also needs to be attractive and easy to use. For many companies, especially larger ones, that will mean using professional artists, writers, and designers. Beginning this task can be daunting, and will require a reasonable budget—which may be intimidating when management isn't sure what the benefits will be.

◆ **Maintenance and Timeliness**—One of the worst things that can happen to a Web site is for it to sit dormant for weeks or months because it's the pet project of an interested employee who has less time for it than she originally anticipated, or because every change to the Web site must first be approved by a committee. It's important that a Web developer be relatively free to spend time on the project, and that someone be available to make timely decisions. Without this, the Web site loses some of its inherent advantages.

◆ **Security**—Transmitting data via Internet technology, including the Web, is inherently a rather unsecure process. For data to be transmitted over the Web, it has to pass through a number of different servers and hosts—and any of the information you offer could potentially be read or held by any of these people. This has been a strong argument against commerce on the Web, as people recognize the dangers in revealing personal information (for instance, credit card numbers). Currently, it's difficult to create completely secure Web sites that offer access only to password-bearing users, and those passwords are often not impossible to intercept.

◆ **Copyright Issues**—The lack of security holds true for the Web designer— nearly anything you create on the Web can easily be read or copied by anyone with Web access. This is intimidating both to artists and publishers who want to make sure that Internet access doesn't, in some way, devalue their published (and profitable) efforts.

◆ **Cost**—Depending on the size of your organization and the expertise of its people, a Web site can quickly become expensive. Learning HTML and creating a reasonable site isn't that difficult (as you'll see in this book), but maintaining the appropriate equipment, paying the dedicated staffers, and bringing in consultants, designers, programmers, and IS technicians as the site grows can quickly expand the budget. The advantages will often outweigh these costs, but any Web developer should be aware that Web sites tend to get bigger and more time-consuming as time goes on.

Secure Connections on the Internet

Some Web server software packages offer an implementation of the Secure Sockets Layer (SSL), a protocol that sits "on top" of TCP/IP (the Internet networking protocol) and "below" HTTP. Its purpose is to secure the transmission of HTTP data over the Web.

With an SSL server (usually noted by its **https://**-protocol URL) and an SSL-capable browser program, transmissions over the Web are encrypted in such a way that users trying to read the data as they pass over the Internet are treated to nothing but garbled text.

SSL is a feature of, among others, the Netscape Enterprise Server, which is designed to allow users to access a Web site in a secure fashion so that credit cards and other personal information can be passed with relative assurance.

Although this is not directly relevant to HTML designers, if you have the opportunity to create a commercial Web site (or otherwise ask for personal information from users), you might look into the possibility of using an SSL-based secure Web server to offer your users peace of mind. And, while SSL isn't the only security scheme, it's the most widely supported.

HTML and the Changing World Wide Web

You already know that the Web is really only a few years old, and that graphical browsers have been around since only mid-1993. So how could the Web have had enough time to change dramatically? In the computer world, it doesn't take long.

The Web and HTML were initially designed for use by academics in a fairly limited way—they planned to collaborate on physics projects and share information in a hypertext format. Publishing on the Web meant they could put experimental data and their conclusions on the Internet, with links to other data and other researcher's notes, or even links that would download graphs and charts.

A few years later, people are talking about the Web as if it were literally the greatest thing since sliced bread. The World Wide Web is touted as the next logical medium for publication. It's the printing press of the future, where everyone who puts together a newsletter, magazine, sales brochure, and (in some cases) a television show will have to have a presence.

Sounds pretty demanding, doesn't it?

The Forced Evolution of HTML

Along with these changing demands for the Web have come changing demands for HTML. It's only in the last year or so that professional designers, writers, layout artists, and their ilk have begun to take an interest in the Web. And what did they find when they got there? You have to use HTML, with no control over justification, no wrapping text around graphics. In the Henry Ford tradition, you could use any color for a background—as long as it was gray. And HTML itself is some bizarre cross between word processing and programming that designers aren't always thrilled to learn.

Given this atmosphere, it becomes clear why programs like Netscape Navigator—with their special layout commands—are so popular. Many professionally developed Web sites have shunned users other than those with Navigator, thinking, "If they can't see it, too bad. The design can't be compromised." It's up to each designer, right?

> **Tip:** Aside from Chapters 19 and 20, a very useful discussion of Netscape versus HTML standards can be found at Andrew King's web site at **http:// webreference.com/html3andns/**.

The problem with these extensions and extras is that HTML's entire philosophy goes against the idea of strict layout and design. From the beginning, HTML was conceived as a very nonspecific method for presenting pages. With many implicit commands, it allowed browser programs considerable flexibility when it came to emphasizing text. Essentially, an HTML browser is given a suggestion like "emphasize the word 'weight,'" but it isn't told exactly how to do it. It could choose italics or bold or place the word in a slightly different font face. In HTML 2.0, the font family isn't specified, nor is alignment on the page. That's up to the HTML browser—at least according to the original theorists.

But then again, HTML was only originally intended for scientists to share ideas and figures—not for Madison Avenue to share its latest campaigns.

The Current State of HTML

With these commercial demands, however, have come different solutions. For every extension Netscape adds to HTML, there is generally (eventually) a standard agreed to by the World Wide Web Consortium (W3C) that meets the same need. Unfortunately, the implementation isn't always the same. So, it's possible for an HTML 3.0 level standard, for instance, to provide for exactly the same layout functions as Netscape—but do it in a way that isn't compatible with Netscape's browser.

So HTML is currently in a bit of a flux. The best you can hope for is that the HTML standard is agreed upon and maintained more quickly in the future as more ideas pop up. At the same time, it's important that the standard remain well thought-out, and that it isn't allowed to become bloated and unworkable.

In fact, this is probably the justification for recent changes to the standard's bodies. With the W3C taking control of HTML, it suggests a shift in the ultimate power over HTML to the corporate players. From now on, you can probably assume that HTML extensions beyond what is generally considered HTML 2.0 will become standard on a case-by-case basis. Overall, this is probably a good thing, since standards can be agreed on as technology emerges—and competing browsers can all use the same methods to incorporate new technology.

Deciding What Type of HTML To Use

So the question becomes, which side do you choose? Do you develop pages that use Netscape-only commands? Do you develop two sets of pages—for HTML 3.0 and for Netscape? What about those special Internet Explorer commands?

There are a couple of different scenarios you should consider when putting together your HTML pages. You'll need to know more about HTML, but once you do, you can make an informed decision about the types of commands you're most likely to use and which ones you can do without. Of course, you can use as many different flavors of HTML as you choose—as long as you remember to give your users a choice (see fig. 4.4).

> **Tip:** You can add to your site CGI scripts that identify a user's browser and serve it the correct type of HTML.

Figure 4.4

A "front door" page allows users with different browser programs to choose how they'd like to view the Web site.

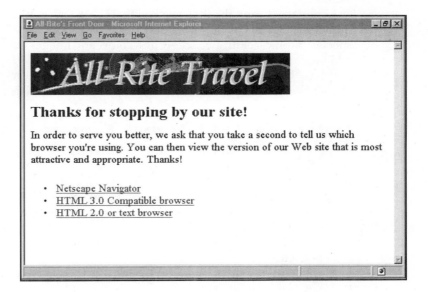

With that in mind, then, let's look at the possibilities.

The HTML 2.0 Standard

If you can get by with less sophisticated layout functions, go with the lowest common denominator—currently HTML 2.0. This level of HTML lets you add text, graphics, and different types of links so that pages are very complete and useful. With any level of HTML, hypermedia links can be made available, but they'll still be limited to the browser's ability to handle them. Even text browsers can save hypermedia files (like sound and video) which the user can view or hear later using other programs.

What HTML 2.0 doesn't include are a great deal of explicit formating tags. There's no way to center text and graphics, for instance, and only limited ways you can format graphics on the page. Aside from clickable graphics links and some calls to external scripts and programs, there isn't much "interface design" you can accomplish with HTML 2.0, either. Data-entry forms, tables, frames, and other elements are all added by other levels of HTML.

The HTML 3.0 Level Standards

As the HTML 3.0 level standards become more and more widely recognized, you can easily update your pages from HTML 2.0 to HTML 3.0. It may be a while before this is necessary—browsers have only just begun to recognize some HTML 3.0 elements.

Remember, though, that even with HTML 3.0 you'll be preventing a good number of viewers from getting the full effect of your pages. HTML 3.0 incorporates special graphics features, background colors and images, tables for displaying data, and other features that may seem indispensable, but will be lost on users of older graphical browsers—and any of the text browsers. If you're going to use HTML 3.0 elements, you should include at least a text-only option as well.

Netscape and Internet Explorer HTML

If you've spent any amount of time on the Web, you're sure to have encountered pages that say something like "Netscape Navigator is recommended for viewing these pages." With Netscape controlling around 60 percent of the browser market, a number of HTML designers have felt free to use HTML elements that can be interpreted only by Netscape—including certain implementations of tables, Netscape frames, special layout tags for centering or right-aligning pages, and other features. You'll have to decide for yourself if leaving out 40 percent of your potential users is a good idea.

It's absolutely true that some of the most attractive Web sites are designed using Netscape's variant of HTML (or special Internet Explorer tags), and that might be most important to you. If so, you should at least consider adding additional text-only or HTML 2.0-only pages to your site for other users.

Making the HTML Decision

The bottom line is that you should always consider your HTML 2.0 and text-only users, and make efforts to include them in your Web sites. Other extensions to HTML and add-ons for Web sites—including the Virtual Reality Modeling Language (VRML), Java and JavaScript programs, and others—will work only with certain browsers. Much of the time, noncompliant browsers will simply ignore these commands, but if this is the case, you need to be aware that some users aren't seeing everything you have to offer.

When you use a non-HTML 2.0 element, it's a good idea to let your users know. A simple statement such as "These pages are best viewed in..." is a nice way to let folks know that they might be missing out on something. If your first priority is the appearance of your page, this is a decent compromise to make.

If your first priority is giving your users information, though, then you're best off either using the lowest common denominator of HTML (HTML 2.0 and, over the next few years, HTML 3.0) or offering different ways to view your sites to your different users.

Summary

There are certain advantages to the Web, such as multimedia, interactivity, timeliness, and a certain air of "tech awareness" that make creating HTML pages something of a necessity for businesses and a good idea for families, too. There are disadvantages as well, including the cost in time and money, the learning curve for Web design, and the constant need to update.

HTML has been forced to evolve over the last year because of the involvement of millions of people, larger businesses, and commercial artists. Spearheaded by Netscape Navigator, a number of extensions to HTML for page-layout purposes have confused the mission of the Web. As a designer, it's up to you to decide who your audience will be and the most appropriate flavors of HTML to use in order to reach that audience.

Review Questions

1. Is it possible for a Web site to actually save businesses money? What business services are often enhanced by Web sites?

2. Why is the Web's multimedia capability an advantage in using the Web for your business?

3. Explain why the Web's "flexibility" was an advantage for our fictional travel agent in the Travel Agent Web Site example.

4. What's one of the worst things that can happen to a Web site?

5. What is a Web application?

6. The Web was originally conceived as a research tool—what has it been touted as recently?

7. What HTML standard is considered the lowest common denominator of HTML?

8. Give an example of an HTML extension to Netscape that doesn't appear in the HTML 2.0 specification.

Review Exercises

1. Use a browser other than Netscape (preferrably an older version of Mosaic or a text-based browser) to access the Netscape home page at **http://home.netscape.com/**. Anything look different?

2. With your browser, access some big-name corporate sites like **http://www.microsoft.com/**, **http://www.apple.com/**, and **http://www.ibm.com/**. Notice the types of information they offer and how the information is presented.

3. If your ISP offers a page of local business links (or if you can find some via a Web search engine), take a look at those and consider how (and if) you would improve on them in some way. What do they do better or worse than the large corporate sites?

## CHAPTER 5

What You Need for a Web Site

Although creating HTML pages is easily the most time-consuming part of building your Web site, another equally important part is figuring out how you're going to get those pages on the Web. You'll need Web server software, an Internet connection, a Web URL for your pages, and a system for organizing your pages and graphics. Depending on how you gain access and how complicated your site is, just getting your first page up on the Web can take a certain amount of planning.

Finding a Web Server

Before you can display your HTML pages on the Web, you'll need access to a Web server. This may already be taken care of for you, especially if you work with an Information Systems (IS) department in a larger corporation. If this is the case, you'll just need to know how and where to send your HTML files when you want to update the site. Otherwise, you'll need to make some arrangements on your own.

It isn't terribly difficult to set up your own Web server—especially if you already have a high-speed connection to the Internet. If you access the Internet through an Internet service provider (ISP), you'll want to discuss this with them, though. More than likely, they're willing to provide you with space on their Web server computers. If your Web site is a fairly small venture, or if you're not ready for a heavy investment in equipment, then using your ISP's Web server is a great (and very common) alternative.

What is a Web Server?

In its essence, it's the job of a Web server to accept connections from Web browsers all over the Internet and, when requested, send them the HTML documents that are available from your site. This is done using the HTTP protocol discussed in Chapter 2.

A Web server is simply a computer with an Internet connection that runs software designed to send out HTML pages and other file formats (such as multimedia files) (see fig. 5.1). The server computer should have a relatively high-speed connection to the Internet (faster than any available modem connections, for instance) and be powerful enough to deal with a number of simultaneous connections from the Internet.

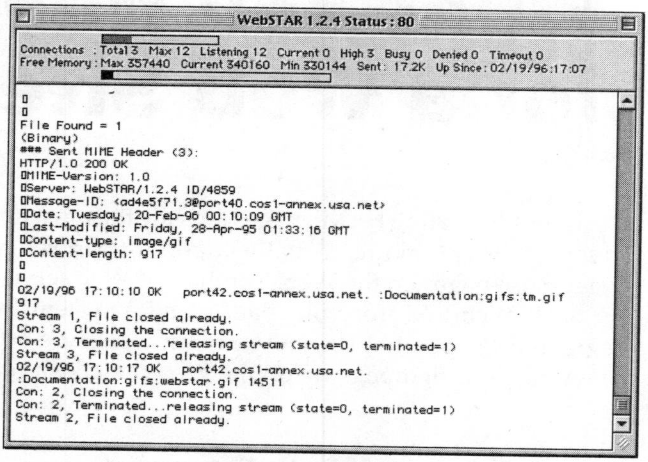

Figure 5.1

WebSTAR Web server software running on a Macintosh computer.

Web server software generally requires a fairly robust operating system (like UNIX, Windows NT, or OS/2), although software is available for other versions of Microsoft Windows, and the Macintosh OS is a very popular choice for Web server computers. The software you use depends on your level of experience with Internet connections and various operating systems.

Speed of the Server

The other major consideration is how popular your Web site will be. The more *hits*, or connections, your Web server receives at one time, the more powerful the computer should be—and the faster your connection to the Internet. What do I mean by a fast connection?

Most Internet connections are measured in terms of *bits per second* (*bps*), which translates loosely as "how many bits of data can be transmitted across the Internet in a second." In computerese, it takes eight bits to make up one *byte* of computer information—and a byte is what is required to create a character of text.

The typical modem connection is 14,400 bps, which translates to roughly 1,800 characters (bytes) transferred every second. If a typical page of text contains 300 words then, and each word averages six characters per word, this connection would yield roughly a page-per-second transmission rate. A 25-kilobyte (KB) file (such as a very small GIF file) would take about 14 seconds to transmit over this connection.

This doesn't sound terribly slow, until you start to take into account the idea that more than one connection might occur with the Web server. If ten people connect to our server over this connection, it will take ten seconds to complete the task of sending each of them a single page of data. If that page totaled 25 KB in size (that is, if it included graphics and other elements), it could take over 140 seconds to complete that same task.

Note: These transmission rate numbers all reflect ideal conditions. In real life, phone line noise, traffic on the Internet, and other factors will slow down transmission rates. Throughput on a 14,400 bps connection is often somewhere between 1,100 and 1,300 characters per second.

If the typical well-designed Web page is between 30 KB and 50 KB in size, you can see that we're going to start running into problems with this type of connection. There's the potential for someone to wait a number of minutes between the transfer of each page they request on your Web site. If the average commercial break on television is three minutes, just think how annoyed your users are going to get.

Types of Internet Connections

So your server will need a faster connection. But how do you get one? If Internet access is available to you through your company's Local Area Network (LAN), you probably already have a high-speed connection. Ask around your IS department. If you're running a small business or home office, you won't have to worry about high speed if you make your Web pages available on your ISP's Web server.

If you're going to use your own Web server computer, though, you'll need a high-speed Internet connection that you can connect to that computer. Table 5.1 details some of the possible connections.

Table 5.1 Internet Connection Speeds and Technologies

Connection Speed	Connection Technology
14.4/28.8 Kbps	High-speed modem
56 Kbps	56K leased line
64 Kbps	Single–B-Channel ISDN
128 Kbps	Basic Rate ISDN
up to 1.5 Mbps	Primary Rate ISDN (U.S.)
1.5 Mbps	T-1 dedicated line
45 Mbps	T-3 dedicated line

The minimum for an acceptable Web server connection is probably a basic-rate ISDN (Integrated Services Digital Network) connection, which offers 128,000 bps connections to the Internet. ISDN technology uses your existing phone wiring to provide an enhanced, digital, telephone connection. Using a special network adapter card for your computer, you can use the ISDN line to dial an appropriately equipped ISP. You can also use the ISDN connection for regular telephone calls.

Note: ISDN is a service of your local telephone company, and you should contact them for more information. Also be aware that emerging technologies such as cable modems (offered by your cable TV company) may be another high-speed alternative.

The basic-rate ISDN connection is still somewhat slow, depending on your Web site's traffic (that is, the number of visitors to your site). But it's also the most reasonably priced, generally falling between $50 and $150 a month for the ISDN line (from your local phone company), with $50 to $100 for the ISDN account (from your ISP), and $300 to $1,000 to purchase the ISDN equipment.

Tip: Relatively low-cost ISDN "modems" are becoming more common for both PCs and Macs in the $300 to $500 range.

A T-1 line is the typical connection for an ISP or a large business, and these lines generally cost thousands of dollars per month for Internet access, as do primary-rate ISDN connections. T-3 lines currently serve as the backbone of the Internet, and are generally only found connecting university, government, and supercomputing organizations.

Dealing with an ISP

For any sort of connection to the Internet, you'll probably need to deal with an Internet service provider. These companies offer dial-up and special high-speed connections to the Internet, as well as generally offering Web and other types of Internet servers for your use.

> **Note:** Looking for a provider for your Web page? With your Web browser, you can access some lists of ISPs around the country (and world) at **http://thelist.com** or **http://www.yahoo.com/Business_and_Economy/Companies/ Internet_Services/Web_Presence_Providers/** which includes a listing of free Web page providers. You might also check with your current ISP for Web deals, and realize that many popular online services offer free or cheap Web space.

For the typical smaller Web site, you'll want to buy space on the ISP's Web site. Generally this will give you an URL that begins with the name of the ISP's host computer, but points to a special directory for your HTML pages, such as **http:// www.isp.com/username/index.html**.

With most Web server programs, the default page that is first loaded is named `index.html`, so that's the name you'll use for the first page you'd like presented to users when they access your Web site.

Determining Costs

If you're looking for an ISP for your Web site (as opposed to using your company's computers or your current ISP), it's important to consider two factors. Most ISPs will charge you based on how much *disk space* your Web site consumes and how much *throughput* is registered for your pages.

Throughput can be seen as the average amount of information transferred from your site to a user multiplied by the number of users who access your Web site:

```
average amount of information X number of users = throughput
```

If, for instance, each user who accesses your site transfers an average of 50 KB, and 1,000 users access your site in a month, then your throughput for that month would be 5 MB of data. If your ISP charges $1 per megabyte of throughput, you'll be charged $5 (not including the disk space charges and any monthly fees the ISP may charge).

So why charge for throughput? If hundreds of people access your site at any given time, this means that many fewer people can access other services provided by the ISP, so they charge you more. Consider the scenario where everyone is downloading a 250 KB shareware program from your Web site, and over 10,000 people access your Web site in a month. This is approximately 2.5 gigabytes of data transferred, for which you might be charged $2,500 (at $1 per megabyte).

> **Tip:** Look for Web sites that offer monthly maximums and special deals to avoid surprise bills for hundreds or thousands of dollars.

A sum of $2,500 is a little high for that sort of traffic, but it does make a good point—many ISPs will limit your site to a certain amount of data transferred or a certain number of visitors per month (for a particular price plan). To get past these limitations, you may have to opt for the next higher plan available from the ISP, or accept additional charges for extra throughput.

What You Need To Know

Once you've decided on an ISP that you feel is reasonably priced, you're ready to create your HTML pages and upload them to the server. To do all this correctly, though, you'll probably need to ask a few questions:

♦ **What is my site's default URL?**—This should be something like the ISP's host address and a directory for your username. For instance, if my username is **tstauffer** and my ISP's Web server is **www.webco.net**, then the default URL for my site might be **http://www.webcom.net/tstauffer/**. Different ISPs will organize this in different ways, so you'll need to make sure you get this right.

> **Note:** Many ISPs will give you the option, at an increased price, of creating your own domain name for your site. Then users could access your site at **http://www.yourname.com/**.

♦ **How do I upload files to my site's directory?**—You should get instructions for accessing your Web site's directory on the Web server computer using either FTP or a UNIX shell account. We'll discuss this more in the section "Updating Your Web Site," later in this chapter.

♦ **Are there any limitations to the names I can give my files?**—The operating system in use by the Web server may not be instantly obvious to you. If this is the case, you'll want to ask if there is a certain filename length or a certain format for naming files you need to follow.

> **Tip:** When in doubt, use the DOS 8.3 filename convention in the style *filename.ext* where *filename* can be no more than eight letters, and *.ext* is a three-letter filename extension, such as .htm.

♦ **Can I create subdirectories within my main Web site directory?**—Most Web servers will give you this capability, but some will not allow you to create new subdirectories.

♦ **What support is offered for CGI programming?** Some servers won't allow you to add CGI scripts to your Web site for processing forms or adding other interactive features. At the same time, some will, but require you to pay extra or pay to have the provider write those scripts (regardless of your ability). If you plan a highly interactive site, then you should ask about CGI support.

Organizing a Web Site

The most important thing to remember when organizing a Web site is how the server computer you're using will differ from the computer you use to create Web pages. This is because you'll need to know the exact path to HTML pages and multimedia files you use in creating your Web page. As we've seen before, an URL requires both a server name and a path statement to the file. This includes files that you've placed on your own Web server—so while you're creating your Web pages, you'll need to know where your files will eventually be.

Although there are a number of different ways to arrange a Web site, there are some rules of thumb to keep in mind. For the most part, any organization you create for your Web site files should be designed to make updating your pages easy in the future. If you have to move all your files around every time you change something on a Web page, you'll also be forced to change all the hypertext links on many other pages—and that can be incredibly time-consuming.

Let's look at a couple of different types of organization for Web sites:

♦ **Single-directory sites**—Smaller sites (with just a few HTML pages and graphics) can often get by with a single directory on the Web server. All your graphics and HTML pages are in this one directory. One of the biggest advantages of this system is that links to local files and graphics require no special path statements.

♦ **Directory by function**—One way to organize more complicated sites is to put each section of related Web pages in the same directory. For instance, in your main directory you might offer only your first (index) page and its associated graphics. For a business site then, you'd have subdirectories for About the Business, Product Information, Technical Support, and so on. In each of these subdirectories, you'd include all the related HTML files and the graphics for those pages.

♦ **Directory by file type**—Some people prefer to create subdirectories according to the type of file as opposed to the content of the page. Your main directory may have only the index page of your site. Other subdirectories might be Graphics, Web Pages, Downloadable Files, and so on. The main advantage in organizing this way is that files generally have to be replaced only once. If you use a graphic on a number of different pages, for instance, you replace it once in the Graphics subdirectory, and all the HTML pages that access this graphic will use the new one.

♦ **Hybrid**—The best way to organize a large site might be a hybrid of the last two methods above. Creating separate subdirectories for nonrecurring items (such as individual Web pages in each category) while creating other subdirectories for items used multiple times (such as graphics) lets you get to all the files in an efficient way.

Naming Your Files

We've already mentioned that file extensions are an important part of all the filenames you use for your Web site. Because other Web browsers may rely on the file extension to know what sort of document or file it is, you'll need to include the appropriate extensions with all your Web site files.

Your Web site will almost always begin with a file called `index.html`. Most Web server software programs will automatically load this page if the URL of your site is accessed without a specific path and file reference. For example, entering **http://www.sun.com/** in your browser actually results in the URL **http://www.sun.com/index.html** being loaded in your browser. Your Web site's first page (whether it's a "front door" page or the first page of your site) should be designed with this in mind. If you plan to offer only Netscape-enhanced pages, for instance, you'll want to let your users know this on the `index.html` page.

The other consideration for naming your files is the organization you plan to use for your site. If you're using a single-directory organization, your filenames should be as unique as possible, and graphics and other files should probably have names that relate to associated Web pages. For instance:

```
about_company.html
about_header.jpeg
about_ceo_photo.jpeg
```

When possible, these names will help you determine which files are associated with which HTML pages when you go to update those files.

> **Note:** Remember that it's important to know what operating system your server uses. Some of the suggestions in this section for styles of filenames will not be helpful if you're using a DOS-based server, since names are limited to the 8.3 format.

For graphics and other files that show up on multiple pages, you might want to come up with a memorable prefix, like `gen_` or `site`, just so you can easily replace these universal files when necessary.

Example: Organizing a Site

To create a reasonably sized site for my home-business Web site, I'm going to use the hybrid style of organization. I have three different sections on my site: About My Business, Services, and Samples. Each of these sections will have its own directory structure. Graphics will be in their own subdirectory, as will downloadable files that I'm including (see fig. 5.2).

Figure 5.2

The directory organization for my site.

The directory names, then, will be as follows:

```
about_pages
service_pages
sample_pages
graphics
sample_files
```

Files and graphics are named for where they appear, unless they show up in multiple Web pages. For this site, the prefixes I'm using are as follows:

```
about_
serv_
samp_
gen_
index_
```

By naming files in this way, I'll be able to replace any graphics or update my sample files easily—without being forced to load each file or graphic to figure out what it is. Making the names as descriptive as possible (aside from the prefix) will help too, as in the following:

```
about_photo_me.jpeg
samp_resume1.doc
sampl_catalog_copy.txt
```

Updating Your Web Site

If you organize your site well, updating the site is simply a matter of replacing an outdated file with a new file using the same filename. For instance, if I wanted to replace the picture of me in the previous example, I'd simply name the new file about_photo_me.jpeg, and save it in the same directory. Now the associated Web page will load the new graphic without requiring any changes to the HTML codes.

You'll need to check with your company's IS contact or your ISP to figure out exactly how you'll update files. With an ISP, you can generally use an FTP program to put new files in your directory organization on the Web site. You might instead be required to use a UNIX-based shell account for your uploading. In either case, it's a fairly simple process.

Your Web space provider will require you to enter a username and password to gain access to the Web server, whether by FTP or shell account. Generally, you will point your FTP server to the Web server itself (for instance, **www.isp.com**), unless the provider has created a *mirror* site to avoid direct access to the Web server.

Note: A mirror site is generally an exact replica of a Web server's hard disk, but it is kept separate for security reasons. For instance, you might not be able to directly access your company's Web site files—but you can change a mirror of that Web server, and your changes will be handled by knowledgeable Internet specialists. Many companies prefer to isolate their Web servers from their corporate network so that important data is impossible to access from outside the company.

"Mirror" is more generally used to represent any more-or-less exact copy of an Internet server. The FTP site **mirrors.aol.com**, for instance, offers copies of nearly every shareware file available on other popular FTP servers around the world. This gives more users access to the same files at the same time.

After clearing the security procedure, you'll most likely be in your personal Web site's main directory. (If not, you'll need to use the `cd` command in UNIX or otherwise change directories in your FTP program.) From that point, you can update files using the Put command. Simply upload the updated files with the same names as the outdated files—in nearly every case, the old files will simply be overwritten. If you're using new files, upload them using the names and paths that your Web page links use to refer to them.

Tip: It's a good idea to maintain a folder or directory on your own hard drive that is as identical as possible to the Web site you make available on a server—so you can test your organization and filenames.

Summary

Before you can start showing the world your HTML pages, you'll need to find a Web server where you can store them. This server can be a corporate server, an Internet service provider, or a computer you maintain yourself. In any case, it needs to run Web server software and have a high-speed Internet connection.

Once you've established where you're going to put your HTML files, you need to decide how you'll organize them. There are four basic ways to do this: in one directory, in directories organized by functions, in directories organized by file type, or a hybrid of the latter two. For larger sites, a hybrid is most effective.

An important part of your Web site organization is the way you name files. The best way to do this is to be as descriptive as possible, while using name prefixes that best describe what Web pages are used to access these files. This will also help immensely when it's time to troubleshoot your Web site or update some of the files.

Review Questions

1. True or false. You'll need an extra, very powerful computer if you expect to have a Web site on the Internet.

2. Aside from the computer itself, what two basic things does a Web server require to operate?

3. If *bps* stands for bits per second, what does *Kbps* stand for? How is this different from *Mbps*?

4. How can you find out if ISDN phone service is available in your area?

5. What is throughput? Why do some Internet service providers charge based on throughput?

6. If your Web server runs the MS-DOS operating system, what are your filename limitations?

7. Explain the hybrid style of Web site organization.

8. The file about_ceo_photo.jpeg is most likely what sort of file? What might the HTML page that it is linked to be about?

9. What is the FTP command for uploading files over the Internet? Does "uploading" mean you're currently sending the file or receiving the file?

Review Exercises

1. After you have a Web site available to you, test it by creating a text file called text.txt. (Just use WordPad, SimpleText, VI, or a similar text editor and type something in this file.) Then, upload the file to your Web server. After it's there, use your Web browser to access it, using the appropriate URL. An example might be **http://www.webcom.net/tstauffer/text.txt**. After you get it to appear in your browser, you'll know you're on the right track!

2. Create a special hierarchy of directories on your own hard drive that mirror the type of organization you're going to use for the Web site. When possible, your lowest-level directory should be named the same as your directory on the Web server.

3. Access your ISP's other Web pages and, from the URLs, attempt to determine what OS the ISP is using for its Web server. (Is it Mac? UNIX? PC? This may be difficult, but not impossible to tell.) Once you've guessed, contact your ISP to figure out if you're right. Don't forget that you'll need to use that OS's naming conventions when you create your site.

Part II

Creating Basic Pages with HTML 2.0

## CHAPTER 6

Creating a Web Page and Entering Text

With the basics behind you, it's time to start creating your first HTML pages. As has already been mentioned, the basic building block of an HTML page is text. To create these pages, all you really need is a text editor and a Web browser for testing your creation (you'll eventually need a graphics program to create and edit your graphics, too). So let's look at the basic tools for Web publishing, and then create your own HTML template.

The Tools for Web Publishing

I've already mentioned it above—all you need is a text editor. In Windows 95, that's Notepad or WordPad. For Mac users, SimpleText is the perfect HTML editor. UNIX users can opt for VI or Emacs. Basically, all you need to remember is that HTML pages, while they include the .htm or .html file extensions, are simply ASCII text files. Any program that generates ASCII text files will work fine as an HTML editor—even a word processor like WordPerfect or Microsoft Word.

> **Tip:** If you create an HTML page in a word processor, don't forget to use the Save As command to save it as an ASCII text file.

You'll also need a Web browser to check on the appearance of your Web page as you create it. All Web browsers should have the ability to load local pages from your hard drive, just as they can load HTML pages across the Web. Check the menu of your Web browser (if it's a graphical browser) for a command like File, Open (see fig. 6.1).

Figure 6.1

In Microsoft Internet Explorer for Windows 95, the File, Open command opens the Open Internet Address dialog box which contains an Open File command button to open a file from a drive.

You may have heard of some dedicated HTML editing programs that are designed to make your work in HTML easier. They do indeed exist, and they can be very useful. Unfortunately, many of them also hide the HTML codes from the designer, so they would be difficult for us to use as you learn how HTML works. Once you understand HTML, though, it can be a great benefit to use one of these browsers. I'll talk about some of them in Chapters 27, 28, and 29.

Document Tags

The first HTML tags you're going to look at are the document tags. These are the tags that are required for every HTML page you create. They define the different parts of the document.

Just like a magazine article, an HTML document has two distinct parts—a head and a body. The head of the HTML document is where you enter the title of the page. It's also used for some more advanced commands that you'll study later in Chapters, 10, 19, 22 and 23.

To create the head portion of your HTML document and to give the document a title, type the following in your text editor:

```
<HEAD>
<TITLE>My First Page</TITLE>
</HEAD>
```

This tells a Web browser what information should be considered to be in the head portion of of the document, and what it should call the document in the title bar of the browser window.

If you've got a head, then you'll need a body, right? The body is where you'll do most of your work—you'll enter text, headlines, graphics, and all your other Web goodies. To add the body section, start after the <code></HEAD></code> tag, and enter the following:

```
<BODY>

</BODY>
```

Between these two tags, you'll eventually enter the rest of the text and graphics for your Web page.

There's one last thing you need to consider. In order that all Web browsers understand that this is an HTML document (remember that you're saving it as ASCII text, so the browser could be confused), you need to add some tags on either side of the head and body tags you've created. Above the first <HEAD> tag, enter the following:

```
<HTML>
```

After the last </BODY> tag, type the following:

```
</HTML>
```

Now, at least as far as your Web browser is concerned, you have a complete Web document!

Example: Creating an HTML Template

Let's take what you know and create a template. By saving this template as a generic text file, you'll have a quick way to create new HTML files—simply load the template and use the File, Save As command to save it as your new Web page.

Start by entering the following in a blank text file:

```
<HTML>
<HEAD>
<TITLE>Enter Title Here</TITLE>
</HEAD>
<BODY>

</BODY>
</HTML>
```

And that's it. Now save this as an ASCII text file called `template.html` (or `template.htm` if you're using DOS or Windows 3.1). Now, whenever you're ready to create a new HTML document, simply load `template.html` into your text editor and use the Save As command to rename it.

Note: If you use a word processor to create your HTML files, you may notice that sometimes you get more than one option for saving files as ASCII text. So which one is right? Fortunately, it doesn't really matter. The big problem comes in editing the text on different platforms since DOS-based machines (including Windows) and Macs treat returns and linefeeds differently. If you plan to edit a Mac-created HTML file on a DOS machine, for instance, choose DOS text when you save it. Funny little newline characters will now appear in a Mac text editor, but everything will look good on the DOS side.

Example: Hello World

When learning a new programming language, it's traditional that the first program you create is designed to say "Hello World." Well, HTML isn't a programming language—but I can use the Hello World example to prove that your template is a complete Web document.

Load the `template.html` file into your text editor, and use the Save As command to rename it `hello_world.html` or something similar. Now, edit the document so that it looks like this:

```
<HTML>
<HEAD>
<TITLE>Hello World Page</TITLE>
</HEAD>
<BODY>
Hello World!
</BODY>
</HTML>
```

Select the File, Save command from your text editor. Now load your Web browser and select the Open File (or similar) command from the File menu. In the dialog box, find the document `hello_world.html` and select OK to load it into your Web browser. If everything goes as planned, your browser should display something similar to figure 6.2.

Figure 6.2

The Hello World page as viewed in Microsoft Internet Explorer.

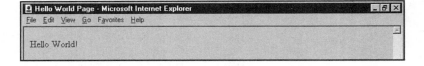

And that's a Web page!

Understanding Tags: Container and Empty Tags

In creating your HTML template, you've already dealt with some of the most basic tags in HTML. The first thing you should notice about these HTML tags is that all tags include < and > on either side of the tag's command. This is how HTML recognizes tags. If you don't use the brackets, then a Web browser will assume your commands are text that you want displayed—even if that text is the same as an HTML command.

While a Web browser would consider the following to be a tag:

```
<HTML>
```

that same Web browser would interpret the following as text to be displayed on-screen:

HTML

> **Tip:** Tags are not case-sensitive, so they don't have to be all uppercase—even though that's how they appear in this book. I suggest you type them as uppercase, though, since it makes them stand out in your text editor.

Because tags aren't considered text by the document, they also don't show up in the document. If the browser interprets something as a tag, it won't appear in the browser window.

Container Tags

You may have noticed that for every tag, such as the title tag, you actually entered two different HTML commands—an "on" tag and an "off" tag. The off tag is the same as the on tag, except for the / after the <.

In HTML, tags that include both an on and an off tag are called *container tags*. These tags wrap around text in your document and perform some sort of formatting on the text. They hold, or contain, the text between the two tags. The title, HTML, head, and body tags are all container tags—the relevant text goes between the on and off tags.

Container tags always have the following form:

```
<TAG>text being formatted or defined</TAG>
```

In fact, you've already been introduced to a fairly common container tag in the first chapter of this book, the <EM> (emphasis tag). An example of the emphasis tag would be:

```
Here's some <EM>really important</EM> text.
```

Because <EM> is an implicit formatting tag, it's up to the browser to decide what to do to the text between the on and off tags. But only the words `really important` will be affected in this example, since they're the only text that is being "contained" by the tags.

Empty Tags

All other tags in HTML fall into one other category, called *empty tags*. These tags have only an on tag—there are no off tags. The reason for this is that empty tags don't act on blocks of text. Instead, they do something all on their own. An example of this would be the <HR> (horizontal rule) tag. This tag draws a line across the width of your document. For example:

```
The following is a horizontal line:

<HR>
The rest of this is just more text.
```

When viewed in a Web browser, the two sentences will be separated by a horizontal line, as in figure 6.3.

Figure 6.3

Here are your two sentences, separated by a horizontal line.

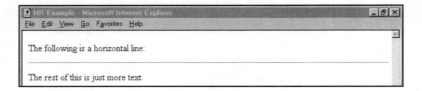

Entering Paragraph Text on Your Web Page

With your template prepared, and with an understanding of the two types of tags in HTML, you're ready to enter text on a Web page. As mentioned earlier, all the text that you enter on a page should come between the <BODY> and </BODY> tags. Like <EM>, the body tags are container tags that tell a Web browser what parts of the HTML document should be displayed in the browser window.

You've seen that you can just type text into an HTML document and it will be displayed in the browser. Technically, though, most of the text you type should be in another container tag: the <P> (paragraph) tag. This tag is used to show a Web browser what text in your document constitutes a paragraph. For the most part, Web browsers ignore more than one space between words and will ignore returns that you add to your HTML file while you're creating it.

In order to give the appearance of paragraphs, then, you have to use the paragraph container tag. The paragraph tag uses the following format:

```
<P>Here is the text for my paragraph. It doesn't matter how long it is,
how many spaces are between the words or when I decide to hit the return
key. It will create a new paragraph only when I end the tag and begin
with another one.
</P>

<P> Here's the next paragraph. </P>
```

Note: Although it is technically a container tag, the </P> tag is not required at the ends of paragraphs by HTML 2.0. This tends to cause a little confusion. Many people end up using <P> as an empty tag, assuming that it's designed to insert a line break at the end of paragraphs (or even to create multiple blank lines). That's not its purpose. Using <P> as a container, as I've shown previously, gets the most reliable results in all different types of browsers. In the spirit of good HTML, the container is used to isolate all the text you want to call a "paragraph." Then it lets the browser render that in the way its programmers feel is most appropriate.

Like the emphasis tag, the paragraph container tells the Web browser that all of the text between the on and off tags is in a single paragraph. When you start another paragraph, the Web browser will drop down a line between the two.

Here's that same example, except you'll throw in some spaces. Remember, spaces and returns almost never affect the way the text will be displayed on the screen. In a paragraph container, the browser will ignore more than one space and any returns.

```
<P>Here is the text for my paragraph.
It doesn't matter how long it is, how many spaces are between the words
or when I decide to hit the return key. It will create a new paragraph
only when I end the tag and begin with another one. </P>

<P> Here's the next paragraph. </P>
```

Both this example and the previous example will be displayed in the Web browser in exactly the same way.

The *
* Tag for Line Breaks

But what if you want to decide where a line is going to end Consider the example of entering an address in a Web document, as follows:

```
<P>
Richard Smith
14234 Main Street
Anycity, ST 00001
</P>
```

It looks about right when you type it into your text editor. However, when it displays in a Web browser, it looks like figure 6.4.

We already know what the problem is: Web browsers ignore extra spaces and returns! But if you put each of those lines in a paragraph container, you'd end up with a space between each line—and that would look wrong, too.

The answer is the empty tag <BR>, which forces a line return in your Web document. Properly formatted, your address would look like this:

```
<P>
Richard Smith<BR>
14234 Main Street<BR>
Anycity, ST 00001<BR>
</P>
```

Figure 6.4

The Post Office would never deliver this.

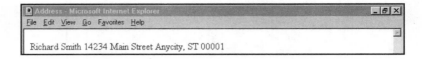

And it would look just right in your Web browser, just as in figure 6.5.

Figure 6.5

This address looks much better.

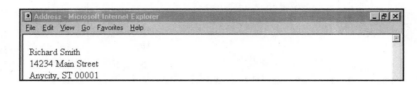

The Comment Tag

There's one other tag I'd like to discuss in this chapter, called the comment tag. This tag is fairly unique, in that it's actually used to make the Web browser ignore anything the tag contains. That can be text, hypertext links, image links, even small scripts and programs.

> **Tip:** It's best to delete obsolete links and tags from your documents, rather than just using the comment tag. Some browsers will display certain tags even if they are "commented out."

For now, you'll use the comment tag to hide text. The point in hiding the text is that it allows you to create a private message that is intended to remind you of something or to help those who view the raw HTML document to understand what you're doing. That's why it's called the comment tag. For instance:

```
<!--This is a comment that won't display in a browser-->
```

The comment tag isn't the most elegant in HTML, but it usually works. Anything you type between `<!--` and `-->` should be ignored by the browser. Even multiple lines are ignored—as with most tags, the comment tag ignores returns.

Generally, you'll use the comment tag for your own benefit—perhaps to mark a point in a particular HTML document where you need to remember to update some text, or perhaps to explain a particularly confusing part of your page. Since it's fairly easy for anyone to view your raw HTML document, you might also use the comment tag to create a copyright message or give information about yourself (see the sidebar).

Viewing the Source of Web Pages

Ever been out on the Web looking at a particularly well-designed HTML document—and wondering how they did it?

If you'd like to, most browsers will let you view the *document source* for any Web page they can load. This allows you to download the raw HTML codes and ASCII text, just as if you'd created the page yourself.

To do this, select the View Document command in the Edit menu of your Web browser (the command may differ slightly, so look for a similar name if you can't find View Document). What results is the plain ASCII text file that was used to create that Web page.

Depending on your browser, this source file will either be displayed in the browser window, or saved to your hard drive and displayed in the default text editor. If the source is displayed in the browser window, then select File, Save As to save the source to your hard drive.

Now you might be able to imagine how comments can come in handy. If you would rather not have people copy and use the source from your Web pages (or if your pages contain otherwise copyrighted material that you want to protect), you can use the comment tag to let others know that you consider the page your property. For instance:

```
<!--Contents of this document Copyright 1996 Todd Stauffer. Please
do not copy or otherwise reproduce the source HTML code of this
document without permission.-->
```

Of course, that's not to say that you shouldn't also offer a visible copyright notice or other legal disclaimers. But comments within the code tend to talk directly to folks a little more HTML-savvy. Using a comment tag like this is a great way to encourage other Web designers to ask you before using your HTML pages for their own private use. (But if they don't ask, any legal problems are your own I'm afraid.)

Note: Don't let this confuse you, but the comment tag is an unusual one. It's not really a container tag, since it doesn't have two similar tags that are differentiated only by / in the second tag. At the same time, it's difficult to describe as an empty tag, since it does do something to text in the document.

Example: Creating a Complete Web Page

Let's take everything you've learned and build a complete Web page. Start by loading the template and using Save As to create a new document for this example. (Call it test1.html or something similar.)

Now, create a document that looks something like Listing 6.1. You should have to change only the title text; enter the other text between the body tags.

On the CD

Listing 6.1 *test1.html* **Testing Tags**

```
<HTML>
<HEAD>
<TITLE>The Testing Tags Page</TITLE>
<!--This page is Copyright 1996 Todd Stauffer-->
</HEAD>
<BODY>
<P>On this page we're reviewing the different types of tags that we've
learned in this chapter. For instance, this is the first paragraph.</P>
<P>In the second paragraph, I'm going to include the name and address of
one of my favorite people. Hopefully it's formatted correctly.<BR>
Tom Smith<BR>
1010 Lovers Lane<BR>
Anywhere, US 10001<BR>
</P>
<HR>
<P>Now I'll start a <EM>completely new</EM> idea, since it's coming after
a horizontal line.</P>
<!--Don't forget to update this page with the completely new idea here.-->
</BODY>
</HTML>
```

When you've finished entering the text and tags (you can use your own text if you like; just try to use all of the tags we've reviewed in the chapter), use the Save command in your text editor. Now switch to your Web browser, and load your new page using the Open File (or similar) command.

If everything went well, it should look something like figure 6.6.

Figure 6.6

Here's how the example should appear in Netscape Navigator. Notice how the comments do not appear.

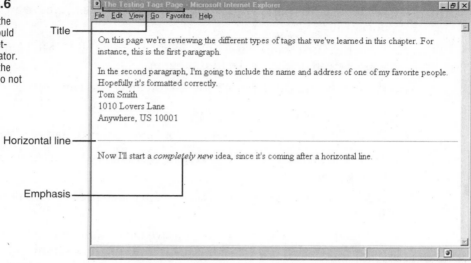

Title ──

Horizontal line ──

Emphasis ──

Summary

A good text editor and a Web browser program are all you need to start creating Web pages. Using these tools, you can create a template for your Web pages that includes all of the appropriate document tags. Since these are almost always the same for every HTML document, you can reuse the template without retyping.

There are two basic types of HTML tags: container tags and empty tags. The major difference between the two is that container tags feature both an on and an off component (usually the same tag, with a slash (/) before the name of the off tag). This is because container tags act on specific blocks of text, while empty tags generally perform some function on their own.

The most basic tags for entering text are the paragraph, line break, comment, and horizontal line tags. The comment tag is a special case—it's designed to keep text from being displayed by a Web browser. Entering text on a Web page is a simple matter of typing between the body tags, with an eye given to using the basic tags correctly.

Review Questions

1. Is it necessary to use a special program to create HTML pages?

2. In what file format are HTML pages saved? What file extension should be used for an HTML document?

3. What are the three basic document tags?

4. What tag have you learned is appropriate for the head area of an HTML document?

5. What's the first thing you should do after loading an HTML template you've created into a text editor program?

6. What is the main difference between container and empty tags?

7. Give one example of an empty tag.

8. Why is the comment tag different from most other container tags?

9. True or false. All text for your Web page should be typed between the body container tags.

10. Aside from line spacing, what is the main difference between the <BR> and <P> tags?

11. Use your Web browser to view and save the main source code for the following Web document: **http://www.ibm.com/index.html**. (You may also need to use a text editor, depending on your Web browser's capabilities.)

Review Exercises

1. Create a document that uses nothing but <P> container tags to break up text. Then, create a document that uses nothing but <BR> tags. What's the difference in your browser?

2. Try adding additional <P> or <BR> tags to your documents between lines or text or paragraphs. Do they add extra lines in your browser? View them from more than one browser. (Hint: adding lines between paragraphs for multiple <BR> or <P> tags is not supported by the HTML standard, although some popular browsers recognize them.)

3. Add a standard "header comment" to your template using the comment tag. This is a great idea, especially if you develop HTML pages for your company—after all, documenting your efforts is what the comment tag is all about. Here's an example for a template, which can be altered every time you create a new document:

```
<!--
Page Designer: Todd A. Stauffer
Creation Date: 00 Month 9?
Revision Date: 00 Month 9?
File type: HTML 2.0     -->
```

## CHAPTER 7

Changing and Customizing HTML Text

HTML 2.0 is a standard created after the fact. What I mean is that HTML was already in wide use when the standard was finally written. As a result, there tend to be a few different ways to do the same things. You'll take a look at most of them, and I'll try to explain the theory behind each. I'll also recommend one or two options that best do what you're interested in accomplishing—and just leave the rest of the options for you to consult if the occasion ever demands.

Creating Headers and Headlines

One of the first things you might have wondered when you were entering text in Chapter 6 is, "How can I change the size of the text?" HTML 2.0 doesn't have any explicit tags or commands for changing the font size within a document (although Netscape HTML does). Instead, it relies on the implicit header tags to do this.

Header tags are containers, and unlike many other HTML tags, they double as paragraph tags. Ranging from level 1 to level 6, headers allow you to create different levels of emphasized headlines to help you organize your documents. The following is an example; see figure 7.1 for the results:

```
<H1>Header Level One is the largest for headlines or page titles</H1>
<H2>Level Two is a little smaller for major subheads</H2>
<H3>Level Three is again smaller, for minor subheads</H3>
<P>This is regular text.</P>
<H4>Level Four is about the same size as regular text, but emphasized</H4>
<H5>Level Five: again emphasized, but smaller than regular text</H5>
<H6>Level Six is generally the smallest header</H6>
```

Figure 7.1

HTML header tags at work. Notice that the fourth entry is regular text between <P> and </P> tags.

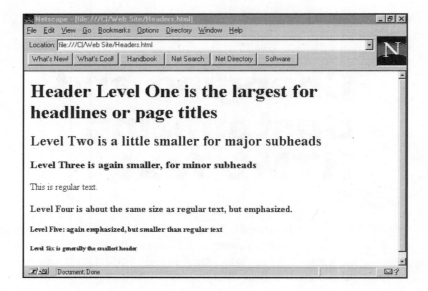

You cannot include a header tag on the same line as regular text, even if you close the header tag and continue with unaltered text. A header tag has the same effect as a <P>, in that it creates a new line after its "off" tag. The following:

```
<H1>This is a header</H1> And this is plain text.
```

offers the same results as:

```
<H2>This is also a header</H2>
<P>And this is also plain text</P>
```

In both cases, the Web browser will place the header text and plain text on different lines, with the header text appearing larger and the plain text appearing "normal" in size.

Note: The HTML standard technically requires that using a particular header level requires that the larger header tags be used previously. So, for instance, if you use an <H2> tag, you should have an <H1> tag somewhere before it. Very few browsers (if any) actually require this and, for the most part, HTML designers use header tags as simply a way to change the size of text for emphasis. That's how I use them, even going so far as to use <H5> or <H6> for "fine print" on my pages. If you're an absolute stickler for standards, though, realize that it's more correct to only use header tags for true headers in your documents, and then only in order (i.e., <H1>, <H2>, <H3>, and so on).

Example: A Topical Discussion

Now, with the addition of the header tags, you're suddenly able to add a level of organization to your pages that was lacking previously. Using the horizontal line and emphasis tags you saw in Chapter 6, it's possible to create a very useful text-oriented HTML document with what you now know.

Let's start just with headers and regular text. Load your HTML template into a text editor and save it as a new HTML document (headers.html or something similar). Then fill in the template's body section using both header containers and paragraph containers (see Listing 7.1).

On the CD

Listing 7.1 *headers.html* **The Template's HTML Body Section**

```
<BODY>
<H1>Welcome to my home on the Web</H1>
<P>Hi there! My name is Mark Williamson, and I'm an active participant
in the Web. Aside from my Internet journeys I'm also a big fan of the
science-fiction writer Wilhelm Norris, and I love collecting models of
television spacecraft. As far as the boring stuff goes, I work as a
Macintosh programmer in Carmel, California.</P>
<H2>My Work</H2>
<P>I've recently moved from programming in a Microsoft Windows
environment to a Macintosh environment, and I must admit that I've been
more than a little overwhelmed. Fortunately I've had good help from local
user groups and my co-workers...plus, they've introduced me to some
exceptional tools for Mac programming.</P>
<H3>ProGraph</H3>
<P>If you've never worked in a visual programming environment, you're
in for a treat. With my background in Windows and UNIX C programming, I
was surprised how quickly I picked up this object-oriented concept. I
definitely recommend it!</P>
```

continues

Listing 7.1 Continued

```
<H3>MetroWerks</H3>
<P>I can't imagine I even need to say anything about this. It's hands-
down the best C and C++ development environment ever created for
Macintosh. In my opinion, it's the best created for any platform!</P>
<H5>This document contains opinions that are my own and do not
necessarily reflect those of my employer.</H5>
</BODY>
```

Entering text and using header tags in this way allows us to create a document that has more of the feel of a well-outlined magazine article, or even a chapter in a book. You may have noticed that this book uses different-sized headlines to suggest that you're digging deeper into a subject (smaller headlines) or beginning a new subject (bigger headlines). HTML allows you to do the same thing with the header tag (see fig. 7.2).

Figure 7.2

Inserting header containers between paragraphs makes for a more readable page.

Larger header indicates broader subjects

Smaller header is digging deeper

Implicit and Explicit Text Emphasis

Implicit tags are those that allow the browser to choose, within limitations, how the marked-up text will be displayed. Header tags are actually an example of an implicit tag, since the HTML designer has no control over how much bigger or smaller a header tag will be. Although most browsers will render header tags in somewhat similar ways, others (for instance, nongraphical browsers) have to come up with another system for emphasis, such as underlining or highlighting the text.

Because HTML was originally created with the overriding mission of being displayed on nearly any computer system, implicit tags for emphasis were a necessity. HTML allows the designer to decide what text will be emphasized. But only explicit tags tell the Web browser how to render that text.

Explicit Styles

Explicit tags are also often called *physical tags,* since they very specifically tell the Web browser how you want the text to physically appear. The browser is given no choice in the matter.

The basic explicit tags are containers that let the user mark text as bold, italic, or underlined (see Table 7.1).

Table 7.1   HTML Physical Container Tags

Tags	Meaning
<B>, </B>	Bold text
<I>, </I>	Italic text
<U>, </U>	Underlined text

> **Note:** Not all browsers will render underlined text (notable among them is Netscape Navigator), because hypertext links are also often displayed as underlined, which could potentially be confusing.

With these tags, the browser really has no choice—it must either display the text as defined or, if it can't do that, then it must add no emphasis to the text. This is both good and bad for you as the designer. If you prefer that text not be emphasized at all if it can't be italic, for example, then you should use the <I> tag.

Another feature of explicit (physical) tags is that they can generally be used in combination with other tags. As you'll see in the next section, this isn't always a good idea with implicit tags. For instance, most graphic browsers will render the following example by applying both tags to the text (see fig. 7.3).

```
<H1><I>Welcome Home!</I></H1>
<B><I>This is bold and italic</I></B>
```

Figure 7.3

Most browsers can render two physical tags applied to the same selection of text.

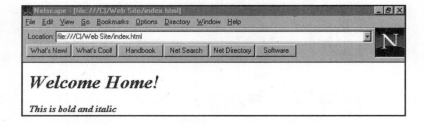

Implicit HTML Tags

Implicit styles are often called *logical styles*, since they allow the browser some freedom in how it will display the text. These tags, like the header tags, are generally relative to one another, depending on the browser being used to view them. See Table 7.2 for some of the common implicit (logical) tags.

Table 7.2 Some Basic Logical HTML Tags

Tags	Meaning	Generally Rendered as…
<EM>, </EM>	Emphasis	Italic text
<STRONG>, </STRONG>	Strong emphasis	Bold text
<TT>, </TT>	Teletype	Monospaced text

Table 7.2 includes a section that tells you how these tags are often rendered in graphical Web browsers. There's no rule for this, though, and the tags don't necessarily have to be rendered in that way.

There are two other distinctions between these tags and the physical tags (such as bold and italic) that you've already discussed. First, these logical tags will always be rendered by any Web browser that views them. Even text browsers (which are unable to show italic text) will display the <EM> or <STRONG> tags by underlining, boldfacing, or highlighting the text.

Second, these tags are generally not effective when used together. Where <B><I>text</I></B> will sometimes offer useful results, <EM><STRONG>text</STRONG></EM> rarely will. Combining these tags with other tags (such as header tags or physical tags) is often either ineffective or redundant.

Note: My warning about combining logical tags isn't always applicable, even though it's a good rule to follow. Netscape Navigator, for instance, will render both <EM> and <STRONG> tags simultaneously with others. (Used together, the tags would result in bold, italicized text in Navigator.)

Example: Physical versus Logical

Here's a great way to kill two birds with one stone. With this example you can get a feel for using both the physical and the logical tags discussed above. At the same time, you can also test these tags in your browser to see how they're displayed. (If you have more than one browser, test this example in all of them. That way you can see how different browsers interpret logical tags.)

To begin, load your template file in a text editor, and rename it something intuitive, like tagtest1.html. Then, enter the text between the body tags as it appears in Listing 7.2.

On the CD

Listing 7.2 *tagtest1.html* **HTML Body Tags Text**

```
<BODY>
<P>
This is a test of the <B>bold tag</B><BR>
This is a test of the <STRONG>strong emphasis tag</STRONG><BR>
</P>
<P>
This is a test of the <I>italics tag</I><BR>
This is a test of the <EM>emphasis tag</EM><BR>
</P>
<P>
This is a test of the <B><I>bold and italics tags together</I></B><BR>
This is a test of the <STRONG><EM>strong and emphasis tags together</EM>
</STRONG><BR>
</P>
<P>
While we're at it, does <U>underlined text</U> appear in this
browser?<BR>
And what does <TT>teletype text</TT> look like?<BR>
</P>
</BODY>
```

Note: Remember that using <STRONG> and <EM> together is not recommended in the HTML 2.0 standard. We did it just as an example to see how it renders in your browser.

When you've finished entering this text, save the file again in your text editor, then choose the Load File command in your Web browser to display the HTML document. If you have other Web browsers, see how those respond to the tags, too (see fig. 7.4).

Figure 7.4

Implicit and
explicit HTML
codes in Internet
Explorer for
Windows 95.

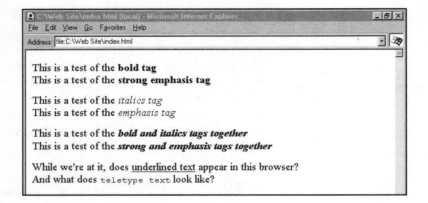

Other Implicits: Programming, Quoting, and Citing

At the beginning of this chapter, I mentioned that the proliferation of HTML tags took place before the standard was ever conceived of—which might explain some of the tags that we discuss in this section. For the most part, these tags are implicit (logical) and aimed directly at certain areas of expertise. At the same time, however, the bulk of these tags will look exactly the same in a Web browser.

Programmer's HTML Tags

One of the early, more common uses for HTML was for documenting computer programs and offering tips or advice to computer programmers. Part of the HTML 2.0 standard, then, offers some implicit (logical) HTML tags that allow HTML designers to mark text in a way that makes it easier to present computer programming codes. Those tags are in Table 7.3.

Table 7.3   HTML Tags for Computer Programming

Tags	Meaning	Generally Rendered as...
<CODE>, </CODE>	Programming lines	Monospaced (like <TT>)
<KBD>, </KBD>	Keyboard text	Monospaced
<SAMP>, </SAMP>	Sample output	Monospaced
<VAR>, </VAR>	Variable	Italic

Notice that the majority of these tags are often displayed in exactly the same way—in the default monospaced font for the browser. Then why use them?

First, not all browsers will necessarily follow the "general" way. Some browsers will actually render these tags in slightly different ways from one another, so that <SAMP>, for instance, might appear in a slightly larger font than <CODE>.

> **Note:** These tags had more meaning with earlier browsers like Mosaic, which used to allow users to define their own fonts and sizes for specific tags. In an era where browsers give the designer control over actual font families and sizes (see Chapters 19 and 21), these tags are used less and less.

Second, using these tags is a great way to internally document your HTML pages, so that you can tell at a glance what certain text is supposed to be. This will help you later when you return to the document to update it or fix errors—especially as the document becomes more complex.

Quoting, Citing, Definitions, and Addresses

Along the same lines as the HTML "programmer's" tags, you have available certain implicit tags that work as typographer's or publisher's codes. As shown in Table 7.4, these codes often work in ways similar to others you've already seen—with a few twists.

Table 7.4   HTML Publisher-Style Tags

Tags	*Meaning*	*Generally Rendered as...*
<CITE>, </CITE>	Bibliographical citation	Italic text
<BLOCKQUOTE>, </BLOCKQUOTE>	Block of quoted text	Indented text
<DFN>, </DFN>	Term definition	Regular text
<ADDRESS>, </ADDRESS>	Street or e-mail address	Italic text

Again, notice that the <CITE> tag isn't going to be rendered any differently from the italics, emphasis, or variable tags you've seen previously. The <DFN> tag is often not rendered as any special sort of text at all, whereas the <ADDRESS> tag is identical in function to the italics tag.

So the best use for these tags (with the exception of the <BLOCKQUOTE> tag) is as internal documentation of your HTML documents. Remember, of course, that some browsers may render them slightly differently from what is suggested in Table 7.4.

Example: Using the *<BLOCKQUOTE>* and *<ADDRESS>* Tags

The only really new tag in the Table 7.4 is the <BLOCKQUOTE> tag. This tag usually indents the left margin of regular text in the browser window, just as you might find a blocked quotation formatted in a printed document.

Also as part of the tag, <BLOCKQUOTE> generally adds a return or one extra line on either side of the tag, so no paragraph tags are needed. Paragraph tags should, however, be used to contain text on either side of the blockquote.

Although the <ADDRESS> tag is similar to italics or emphasis, I've thrown in an example of using it correctly. Remember to include a line break after each line of the address.

To begin this example, create and save a new HTML document from the template you created in Chapter 6. Enter Listing 7.3 between the body tags.

On the CD

Listing 7.3 *emphasis.html* The *<BLOCKQUOTE>* and *<ADDRESS>* Tags

```
<BODY>
<P>I believe it was Abraham Lincoln who once said (emphasis is mine):
<BLOCKQUOTE>Four score and seven years ago our <B>forefathers</B> brought
forth on this continent a new nation, conceived in <I>liberty</I> and
dedicated to the proposition that all men are created <EM>equal</EM>.
</BLOCKQUOTE>
It was something like that, wasn't it?
</P>
<P>If you liked this quote, feel free to write me at:<BR>
<ADDRESS>
Rich Memory<BR>
4242 Sumtin Street<BR>
Big City, ST 12435<BR>
</ADDRESS>
</P>
</BODY>
```

Notice that an off paragraph tag isn't required before you get into the address tag—remember, <ADDRESS> works very much as italics does, and the <BR> tag is designed to work as well inside a paragraph container as it does outside one. So you can put the paragraph tag after the address, to contain both address listing and the text in the same paragraph.

What does all of this look like? Take a look at figure 7.5. <BLOCKQUOTE>, unlike some of the tags you've looked at, really does offer unique abilities that make it worth using in your documents.

Figure 7.5

Blockquote and address HTML tags.

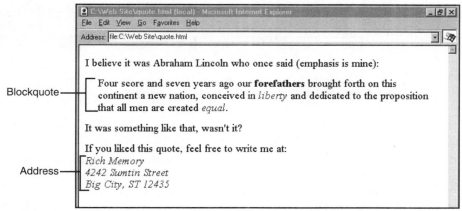

Preformatted Text
==================

Preformatted Text

Are you ready to break some of the rules of HTML that I've been harping on over the last two chapters? That's what you're about to do—in fact, you're going to break two. I've said over and over that the HTML 2.0 standard is not designed for layout. In fact, you haven't even learned how to put two blank lines between paragraphs.

I've also said that spaces and returns in between tags (like the paragraph tag) don't matter. Well, there is at least one exception to this rule: the <PRE> tag.

The <PRE> (preformatted text) tag is designed to allow you to keep the exact spacing and returns that you've put between the on and off tags. The basic reasoning behind this tag is the notion that every once in a while you'd like your text to stay exactly as you put it—for instance, in a mathematical formula, or if you create a table. While there are other ways to do both tables and math, they don't fall under the HTML 2.0 standard. On top of that, you can use <PRE> for a number of other reasons: lists, lining up decimals for dollar figures, and even poetry.

Consider the following example:

```
<P>Oh beautiful, for spacious skies,
For amber waves of grain.
For purple mountains' majesty,
Above the fruited plains.</P>
```

Sure it's a familiar refrain, but it won't look so familiar in a browser if you leave it between paragraph tags. Instead, you can use the <PRE> tag to keep things exactly the way you want them:

```
<PRE>Oh beautiful, for spacious skies,
     For amber waves of grain.
For purple mountains' majesty,
     Above the fruited plains.</PRE>
```

In a browser, it'll look exactly the way you want it to (see fig. 7.6).

Figure 7.6

Paragraph versus
preformatted text.

Using the
<P> tag

Using the
<PRE> tag

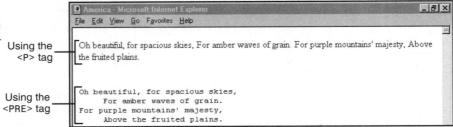

You may have noticed that the preformatted text is in a monospaced font—it will always be that way. Otherwise, the <PRE> tag works pretty much like the paragraph font, except that it lets you decide where the line breaks and spaces will appear. Look at the following example:

```
<PRE>I    simply want to make this <B>really</B> clear to you.

</PRE>
```

With the above code, the browser will display this line in nearly exactly the same way as it would using the <P> tag, except that it will be in a monospaced font, and the extra spaces and extra return will appear as well. In fact, there will be two blank lines below the line of text—one for the return, and one for the </PRE> tag itself.

You can even use the <PRE> tags to create extra lines in a document without typing any text between them. This example adds two blank lines to a document:

```
<PRE>
</PRE>
```

For each additional blank line you want to add, just press Enter after the first tag one time.

> **Note:** There is one potential drawback to the <PRE> tag. It doesn't allow the browser screen to wrap text automatically—instead, users need to expand their browser window if you use particular long lines within a <PRE> container. Just keep this in mind, and make sure your lines of text are reasonably short so that all browsers can view them without scrolling.

Example: Creating Your Own Layout with the *<PRE>* Tag

Let's take a look at a couple of different reasons why you might want to use the <PRE> tag in your HTML documents. Start by loading your template and choosing the

Save As command in your text editor to save the file as `pre_test.html`, or something similar.

Now between the body tags, let's create an example that uses some of the benefits of preformatting—the ability to center text and choose your own margins, for example. How? Let's format some screenplay dialogue (see Listing 7.4).

Tip: Text between `<PRE>` tags is easier to align if you hit Enter after the on tag, then start typing. Doing so will add an extra line, though.

On the CD

Listing 7.4 *pre_test.html* **Create Your Own Layout**

```
<BODY>
<P>
<TT>
<B>(Int) Rick's Apartment, Late Afternoon</B><BR>
Rick is busying himself with his personal computer when Linda walks
through the door from the kitchen. Startled, Rick bolts upright from his
chair and swats frantically at the keyboard trying to make something
disappear. Linda moves closer to the computer.</TT></P>
<PRE>

                    Linda
                     (confused)
          What were you doing?

                    Rick
          Just the finances.

                    Linda
          But you already printed checks
          last Sunday.

                    Rick
          I know. But Tuesday is when I, uh,
          enter my gambling debts. (Sighs deeply.)
          Honey, I'm in big trouble.
</PRE>
</BODY>
```

It takes a little tapping on the space bar, but with the `<PRE>` tag you can create some fairly elaborate layouts for getting your point across—especially when layout is just as important as the text itself. In a browser, it comes out looking like a big-budget picture script (see fig. 7.7).

Figure 7.7

The <PRE> tag at work.

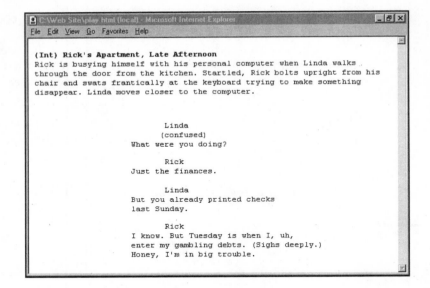

Example: Using *<PRE>* for Spaces and Tables

In the same way that you created the film script using the <PRE> tag, you can also format a primitive table using the <PRE> tag along with some others. The key to making this work correctly is alignment. Realize that each space taken up by a character of an invisible tag (like <B>) will not appear in the browser's display, so you'll need to compensate.

> **Tip:** One way to keep the columns in a table straight is to type your table first, and then add emphasis tags afterward.

Load your template and save it as `pre_tbl.html`. Now enter Listing 7.5 between the body tags.

Listing 7.5 *pre_tbl.html* **Creating Spaces and Tables**

```
<BODY>
<PRE>

</PRE>
<HR>
<H2>Price Per Item in Bulk Orders</H2>
<PRE>
```

```
Quantity        XJS100      RJS200      YJS50       MST3000

1-50            $40         $50         $75         $100
50-99           $35         $45         $70         $95
100-200         $30         $40         $65         $90
200+            $25         $35         $55         $75

</PRE>
<H5>Prices do not include applicable sales taxes.</H5>
</BODY>
```

You may need to play with the spacing a bit to line everything up. Save the HTML document, then choose the Open File command in your browser to proof it. Keep playing with it until it looks right.

> **Tip:** If you use a more advanced text editor or word processor, fight your urge to use the Tab key to align <PRE> elements. Use the spacebar instead.

Once you have everything aligned correctly, it's actually a fairly attractive and orderly little table (see fig. 7.8).

Figure 7.8

Use the <PRE> tag to create a table.

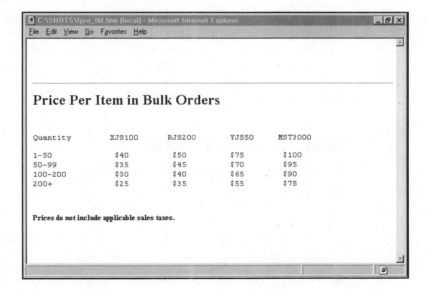

> **Note:** You may be tempted to use <B> or another emphasis tag for the column heads in your table. Realize, however, that it is nearly impossible to align columns so that they will appear correctly in every browser when one row is bold and other rows are plain text. Different browsers make bold text a fraction wider than regular text, making the row increasingly misaligned. Even if it looks good in your browser, chances are it won't work in all of them.

Summary

HTML 2.0 offers us both explicit (physical) and implicit (logical) tags with which to mark up text. The explicit tags are designed to do something specific to the text, such as turn it bold or italic. If a browser can't do what's asked, it doesn't do anything.

Implicit tags are more general commands, such as Emphasis or Strong Emphasis. While most browsers will show these tags in a similar way, there's no specific rule. Each individual browser will display an implicit tag somehow, but not always in the same way that other browsers do it.

There are a good number of implicit tags, many of which duplicate certain types of emphasis. These are good for internally documenting HTML documents, though, since the tags are generally designed for some specific task—such as displaying computer programming code or certain typographical elements.

The <PRE> tag is also a very useful tag, although it breaks some of the rules for other tags. It allows you to maintain the spaces and returns you've entered between the two tags. This lets you preformat your HTML documents so that tables and other elements are displayed correctly.

Review Questions

1. What are the other names for explicit and implicit tags?

2. What is the difference between an explicit and an implicit tag?

3. Why is the <B> (bold) tag considered explicit?

4. Will the <I> tag work in a text-based browser like Lynx? How about the <EM> tag?

5. What programmer's HTML tag is usually displayed differently from the others?

6. Why would you use a programmer's HTML tag?

7. Is it possible to have more than one paragraph of text in a single <BLOCKQUOTE> container?

8. What other common HTML tag is similar to the <PRE> tag?

9. Can you use other tags, such as <B> or <I>, within <PRE> containers?

Review Exercises

1. Create a document that uses all of the different implicit and explicit layout tags discussed, and note how your browser(s) render them. Also note what happens when you combine tags and view them in your browser(s).

2. What creates spaces in your browser? Create a document that uses multiple <BR> and <P> tags, and returns between <PRE> tags to add blank lines to your document. Then test the page in your browser to see which are most reliable. (In most cases, it should be <PRE>, but it's interesting to note the differences from browser to browser.)

3. Create a document using the <PRE> tag to work as an invoice or bill of sale, complete with aligned dollar values and a total. Remember not to use the Tab key and avoid using emphasis tags like <B> or <EM> within your list.

## CHAPTER 8

Displaying Text in Lists

You've probably all heard that one of the best ways to communicate a great deal of information in a short amount of time is by using bulleted lists to convey the message. That philosophy was not lost on the early creators and designers of Web pages, and various tags allow for easy formatting of a number of styles of lists, including both bulleted and nonbulleted incarnations.

Using Lists in HTML

List tags, like paragraphs and preformatted text, are generally HTML containers that are capable of accepting other container and empty tags within their boundaries. These list tags are responsible for affecting the spacing and layout of text, not the emphasis, so they are applied to groups of text, and allow individual formatting tags within them.

Most HTML lists are created following the form:

```
<LIST TYPE>
<ITEM> First item in list
<ITEM> Second item in list
<ITEM> Third item
</LIST TYPE>
```

Each of the items appears on its own line, and the <ITEM> tag itself is generally responsible for inserting either a bullet point or the appropriate number, depending on the type of list that's been defined. It's also possible that the <ITEM> tag could insert no special characters (bullets or otherwise), as is the case with definition listings.

You'll look at each type in the following sections. The basics to remember are to use the main container tags for list type and the individual empty tags to announce each new list item. The type of list you choose is basically a question of aesthetics.

Ordered and Unordered Lists

It might be better to think of these as *numbered* (ordered) and *bulleted* (unordered) lists, especially when we're talking about their use in HTML. The only drawback to that is the fact that the HTML codes for each suggest the ordered/unordered names. For numbered/ordered lists, the tag is <OL>, and for bulleted/unordered lists, the tag is <UL>. Confused yet? That's my job.

For either of these lists, a line item is designated with the empty tag <LI>. In the case of ordered lists, the <LI> tag inserts a number; for unordered lists, it inserts a bullet point. Examples of both follow. The following is an ordered list:

```
<OL>
<LI> Item number one.
<LI> Item number two.
<LI> Item number three.
</OL>
```

And here's an unordered list:

```
<UL>
<LI> First item.
<LI> Second item.
<LI> Third Item.
</UL>
```

Once you've got one of these under your belt, the other looks pretty familiar, doesn't it? To see how these look in a browser, check figure 8.1. (Note that I've added a line of text before each to make each list easier to identify.)

Figure 8.1

The subtle differences between ordered and unordered lists.

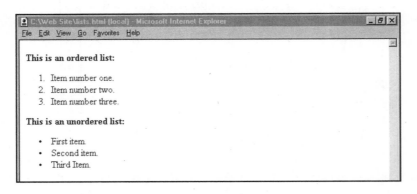

As I've already mentioned, both ordered and unordered lists can take different types of internal HTML tags. It's even possible to include paragraph, line break, and header tags in lists.

> **Note:** In the HTML 2.0 standard, it's considered bad form to use the header tags in bulleted lists, since your goal is probably only to change the size of the text for emphasis. Header tags are designed for page organization, not emphasis. Most browsers will interpret them correctly, but you should also stop to consider that they usually look pretty ugly in lists.

While you may see the potential in creating ordered lists that conform to standard outlining conventions (for instance, Roman numerals and letters), HTML 2.0 doesn't really help much. There is no way to change the <LI> number from Arabic numbers, and there's no way in HTML 2.0 to create a list that starts with something other than 1.

Netscape, however, has added both of these abilities, and you can be much freer in your outline, as long as you warn your users ahead of time to view your page with Netscape Navigator (or a Netscape-compatible browser). Refer to Chapter 19 for more on this.

Example: Formatting Within Lists

Different formatting within lists can offer some dramatically different results, and you should take some time to experiment. Load and save your template as a new HTML document, and enter Listing 8.1 (or similar experiments) within the body tags.

On the CD

Listing 8.1 *lists.html* **Formatting Example**

```
<BODY>
<P>The following are some of the things that little boys are made of:</P>
<UL>
<LI> Dirt
<LI> Snails
<LI> Puppy-dog <B>tails</B>
<LI> Worms
<LI> Various ramblings from <I>Boy Scout Magazine</I>
<LI> An affinity for volume controls
</UL>
```

continues

Listing 8.1 Continued

```
<P> And, in order of importance, here are the things that little girls
are made of:</P>
<OL>
<LI><P>An instinctive ability to listen and reason. Although relational
in their logic, and often not as <I>spatial</I> and detached in their
thinking, a superior empathetic capability general makes little girls
better at conflict resolution.<P>
<LI> Outstanding memories. Little girls can remember things like
addresses with little or no difficulty. Consider this long lost professor
of my aging mother whose address she can still recall:<BR>
<ADDRESS>
1472 Wuthering Heights Circle<BR>
Poetsville, CT 31001<BR>
</ADDRESS>
She visited once, and his dogs were mean to her.</P>
<LI> The gift of <STRONG>Absolute control</STRONG> over all things
sentient.
</OL>
</BODY>
```

Notice that, in every instance, only a new `<LI>` tag is capable of creating a new line in the list. Nearly any other type of HTML markup is possible within a given line item. Once you've saved this document, call it up in a browser and notice how it's formatted (see fig. 8.2).

Figure 8.2

Ordered and unordered lists with special HTML formatting.

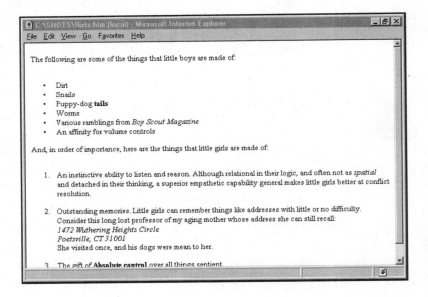

Directories, Definitions, and Menus

Your other lists have something in common with one another that they don't share with ordered and unordered lists: all of them use some permutation of the previous line-item system, but none of them consistently use numbers or bullets. Directories and menus are basically just plain lists. Definitions are unique among all lists because they offer two levels of line items within the list structure—one for the definition item and one for the definition itself.

Directory and Menu Lists

To create a directory or menu list, you start with its respective container tag: <DIR> or <MENU>. Of these two, the directory list is probably more useful. Most browsers don't currently render the <MENU> command consistently—some use a bulleted list, others use no bullets. The following is an example of <MENU>:

```
<MENU>
<LI>House Salad
<LI>Fresh <B>Soup of the Week</B>
<LI>Buffalo Wings
<LI>Escargot
<LI>Liver and Onions
<LI>Turkey Sandwich, <EM>open faced</EM>
<LI>Turkey Sandwich, <EM>pre-fab</EM>
</MENU>
```

> **Note:** You might use the <MENU> tag when creating a list of hypertext links. It's thought that future interpretations of the menu list may be built into future browsers, and that designers will eventually see more benefit in using the <MENU> tag.

In theory, the <DIR> tag is a little more limiting. It's designed as a mechanism for listing computer file directories in HTML pages. Technically, it doesn't support interior HTML tags, although most browsers will display them. The <DIR> tag is also supposed to be limited to 24 characters (for some unknown reason) and show the filenames in rows and columns, like a DIR/W command in MS-DOS, but the bulk of browsers seems to ignore both of these constraints as well, as in the following example:

```
<DIR>
<LI> autoexec.bat
<LI> config.sys
<LI> .signature
<LI> .password
<LI> System Folder
<LI> commaand.com
<LI> .kernel
</DIR>
```

Most browsers (including Netscape) will use the same font and layout for menus and directories as they will for unordered lists. In some cases, browsers will display one or the other (more often directory lists) without a bullet point, which can make them mildly useful. Some browsers can be set to a different font for directories and menus (versus ordered lists). So you may want to use these types, if only because some Web-savvy users' browsers will make an effort to display them differently (see fig. 8.3).

Figure 8.3

Menu and directory lists in MS Internet Explorer.

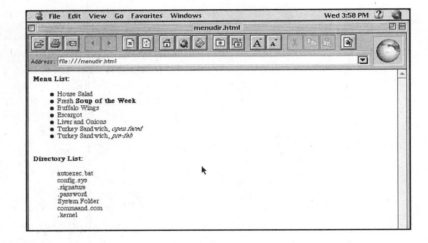

Definition Lists

The final list tag is the definition list, which is designed to allow for two levels of list items, originally conceived to be the defined term and its definition. This is useful in many different ways, though, and is also nice for its consistent lack of bullet points or numbering items (as opposed to the menu and directory listings, which are often rendered haphazardly by browsers).

The tags for this list are the container tag <DL> (definition list) and two empty tags, <DT> (definition term) and <DD> (definition). The <DT> tag is designed (ideally) to fit on a single line of your Web page, although it will wrap to the beginning of the next line if necessary. The <DD> tag will accept a full paragraph of text, continuously indented beneath the <DT> term. The following is an example of all three tags:

```
<DL>
<DT><B>hero</B> <I>(n.)</I>
<DD>A person admired for his or her brave or noble deeds.
<DT><B>hertz</B> <I>(n.)</I>
<DD>A unit used in the measurement of the frequency of electromagnetic
    waves
<DT><B>hex</B> <I>(n.)</I>
<DD>An evil spell or magical curse, generally cast by a witch.
</DL>
```

Notice that standard HTML mark-up is permissible within the boundaries of a definition list, and that using bold and italics for the defined terms adds a certain dictionary-like quality (see fig. 8.4).

> **Tip:** Not all browsers will display definition lists in the same way, so adding spaces to <DT> items (to get them to line up with the <DD> text) is often a waste of time.

Figure 8.4

A basic definition list.

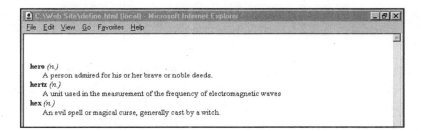

It should also be pointed out that just because definition lists allow for two different types of list items, you needn't necessarily use both. Using just the <DT> tag in your list, for instance, will result in a list not unlike an unordered list—except that nearly all browsers will display it without bullets:

```
<DL>
<DT>Milk
<DT>Honey
<DT>Eggs
<DT>Cereal
</DL>
```

And, although more difficult to find a use for, the <DD> item could be used on its own to indent paragraphs repeatedly. This book occasionally uses a similar device.

```
<P>I must say that I was shocked at his behavior. He was:
<DL>
<DD><I>Rude.</I> Not rude in your standard sort of affable way, or even
in a way that would be justifiable were he immensely weathly or criti-
cally wounded. It was just a rudeness spilling over with contempt.
<DD><I>Unjust.</I> If there was something he could accuse you of falsely,
he would do it. I could almost see him skulking around his apartment
after a particularly unsucessful party, doing his best to find things
stolen, which he could blame on people who hadn't actually bothered to
show up.
</DL>
</P>
```

The definition list offers some additional flexibility over the standard lists, giving you more choices in the way you layout the list items (see fig. 8.5).

Figure 8.5

Definition lists using only one of the two elements.

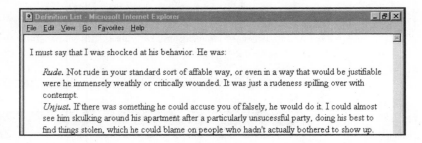

Example: HTML Within Lists

With the definition list, there are many things you can accomplish with formatting. You can experiment with different HTML tags to see how they react within the list. Remember that, within the `<DL>` and `</DL>` tags, the two data item tags, `<DT>` and `<DD>`, reign supreme. For instance, even a new paragraph within a `<DD>` tag will stay indented in most browsers.

Load your template and choose the Save As command to give it a new name. Then type Listing 8.2 between the body tags (see fig. 8.6).

On the CD

Listing 8.2 *lists2.html* **HTML Within Lists**

```
<BODY>
<H1>Computer Terms</H1>
<DL>
<DT><B>CPU</B>
<DD>Central Processing Unit. This is the "brain" of a computer, where
instructions created by the computers system software and application
software are carried out.
<DT><B>Hard Drive</B>
<DD>Sometimes called a <I>fixed drive</I>, this is a device (generally
mounted inside a computer's case) with spinning magnetic plates that is
designed to store computer data. When a file is "saved" to the hard
drive, it is available for accessing at a later time.<BR>
Most system software and application programs are also stored on the
computer's internal hard drive. When an applications name is typed or
icon is accessed with a mouse, the application is loaded from the hard
drive in RAM and run by the system software.
<DT><B>Application Software</B>
<DD>Computers programs used to create or accomplish something on a
computer, as distinct from system software. Examples of computer applica-
tion software might include:<BR>
```

```
WordPerfect (a word processing application)<BR>
Microsoft Excel (a spreadsheet application)<BR>
QuarkXPress (a desktop publshing application)<BR>
Corel Draw (a computer graphics application)<BR>
</DL>
<BODY>
```

Figure 8.6

Using extensive
HTML formatting
in a list.

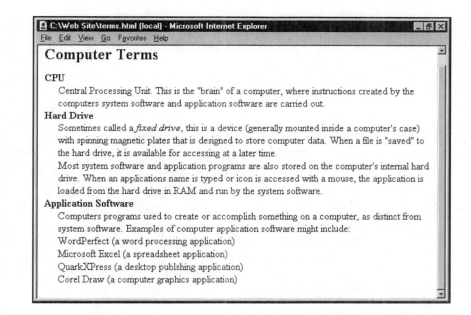

Using the <BR> tag allows you to create an impromptu list within the list, although everything remains indented because it's ultimately under the influence of the <DD> tag. The definition item tags (<DT> and <DD>) stay in effect until another instance of a definition item tag is encountered or until the </DL> tag ends the definition list.

Nesting Tags and Combining List Types

Since most of your HTML lists can accept HTML tags within their list items, it stands to reason that you could potentially create lists within lists. In fact, creating a list, then creating another list as part of an item in that first list is how you can create an outline in HTML.

Nesting Tags

The idea of nesting comes to us from computer programming. Nesting is essentially completing an entire task within the confines of another task. For HTML, that means completing an HTML tag within the confines of another container tag. This could be something like the following:

```
<P>She was easily the most <EM>beautiful</EM> girl in the room.</P>
```

This is an example of correctly nesting the <EM> tag within a paragraph container. On the other hand, many browsers would still manage to display this next code:

```
<P>She was easily the most <EM>beautiful</P> girl in the room.</EM>
```

But this second example is really poorly constructed HTML. It often works, but the <EM> tag isn't properly nested inside the <P>. In this example, that doesn't matter too much, since you can still reason out what this statement is trying to do.

With lists, however, things can get complicated. So it's best to remember the "nesting" concept when you begin to add lists within lists. As far as HTML is concerned, a nested list works as marked-up text within the previous list item. When the next list item is called for, HTML moves on.

Lists Within Lists

Let's look at an example of a simple nested list:

```
<OL>
<LI>Introduction
<LI>Chapter One
    <OL>
    <LI> Section 1.1
    <LI> Section 1.2
    <LI> Section 1.3
    </OL>
<LI>Chapter Two
</OL>
```

> **Tip:** It's a good idea to indent nested lists as shown in the example. The browser doesn't care—it's just easier for you (or other designers) to read in a text editor. (Regardless of your spacing, most browsers will indent the nested lists—after all, that's the point.)

Notice that the nested list acts as a sublevel of the Chapter One list item. In this way, you can simulate an outline in HTML. Actually, the nested list is just HTML code that is part of the <LI>Chapter One list item. As you saw in Listing 8.2, you can use the <BR> tag to create a line break in a list element without moving on to the next list item. Following the same theory, an entire nested list works as if it's a single list item in the original list.

The following:

```
<OL>
<LI>Section Five<BR>
   This section discusses ducks, geese, finches and swans.
<LI>Section Six
</OL>
```

is essentially the same as the list that follows:

```
<OL>
<LI>Section Five
     <OL>
     <LI> Ducks
     <LI> Geese
     <LI> Finches
     <LI> Swans
     </OL>
<LI> Section Six
</OL>
```

In both cases, the nest HTML container is simply a continuation of the first list item. Both the text after the <BR> in the first example and the ordered list in the second example are part of the list item labeled Section Five. That list item is over when the next list item (Section Six) is put into effect (see fig. 8.7).

Figure 8.7

In both of the examples, the HTML container is simply part of the list.

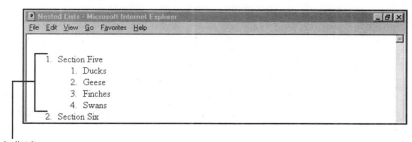

A single list item

Combining List Types

When nesting lists, it's also possible to nest different types of lists within one another. This is useful when you'd like to vary the types of bullets or numbers used in an outline form. For instance:

```
<OL>
<LI>Introdution
<LI>Company Financial Update
     <UL>
     <LI>First Quarter
     <LI>Second Quarter
     <LI>Third Quarter
     <LI>Fourth Quarter
     </UL>
<LI>Advertising Update
     <UL>
     <LI>Results of Newspaper Campaign
     <LI>Additions to Staff
     <LI>New Thoughts on Television
     </UL>
<LI>Human Resources Update
</OL>
```

There's nothing terribly difficult to learn here—just the added benefit of being able to nest different types of lists within others. You're still simply adding HTML markup code to items in the original list. This time, however, you have more choice over how your outline looks (see fig. 8.8).

Figure 8.8

Nesting different types of lists.

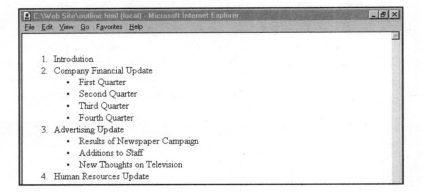

Example: Nesting Definition Lists

Although creating outlines is nice, more often you're interested in presenting actual information on your Web pages. Doing that in an outline form can often be helpful to your Web users. You have a number of different ways you can do that, including nesting paragraphs within ordered and unordered lists. Or you can just use definitions lists.

Load your template and choose the Save As command to rename it. Then enter the following text between the body tags:

```
<BODY>
<H2>About Our Company</H2>
<OL>
<LI>Our Leaders
     <DL>
     <DT><B>Richard B. McCoy, CEO</B>
     <DD> Raised on small farm in Indiana, Dr. McCoy dreamed of something
bigger. By the time he'd graduated from Harvard Business School with an
MBA, he'd already realized part of his dream. He'd married the most
beautiful woman he'd ever met and was the proud father of a baby girl.
From there, his life took control of his career, and his new found
interest in parenting launched his idea of building the better baby bed.
His invention, the SleepMaker 3000, was an instant success. Twenty years
later, he finds his family room couch is enough incentive for him to take
a long nap on Saturdays after a good morning round of golf.
     <DT><B>Leslie R. Gerald, CFO</B>
     <DD> Denying the fact that she's an accountant is nearly a full-time
pursuit for Ms. Gerald. Having graduated at the top of her class at
Northwestern University, her life has been about 1/3 accounting, 1/3
daredevil athleticism and 1/3 sleep. In the meantime she's found time for
a steady beau, decorating her mountain retreat and writing a book called
<I>It's More Exciting Than You Think </I> about, believe it or not,
flying ultra-light aircraft.
     <DT><B>David W. Deacon, VP of Marketing</B>
     <DD> Known as "Dave" to anyone he's ever spoken to for more than
five minutes, Mr. Deacon displays the calm friendliness of the consummate
salesman, with a twist. He actually is a nice guy. When he's not doing
his best to promote our products, Dave is well known in the community as
a service volunteer. Last year he was awarded Seattle's prestigous Man of
the Year award in recognition of over 500 volunteer hours and over
$50,000 in personal contribution to various area charities.
     </DL>
      <BR>
<LI>Employees of the Month
     <UL>
     <LI> January: Bill Cable, IS
     <LI> February: Janet Smiles, Marketing
     <LI> March: Rich Lewis, Finance
     <LI> April: Wendy Right, Vendor Relations
     <LI> May: Alice Cutless, Area Sales
     <LI> June: Dean Wesley, Training
     </UL>
</OL>
</BODY>
```

Combining different types of lists, then, is a great way to organize your Web site in such a way that it's easy to get at interesting information. At the same time, it's still possible to present that information in many different ways using various list tags (see fig. 8.9).

Figure 8.9

Nesting and combining the various types of HTML lists.

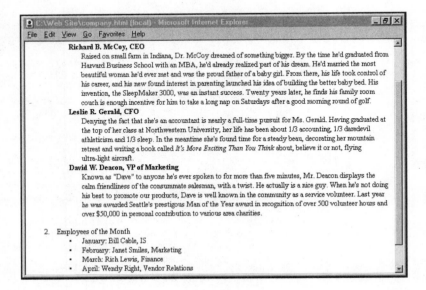

Summary

HTML lists are an effective way to communicate a great deal of information in a relatively small amount of space. HTML provides tags for both ordered (numbered) lists and unordered (bullet-style) lists. In addition to those, you can add menu lists, directory lists, and definition lists.

The ordered and unordered lists are easily the most commonly used, while the menu and directory lists don't often add much value to your Web pages. Definition lists, however, are unique because they allow you to have two different types of list items with the lists—a term and its definition.

All of these lists can be used together in what's called nesting, or creating lists within other lists. The definition list is especially good for this because you can add all different types of lists (such as bullet and numbered lists) within the descriptions in your definition list.

It's also possible to nest different types of lists within numbered lists to create multilevel outlines in your HTML documents.

Review Questions

1. What are the two basic tags in an HTML list?

2. What does a `<LI>` create when used in an unordered list?

3. Can you change the style of numbers in an ordered list (using HTML 2.0 standards)?

4. Which is less likely to display with bullet points—a directory list or a menu list?

5. Can you use other HTML tags (such as `<B>` or `<EM>`) within HTML list containers?

6. What is unique about the definition list style?

7. Do definition lists have to be used for words and their definitions?

8. Does HTML force you to include both a `<DT>` and a `<DD>` tag in your definition lists?

9. Is nesting something that happens only in HTML lists?

10. Which of these is an example of a nested list?

(A)

```
<OL>
<LI>Groceries<BR>
    Milk<BR>
    Soup<BR>
    Ice Cream<BR>
<LI>Other groceries
</OL>
```

(B)

```
<OL>
<LI>Groceries
    <UL>
    <LI> Milk
    <LI> Soup
    <LI> Ice Cream
    </UL>
<LI>Other Groceries
</OL>
```

11. What type of HTML lists would you use to create an outline, the major points of which were numbered and the minor points used bullets?

Review Exercises

1. Create a list using the <DIR> and <MENU> tags. View each in your different browser and note how some browsers render these differently from one another.

2. Create a <DL> definition list with nothing but <DD> elements, and one with nothing but <DT> elements. Notice how they're rendered in your browser. Definition lists used in this way are often very useful.

3. Use nested definition lists to create your own HTML "outline." You can use the <DL> elements to number your own outline elements, like the following:

```
<DL>
<DT> I. Introduction
   <DL>
   <DT> A. Welcome!
   <DT> B. Description of Mission Statement
   <DT> C. Conventions in this Report
   </DL>
<DT> II. Chapter One
</DL>
```

## CHAPTER 9

Adding Graphics to Your Web Pages

Now that you've seen the many ways you can add some character to your text—and use different tags to better communicate your ideas—it's time to jazz up your pages a little bit. Let's add some graphics!

First, though, you should know a couple of important things about placing graphics. Some of these considerations may seem a bit foreign to you, especially if you're a graphic designer or commercial artist. You have to think in a slightly different way about graphics for your HTML pages.

The Special Nature of Graphics on the Web

You may be comfortable using a program such as CorelDRAW! or Adobe Photoshop to create and manipulate graphics. You may already know the difference between a PICT file and a TIF file (and why that difference might be important). You may even know a lot about preparing graphics for professional printing or adding graphics to desktop publishing documents.

But if you've never done any design for the World Wide Web, there's also a good chance that you've never worried about one special graphics issue, even if you are a print design expert. How big is the graphics file that you created? Aside from using the correct graphics format, this issue is the single most important consideration in graphical Web design.

The Size of Graphics Files

Why is the size of graphics files so important? Your Web users have to download your pages to view them, including all the graphics associated with the pages. Couple that fact with the Web speed issues discussed in Chapter 5, and the need for smaller graphics files becomes apparent.

The high-color, high-resolution graphics files that color printers and professional designers work with are generally measured in the number of megabytes of information required to create the graphics file. Each image can take up more space than is available on a floppy disk. Often, special tapes and cartridges are required to transfer these files from the graphics shop to the printer.

A good average size for a Web graphic, on the other hand, is between 10K and 30K—about one to three percent of the size of those high-color, high-resolution graphics. This could be tough.

Example: Watching Graphical Sites Download

Just to get a feel for how all this graphics stuff works, start your Web browser and Internet connection. Make sure that your browser has its preferences or options set so that it downloads graphics automatically.

If you're using Netscape Navigator, use the Netscape home page as your benchmark. If you're not using Netscape Navigator, point your Web browser to **http://www.netscape.com/**.

Now, as the page downloads, watch the status bar at the bottom of your browser's window. You should be able to watch as your browser downloads the page and the various graphics, and your browser may even tell you how large each graphics file is as you're downloading.

Next, select an individual graphics file on the page, and save it to your hard drive. In Windows 95, right-click a graphic and then choose to save the graphic as a file (in Navigator or Internet Explorer). On a Mac, hold down the mouse button and then choose to save the graphic when the pop-up menu appears (see fig. 9.1).

Finally, look at the file, using the Windows Explorer or Mac Finder. Check the file size of the graphic. Notice how small the file is, and remember how long downloading it took. You'll have to be aware of these considerations when you create your Web graphics.

Figure 9.1

Use Netscape
Navigator to
download Web
graphics.

Saving a graphic ————

The status bar

Picking Your Web Graphics File Type

The other thing that you need to concern yourself with is the file type that you're
going to use for Web graphics. In general (at least currently), you can choose either
of two file types: GIF and JPEG. *GIF* (CompuServe Graphics Interchange Format)
is the more popular among Web browsers, but *JPEG* (Joint Photographic Experts
Group) is gaining popularity and becoming more widely used.

Why have two standards? GIF and JPEG bring different advantages to the table.
Let's take a look.

GIF Format Graphics

Any graphical browser supports the display of GIF format files *inline,* meaning that
the browser doesn't require a special viewer for these files. GIFs are compressed
graphics, but they tend to lose less image clarity than JPEGs. Images that have
smaller color palettes (those that use 256 colors or fewer) often look better in GIF
format. GIF is also the file format of choice for creating transparent graphics—
graphics that make the Web page appear to be the actual background of the GIF
graphic (see the section,"Creating Transparent GIFs," later in this chapter).

Although GIF files are compressed, they tend to be a bit larger than JPEGs, but they decompress more quickly and tend to be drawn more quickly than JPEGs (given the same file size). Another problem with the GIF file format is the fact that it includes certain copyrighted elements that make it less than an open standard for graphics interchange.

> **Note:** Folks in the press took the ball and ran with it in late 1994 when they became aware of the fact that the GIF file format, created by CompuServe, used a compression scheme called LZH—a scheme patented by the Unisys corporation. At the time, CompuServe and UniSys had a licensing agreement under which CompuServe paid a royalty to Unisys but was granted the right to sublicense GIF and LZH technology to companies that made use of the graphics format in their programs. This publicity shifted some users and developers to unrestricted file formats such as JPEG, although GIF remains the most popular format for Web graphics.

The JPEG Format

Gaining on GIF in popularity is the JPEG format, which is widely used by Web designers. JPEG graphics can be viewed in most new graphical browsers without a special helper application. JPEG graphics have the advantage of being better for graphics that have more colors (up to 16.7 million, in most cases) than similar GIF files; in addition, the JPEG files are smaller (look ahead to fig. 9.2). Also, the compression scheme is in the public domain.

On the down side, JPEGs can be a little more *lossy* than GIFs, meaning that the higher rate of compression results in slightly lower image quality. JPEGs also take a little longer to decompress than do GIF files. So although the smaller size of JPEG files allows them to be transmitted over the Internet more quickly, the amount of time that it takes to decompress those files sometimes negates this advantage.

> **The Future of Web Graphics Formats**
>
> In the spring of 1996, the World Wide Web Consortium (W3C) announced a working paper standard for a new graphics format—the Portable Network Graphic (PNG) file type—as a possible replacement for the GIF and JPEG formats.
>
> The PNG file format provides for high, lossless compression of graphics up through "true-color" depths, allowing transmission of very clean, crisp graphics over the Web. The specification uses public-domain compression schemes to avoid the sublicensing issues associated with GIF.

The format is designed to be highly machine-independent, so that different types of computers and operating systems can easily deal with the creation and display of PNG graphics. The PNG format allows for transparency effects (like the GIF format). These graphics often display more quickly in browsers that display graphics *progressively* (as the graphics are being downloaded).

Although the transition most likely will take some time, PNG is already making progress on the Web. You can expect many more browsers, graphics applications, and helpers to support the format in the future.

Creating and Manipulating Graphics

It's no secret that a lot of Web design has transitioned from manipulating text-based HTML documents to designing and integrating compelling graphics into Web pages. As the Web has become more commercial, its graphical content has become more professional. If you're not up to the task of creating professional graphics, don't worry too much; programs are available that will help you. Also, it's more important that graphics further the usefulness of the text. The graphics in and of themselves are not the point. The point is to make your Web pages more exciting and informative.

It is a fact, however, that Web sites are leaping forward daily into a more professional, more graphical presentation of Web-based information. Commercial artists and designers are continuing to find new niches on the Web. If you're a skilled computer artist, congratulations; this is where you'll put your skills to use. If you're not, that's OK, too. Any Web designer needs to be able to manipulate and edit graphics in a program such as Adobe Photoshop or CorelDRAW!, but you don't necessarily have to *create* those graphics, if that's not your forte.

Creating Graphics for the Web

As you get started with a program such as Photoshop or CorelDRAW!, keep in mind that the most important consideration in creating Web graphics is the file size. File size isn't generally the first consideration for creating print graphics; almost any print shop or prepress house will accept large storage cartridges or tapes that provide access to your huge full-color graphics. Not so on the Web. Your target is as small as possible—between 15K and 35K for larger (bigger on the screen) files.

You can come up with graphics to use on your Web pages in many ways. Eventually, any graphic that you use needs to be in a standard file format (for example, GIF or JPEG) and relatively small. But how you come up with the final graphic has a lot to do with the information that you're trying to communicate and with your skills as an artist. The following are some of the different ways you might come up with Web graphics:

◆ **Create graphics in a graphics application**. Many programs for both professional and amateur artists can output GIF- or JPEG-format files for use on the Web. Among these programs are Adobe Photoshop, CorelDRAW!, Fractal Painter, and Fractal Dabbler.

> **Tip:** Any graphics program, even Microsoft Paint, can create Web graphics, although you may need to use another program to change the graphic to an acceptable file format.

◆ **Download public-domain graphics**. Tons of sites on the Internet allow you to download icons, interface elements, and other graphics for your Web site. At the same time, public-domain clipart collections (such as those available on CD-ROM) can be useful for Web pages.

◆ **Use scanned photographs**. Using scanned photographs (especially those that you've taken yourself) is a great way to come up with graphics for your Web pages. Unless you have access to scanning hardware, though, you may need to pay someone to scan the photos.

◆ **Digital cameras**. Cameras are available that allow you to take photos that can be downloaded directly from the camera to your computer. While some of this equipment can be very expensive, cameras under $500 do exist, and those photos can easily be converted for use on the Web.

◆ **Use PhotoCDs**. Many photo development shops can create digital files of your photographs (from standard 35mm film or negatives) and save those files in PhotoCD format. Most CD-ROM drives allow you to access these photos, which you can then change to GIF or JPEG format and display on your Web pages.

Example: Creating Graphics in Paint Shop Pro

A popular program for creating Web graphics in Windows and Windows 95 is Paint Shop Pro, which has the added advantage of being try-before-you-buy shareware. To download Paint Shop Pro, access the URL **http://www.jasc.com/pspdl.html** with your Web browser, and find the hypermedia link for downloading the program for your particular version of Windows.

> **Note:** As with any shareware program, you should register Paint Shop Pro (by sending in the requested fee) if you find it useful.

Paint Shop Pro arrives as a PKZip-compressed file archive, so you also need a program on your hard drive to unzip it when the download is complete. (WinZip is available from **http://www.winzip.com/**.) Then install the program in Windows and start it. You should see a window like the one shown in figure 9.2.

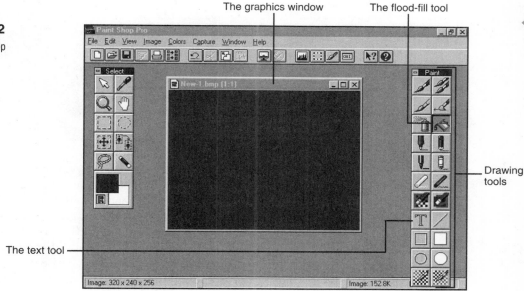

Figure 9.2
The Paint Shop Pro interface.

You can use Paint Shop Pro to create a simple graphic, such as a logo or title, for your Web pages. Using the flood-fill tool, for example, allows you to select a color and "pour" it into the window, creating a background color for the rest of your graphic.

Click the fill-tool icon and then choose a color from the color palette. To apply that color to your graphic, click in the graphic window.

Now select the text tool, choose another color from the palette, and click the graphic window. Type your text (your company name, for example) in the dialog box; then click OK. Now you should be able to drag the text around the window. When you have the text arranged correctly, click anywhere in the window to place the text permanently (see fig. 9.3).

Text with a background

Figure 9.3

Creating a simple graphic.

The rectangular selector tool

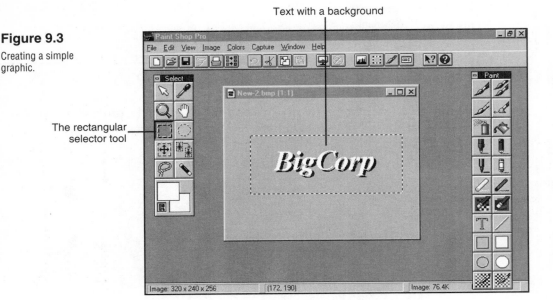

Before you save this graphic, you should make it as physically small as possible so that it works well on your Web page. To cut the image down a bit, select Paint Shop Pro's rectangular selector tool. Click somewhere near the top left corner of the graphic (at the point you want to make the new top left corner of your cropped image), and drag the mouse pointer to the other side (bottom right corner) of the image. When you release the mouse pointer, a thin box should appear around this slightly smaller portion of your graphic. From the menu, choose Image, Crop, and the graphic is cropped to that size. If everything went well, you have a smaller graphic that is just as useful for your Web site.

Our last step is to save the graphic in a file format that's useful for the Web. Choose File, Save As. In the Save As dialog box that appears, you can select the file type from a drop-down list (see fig. 9.4). Select either GIF or JPEG, type a filename, and click OK.

Now you've created a graphic for use on your Web page. Use the Windows Explorer or File Manager to check the file size. You want the file to be somewhere around 20K—an ideal size for a Web page graphic.

Figure 9.4

Saving your graphic in a Web-compatible format.

Name file with extension

Choose graphic type

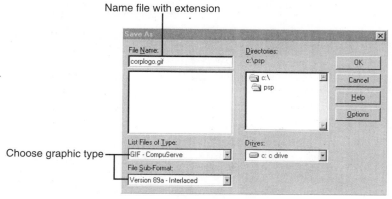

Manipulating Web Graphics

After you decide what graphics to use, the next step is to manipulate and edit those graphics for best use on the Web. The preceding section discussed some of this manipulation (cropping and saving a graphic to make it as small as possible). Following are some other ways to use graphics applications to make your images lean, attractive, and useful:

♦ **Keep graphics small**. Creating smaller graphics in the first place, and using the cropping tool to take out backgrounds and extra space, are great ways to keep graphics to a manageable size.

♦ **Use fewer colors**. Many graphics applications allow you to decide how much color information should be included in the file. Do you want to use a possible 256 colors or millions of colors? The fewer colors you choose, the smaller your image file will be (see fig. 9.5).

> **Note:** Programs will often describe the number of colors in a graphic using either a number or something called *bit-depth*. An 8-bit graphic, for instance, offers 256 colors. How do you calculate these numbers? Two to the power of the bit-depth is the number of possible colors ($2^8 = 256$ colors; $2^{16} = 65536$ colors).

Figure 9.5

Adobe Photoshop allows you to chose the color bit-depth for a particular graphic.

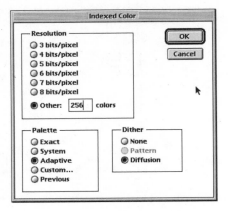

♦ **Create thumbnail graphics**. At times, displaying a large graphic may be necessary, especially if your user chooses to view it. You can give users this option by creating thumbnail graphics in your graphics programs and then using the thumbnails as links to identical (but much larger) graphics files. This method allows you to create pages that contain many images, all of which are scaled down considerably (and, therefore, download more quickly). If a user wants to view one of the graphics at full size, he or she can simply click the thumbnail graphic.

> **Note:** Some browsers (notably, Netscape) can be used to resize the graphics on-the-fly. Although this is convenient for the designer, the entire file still must be transferred across the Internet, thereby negating the benefits that smaller thumbnail graphics offer in terms of downloading speed.

Example: Creating Thumbnails with LView Pro

Another must-have program for most Windows-based Web designers is LView Pro, a shareware graphics-manipulation program. Although the program has some of the same features as Paint Shop Pro, LView is designed less for creating images and more for changing them from one size to another or from one file format to another.

You can download LView by accessing the Web URL **http://world.std.com/~mmedia/lviewp.html**. Choose the version for your flavor of Windows, download it to your computer, extract it from its Zip archive, install it in Windows, and start it.

To resize an image to create a thumbnail, follow these steps:

1. Choose File, Open. The Open dialog box appears.

2. In the Open dialog box, find the image that you want to resize.

3. With the image in a window on the desktop, choose Edit, Resize. The Resize Image window appears (see fig. 9.6).

Figure 9.6

Resizing graphics in LView Pro for Windows.

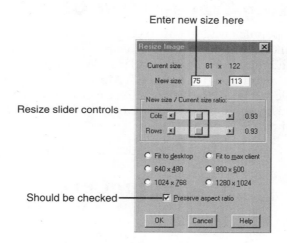

4. Now you can use the slider controls or enter a new size for your thumbnails. A good rule is somewhere around 75 pixels wide (width is the first field after New Size in the dialog box). Changing the width also changes the height in order to preserve the aspect ratio of your images.

5. When you have finished resizing, click OK.

> **Tip:** If you plan to offer many thumbnails on one page, it's a good idea to make them a uniform width (or height) to keep the page orderly.

When you create thumbnails, you'll probably want to maintain the aspect ratio of the current graphic in resizing, so that LView keeps the height and width of the new graphic at the same ratio as the original graphic, making the thumbnail smaller but similarly proportioned. Don't forget to save the new file with a slightly different name, using the appropriate file extension (GIF or JPG).

> **Tip:** Whenever an application gives you the choice, you should save GIF files as interlaced GIFs and JPEGs as progressive JPEGs. This lets the graphics display faster in many browsers.

Creating Transparent GIFs

One very popular way to edit Web graphics is to create transparent GIFs. This process allows you to make one of the colors of your graphic (generally the background color) transparent, so that the Web page's color scheme or background graphics shows through (see fig. 9.7). Most often, it's used to give the illusion that the graphic is part of your Web page. You can use this method to add impact to your pages and to limit the size of your graphics by doing away with elaborate backgrounds.

Figure 9.7

Regular vs. transparent GIFs.

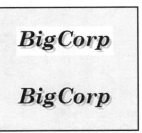

To be rendered with a transparent background, a GIF file must be saved in the GIF89a file format. This can be done with Paint Shop Pro, LView Pro, Transparency for the Mac, and many other programs. Saving a file in this format is simply a matter of deciding what color is going to be the transparent color when the GIF is displayed.

> **Tip:** Giving the image in your transparent GIF a shadow (in a graphics application) enhances the appearance of a graphic floating directly over the page.

Creating Transparent GIFs in Transparency for the Mac

One of the easiest ways to create a transparent GIF on the Mac is to use a simple application called Transparency. You can download the program from the Web page **http://www.med.cornell.edu/~giles/projects.html** or **http://www.med.cornell.edu/~giles/projects.html**.

After you download and install Transparency, double-click the program icon to start it. Pull down the File menu and choose Open. In the Open dialog box that appears, open the GIF file that you want to change to a transparent GIF. Your image is then presented in its own window (see fig. 9.8).

Figure 9.8

Transparency for the Mac, changing a white background to transparent.

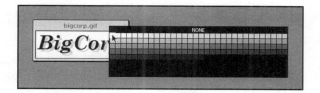

Point to the color in the GIF that you want to turn transparent. As you hold down the mouse button, a color palette appears, with the current color selected. If you want that color to turn transparent, release the mouse button. If you want some other color to be transparent (or if you prefer to use no transparency), point to the color that you want to make transparent and release the mouse button. To turn off transparency, simply select the box marked None at the top of the palette.

Now pull down the File menu and choose the Save As GIF89a command. Rename the file (or use the same name, if you want), and save it. The file now should appear in a Web browser as a transparent GIF.

Example: Creating Transparent GIFs in LView Pro

Windows users can create transparent GIFs in LView Pro. To do so, follow these steps:

1. Load the program, and choose File, Open to open a graphics file. The Open dialog box appears.

2. If the file isn't already a GIF image, choose Retouch, Color Depth, and convert the file to a Palette Image.

3. Select 256 colors in the palette creation and quantizing options, and uncheck the Enable Floyd-Steinberg Dithering checkbox.

4. Click OK.

5. Now you can decide which color will appear transparent. Choose Retouch, Background Color and then click the color that should be transparent. You can also use the dropper (click the Dropper button) to select the color that should be transparent (see fig. 9.9).

Figure 9.9

Click the dropper to choose the transparent color.

BigCorp —————— The dropper icon

6. With the correct color selected, choose File, Save As, and save the graphic as a GIF89a. The background color will appear transparent in a Web browser's window.

Embedding Graphics in Web Pages

When your graphics are created, cropped, resized, and saved in the appropriate formats, you're ready to add them to your Web pages. To add graphics, you use an empty tag called the <IMG> (image) tag, which you insert into the body section of your HTML document as follows:

```
<IMG SRC="image URL">
```

or

```
<IMG SRC="path/filename">
```

SRC accepts the name of the file that you want to display, and *image URL* (or *path/ filename*) is the absolute (full URL) or relative path (for a local file or a file in the current directory) to the image. As the first example shows, you can display on your page any graphic file that is generally available on the Internet, even if the file resides on a remote server. For graphics files, however, it is much more likely that the file is located on the local server, so a path and filename are sufficient.

You could enter the following text in a browser:

```
<HR>
<P>This is a test of the Image tag. Here is the image I want to
display:</P>
<IMG SRC="image1.gif">
<HR>
```

In this case, `<IMG SRC="image1.gif">` is a relative path URL, suggesting that the file `image1.gif` is located in the same directory as the HTML document. The result would be displayed by a browser as shown in figure 9.10.

Figure 9.10

Displaying inline graphics on a Web page.

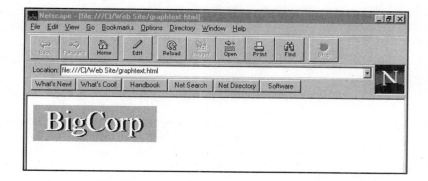

> **Tip:** You'll learn more about absolute and relative URLs in Chapter 10, "Hypertext and Creating Links."

An absolute URL is essential, however, if you were accessing an image on a remote site, as in the following example:

```
<IMG SRC="http://www.graphcom.com/pub/graphics/image1.gif">
```

(This example is fictitious.) Please realize that using a URL to a distant site on the Internet causes that site to be accessed every time this `<IMG>` tag is encountered on your page, so you should probably have some sort of arrangement with that Web site's system administrator before you link to a graphic on their server.

Adding Graphics to Other HTML Tags

You can add graphics links to HTML tags to do various things, including placing graphics next to text (within paragraphs) and even including graphics in lists. The following example displays the graphic flush with the left margin, with the bottom of the text that follows the image aligned with its bottom edge:

```
<P><IMG SRC="start.gif"> It's time to start our adventure in the world of
the Web. As you'll see below, there is much to learn. </P>
```

Words at the end of the first line wrap below the image (see fig. 9.11).

Figure 9.11

Graphics within paragraph containers.

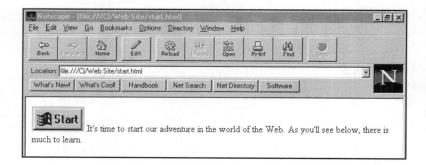

Another popular use for graphics is including them in HTML lists. Best suited for this task is the `<DL>` (definition) list, which allows you to use your own graphics as bullet points. (Ordered and unordered lists display their numbers or bullets in addition to the graphic.)

A `<DT>` (definition term) tag can accept more than one `<DD>` (definition) element, so you can create a bulleted list as follows:

```
<DL>
<DT>
<DD><IMG SRC="bullet.gif"> This is the first point
<DD><IMG SRC="bullet.gif"> This is the second point
<DD><IMG SRC="bullet.gif"> Here's the third point
<DD><IMG SRC="bullet.gif"> And so on.
</DL>
```

Tip: If you're not up to creating your own bullet points, many archives of common bullets, graphics, and clipart images exist on the Web. Try CERN's images at **http://www.w3.org/hypertext/WWW/Icons** or a popular site like Randy's Bazaar at **http://www.infi.net/~rdralph/icons/**.

At the same time, you could use a definition list in conjunction with thumbnail graphics in a list that uses both the `<DT>` and `<DD>` tags. An example might be the following real estate agent's pages (see fig. 9.12):

```
<DL>
<DT><IMG SRC="Small_House14101.GIF">
<DD><EM>14101 Avondale</EM> This executive 3/2/2 is nestled among the
live oak, with a beautiful view of the foothills. $139,900.
<DT><IMG SRC="Small_House3405.GIF">
<DD><EM>3405 Main</EM> This timeless beauty is a cottage made for a
prince (and/or princess!) Spacious 2/1/1 is cozy and functional at the
same time, with all-new updates to this 1880s masterpiece. $89,995.
</DL>
```

Figure 9.12

Use a <DL> tag to create custom bulleted lists and thumbnail lists.

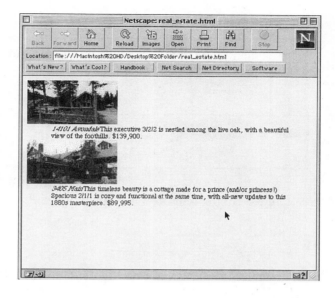

The *ALT* Attribute

None of the HTML tags that you've encountered so far offer the option of a *tag attribute*—an option that somehow affects or enhances the way the tag is displayed on-screen.

The ALT attribute for the <IMG> tag is designed to accept text that describes the graphic, in case a particular browser can't display the graphic. Consider the plight of users who use Lynx or a similar text-based program to surf the Web (or users of graphical browsers that choose not to auto-load graphics). Because those users can't see the graphic, they'll want to know what they're missing.

The ALT attribute works this way:

```
<IMG SRC="image URL" ALT="Text description of graphic">
```

The following is an example:

```
<IMG SRC="image1.gif" ALT="Logo graphic">
```

For people whose browsers can't display the graphic, the ALT attribute tells them that the graphic exists and explains what the graphic is about.

Tip: Test your site with the Load Images option turned off so that you can see how your ALT text displays.

The *ALIGN* Attribute

`<IMG>` can accept another attribute that specifies how graphics appear relative to other elements (like text or other graphics). Using the ALIGN attribute, you can align other elements to the top, middle, or bottom of the graphic. It follows this format:

```
<IMG SRC="image URL" ALIGN="direction">
```

Note: The ALIGN="BOTTOM" attribute isn't necessary, because it is the default setting for the `<IMG>` tag.

The ALIGN attribute is designed to align text that comes after a graphic with a certain part of the graphic itself. An image with the ALIGN attribute set to TOP, for example, has any subsequent text aligned with the top of the image, like in the following example:

```
<IMG SRC="image1.gif" ALIGN=TOP> Descriptive text aligned to top.
```

Giving the `<IMG>` tag an ALIGN="MIDDLE" attribute forces subsequent text to begin in the middle of the graphic (see fig. 9.13):

```
<IMG SRC="image1.gif" ALIGN="MIDDLE"> Descriptive text aligned to middle.
```

Figure 9.13

The ALIGN attribute for the `<IMG>` tag.

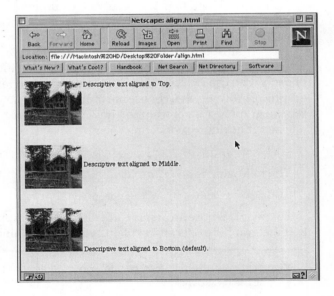

Order among the attributes that you assign to an image tag is unimportant. In fact, because SRC="*URL*" is technically an attribute (although a required one), you can place the ALIGN or ALT attribute before the SRC information. Anywhere you put attributes, as long as they appear between the brackets of the <IMG> tag, is acceptable.

Example: Adding Graphics to Your Web Site

Now that you've learned how to add images to your Web pages, you have almost doubled the things that you can do on the Web. In this example, you add graphics to a typical corporate Web page, using a couple of methods that you've learned.

To start, you need to create some graphics for your home page. If you have a corporate logo and a scanner handy, go ahead and scan in some graphics. Alternatively, you can use a graphics program to create, crop, and save your graphics as GIF or JPEG files. While you're at it, you may want to create some of your GIFs as transparent GIFs.

Create a logo, a special bullet, and a photo for use on the page. Name your GIFs LOGO.GIF, BULLET.GIF, and PHOTO.GIF, or something similar. (If you have already created a Web site, feel free to name the files according to the organizational system that you're using for the site. You can also use JPEG graphics if you so desire.) Then load your HTML template, and save it as a new HTML document. Between the body tags, type something like Listing 9.1.

On the CD

Listing 9.1 *images.html* **Using** *<IMG>* **to Create Images**

```
<BODY>
<IMG SRC="logo.gif" ALT="RealCorp Logo">
<H1>Welcome to RealCorp's Web Site</H1>
<H2><IMG SRC="photo.gif" ALT="Photo of CEO Bob MacFay"
ALIGN=MIDDLE><EM>I'm Bob MacFay, CEO of RealCorp...</EM></H2>
<P>We at RealCorp make it our business to be as productive and hard
working as you are. That's why we've set up this Web site...to work a
little harder, so you don't have to. Take a look at the various services
our company offers, and maybe you'll see why we like to say, "We're the
hardest working corporation all week, every week."</P>
<DL>
<DT>
<DD><IMG SRC="bullet.gif" ALT="·" ALIGN=MIDDLE> Full service plans for
any size of customers
<DD><IMG SRC="bullet.gif" ALT="·" ALIGN=MIDDLE> On-time service calls,
any time, any day of the week
```

continues

Listing 9.1 Continued

```
<DD><IMG SRC="bullet.gif" ALT="-" ALIGN=MIDDLE> Fully-equipped mobile
troublshooting vans
<DD><IMG SRC="bullet.gif" ALT="-" ALIGN=MIDDLE> Time honored appreciate
for quality over expediency
</DL>
</BODY>
```

Although the ALT attribute is optional and the bulleted list may survive without it, the example uses ASCII to substitute hyphens for the bullet graphics if the browser can't display images. In most cases, you'll want to describe an image that a user can't view. For an element such as a bullet, though, you can use the ALT attribute to substitute an ASCII character for the graphic.

For the photo of the CEO, the <IMG> tag is called within the <H2> tag, because the <H2> container (like a paragraph) otherwise would insert a carriage return and force the words I'm Bob MacFay... to appear below the photo. Including the <IMG> tag inside the <H2> tag allows the text to appear next to the photo (see fig. 9.14).

Figure 9.14

Sample Web page, including some different attributes for the <IMG> tag.

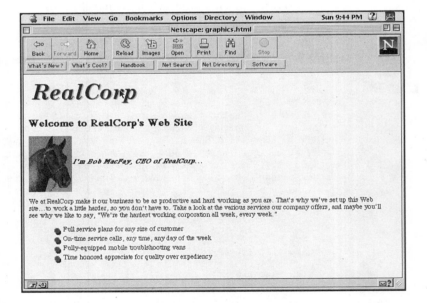

Play with this example a little bit to get a feel for when you should place the <IMG> tag within another HTML container and when you can leave the tag out on its own. A page sometimes looks completely different, based only on where you place your image tags.

Summary

Creating and manipulating graphics for display on the World Wide Web is somewhat different from the procedures for many other media, because Web graphic files need to be much smaller. The smaller a graphic, the fewer colors it uses; and the more compressed a file, the better the experience for the user. Web designers need to know how to use some fairly specialized graphics programs.

One of the most interesting manipulations of a Web graphic is the transparent GIF file, which makes the graphic seem to be floating above the Web page—or makes the Web page the actual background for the graphic. You need special techniques and programs to create such a file.

After you create some fast-loading, attractive graphics, placing them on your Web pages is fairly simple. All you need is the <IMG> tag, complete with a path and filename to the graphic. Our discussion of the <IMG> tag introduces something new for HTML tags: attributes. Various attributes for the <IMG> tag allow you to add text to a graphic (for text-based browsers) and to align the text with the top, middle, or bottom of the graphic.

Review Questions

1. What's the single most significant concern in creating graphics for display on the Web?

2. True or false. The number of colors used to create a graphic can affect the size of the graphic file.

3. What are the two most common graphic formats used on the Web? Can you use other formats?

4. What does it mean when a graphic format (such as JPEG) is lossy?

5. Name four ways that you can obtain graphics for your Web site.

6. What is the ideal size range for Web graphics?

7. What are thumbnail graphics?

8. What specific file format must a GIF be saved in for it to work as a transparent GIF?

9. When used with the <IMG> tag, what sort of command or HTML element is SRC?

10. What is the purpose of the ALT attribute?

11. True or false. The <IMG> tag automatically inserts a carriage return after displaying its graphic.

12. Why do you never have to set the ALIGN attribute to BOTTOM?

Review Exercises

1. Use your graphics program to save the same graphic as both a GIF and a JPEG image. Then create a Web page that loads both. Note the differences in size and quality.

2. Create a GIF image and turn the background transparent with your graphics program (Paint Shop Pro, LView Pro, or Transparency for the Mac, among others). Load both the original and the transparent GIF into your browser (create a Web page if necessary), and notice the difference that transparency makes. Also note whether or not the file size changes.

3. Use the ALIGN attribute to an <IMG> tag to align another image to the top of the first image. Play with this feature, aligning images to TOP, MIDDLE, and BOTTOM.

## CHAPTER 10

Hypertext and Creating Links

Now that you've seen in detail the ways you can mark up text for emphasis and add images to your Web pages, it's time to take the leap into making these pages useful on the World Wide Web by adding hypertext links. The anchor tag for hypertext links is simple to add to your already-formatted pages. You'll see how URLs are useful for creating hypermedia links and links to other Internet services.

Using the <A> Tag

The basic link for creating hypertext and hypermedia links is the <A>, or anchor, tag. This tag is a container, which requires an </A> to signal the end of the text, images, and HTML tags that are to be considered to be part of the hypertext link. Here's the basic format for a text link:

```
<A HREF="URL">Text describing link</A>
```

Be aware that HREF, although it's something that you'll use with nearly every anchor tag you create, is simply an attribute for the <A> tag. Displayed in a browser, the words *Text describing link* would appear underlined and in another color (on a color monitor) to indicate that clicking that text initiates the hypertext link.

The following is an example of a relative link:

```
<A HREF="products.html">Our Product Information</A>
```

If the HTML document to which you want a link is located elsewhere on the Internet, you simply need a more complete, absolute URL, such as the following:

```
<A HREF="http://www.bignet.net/realcorp/products.html">Our Product
Information</A>
```

In either case, things end up looking the same in a browser (see fig. 10.1).

Figure 10.1

These are the hypertext links that you've created.

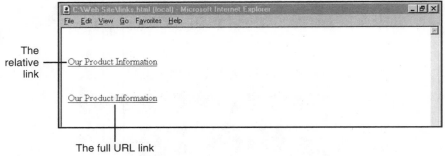

The relative link

Our Product Information

Our Product Information

The full URL link

Section Links

Aside from creating hypertext links to documents on your local computer or elsewhere on the Internet, you can create links to other parts of the same document in which the link appears. These "section" links are useful for moving people to a new section that appears on the same Web page without forcing them to scroll down the entire page.

Doing this, though, requires two instances of the anchor tag—one that serves as the hypertext link and another that acts as a reference point for that link, following this format:

```
<A HREF="#section_name">Link to another section of this document</A>
<A NAME="section_name">Beginning of new section</A>
```

Notice that the anchor tag that creates the hyperlink is similar to the anchor tags that you have used previously. The only difference is the pound sign (#) used at the beginning of the HREF text. This sign tells the anchor that it is looking for a section within the current document, as opposed to within an external HTML document.

The NAME attribute is used to create the actual section within the current HTML document. The text that the NAME attribute contains is relatively unimportant, and it won't be highlighted or underlined in any way when displayed by a browser. NAME is nothing more than an internal reference; without it, though, the link won't work.

> **Note:** Remember to use the pound sign (#) only for the actual hypertext link, not the NAME anchor. Also, realize that the NAME text is case-sensitive and that the

associated HREF text should use the same case for all letters as does the NAME. If the HREF calls for Section_ONE, and the NAME is actually Section_One, the link will not work.

Example: A More Effective Definition List

In Chapter 8, "Displaying Text in Lists," you worked with the definition list tags available to use in HTML and, in some cases, actually used them for a list of definitions. You do that again in this section, but this time you use section links to move directly to the words that interest you.

Load the HTML template into your text editor, and choose the Save As command in your text editor to create a new file. In the body of your HTML document, type Listing 10.1 or something similar.

On the CD

Listing 10.1 *listlink.html* **Creating a Definition List**

```
<BODY>
<H2>The Definition List</H2>
<P>Click one of the following words to move to its definition in the
list:
<BR>
<A HREF="#EPITHET">epithet</A><BR>
<A HREF="#EPITOME">epitome</A><BR>
<A HREF="#EPOCH">epoch</A><BR>
<A HREF="#EPOXY">epoxy</A><BR>
<A HREF="#EQUAL">equal</A><BR>
</P>
<HR>
<DL>
<DT><A NAME="EPITHET"><B>ep i thet</B></A>
<DD><EM>noun.</EM> a descriptive, often contemptuous word or phrase
<DT><A NAME="EPITOME"><B>ep it o me</B></A>
<DD><EM>noun.</EM> someone who embodies a particular quality
<DT><A NAME="EPOCH"><B>ep och</B></A>
<DD><EM>noun.</EM> a division in time; a period in history or geology
<DT><A NAME="EPOXY"><B>ep ox y</B></A>
<DD><EM>noun.</EM> a synthetic, heat-sensitive resin used in adhesives
<DT><A NAME="EQUAL"><B>e qual</B></A>
<DD><EM>adj.</EM> having the same quality or status; having enough
strength, courage, and so on.
<DD><EM>noun.</EM> a person or thing that is equal to another; a person
with similar rights or status
</DL>
</BODY>
```

In the example, clicking one of the words that appears as a hyperlink in the first section of the paragraph moves the browser window down to that link's associated

NAME anchor, so that the definition becomes the focal point of the user's attention. Obviously, using section links would be of greater use in a larger list. Consider the implications for turning an entire dictionary into HTML documents.

Also notice that anchors can be placed within the confines other HTML tags, as in the first paragraph container and in the definition lists of the example. In general, anchor tags can be acted on by other HTML tags as though they were regular text. In the case of hyperlinked text, the underlining and change in color in graphical browsers take precedence, but the hyperlinked text also has any other qualities of the surrounding text (for example, indenting with the rest of the definition text).

In figure 10.2, notice which anchors cause the text to become a hyperlink and how the anchor tags respond within other container tags.

Figure 10.2

Anchor tags are used to define and move between sections of an HTML document.

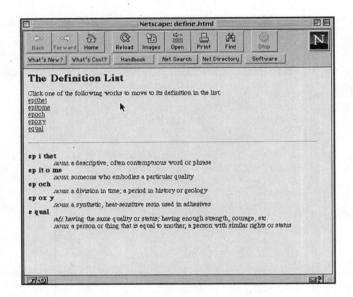

Using Relative URLs

Go back and look at the hypertext links that we discussed at the beginning of this chapter (as opposed to section links). In most cases, the URL referenced by the HREF attribute within the anchor tag needs to be an absolute URL, unless it references a file located in the same directory as the current HTML document.

But consider the case of a well-organized Web site, as set out in Chapter 5, "What You Need for a Web Site." That chapter discussed the fact that it's not always the best idea to drop all your Web site's files into the same directory, especially for large sites that contain many graphics or pages. How do you create links to files that may be on the same server but not in the same directory?

One obvious way is to use an absolute URL for every link in your Web site. If the current page is **http://www.fakecorp.com/index.html**, and you want to access a specific page that you organized into your products directory, you could simply create a link like the following, using an absolute URL:

```
<A HREF="http://www.fakecorp.com/products/new_prods.html>Our new
products</A>
```

These absolute URLs can get rather tedious, not to mention the fact that if you happen to change the name of your Web server or move your site to another basic URL, you'll probably have to edit every page in your site to reflect the new URLs.

Adding the *<BASE>* Tag

The <BASE> tag is used to establish the absolute base for relative URLs used in your document's hypertext links. This tag is especially useful when your Web pages may appear in different subdirectories of a single main directory, as in some of the organizational types discussed in Chapter 5. The format of the <BASE> tag is as follows:

```
<BASE HREF="absolute URL">
```

Note that the <BASE> tag is designed to appear only between the <HEAD> tags.

It may be helpful to think of <BASE> as doing something similar in function to a DOS path statement. The <BASE> tag tells the browser that relative URLs within this particular Web document are based on the URL defined in the <BASE> tag. The browser then assumes that relative URLs derive from the URL given in the <BASE> tag and not necessarily from the current directory of the HTML document.

Consider a document named **http://www.fakecorp.com/products/list.html** that looks something like this:

```
<HEAD>
<TITLE>Page One</TITLE>
</HEAD>
<BODY>
<A HREF="index.html">Back to Index</A>
</BODY>
```

In this example, the browser tries to find a document named index.html in the directory products, because the browser assumes that all relative addresses are derived from the current directory. Using the <BASE> tag, however, changes this example a bit, as follows:

```
<HEAD>
<BASE HREF="http://www.fakecorp.com/">
<TITLE>Page One</TITLE>
</HEAD>
<BODY>
<A HREF="index.html">Back to Index</A>
</BODY>
```

157

Now the browser looks for the file index.html in the main directory of this server, regardless of where the current document is stored (such as in the products directory). The browser interprets the relative URL in the anchor tag as though the complete URL were **http://www.fakecorp.com/index.html**.

> **Tip:** If you plan to create a large Web site, you may want to add the <BASE> tag (complete with the base URL) to your HTML template file.

Using the <BASE> tag to point to your Web site's main directory allows you to create the different types of organization systems described in Chapter 5 by using relative URL statements to access HTML documents in different subdirectories.

Example: A Hybrid-Style Web Site

Chapter 5 discussed the hybrid style of Web site organization, which allows you to put some common files (such as often-used graphics) in separate directories and to organize unique files with their related HTML pages.

In this example, you create an HTML document called products.html, located at the URL **http://www.fakecorp.com/products/products.html**. Some of your graphics are maintained in a subdirectory of the main directory of this Web site; the subdirectory is called graphics/. You also have links to other pages in the main directory and in a subdirectory called about/. Figure 10.3 shows this graphically.

Figure 10.3

Graphical look at your fictitious Web site's organization.

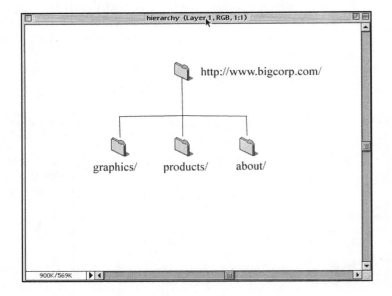

For this example, you create only one Web page. To test the page, however, you want to create a directory structure similar to the previously outlined directory structure and include all the files mentioned.

Begin by saving your template file as `products.html`. Then, in your text editor, enter Listing 10.2.

On the CD

Listing 10.2 *basetag.html* Creating a Directory Structure

```
<HTML>
<HEAD>
<TITLE>Our Products</TITLE>
<BASE HREF="http://www.fakecorp.com/">
</HEAD>
<BODY>
<IMG SRC="products/prod_ban.gif">
<H2>Our Products</H2>
<P>Here's a listing of the various product types we have available. Click
the name of the product category for more information:</P>
<DL>
<DT>
<DD><IMG SRC="graphics/bullet.gif"> <A HREF="products/pc_soft.html">
PC Software</A>
<DD><IMG SRC="graphics/bullet.gif"> <A HREF="products/mac_soft.html">
Macintosh Software</A>
<DD><IMG SRC="graphics/bullet.gif"> <A HREF="products/pc_hard.html">
PC Hardware</A>
<DD><IMG SRC="graphics/bullet.gif"> <A HREF="products/mac_soft.html">
Macinotsh Hardware</A>
</DL>
<HR>
<A HREF="index.html">Return to Main</A>
</BODY>
</HTML>
```

Notice that all the hypertext link HREF commands are pointing to pages that are relative to the <BASE> URL, which is set for the main directory of the Web site. With <BASE> set, it's no longer appropriate simply to enter a filename for your relative URL, even if the file is in the current directory (for example, products/). If all goes well and all your references hold up, your page is displayed as shown in figure 10.4.

Note: Notice that the <BASE> HREF also affects graphics placed with the <IMG> tag. Remember to use relative addresses for images that take the <BASE> address into account. Only HTTP documents and images are affected by <BASE>, though, and not other URL types (like **ftp://** and **gopher://**).

Figure 10.4

Your Products
page, complete
with relative links
to other parts of
the Web site.

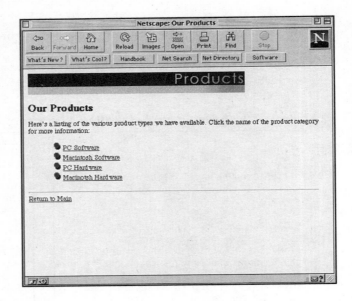

Creating Links to Other Internet Services

Here's where the real power of URLs comes into play. Remember that an URL can be used to describe almost any document or function that's available on the Internet? If something can be described in an URL, a hyperlink can be created for it. In the following section, you start with e-mail.

Hyperlinks for E-Mail Messages

Creating a hyperlinked e-mail address is simple. Using the mailto: type of URL, you can create the following link:

```
<A HREF="mailto:tstauffer@aol.com">Send me e-mail</A>
```

In many graphical browsers, this URL often loads an e-mail window, which allows you to enter the subject and body of an e-mail message and then send it via your Internet account (see fig. 10.5). Even many of the major online services support this hyperlink with their built-in e-mail systems.

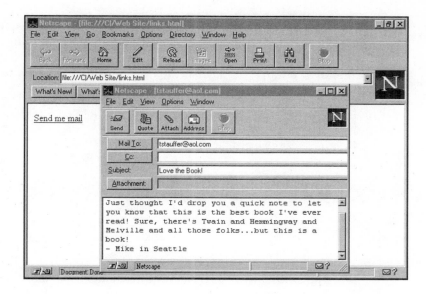

Figure 10.5

Clicking a
`mailto:` link
brings up an
e-mail message
window in
Netscape.

Not all Web browsers accept the `mailto:` style of URL, however, and most of those don't return an error message. If you use this type of link, you may want to warn users. Something like the following text should work well for users of nongraphical browsers:

```
<P>If your browser supports the mailto: command, click <A
HREF="mailto:tstauffer@aol.com">here</A> to send me an e-mail message.
</P>
```

Other Internet Services

Using the various types of URLs discussed in Chapter 3, you can create links to nearly all other types of Internet services as well. For Gopher sites, for example, a hypertext link might look like the following example:

```
<A HREF="gopher://marvel.loc.gov/">the Library of Congress Gopher</A>
```

Most Web browsers can display Gopher menus. In most cases, clicking a gopher link points the browser at the Gopher site, and the Gopher menu appears in the browser window.

You can create links that cause the Web browser to download a file from an FTP server, as follows:

```
<P>You can also <A HREF="ftp://ftp.fakecorp.com/pub/
newsoft.zip">download</A>the latest version of our software.
```

When the connection to the FTP server has been negotiated, the file begins to download to the user's computer (see fig. 10.6). Depending on the Web browser, this file may not be formatted correctly. Each browser needs to be set up to accept files of a certain type (such as the PKZip format file in the preceding example).

> **Note:** Most browsers can accept hyperlinks only to anonymous FTP servers. You generally should not include in your HTML documents links to FTP servers that require usernames and passwords.

Figure 10.6

Netscape is downloading a file from an FTP server.

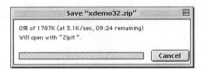

Again, most browsers have some mechanism (sometimes built into the browser window) for reading UseNet newsgroups. Some browsers launch a separate program to read UseNet groups. In either case, you can create a link like the following:

```
<A HREF="news:news.answers">UseNet Help Newsgroup</A>
```

This link loads whatever UseNet reading features the browser employs and displays the specified newsgroup (see fig. 10.7). As discussed in Chapter 3, the news: URL type does not require a particular Internet server address to function. Each browser should be set up with its own links to the user's news server.

Figure 10.7

MS Internet Explorer after clicking a link to the newsgroup news.answers.

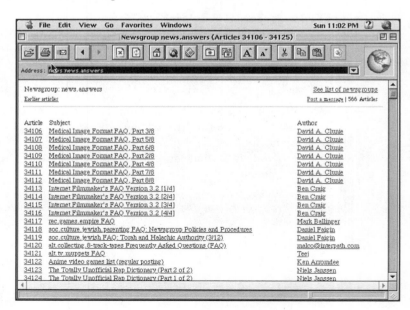

Other Links for the *<HEAD>* Tag

You can create a couple more tags in the <HEAD> section of your HTML documents. These tags are of varying levels of real-world usefulness, so you may want to read this section quickly and refer to it again later if you have a question. The two tags discussed in the following sections are <LINK> and <ISINDEX>.

The *<LINK>* Tag

The <LINK> tag is designed to establish a hypertext relationship between the current document and another URL. Most of the time, the <LINK> tag does not create a clickable hypertext link in the user's Web viewer window. It's a little beyond the scope of this book, but programs can be written to take advantage of the <LINK> tag, such as a program that creates a toolbar that makes use of the relationship defined.

The <LINK> tag generally has either of the following formats:

```
<LINK HREF="URL" REL="relationship">
```

or

```
<LINK HREF="URL" REV="relationship">
```

For the most part, <LINK> is used to create an author-defined structure to other HTML documents on a Web site. The attribute REL, for example, defines the relationship of the HREF URL to the current document. Conversely, REV defines the relationship between the current document and the HREF'ed URL.

Following are two examples of <LINK> statements:

```
<LINK HREF="http://www.fakecorp.com/index.html" REL="PARENT">
<LINK HREF="http://www.fakecorp.com/product2.html" REV="CHILD">
```

In the HTML 2.0 standard, these definitions are relatively irrelevant—at least publicly on the Web. You more commonly find these statements used within certain organizations (perhaps companies employing an intranet), especially for advanced Web-based documentation efforts and for efforts that use HTML and SGML (as discussed in Chapter 1, "What is HTML?") together.

HTML 3.0 more than likely will introduce more widespread use of the <LINK> statement and other <HEAD> tags for more tangible benefits.

You may want to use one <LINK> frequently: the REV="MADE" link, which tells users who created the HTML page. Although this use of <LINK> doesn't actually call up a mailto: link in most browsers, some may recognize it eventually. In the meantime, it gives people who view your source code the e-mail address of the author, as in the following example:

```
<LINK HREF="mailto:tstauffer@aol.com" REV="MADE" REL="AUTHOR">
```

You also should include a mailto: anchor tag in the body of your document to allow people to respond to your Web page. Using both is encouraged, but it's ultimately up to you.

> **Tip:** You can find more information about `<LINK>`, and the various values for `REL/REV`, at **http://www.sq.com/papers/Relationships.html**.

The *<ISINDEX>* Tag

Adding the `<ISINDEX>` tag to the `<HEAD>` of your document allows some Web-server search engines to search your Web pages for keywords. If your Web server offers such a search engine and the user's browser supports these searches, the user will be presented with a simple search box when this page is loaded. The user can then enter the text he or she wants to search for on your page.

The tag itself is very straightforward and requires no further attributes, as the following example shows:

```
<HEAD>
<ISINDEX>
</HEAD>
```

> **Note:** If someone else runs your Web server, you may want to ask that person whether you should include the `<ISINDEX>` tag. If the administrator offers a server-based search engine, he or she may have you use the `<ISINDEX>` tag, or he or she may insert it into your document himself or herself.

Summary

The `<A>` (anchor) tag is the basis for creating hyperlinks on your Web pages. This tag is fairly straightforward; you can use it in conjunction with other tags (such as definition lists) to make hypertext links easy to understand and presentable to the user.

You also can create links to other parts of the same document: relative links and links for special services, such as e-mail. In the case of some of these links (especially relative links), you must seriously consider the way in which your Web site is organized.

The head section of your HTML page can accept several other link-related tags. To keep relative links in check, you can use the `<BASE>` tag. The `<LINK>` tag is used mainly for internal reference, and the `<ISINDEX>` tag can be used on Web servers that provide search engines for your Web pages.

Review Questions

1. Is HREF a tag or an attribute?

2. Do local links and distance links look any different when they are viewed in a browser?

3. What type of link is `<A HREF="#intro">Intro</A>`? Can you tell from the link what document will be accessed?

4. Is it possible to include HTML markup tags (such as emphasis tags) inside anchor tags?

5. What is the purpose of the `<BASE>` tag, and in what part of the HTML document does it appear?

6. True or false. The `<BASE>` tag's HREF attribute requires a relative URL.

7. Would the following link succeed? (Assume that the e-mail address is correct.)

   ```
   <A HREF="mailto://buddy@aol.com">Mail me!</A>
   ```

8. What two attributes for the `<LINK>` tag are discussed in this chapter?

9. Does the `<LINK>` tag create a hypertext link in the browser window?

10. If your Web server is administered by someone else, what's the best way to find out whether the `<ISINDEX>` tag will do you any good?

Review Exercises

1. Create a hypertext link that points to a section of another document. (Hint: use the URL and a section name, like **http://www.fakecorp.com/ products.html#clothing**). Don't forget the NAME anchor in the second document.

2. Using the `<BASE>` tag, change the following so that the URL and image SRC attribute are relative:

   ```
   <BODY>
   <IMG SRC="http://www.fakecorp.com/images/logo.gif">
   <P> Welcome to <A HREF="http://www.fakecorp.com/
   about.html">BigCorp</A> on the World Wide Web!</P>
   </BODY>
   ```

3. Create a page about your hobbies and interests. (This might be a great About page for your personal Web site.) On the page, include links to interesting sites that coincide with your description. (For instance, if you like sports, you might create a link to **http://www.cnn.com/SPORTS/** for the benefit of your users.)

## CHAPTER 11

Using Links with Other HTML Tags

Creating links to other local and distance HTML documents is a relatively straight-forward process, as Chapter 10, "Hypertext and Creating Links," showed. But you also can include links within and together with other HTML tags to make them more interesting, better organized, and more accessible to your users.

As you read this chapter, it may strike you that very little new information about HTML is presented. That's done somewhat purposefully. The point of most of this chapter is simply to explore the various ways that hypertext links can be added to fully formatted HTML documents.

In this chapter, you'll take what you know about hypertext links and integrate them more completely into your Web pages. You'll also look at how to create *graphical links*—links that are initiated by allowing the user to click images in your documents, instead of just text. You'll also create *menubar links* (a series of graphical links) in an effort to design an attractive interface for your Web sites. And, you'll see how to call multimedia files using hypertext links.

Using Links with HTML Formatting Tags

You can include the anchor tag (`<A>`) for hypertext links inside or with nearly any other HTML formatting tags. Although it's important to remember that anything inside the actual `<A HREF>` statement needs to remain intact, the `<A>` tag acts almost exactly like the `<P>` tag (except that it doesn't insert a return). Entire sentences, paragraphs, and even lists and headers can be a single hypertext link. Although this would be unsightly and bad HTML design, it is possible.

You can also include links within nearly all other HTML container tags. Even emphasis tags, such as <EM> and <B>, can accept an entire anchor container within their confines; they still allow the hypertext link to be created and the descriptive text to be emphasized. The following section shows how this might work.

Emphasis Tags and Hyperlinks

The first, most obvious example of using emphasis tags and hyperlinks involves emphasizing the descriptive text of the link within the <A> tag itself. What if you need to create a link that is also the title of a book and that, as such, must be italicized? You could actually do this in either of the following two ways:

```
<A HREF="book1.html"><I>The Young and the Dirty</I></A>
<I><A HREF="book2.html">The Old and the Unkempt</A></I>
```

Either method is acceptable, although the first probably makes a bit more sense to someone viewing your source document.

As usual, the best practice is to finish inside tags first and then close off outside tags. In the first example shown earlier in this section, the closing </I> tag should come before the </A> tag, because the italics tag is the interior tag and the <A> tag is acting as a container for the entire line.

The <EM>, <STRONG>, <BOLD>, and <TT> tags can be used the same way with hypertext links. The <U> (underline) tag, although legal, is redundant, because most browsers display hyperlinks by turning them a different color and underlining the descriptive text.

Hyperlinks can appear within the confines of any of the container tags that this book has described so far. The <PRE> tag, header tags, the special formatting tags (such as <ADDRESS>, <CITE>, and <CODE>), and the <P> tag can contain hyperlinks.

Example: Hyperlinks in Context

This example shows you a few more ways to use emphasis tags with hyperlinks in an HTML document. For this example, give your HTML template a new name, and type Listing 11.1 between the <BODY> tags.

On the CD

Listing 11.1 *links.html* **Creating Hyperlinks**

```
<BODY>
<H2>The Page of Links</H2>
<ADDRESS>
Todd Stauffer<BR>
Colorado Springs<BR>
<A HREF="mailto:TStauffer@aol.com">TStauffer@aol.com</a><BR>
</ADDRESS>
<P>On the following pages, I offer a series of <A HREF="
http://www.ncsa.uiuc.edu/demoweb/html-primer.html#A1.3.3"> links </A>
to WWW sites that I think you may find interesting.<BR>
```

```
<B>Also, if you haven't yet read <A HREF="
http://home.netscape.com/escapes/whats_cool.html">
<I>The Cool Links Page</I></A> from Netscape Corp., you can't imagine how
much you're missing on the Web.</B></P>
<HR>
<P>The following table will lead you to some of my favorite links on a
variety of topics:
<PRE>
My Favorite Corporate Web Sites By Topic:

<B>Topic            Site</B>
Windows     <A HREF="http://www.microsoft.com/windows/">The Microsoft
Windows95 Site</A>
Macintosh  <A HREF="http://www.apple.com/">Apple Corp. Home Pages</A>
OS/2        <A HREF="http://www.austin.ibm.com/pspinfo/os2.html">
IBM's OS/2 Warp Web Site</A>

</PRE>
</P>
<CITE>Some of the addresses in this Web site are based on results ob-
tained from the <A HREF="http://guide.infoseek.com/">Infoseek Web Search
Pages</A>.</CITE>
</BODY>
```

When displayed in a browser, all the links should appear properly formatted and ready for the user to click (see fig. 11.1).

Figure 11.1

Hypertext links, formatted with other HTML tags.

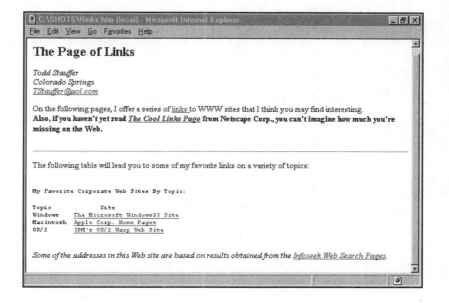

Using Hypertext Links in HTML Lists

In Chapter 10, you saw an example of using the <DL> (definition list) tag to create a better organization for section links within a hypertext document. But, like other types of HTML container tags, HTML lists can easily accept any sort of hypertext link as a <LI> (list item), <DT> (definition term), or <DD> (definition).

Any HTML list type that accepts the <LI> tag to create a new list item can include a hypertext link. An unordered (bullet-style) list can easily accept hypertext links by themselves, as the following example shows:

```
<UL>
<LI> <A HREF="http://www.microsoft.com/">Microsoft Corp.</A>
<LI> <A HREF="http://www.apple.com/index.html">Apple Corp.</A>
<LI> <A HREF="http://www.ibm.com/index.html">IBM Corp.</A>
</UL>
```

Or even hypertext links mixed with other text (see fig. 11.2):

```
<UL>
<LI> For a discussion of Windows 95, try <A HREF="http://
www.microsoft.com/">
Microsoft Corp.</A>.
<LI> Mac users might check out the <A HREF="http://www.apple.com/
index.html"> Apple Corp.</A> Web site.
<LI> OS/2 and PC folks: <A HREF="http://www.ibm.com/index.html">
IBM Corp.</A>
</UL>
```

Figure 11.2

Hypertext links in unordered lists.

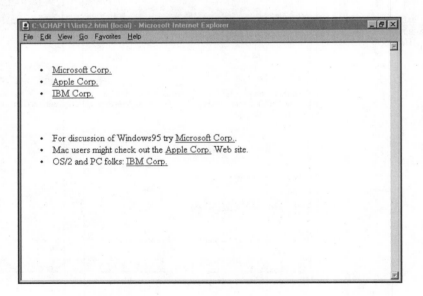

Adding hypertext links works just as easily with other HTML list types, including ordered (numbered) lists, menu lists, directory lists, and definition lists.

Example: An HTML Table of Contents

One of the most common reasons for using a combination of HTML lists and hypertext links is to create a table of contents for a particularly long HTML site (or the HTML version of an academic thesis, scientific study, or book). Using nested HTML lists (like those that you created in Chapter 8), you can add different levels of links under each different subject heading in your outline.

Using your HTML template, create a new HTML document and enter Listing 11.2 or something similar (see fig. 11.3).

On the CD

Listing 11.2 *listlink.html* **HTML Table of Contents**

```
<BODY>
<H2>The Guidebook to Local Hangouts</H2>
<P>Choose from the following links to jump directly to that section of
the text:</P>
<OL>
<LI><A HREF="intro.html#thanks">Credits</A>
<LI><A HREF="intro.html#unique">What is unique about this guide?</A>
<LI><A HREF="intro.html#included">Included clubs</A>
<LI><A HREF="intro.html#ratings">How the rating system works</A>
<LI><A HREF="guide.html#general">Type of Club</A>
    <UL>
    <LI><A HREF="guide1.html#sports">Sports Bars</A>
    <LI><A HREF="guide1.html#country">Country (& Western) Bars</A>
    <LI><A HREF="guide.html#alternative">Alternative Bars</A>
    <LI><A HREF="guide.html#rock">Album/Hard Rock Clubs</A>
    <LI><A HREF="guide.html#jazz">Jazz & Classic Blues Bars</A>
    <LI><A HREF="guide.html#oldies">Big Band/Classical/Torchsong Bars</A>
    <LI><A HREF="guide.html#pool">Pool Halls</A>
    </UL>
<LI><A HREF="restaurant.html#general">Type of Restaurant</A>
</OL>
<BR>
</BODY>
```

A table of contents is a great excuse to use section tags, along with regular URLs, to access parts of remote documents. In the preceding example, the document guide.html contains information on all types of bars in the area, with each section being defined by an <A NAME=> tag. Using the tags enables your Web page users to access parts of the remote document directly.

Figure 11.3

Using lists and hypertext links to create a table of contents.

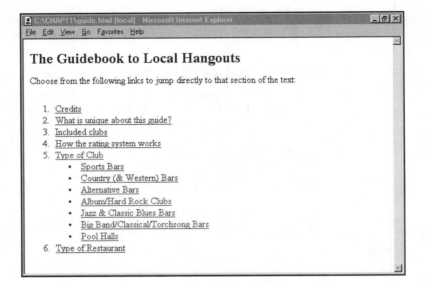

Creating Graphical Links

Now you know that you can place a hypertext link inside nearly any other HTML container tag, and you know that different tags work well inside the anchor tag. But what about graphics?

Graphics work as well as just about all other types of HTML tags. Simply by placing an <IMG> tag inside an anchor tag, you create a clickable image, which can substitute for the descriptive text in a link.

Consider the following example:

```
<A HREF="http://www.fakecorp.com/"> <IMG SRC="biglogo.gif"
ALT="Bigcorp"></A>
```

Notice that the example doesn't include any sort of descriptive text in the link. If a user's graphical viewer can support this type of image, the link displays the graphic, with a colored border. Clicking the image sends the browser to the associated link. If the user isn't viewing this page with a graphical viewer, he or she sees the ALT text, which works as a hyperlink.

If you want, you can include text inside the anchor container, as follows:

```
<A HREF="www.fakecorp.com/"> <IMG SRC="biglogo.gif" ALT="Bigcorp">
Go to BigCorp's Web Site</A>
```

The descriptive text is displayed right next to the graphic image, and both the text and image are hyperlinks (see fig. 11.4).

Figure 11.4

A clickable image and a clickable image with descriptive text.

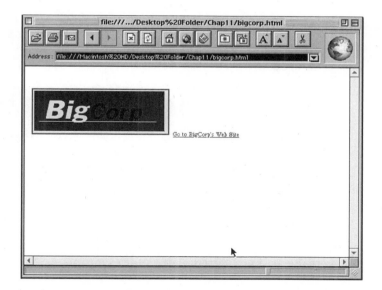

Example: A Graphical, Hyperlinked Listing

Another interesting use of lists and hypertext links features the `<DL>` list, with an interesting twist. This example throws in thumbnail versions of some graphics that suggest what the links access. The user can access a link by clicking the associated graphic.

This example shows a popular HTML menuing format; it offers a low-bandwidth way to offer a visual reference for a database-style Web site. On a page such as this, you could list artwork, movie reviews, other Web sites, a company's products, a list of people, screen shots of computer programs, or just about anything else graphical.

Create a new HTML document from your template, and then enter text and tags according to the example in Listing 11.3.

Listing 11.3 *linkmenu.html* **Creating a Graphics Listing**

```
<BODY>
<H2>Suggested Search and Directory Pages</H2>
<P>Ready to Search the Net? Click the associated icon to jump to that
particular Web search page.</P>
<DL>
<DT><A HREF="guide.infoseek.com"><IMG SRC="infoseek.gif"> The Infoseek
Engine</A>
<DD>Infoseek offers a broad range of searching and directory options, and
is a fine place to start your search on the Web. It's also possible to
```

continues

Listing 11.3 Continued

```
search other services, like UseNet and Classifieds. <I>Tip:</I> For best
results, put proper names or complete phrases in quotes, like "Microsoft
Windows".
<DT><A HREF="www.yahoo.com"><IMG SRC="yahoo.gif"> The Yahoo Directory</A>
<DD> Widely regarded as the earliest attempt to organize the Web, Yahoo
remains a formidable directory of links to useful sites. Searching isn't
as comprehensive as some others, but the directory is the main reason to
use Yahoo, anyway.
<DT><A HREF="www.lycos.com"><IMG SRC="lycos.gif"> The Lycos Search
Engine</A>
<DD> Image isn't everything, and Lycos doesn't give the prettiest search
results. But if you're comfortable with relatively plain listings, Lycos
offers one of the larger databases of Web Sites available.
</DL>
</BODY>
```

This is an attractive way to organize thumbnail graphics into menus and so versatile that you'll find plenty of uses for this style of presentation (see fig. 11.5).

Figure 11.5

Creating a clickable graphic menu.

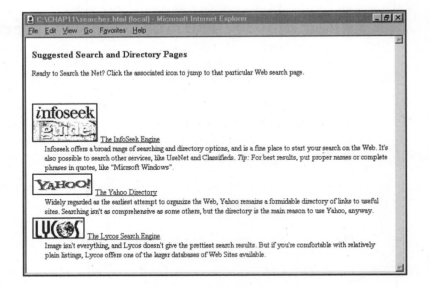

Example: A Clickable Graphic Menu Bar

Wrapping a hypertext anchor tag around a graphic allows you to do something else with graphical links: create clickable menu bars. You'll see this style of interface used frequently on the Web. Menu bars are generally designed to allow you to access the most frequently sought pages or commands on a Web site. By lining up your graphical hyperlinks, you can create your own menu bars.

> **Tip:** The key to a good menu bar is creating graphical buttons of uniform height.

You start by creating a couple of button images in a graphics applications. Save the images as GIF or JPG files. Then create the menu bar in a new HTML file (see Listing 11.4).

Listing 11.4 *menubar.html* Creating a Graphical Menu Bar

```
<BODY>
<A HREF="http://www.fakecorp.com/index.html"><IMG SRC="home_button.gif"
ALT="Back to Home"></A>
<A HREF="http://www.fakecorp.com/products.html"><IMG
SRC="prod_button.gif"
ALT="To Products"></A>
<A HREF="http://www.fakecorp.com/about.html"><IMG SRC="about_button.gif"
ALT="To About Bigcorp"></A>
<A HREF="http://www.fakecorp.com/service.html"><IMG SRC="serv_button.gif"
ALT="To Service"></A>
</BODY>
```

Remember that HTML isn't sensitive to spacing and returns, so, although each of these links is on a separate line in the example (just to enhance readability), the graphic buttons are displayed next to one another without spacing (see fig. 11.6). You've created a graphical menu bar for your Web site.

Figure 11.6

A sample menu bar, created with clickable graphic links.

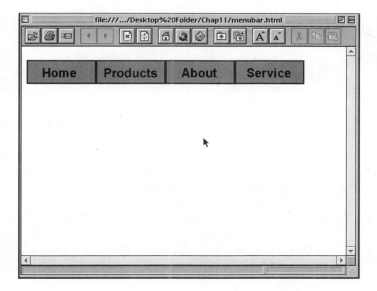

Chapter 12, "Clickable Image Maps and Graphical Interfaces," goes into further depth about creating a graphical interface for your Web site.

Example: Custom Controls

The HTML isn't any different for this example, but it shows something else that you can do with graphical links: add custom controls (such as clickable arrows) to your Web site.

Note: Some great places to get public-domain clickable graphics on the Web include the following:

http://www.widomaker.com/~spalmer/

http://www.fau.edu/student/chemclub/dave/img1.htm

http://ivory.nosc.mil/html/trancv/html/icons-bsdi.html

You can check for other sites at Yahoo's icon pages:

http://www.yahoo.com/Computers_and_Internet/Internet/World_Wide_Web/Programming/Icons/

Start by either creating some arrow controls that you want to use or downloading them from a public-domain graphics site on the Web. Then save your template as a new document, and enter HTML text similar to Listing 11.5.

On the CD

Listing 11.5 *controls.html* Having Controls

```
<BODY>
<PRE><A HREF="index.html"><IMG SRC="left_arrow.gif"></A>
<A HREF="product2.html"><IMG SRC="right_arrow.gif"></A></PRE>
</BODY>
```

The <PRE> tag is used in the example just to offer a little space between the two graphics; the arrows look better that way. Although the example places only the arrows between the <BODY> tags, you have probably much more to say, but the arrows tend to be attractive at the top of the page. Some people duplicate the arrows at the bottom of the page so that users can move on after reading everything.

You'll have to have a fairly strong organization to your pages to make the arrow graphics work. If people are supposed to move through your site page by page, using the arrows is a great idea. If your site is a little more relaxed, the arrows may only confuse people. You can always use only the left arrow to provide a link back to your index or main page.

Using Hypermedia Links

You don't need to remember anything special about transferring multimedia files across the Internet, except for the fact that you need to use the correct transport protocol. In most cases, that just means using the **http://** protocol for transferring files that you expect the browser to hand off to a helper application.

You could easily send a multimedia QuickTime movie, for example, from your Web page with the following link:

```
<A HREF="http://www.fakecorp.com/todd/vacation.qt">Click to see my
vacation movie (218K)</A>
```

By the same token, you could use a relative link to the multimedia file, using the <BASE> tag or putting the multimedia file in the same directory as the HTML document that includes the link, as follows:

```
<A HREF="vacation.qt">Click to see my vacation movie (218K)</A>
```

> **Tip:** It's good netiquette to include an estimate of the size of multimedia files, so that modem users can decide whether to spend time downloading the files.

Using what you've learned about clickable graphics, it's just as easy to include a small single-frame graphic clip of your QuickTime movie in GIF or JPEG format to use as your link, as follows:

```
<A HREF="vacation.qt"><IMG SRC="vacation.jpg" ALT="My Vacation Movie">
(218K)</A>
```

Although you can send multimedia files by using the **ftp://** protocol, some browsers interpret this as an attempt to download the file to the user's computer without invoking the associated helper application (or displaying the file with the browser's built-in abilities).

Suppose that you have a graphics file that you want to display at full size in the browser window, instead of embedding the image in an HTML document. Create the following link:

```
<A HREF="http://www.fakecorp.com/todd/photo.gif">Click here to see the
full 512x240 image</A>
```

This link sends the graphic over the Web to the browser. The browser then attempts to display the full graphic in the browser window.

Now suppose that you use the FTP protocol instead, as shown in the following example:

```
<A HREF="ftp://ftp.fakecorp.com/todd/photo.gif>Click here to see the full
512x240 image</A>
```

In most browsers, the user is prompted for a directory and filename to give the file when it arrives. The file then is saved to the user's hard drive but not displayed automatically.

In fact, such is the case with most multimedia files. The HTTP protocol suggests to the browser that it should display the file, if possible, or pass the file on to a helper application. The FTP protocol, on the other hand, causes some browsers simply to save the file to the hard drive.

> **Note:** The FTP protocol doesn't always cause browsers to simply save the file. One notable exception is HTML documents themselves. Often, an FTP server can successfully serve HTML documents to a Web browser, which then displays the documents in the browser window.

Summary

This chapter took some of the things that you've learned about hyperlinks, graphics, and hypermedia links and rolled them into one. Most of this material isn't new, but most of the ideas for using them are.

You can include hypertext links within most other HTML markup tags, or you can use HTML emphasis tags to mark up the descriptive text of most hypertext links. Remember to keep things organized and mark up your anchor text only for a good reason. Using lists, for example, you can create a table of contents that makes getting around a text-heavy site much easier.

When you put graphics and hypertext links together, ideas start to explode. You can create graphical menus, employ clickable menu bars, and add custom controls to your Web pages. Clickable graphics (especially thumbnail-style images) are among the easiest and most satisfying ways to enhance your Web site.

Review Questions

1. True or false. Like the `<P>` tag, the anchor (`<A>`) tag inserts a return after the closing `</A>` tag.

2. Can you mix hypertext and emphasis tags, and if so, for what purpose?

3. What emphasis tag usually is redundant when it's used with an anchor tag?

4. Are any HTML list types incapable of accepting hypertext links as list items?

5. Is the following link correctly formatted, and what does it access:

```
<a href="chapter1.html#parttwo">Ch.1, Part II</A>
```

6. What might the following link be used for, and is this construct legal?

```
<A HREF="big_photo.gif"><IMG SRC="sm_photo.gif"></A>
```

7. What happens if a link uses the FTP protocol to transfer a multimedia file over the Web? Can the user still view or listen to the multimedia file?

Review Exercises

1. Use the <DIR> and <MENU> HTML containers to create a list of hypertext links. Notice the differences between these and ordered and unordered lists in your browser.

2. Create a "table of contents" style page (using regular and section links) that loads a different document for each chapter or section of the document. For example, clicking the link **Introduction** would load the file intro.html into the browser windows. Clicking the link **Chapter 1.1** would load the link chapter1.html#section1 and so on.

3. Create a vertical (up-and-down) menu bar. (Hint: use <BR> and graphics that are all the same width.) Can you get the images to touch (and appear seamless) like you can with a horizontal menu bar?

4. Using a <DL> definition list, create a "thumbnails" page of graphics (for a catalog, for instance). When users click one of the thumbnail graphics, take them to a product page with a larger graphic and description of the product. Also, place a graphical button or arrow on the product page that lets them click to get back to the thumbnail view.

Part III

Interactive HTML

Clickable Image Maps and Graphical Interfaces

In Chapter 11, "Using Links with Other HTML Tags," you spent some time creating clickable images, which make Web pages more graphically appealing and (ideally) a little more intuitive. This chapter takes creating a graphical interface to your Web site one step further.

With image maps, you can create an entire interface for your Web pages and sites that rivals the interfaces of popular multimedia games, graphical operating environments, and interactive kiosks. The first 11 chapters of this book have said that the Web is about text, but that fact doesn't mean that you can't use some great graphics to spice up your presentation.

Image Maps Defined

The *map* part of *image map* conjures up two separate images. First, image maps on Web sites often act like road maps for the Web site, adding interface elements that make it easier to get around on the Web site. Second, the word *map* also suggests the way that image maps are created. Image maps begin life as normal graphics (usually in GIF or JPEG format), designed with the Web in mind. Then another program is used to map *hot zones* (clickable areas) on top of the graphics.

When put in place on a Web page, an image map allows users to access different HTML pages by clicking different parts of the graphic. Because each hot zone has an associated URL, and because each hot zone corresponds to part of the graphic, maneuvering about a Web site becomes more interesting, graphical, and interactive.

Example: The Apple Web Site

Apple Computer offers a very interesting example of an image map on the main page of its Web site. To check out the page, load your graphical Web browser, connect to the Internet (if you're not already connected), and enter **http://www.apple.com/**.

When the page loads in your browser, you'll see the interface, which looks a little like a futuristic hand-held computer, on-screen.

> **Note:** Notice how long it can take a graphical interface to load over your connection, especially if you use a modem to access the Internet.

This example isn't terribly structured, but it allows you to play with the image map interface. You may already have a good deal of experience with such interfaces, especially if you've spent a lot of time on the Web.

By simply pointing at part of the graphic, you may be able to bring up a URL in the status bar at the bottom of your browser bar (see fig. 12.1). This bar shows you where the various hot zones for the image map are and at what coordinates your mouse pointer appears.

Check out one more thing. If the image map fills your screen, scroll down in your browser window so that you can see what's below the interface on Apple's Web page. The text directly below the interface almost exactly mirrors the hyperlink options you have with the image map, because image maps, unlike clickable graphics, don't offer an ALT statement for the various hot zones. So you have to include additional links to cater to your users of nongraphical browsers.

Figure 12.1

The image map interface at Apple Computer's Web site.

The image map interface

The status bar

Understanding How Image Maps Work

Creating an image map involves three steps: creating the graphic, mapping the graphic for hot zones, and placing the correct information (along with the correct programs) on the Web server itself. This section discusses the Web server; the next section talks about defining hot zones.

For more information on creating graphic images for Web pages, see Chapter 9, "Creating and Embedding Graphics."

To offer your users the option of using image maps, you must have a special map server program running on your Web server. For UNIX-based servers, this program will most often be NCSA Imagemap; other platforms have their own map server programs.

The Map Server Program

When a user clicks an image map on a Web page, the browser determines the coordinates of the graphic (in pixels) that describe where the user clicked. The browser then passes these numbers to the map server program, along with the name of the file that contains the URLs that correspond to these coordinates.

NCSA Imagemap, then, simply accepts the coordinates and looks them up in the database file that defines the hot zones for that image map. When NCSA Imagemap finds those coordinates and their associated URL, it sends a "connect to URL" command (just as a hypertext link does) that causes your browser to load the appropriate HTML document.

> **Note:** If you're running your own WebStar or MacHTTP server from a Macintosh, you can use a map server called MapServe, which you can download from **http://www.spub.ksu.edu/other/machttp_tools/mapserve/mapserve.html**.
>
> For the most part, other commercial Web servers for UNIX and Windows NT include map server capabilities.

The Map Definition File

To determine which parts of the image map are linked to which URLs, the map server program must have a map definition file at its disposal. This file is generally a text file with the extension MAP, stored somewhere in the cgI-bIn directory for your Web site. Exactly where this file is stored depends on the combination of your Web server and map server. Let it suffice to say that you'll need to consult your server's documentation or your ISP.

The map definition file looks something like figure 12.2. You can create this file and save it as a standard ASCII text file with the appropriate extension; fortunately, you probably won't have to.

Figure 12.2

A map definition file.

sets off comments

Defining a rectangular hot zone

The URL to return for this zone

Coordinates of the hot zone

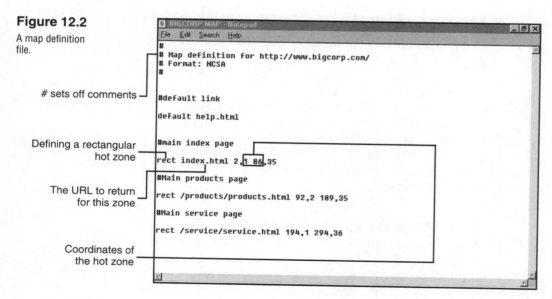

You can define different shapes in the file; these shapes correspond to the shapes of the hot zones that overlay the graphic that you want to use for your image. Each set of coordinates creates a point on the graphic. The coordinates are expressed in pixels, with each pair of numbers representing the number of pixels to the right and down, respectively, from the top left corner of your graphic.

The shapes require a different number of points to define them. Rectangles require two points, for example, and polygons require as many points as necessary. Luckily, the number of points involved isn't something that you'll have to worry about. Simply by using a map editing program for Windows or Macintosh (discussed later in this chapter in the sections, "MapEdit for Microsoft Windows and XWindows" and "WebMap for Macintosh"), you can automatically create the map definition file required for your map server.

> **Note:** You can create image maps without map servers and map definition files by using a technology called client-side image maps. Currently a Netscape technology, this technology eventually may become an HTML 3.0 standard. For more information, see Chapter 17, "Client-Side Image Maps."

The Various Shapes of Hot Zones

This section briefly defines the shapes of hot zones. Hot zones can be in any of the following shapes:

♦ **rect (rectangle)**—This shape requires two points: the upper left coordinates and the lower right coordinates.

♦ **circle**—To create a circular region, you need coordinates for a center point and an edge point. The circle is then computed with that radius.

♦ **point**—A point requires only one coordinate. The map server software decides which point the mouse pointer was closest to when the shape was clicked (provided that the click didn't occur in another hot zone).

♦ **poly (polygon)**—You can use up to 100 sets of coordinates to determine all the vertices for the polygon region.

♦ **default**—Any part of the graphic that is not included in another hot zone is considered to be part of the default region, as long as no point zones are defined. If a point is defined, then default is redundant, since the map server will evaluate any click (outside of a hot zone) and choose the nearest point.

Defining Your Image Map Hot Zones

As a designer, you are responsible for doing two things in the hot zone definition process. First, you need to define the hot zones to create the image map—that is, you need to decide what URL the coordinates will correspond to when the image map is clicked. Second, you need to create the map definition file that makes the hot zone information available to the Web server. For Windows and Macintosh users, luckily, programs that do both are available.

MapEdit for Microsoft Windows and X-Windows

Available for all flavors of Windows (Windows 95, Windows 3.1, and Windows NT) and for most types of UNIX, MapEdit is a powerful program that allows you to graphically define the hot zones for your image maps. You can access and download the latest version of this program via the MapEdit Web site (**http://www.boutell.com/mapedit/**).

When you have the program installed and you double-click its icon to start it, follow these steps to define your map:

1. Choose File, Open/Create from the MapEdit menu. The Open/Create Map dialog box appears.

2. In the Open/Create Map dialog box, enter the name of the map definition file you want to create and the name of the graphic file you want to use for your map. You should also use the radio buttons to determine whether you'll use CERN or NCSA map definitions. (Consult your map server software or ISP if you're not sure whether to use CERN or NCSA.)

3. Click the OK button. The Creating New Map File dialog box appears. In this dialog box, click Yes. After a moment, MapEdit displays your image file.

4. To create a new hot zone, choose the shape from the Tools menu; then click one time for each point required for the shape. For a rectangle, click once to start the rectangle and then click where you'd like the opposite corner of the triangle to appear. For a circle, click for the middle, and then drag out the circle and click when you've got the right radius. The triangle tool is actually a "polygon" tool, so click for each point in the polygon. Then, right-click at the last point (to connect your last point to the first point and complete the shape).

5. When the shape is created, the Object URL dialog box appears (see fig. 12.3). Enter the URL that you want to associate with your new hot zone. (You also can enter comments, if you want.) Then click OK to continue.

Figure 12.3

Associating an URL with the hot zone.

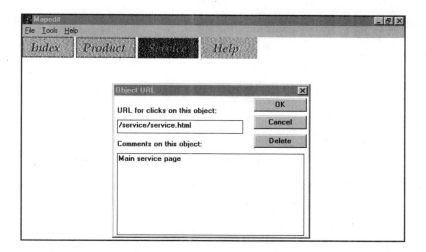

6. Add more shapes by following steps 4 and 5 until you finish mapping your graphic.

7. Choose File, Save. Now you have a .MAP file for your image map.

> **Tip:** By choosing File, Edit Default URL, you can determine whether your image map includes a default URL for clicks outside your hot zones.

Example: MapEdit and a Simple Button Bar

In this example, you use MapEdit to create a simple button bar—a little like the menu bar that you created with clickable graphics in Chapter 11, except for the fact that this one is an image map. Start by drawing an appropriate graphic in a graphics application and saving it as a GIF file. For this example, name the file testbar.gif. Then follow these steps:

1. Open MapEdit, and choose File, Open/Create. The Open/Create Map dialog box appears.

2. In this dialog box, enter **testbar.map** for the map file and **testbar.gif** for the graphics file. (If you saved the GIF file in a different directory, use the Browse button to find and load it.)

3. When the graphic loads, pull down the Tools menu and make sure that Rect is selected.

4. Draw rectangles for the buttons, providing an appropriate URL for each button. For this example (four buttons in all), use the following URLs:

> **http://www.fakecorp.com/index.html**
>
> **http://www.fakecorp.com/product.html**
>
> **http://www.fakecorp.com/service.html**
>
> **http://www.fakecorp.com/help.html**

5. Choose File, Edit Default URL. The Default URL dialog box appears.

6. Enter the following URL:

> **http://www.fakecorp.com/error.html**

7. Choose File, Save.

8. Choose File, Quit.

You've created your map definition file. To look at the file, open Notepad (or a similar text editor), and load the file testbar.map into it. The file should look something like figure 12.4 (although the coordinates are bound to be slightly different).

Figure 12.4

A successful map definition file created in MapEdit.

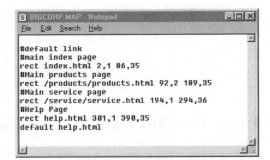

```
#default link
#main index page
rect index.html 2,1 86,35
#Main products page
rect /products/products.html 92,2 189,35
#Main service page
rect /service/service.html 194,1 294,36
#Help Page
rect help.html 301,1 390,35
default help.html
```

WebMap for Macintosh

If you're a Macintosh user, you can use a program called WebMap, which is similar to MapEdit. You can download WebMap from **http://www.city.net/cnx/software/webmap.html**. Install the program; then double-click its icon to start it. To create an image map in WebMap, follow these steps:

1. Choose File, Open.

2. In the Open dialog box, select the graphic that you want to use for your map and the name of the map definition file that you want to create.

3. Click the OK button. After a moment, MapEdit displays your image file.

4. To create a new hot zone, choose the shape from the floating tool palette, and drag to create a hot zone. For a rectangle, circle, or oval, click and hold the mouse in the top left corner of your shape, drag the mouse to make the shape the desired size, and then release the mouse button. To create a polygon, choose the polygon shape from the tool palette and then click once on the graphic for each point in your polygon. To complete the shape, click once on the first point you created.

5. When the shape is created, enter the URL in the space provided above the graphic file (see fig. 12.5). You can use the pointer tool (the one that looks like a mouse pointer) to select different shapes that you've created and then edit their URLs.

Figure 12.5

Using WebMap to create hot zones.

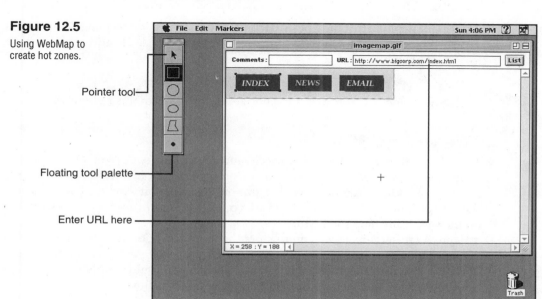

Pointer tool

Floating tool palette

Enter URL here

6. To create a default URL, use the pointer tool to click the graphic background (not a shape). Default URL should appear in the comment window. Then enter the default URL in the URL text box.

To create your map definition file, pull down the File menu and choose Export As Text. In the resulting dialog box, you can name your map file and save it in CERN or NCSA format. Now you're free to save the graphic and quit the program.

Adding Image Maps to Your Web Page

After you create your image map and your map definition file, you're ready to add a link for your image map to your HTML page. You can accomplish this task in a couple of ways, depending on your Web server. In essence, though, the only major difference between an image map and a clickable image (refer to Chapter 11) is a new attribute for the <IMG> tag: ISMAP.

Image maps follow this format:

```
<IMG SRC="graphic.ext" ISMAP>
```

Note: It's perfectly acceptable to add other <IMG> tag attributes (such as ALT) to your image map definition.

Using the ISMAP attribute doesn't do much for you unless the image map is also a hyperlink, so the following code is everything that you need to add an image map to your Web page:

```
<A HREF="URL"><IMG SRC="graphic.ext" ISMAP></A>
```

Our next step is to figure out what to use as the URL in this hyperlink.

The Image Map URL

The URL that you're interested in accessing isn't a particular Web page, because using an URL to a particular Web page would defeat the image map concept; the link would act like a regular clickable graphic. Instead, you want the URL to access the map definition file. You'll have to ask your ISP (or figure out for yourself) where on the server the map file is stored.

Some Web servers allow you to store the map definition file anywhere on the server; the servers are smart enough to figure out that you're accessing a map definition file and take care of the rest. In that case, you could simply store the map definition file in the current directory and access it as follows:

```
<A HREF="mymap.map"><IMG SRC="mymap.gif" ISMAP></A>
```

If you have an understanding server, this method may work for you.

Other servers may require you to access a particular directory on the server, such as the /cgi-bin/ or /bin/ directory, where server scripts (mini computer programs) are stored. In such a case, something like the following examples may be the way to access the image map:

```
<A HREF="http://www.myserver.com/cgi-bin/mymap.map><IMG SRC="mymap.gif"
ISMAP></A>
```

or

```
<A HREF="http://www.myserver.com/bin/mymap.map><IMG SRC="mymap.gif"
ISMAP></A>
```

If the server requires you to access one of these scripting directories, though, it may not want you to access the map definition file directly. Instead, the server will want you to use an alias.

Some servers store all map information in a single database file (often called `imagemap.conf`) and require you to access information within the database by using an alias. You and your Web server administrator have to determine what this alias is. In that case, your link would look more like the following:

```
<A HREF="http://www.myserver.com/bin/mymap"><IMG SRC="mymap.gif" ISMAP></A>
```

Example: Testing Your Link

The best way by far to participate in this example is to confer with your ISP, place your map definition file on the Web server, and test it from a remote location using the correct URL. If that procedure doesn't work, you can manage some testing on your own.

Save your template as a new HTML file, and have an image-mapped graphic handy in the same directory. Then enter Listing 12.1 between the <BODY> tags.

On the CD

Listing 12.1 *img_map.html* Adding Image Maps in HTML

```
<BODY>
<A HREF="http://www.server.com/mymap.map"><IMG SRC="mymap.gif" ISMAP ALT=
"My Image Map"></A>
<H2>Welcome to my page!</H2>
</BODY>
```

> **Note:** If you're going to test this example on an actual Web server, you need to replace the URL with the appropriate one for your Web site (and add the type of link to your map info file that's required for your server). Also, use the real name of the mapped GIF file in the <IMG> tag.

Save the HTML file and then load it in a graphical browser. If your graphic came up, chances are that you set the <IMG> tag correctly. Notice that many browsers do not display a colored link border around the graphic, because the graphic is now considered to be an image map.

Before clicking any of the hot zones, move your mouse pointer around on the image map graphic. If you have a status bar at the bottom of your browser window, you may notice that the link keeps changing (see fig. 12.6). Along with the URL of your map definition file, you should be seeing the current coordinates of your pointer. All this information is sent to the map server to help it figure out what region you clicked. (If you're testing this image map from your local drive, the status bar test is the only part of the example that will work.)

Figure 12.6

An example image map, showing the URL and the coordinates that it will access if clicked.

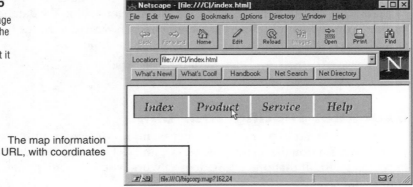

The map information URL, with coordinates

Now, if you are testing your image map on the Web server, go ahead and click the map to make sure that all the links work. If you're viewing the image map locally, turn off the graphics-loading option in your browser, and reload the page. You should notice that there's now no way to access the hyperlinks in the image map—that's why you also need text links for your image map pages.

Image Map Design Tips

This chapter has covered creating and linking an image map to your Web page fairly thoroughly. Image maps are a bit of a departure from standard text-markup HTML, however, so you should learn a little bit of design theory and Web-related netiquette before you leave this chapter. Please try to keep some of the following suggestions in mind when you add image maps to your Web pages:

♦ **Use image maps sparingly**. The best way to use an image map is as a clickable menu bar or some other easy-to-recognize interface element. The point isn't really to see how graphical you can make your Web pages—just how intuitive.

♦ **Remember that image maps are usually little more than big graphics files**. Ultimately, the key to graphics on the Web is keeping them small. Even if your image map is incredibly attractive, users will be annoyed if they have to wait many minutes for their four possible choices to download to their browsers. Use all the tips in Chapter 9 to keep your graphic as small as possible, and use image maps only to enhance usability.

♦ **Image maps require redundant text links**. Unless you plan to leave out everyone who can't view your graphics, you need to create text links that do everything that your image map does. Remember that with clickable graphics, the ALT attribute takes care of the problem. The ALT attribute doesn't work for image maps, because a single image map graphic can have many links, so you need to create an identical text link on your page for every hot zone link in your image map.

♦ **Stick to normal shapes whenever possible**. Rules are made to be broken, but in general, you should try to be conservative with your image maps (see fig. 12.7). A graphic that looks as though it has rectangular buttons should function as though it has rectangular buttons. In other words, make your hot zones correspond logically to the image map graphics. Random hot zones randomly annoy users.

Figure 12.7

Some sites make it their business to use image maps that break the rules. This one doesn't.

Summary

Image maps allow you to create hot zones in individual graphics files. These hot zones point to different URLs, effectively turning a single graphic into a Web interface. By creating creative graphics and pointing different sections of those graphics to pages in your site, you can make it very easy for Web users to get around on your site.

Image maps work in conjunction with your Web server, which must be running a special map server program. In such a case, you need to create a graphic and a map definition file. Fortunately, programs for Windows, UNIX, and Macintosh exist to help you create this definition file.

In conjunction with your system administrator, you place the map definition file in the correct directory on your Web server (most often in the /cgi-bin or /bin directory), and create a link to the image map on your Web page. Placing the image map in your HTML document requires the same anchor and <IMG> tags, but you need to include the ISMAP attribute in the <IMG> tag.

After you finish with all your tags, test your new image map. If all goes well, you'll have a new interface for your Web pages.

You should consider some design rules. Basically, keep the graphics small and fairly standard, so that you don't annoy or confuse your users.

Review Questions

1. Why are the graphics discussed in this chapter called *image maps*?

2. What three steps do you follow to create an image map?

3. What file format is the map definition file saved in?

4. Is it important to know what type of map server program your Web server is using? Why or why not?

5. How do you find out where to store your map definition file?

6. How many points are required for a rectangle in a map definition file? What is the maximum number of points that you can use for a polygon?

7. True or false. You can create an image map without a map editing program.

8. Which files must you create for an image map to work?

9. Do the shapes (rect, poly, point, and so on) that you draw in a map editing program show up in the Web browser window? Why or why not?

10. Why is defining a default map definition redundant if you have already defined a point?

11. Aside from the URL to the map definition file, what information does the Web browser send to the Web server? What does the designer do to make this happen?

Review Exercises

1. Create two different map definition files for the same graphic, one using the CERN method and one using NCSA. Compare the two definition files and notice the differences.

2. Again create two different map definition files for the same graphic, this time using all polygon shapes for one of the definitions and all squares for the other definition. Compare the two definition files. Are polygons considerably more complicated than standard shapes?

3. Create a button bar (or menu bar) using a series of clickable graphics. Then, create a similar button bar using an image map. Which takes more work? Which will take more time to download to a browser (i.e., which method takes up more drive space)?

## CHAPTER 13

HTML Forms

The next set of HTML tags are designed to allow you to enhance the interactivity of your Web pages by increasing your ability to request information from users. Using the forms tags, you can ask users to enter text information, choose from menus, mark checkboxes, make choices from radio buttons, and then send that information to the Web server for processing.

Using Forms and Form-Capable Browsers

Although the forms tags are a part of the HTML 2.0 standard, it's important to recognize that not all browsers are capable of viewing them—especially older browsers and text-based browsers. Users need to have forms-aware browsers, like the current versions of NCSA Mosaic, Netscape Navigator, and Microsoft Internet Explorer, among others. Generally, other browsers will simply ignore the forms commands if they can't deal with them.

> **Tip:** It's a good idea to let your users know that they're about to jump to a form-based page whenever possible. Forms pages are a waste of time for users of older browsers that don't support them.

The idea behind a Web form is simple—it allows you to accept information or answers from your users with varying levels of guidance. Users can be asked to type answers, choose their answers from a list of possibilities you create, or even be limited to choosing one answer from a number of options that you specify.

That data is then passed on to the Web server, which hands it to a script, or small program, designed to act on the data and (in most cases) create an HTML page in response. In order to deal with forms data then, you need to understand a little something about scripting, or programming, for a Web server—or know someone who does. While learning to program is beyond the scope of this book, we'll look at how these scripts work in Chapter 14, "Form Design and Data Gathering with CGI Scripts."

> **Note:** Most Web server scripts are written in Perl, C, or UNIX shell scripts. If your Web server is DOS, Windows, or Mac based, however, you may have other options. Some DOS Web servers allow you to script in the DOS batch language, while some Windows servers can accept Visual Basic scripts (not to be confused with Microsoft's new Visual Basic Script language). Mac Web servers generally allow for AppleScript or Frontier scripting.

Creating the Form

In an HTML document, forms are set between the `<FORM>` container tags. The form container works as follows:

```
<FORM METHOD="how_to_send" ACTION="URL of script">
...form data...
</FORM>
```

Notice that the `<FORM>` tag takes two attributes: METHOD and ACTION. The METHOD attribute accepts either POST or GET as its value. POST is by far the more popular, as it allows for a greater amount of data to be sent. GET is a little easier for Web programmers to deal with, and is best used with single responses, like a single textbox.

The second attribute is ACTION, which simply accepts the URL for the script that will process the data from your form. Most often the script is stored in a directory called `bin/` or `cgi-bin/` located on your Web server.

An example of the `<FORM>` tag then, would be the following:

```
<FORM METHOD="SEND" ACTION="http://www.fakecorp.com/cgi-bin/
register_script">
</FORM>
```

As with any HTML container tag, this implementation of the `<FORM>` tag has actually created a complete form (just like `<P>` and `</P>` is a complete paragraph). Unfortunately, our complete form doesn't *do* anything yet, so that's somewhat academic.

> **Note:** You can't nest forms within one another. You need to add the end tag `</FORM>` for the first form before creating another one in the same document. Generally, browsers will ignore any new occurrences of the `<FORM>` tag, since the purpose of the tag is to tell the browser how to submit data to the server, and different parts of the form can't be submitted in different ways.

Example: Someone Else's Form

Let's take a quick look at a form that's been created by someone else—one that most seasoned Web browsers have encountered at one time or another. Load up your Web browser and point it to **http://webcrawler.com/**.

This is the WebCrawler page, a Web search engine offered by America Online. Your next step is to view the source of this document. Select the View Document Source command in your Web browser's Edit menu. What you see will look something like figure 13.1.

> **Note:** Nearly all graphical browsers have a View Source command. Look in the Edit menu for this command or a command with a similar name. The HTML source of the current Web document will then be displayed or saved as a text file.

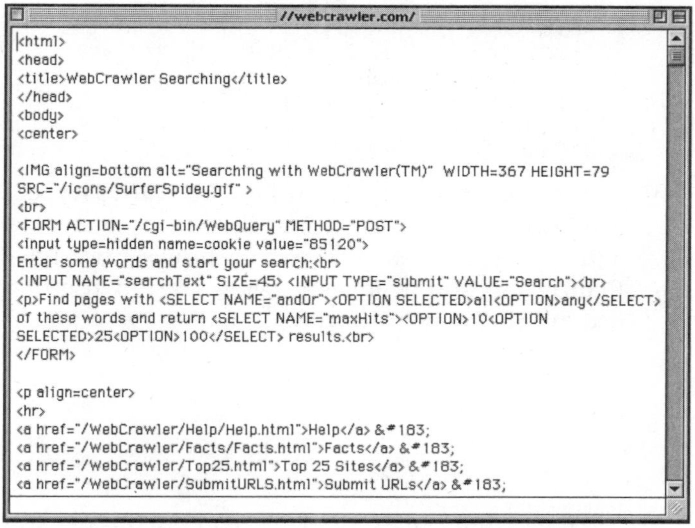

Figure 13.1

Example of an HTML form available on the Web.

```
//webcrawler.com/
<html>
<head>
<title>WebCrawler Searching</title>
</head>
<body>
<center>

<IMG align=bottom alt="Searching with WebCrawler(TM)"  WIDTH=367 HEIGHT=79
SRC="/icons/SurferSpidey.gif" >
<br>
<FORM ACTION="/cgi-bin/WebQuery" METHOD="POST">
<input type=hidden name=cookie value="85120">
Enter some words and start your search:<br>
<INPUT NAME="searchText" SIZE=45> <INPUT TYPE="submit" VALUE="Search"><br>
<p>Find pages with <SELECT NAME="andOr"><OPTION SELECTED>all<OPTION>any</SELECT>
of these words and return <SELECT NAME="maxHits"><OPTION>10<OPTION
SELECTED>25<OPTION>100</SELECT> results.<br>
</FORM>

<p align=center>
<hr>
<a href="/WebCrawler/Help/Help.html">Help</a> &#183;
<a href="/WebCrawler/Facts/Facts.html">Facts</a> &#183;
<a href="/WebCrawler/Top25.html">Top 25 Sites</a> &#183;
<a href="/WebCrawler/SubmitURLS.html">Submit URLs</a> &#183;
```

Notice a couple of things here. The <FORM> tag at WebCrawler is using the ACTION and METHOD attributes that were discussed. ACTION is accessing a script called WebQuery found in the cgi-bin/ directory of the Web server. The METHOD used is SEND.

> **Tip:** Although you shouldn't copy others' work, don't forget that you can always use View Source commands to learn how something was done on the Web.

Text Fields and Attributes

One of the more common uses for forms is to accept multiple lines of text from a user, perhaps for feedback, bug reports, or other uses. To do this, use the <TEXTAREA> tag within your form. You can set this tag to control the number of rows and columns it displays, although it will generally accept as many characters as the user desires to enter. It takes the following form:

```
<TEXTAREA NAME="variable_name" ROWS="number" COLS="number">
default text
</TEXTAREA>
```

It may surprise you to find that <TEXTAREA> is a container tag, since it just puts a box for typing on the page. What's contained in the tag is the default text—so you can guide your users by letting them know what you'd like entered there. For instance:

```
<FORM>
<TEXTAREA NAME="comments" ROWS="4" COLS="40">
Enter comments about this Web site.
Good or Bad.
</TEXTAREA>
</FORM>
```

The default text appears in the textbox just as typed. Notice in figure 13.2 that text inside the <TEXTAREA> tag works like <PRE> formatted text. Any returns or spaces you add to the text are displayed in the browser window. In fact, notice that by hitting Return after the opening <TEXTAREA> tag, I'm inserting a blank line at the top of the textarea (in many browsers).

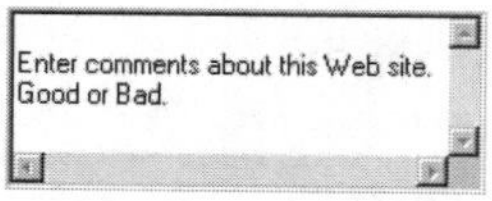

Figure 13.2

The <TEXTAREA> tag in action.

```
Enter comments about this Web site.
Good or Bad.
```

The NAME attribute is a variable name for this string of text. It gets passed on to your processing script on the Web server. ROWS and COLS can accept different numbers to change the size of the textarea box, but you should take care that the majority of browsers can see the entire box on-screen. It's best to limit COLS to 80, and ROWS to something like 24 (the typical size for a text-based computer screen). But it's up to you.

<TEXTAREA> will also accept one other attribute: WRAP. WRAP can be set to OFF (which is the default if WRAP is not included), VIRTUAL, or PHYSICAL. Setting wrap to PHYSICAL forces the browser to include actual line breaks in the text when sending it to the Web server. VIRTUAL makes the textbox seem to offer line wrap, but sends a continuous stream of words to the Web server (unless the user has entered returns on his or her own).

Example: Web-based Feedback Form

I mentioned before that <TEXTAREA> is commonly used to gather feedback from your Web users. To create a small form to do just that, save your default template as a new HTML document and enter the following:

```
<BODY>
<H3>Feedback Form</H3>
<P>Please take a moment to tell us what you thought of the Web site.<BR>
Your Feedback is appreciated!</P>
<FORM METHOD="POST" ACTION="cgi-bin/feedback">
Enter your comments below:<BR>
<TEXTAREA NAME="comments" ROWS="10" COLS="70" WRAP="VIRTUAL">
Dear BigCorp:
</TEXTAREA>
</FORM>
</BODY>
```

You can see how this looks in figure 13.3. Notice in the example that some descriptive text is enclosed inside the <FORM> tag, but outside of the <TEXTAREA> tag. This is completely legal—it just lets you explain what the purpose of the textarea is.

Figure 13.3

Sample textarea HTML form.

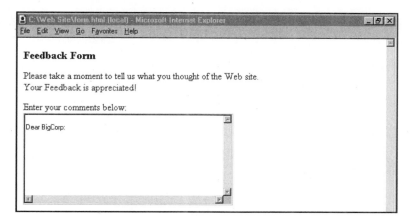

You may have realized that there's something lacking in this sample form. There's no way to submit the user's entry! You'll get to that in the next section, when I discuss this next tag for form entry.

The *<INPUT>* Tag

Our next tag for HTML forms give you the opportunity to be a bit more picky about the type of input you're going to accept from the user. The <INPUT> tag follows the following format:

```
<INPUT TYPE="type_of_box" NAME="variable" SIZE="number"
MAXLENGTH="number">
```

Now, technically, the only required attributes are TYPE and NAME. Some other "types" of the input tag will also accept the attribute VALUE. But first, let's look at the different types of <INPUT>.

> **Note:** By the way, notice that <INPUT> is an empty tag. There's no </INPUT> element.

TEXT

The first possible value for the TYPE attribute is TEXT, which creates a single-line textbox of a length you choose. Notice that the length of the box and the maximum length entered by the user can be set separately. It's possible to have a box longer (or, more often, shorter) than the maximum number of characters you allow to be entered. Here's an example of a textbox:

```
Last name: <INPUT TYPE="TEXT" NAME="last_name" SIZE="40" MAXLENGTH="40">
```

When appropriately entered between <FORM> tags, this <INPUT> yields a box similar to figure 13.4. If desired, the attribute VALUE can be used to give the textbox a default entry, as in the following example:

```
Type of Computer: <INPUT TYPE="TEXT" NAME="computer" SIZE="50"
MAXLENGTH="50" VALUE="Pentium">
```

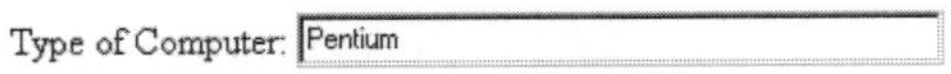

Figure 13.4

Using the TEXT option with the TYPE attribute.

Type of Computer: [Pentium_____]

PASSWORD

The PASSWORD option is nearly identical to the TEXT option except that it responds to typed letters with bullet points or a similar scheme (chosen by the browser) to keep the words from being read. A sample password box could be the following:

```
Enter Password: <INPUT TYPE="PASSWORD" NAME="password" SIZE="25"
MAXLENGTH="25">
```

When characters are typed into this textbox, they are shown on the screen as in figure 13.5.

Figure 13.5

PASSWORD hides text from people looking over your user's shoulder.

Enter Password: [▓▓▓▓▓   ]

Recognize that the text is still stored as the text typed by the user—not as bullet points or similar characters.

CHECKBOX

This value for TYPE allows you to create a checkbox-style interface for your form. This is best used when there are two possible values for a given choice—and no others. You can also determine whether or not a checkbox will already be checked (so that it must be unchecked by the user, if desired), by using the attribute CHECKED. Here's an example of adding checkboxes to a form:

```
Type of computer(s) you own:<BR>
<INPUT TYPE="CHECKBOX" NAME="Pentium" CHECKED> Pentium
<INPUT TYPE="CHECKBOX" NAME="486"> 486-Series PC
<INPUT TYPE="CHECKBOX" NAME="Macintosh"> Macintosh
```

In this example, it's possible to check as many of the options as are presented. CHECKBOX evaluates each item separately from any others. Figure 13.6 illustrates how CHECKBOX is displayed in a browser.

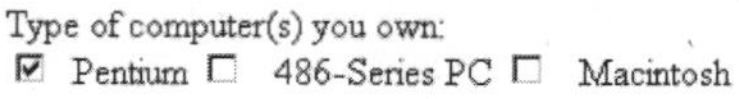

Figure 13.6

Notice that Pentium is pre-checked.

Type of computer(s) you own:
☑ Pentium ☐ 486-Series PC ☐ Macintosh

RADIO

Like CHECKBOX, RADIO is designed to offer your user a choice from pre-determined options. Unlike CHECKBOX, however, RADIO is also designed to accept only one response from among its options. RADIO uses the same attributes and basic format as CHECKBOX.

RADIO requires that you use the VALUE attribute, and that the NAME attribute be the same for all of <INPUT> tags that are intended for the same group. VALUE, on the other hand, should be different for each choice. For instance, look at the following example:

```
Choose the computer type you use most often:<BR>
<INPUT TYPE="RADIO" NAME="Computer" VALUE="P" CHECKED> Pentium
<INPUT TYPE="RADIO" NAME="Computer" VALUE="4"> 486-Series PC
<INPUT TYPE="RADIO" NAME="Computer" VALUE="M"> Macintosh
<INPUT TYPE="RADIO" NAME="Computer" VALUE="O"> Other
```

With RADIO, it's important to assign a default value, since it's possible that the user will simply skip the entry altogether. While the user can't check more than one, he or she can check none. So choose the most common value and set it as CHECKED, just so that the form-processing script doesn't have trouble.

> **Note:** Of course, if you want to give your user the option of choosing none, then you can leave off the CHECKED attribute. It's more complete and obvious for the user, however, to include another radio button with a VALUE of none, and make it the CHECKED choice.

HIDDEN

This <INPUT> type technically isn't "input" at all. Rather, it's designed to pass some sort of value along to the Web server and script. It's generally used to send a keyword, validation number, or some other kind of string to the script so that the script knows it's being accessed by a valid (or just a particular) Web page. The <INPUT TYPE="Hidden"> tag takes the attributes NAME and VALUE.

> **Note:** This isn't really terribly covert, since an intrepid user could simply choose View Source to see the value of the hidden field. It's more useful from a programmer's standpoint. For instance, on a large Web site, the hidden value might tell a multi-purpose script which particular form (among many) is sending the data, so the script knows how to process the data.

RESET

The <INPUT> tag has built into it the ability to clear an HTML form. RESET simply creates a push button (named with the VALUE string) that resets all of the elements in that particular FORM to their default values (erasing anything that the user has entered). An example would be the following:

```
<INPUT TYPE="RESET">
```

With a VALUE statement, you could enter the following:

```
<INPUT TYPE="RESET" VALUE="Reset the Form">
```

The results are shown in figure 13.7.

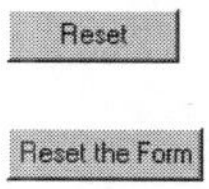

Figure 13.7

Default and
VALUE-attributed
Reset buttons.

SUBMIT

The <INPUT> tag also has a type that automatically submits the data that's been entered into the HTML form. The SUBMIT type accepts only the attribute VALUE, which can be used to rename the button. Otherwise, the only purpose of the Submit button is to send off all the other form information that's been entered by your user. See the following two examples (see fig. 13.8):

```
<INPUT TYPE="SUBMIT">
<INPUT TYPE="SUBMIT" VALUE="SEND IT IN!">
```

Figure 13.8

Creating a Submit
button.

You can use just about anything you want for the VALUE, although it's best to remember that really small words, like *OK*, don't look great as buttons. To make a button larger, enter the VALUE with spaces on either end, like in the following:

```
<INPUT TYPE="SUBMIT" VALUE="         GO         ">
```

Example: A More Complete Form

Along with all the other <INPUT> types, now you've finally got a way to submit data. So, let's create a more involved form that includes some of these examples—a subscription form.

Save your HTML template to create a new document. Then, enter something similar to Listing 13.1.

Listing 13.1 *scrp_frm.html* **Creating a Complete Form**

```
<BODY>
<H2>Subscribe to CorpWorld</H2>
<P>Interested in receiving daily email updates of all the latest exploits
of BigCorp? Well, now you can. And, best of all, it's free! Just fill out
this form and submit it by clicking the "Send it In" button. We'll put
you on our mailing list, and you'll receive your first email in 3-5
days.</P>
<FORM METHOD="Send" ACTION="http://www.fakecorp.com/cgi-bin/subscribe">
Please complete all of the following:<BR>
First Name: <INPUT TYPE="Text" Name="first" SIZE="25" MAXLENGTH="24"><BR>
Last Name:  <INPUT TYPE="Text" Name="last" SIZE="35" MAXLENGTH="34"><BR>
Business:   <INPUT TYPE="Text" Name="business" SIZE="50"
MAXLENGTH="49"><BR>
We must have a correct email address to send you the newsletter:<BR>
Email:      <INPUT TYPE="Text" Name="email" SIZE="50" MAXLENGTH="49"><BR>
How did you hear about BigCorp's email letter?<BR>
<INPUT TYPE="RADIO" NAME="hear" VALUE="web" CHECKED>Here on the Web
<INPUT TYPE="RADIO" NAME="hear" VALUE="mag">In a magazine
<INPUT TYPE="RADIO" NAME="hear" VALUE="paper">Newspaper story
<INPUT TYPE="RADIO" NAME="hear" VALUE="other">Other
<BR> Would you care to be on our regular mailing list?<BR>
<INPUT TYPE="CHECKBOX" NAME="snailmail" CHECKED> Yes, I love junk
mail<BR>
<INPUT TYPE="RESET">
<INPUT TYPE="SUBMIT" VALUE="Send it in!">
</FORM>
</BODY>
```

Notice that, for text type <INPUT> boxes, the MAXLENGTH is one less than the size of the box. This tends to look a little better, but choosing the size is up to you. Figure 13.9 shows how it looks on a Web page. (You'll get to straightening everything out and making it look great in Chapter 14.)

Figure 13.9

The complete form in MS Internet Explorer.

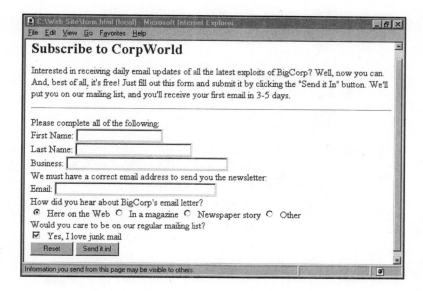

Creating Pop-Up and Scrolling Menus

The last types of input that you can offer to users of your Web page revolve around the <SELECT> tag, which can be used to create different types of pop-up and scrolling menus. This is another element designed specifically for allowing users to make a choice—they can't enter their own text. The <SELECT> tag requires a NAME attribute and allows you to decide how many options to display at once with the SIZE attribute.

Using *<SELECT>*

Also notice that, like <TEXTAREA>, <SELECT> is a container tag. Options are placeed between the two <SELECT> tags, each with a particular VALUE that gets associated with <SELECT>'s NAME attribute when chosen. The following is the basic format:

```
<SELECT NAME="variable">
<OPTION SELECTED VALUE="value"> Menu text
<OPTION VALUE="value"> Menu text
...
</SELECT>
```

The attribute SELECTED is simply designed to show which value will be the default in the menu listing. *value* can be anything you want to pass on to the Web server and associated script for processing. An example might be:

```
Choose your favorite food:
<SELECT NAME="food">
<OPTION SELECTED VALUE="ital"> Italian
<OPTION VALUE="texm"> TexMex
<OPTION VALUE="stek"> SteakHouse
<OPTION VALUE="chin"> Chinese
</SELECT>
```

You can also use the SIZE attribute to decide to display the menu in its entirety, by simply changing the first line of the example to the following:

```
<SELECT NAME="food" SIZE="4">
```

Both examples are shown in figure 13.10.

Figure 13.10

Two <SELECT>
menus—a pop-up
and a fixed.

In the first example, selecting the menu item with the mouse causes the menu to pop-up on the page. The user can then select from the choices. In the second example, it's necessary to click the desired item.

Allowing More than One Selection

One more attribute for the <SELECT> tag allows the user to select more than one option from the menu. Using the MULTIPLE attribute forces the menu to display in its entirety, regardless of the SIZE attribute. An example might be the following: (the result appears in figure 13.11):

```
What type of cars does your family own (select as many as apply)?
<SELECT NAME="cars" MULTIPLE>
<OPTION VALUE="sedan"> Sedan
<OPTION VALUE="coupe"> Coupe
<OPTION VALUE="mivan"> Minivan
<OPTION VALUE="covan"> Conversion Van
<OPTION VALUE="statn"> Stationwagon
<OPTION VALUE="sport"> SUV (4x4)
<OPTION VALUE="truck"> Other Truck
</SELECT>
```

Figure 13.11

A <SELECT> menu can allow multiple choices.

What type of cars does your family own (select as many as apply)?

Example: Order Form

With all of these possibilities for the form, you can manage some fairly complete data entry interfaces for users. Consider this one: an online order form. Used in conjunction with a secure Web site, this form could be used to process purchase orders over the Internet.

Save your template as a new HTML file and enter Listing 13.2's example text between the <BODY> tags.

On the CD

Listing 13.2 *ordr_frm.html* **Creating an Order Form**

```
<BODY>
<H3>Online Order Form</H3>
<P> Please enter your name, billing address and shipping address. Please
don't forget the order number from our online catalog listings. Thanks
for shopping BigCorp!</P>
<FORM METHOD="SEND" ACTION="http://www.fakecorp.com/cgi-bin/order">
<HR>
Please enter a full name and address for BILLING purposes:<BR>
First Name: <INPUT TYPE="TEXT" NAME="first" SIZE="25" MAXLENGTH="24"><BR>
Last Name: <INPUT TYPE="TEXT" NAME="last" SIZE="35" MAXLENGTH="34"><BR>
Address: <INPUT TYPE="TEXT" NAME="address" SIZE="60" MAXLENGTH="59"><BR>
City: <INPUT TYPE="TEXT" NAME="city" SIZE="25" MAXLENGTH="24">
State: <INPUT TYPE="TEXT" NAME="state" SIZE="3" MAXLENGTH="2"> ZIP:
<INPUT TYPE="TEXT" NAME="zip" SIZE="6" MAXLENGTH="5"><BR>
<HR>
<INPUT TYPE="CHECKBOX" NAME="same_add"> Check if Shipping Address is
different from Mailing Address
<HR>
<TEXTAREA NAME="ship_add" ROWS="3" COLS="60" WRAP="PHYSICAL">Enter
shipping address here if different from above.
</TEXTAREA>
<HR>
Please enter the code for the product you wish to purchase: <INPUT TYPE=
"TEXT" NAME="prod_num" SIZE="7" MAXLENGTH="6">
<HR>
How would you like to pay for this?<BR>
<SELECT NAME="credit">
<OPTION SELECTED VALUE="mast"> MasterCard
<OPTION VALUE="visa"> Visa
<OPTION VALUE="amex"> American Express
<OPTION VALUE="disc"> Discover
</SELECT>
```

continues

Listing 13.2 Continued

```
Please enter the card number: <INPUT TYPE="TEXT" NAME="cred_num"
SIZE="17"
MAXLENGTH="16"><BR>
Expiration date (01/99): <INPUT TYPE="TEXT" NAME="exp_date" SIZE="6"
MAXLENGTH="5"><HR>
<BR>
Please take care that everything is filled out correctly, then click
"Submit Order." If you'd like, you can select the "Reset" button to start
again. Clicking the "Submit Order" button will send your order to BigCorp
and your credit card will be charged.<BR>
<INPUT TYPE="reset">
<BR>
<INPUT TYPE="submit" VALUE="Submit Order">
</FORM>
</BODY>
```

Here you've taken advantage of most of the options available to you for forms (see fig. 13.12). Notice that, if the checkbox for Check if Shipping Address is different from Mailing Address is left unchecked, you can assume (in the processing script) that the textarea can be ignored. Also notice how using the MAXLENGTH attribute for State: and ZIP: allows you some very basic error checking in these fields. At least, you know that users are entering the correct number of characters.

Figure 13.12

The completed Web order form.

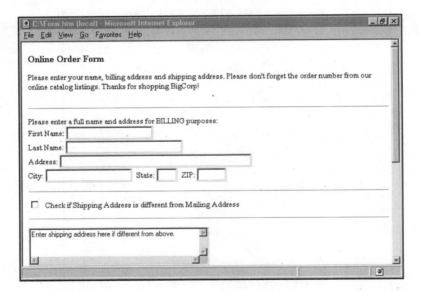

212

Once the user clicks the Submit Order button, the script on your Web server takes over. The script should be designed to accept the data, add it to your internal order-processing database (if appropriate), and respond to the submission with an HTML page confirming the order and offering any additional help or instructions. Then, hopefully, the product will ship on time!

Summary

HTML forms are a powerful way to add interactivity to your Web site. They can be used to elicit information, responses, memberships, or even product orders from your users. They can also be used as an interface for data retrieval.

The basic elements of a form are the <FORM> tag itself, along with a number of different types of form elements, including <INPUT>, <SELECT>, and <TEXTAREA>. Each of these have their own attributes, values, and special cases.

The <TEXTAREA> creates a relatively free-form textarea where comments, messages, and other feedback can be typed by the user. <INPUT> allows for a number of different types of interaction with the user, including single-line textboxes, radio button interfaces, checkboxes, and special buttons for resetting forms or sending in the form data.

<SELECT> types allow you to control how users respond by offering them access to menu listings. Menus can be either pop-up or scrolling, giving the user the ability to make a single choice or multiple choices from each menu.

Review Questions

1. What are the two values for the <FORM> attribute METHOD? Which are you more likely to use?

2. What does the ACTION attribute accept?

3. What is a <TEXTAREA> form element used for? How does the user enter data?

4. <TEXTAREA> is a container tag. What does it contain?

5. Why sort of element is TYPE as it relates to the <INPUT> tag?

6. Aside from how they look, what's the major difference between checkboxes and radio buttons?

7. How do you define a checkbox or radio button as the default value?

8. How do you tell an HTML form to send its data to the Web server?

9. What type of interface element does the <SELECT> tag display?

10. If you use the attribute MULTIPLE with the <SELECT> tag, what happens to the way the menu displays?

11. How do you define the default value in a <SELECT> menu?

Review Exercises

1. Create a simple form that lets your user send you an e-mail message. (Hint: you can use the mailto: type of URL to actually cause the form to mail the form data to your e-mail account.)

2. Create a form that offers the following choices in a pop-up menu, a series of radio buttons, and a list of checkboxes. Make a different value the default in each. The choices are: North, South, East, and West.

3. Using a Select menu, create two different menus of the following items. Make one a pop-up menu and the other a scrolling menu. The choices are: Life, Liberty, Happiness, Death, and Taxes.

## CHAPTER 14

Form Design and Data Gathering with CGI Scripts

Now that you've seen how to create the basic form tags, let's put that knowledge together with some of the HTML tags you've already learned and make your forms more intuitive, attractive, and meaningful to the user. You'll also look at how data is transferred to the Web server and how your scripts need to be written to deal with the data.

Form Design Issues

Central to the idea of form design is making the form as easy for users to understand and underwhelming enough that they follow through and fill out the form. The less incentive you have for them to fill out the form, the less likely they are to try. A clean, short form is more likely to entice users than a long, confusing one.

There are a couple of rules you should consider when building your forms so that they're easier and more effective for users:

♦ **Use other HTML tags to make things clear**. You can use <BR>, <HR>, and paragraph tags to set apart different "chunks" of your form, while <B>, <I>, and even <PRE> can be used to make the form more easily read.

♦ **Keep your forms short**. This isn't always possible, but when your forms are long, it's important to at least use <HR> and similar tags to break it up a bit. If forms have smaller sections, they're easier on the eye.

♦ **Use intuitive design**. Common sense is sometimes the key to a good form. For instance, putting the Submit button in the middle of the form will keep people from filling out the rest of it. Often it's best to use <SELECT>, radio buttons, and checkboxes to keep your users from guessing at the type of info you want.

♦ **Warn users of unsecured transactions**. You should tell your users if your Web server is secure—and how they can make sure that the connection is current. If you ask for a credit card or similar personal information over an unsecured connection, let them know that, too.

Sound simple enough? Let's move on to some of the specifics of this advice—and get these form tags to work.

Line Breaks, Paragraphs, and Horizontal Lines

The first rule of form design tells you to use HTML appearance tags to make your forms more coherent to the user. Doing this will affect the layout in one way or another—it's up to you to decide which is best for your particular circumstance.

Line Breaks

Unlike text-oriented HTML, your best friend in form design is not really the paragraph tag—it's the line break tag. This is because you want to directly affect the layout of the forms, instead of leaving it up to the browser. Therefore, you've got to be a little more proactive. You'll end up with a lot of line break tags before your form is through.

Consider the following example:

```
<FORM>
<B>Enter your name and phone number</B>
First Name: <INPUT TYPE="TEXT" NAME="first" SIZE="30">
Last Name: <INPUT TYPE="TEXT" NAME="last" SIZE="40">
Phone: <INPUT TYPE="TEXT" NAME="phone" SIZE="12">
</FORM>
```

Figure 14.1 illustrates how this would appear in a browser.

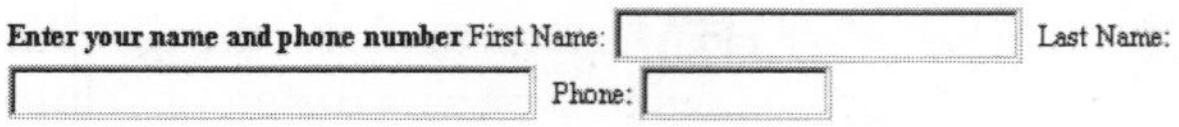

Figure 14.1

These text boxes were inputted without <BR> tags.

Enter your name and phone number First Name: [   ] Last Name:
[   ] Phone: [   ]

It doesn't look terribly clean, does it? To get each of those text boxes on a separate line, and thus more pleasing to the eye, we need to add the <BR> tag:

```
<FORM>
<B>Enter your name and phone number</B><BR>
First Name: <INPUT TYPE="TEXT" NAME="first" SIZE="30"><BR>
Last Name: <INPUT TYPE="TEXT" NAME="last" SIZE="40"><BR>
Phone: <INPUT TYPE="TEXT" NAME="phone" SIZE="12"><BR>
</FORM>
```

Adding <BR> forces each subsequent text box to the next line. This is a more attractive form, and the <BR> tags make it easier for the user to understand (see fig. 14.2).

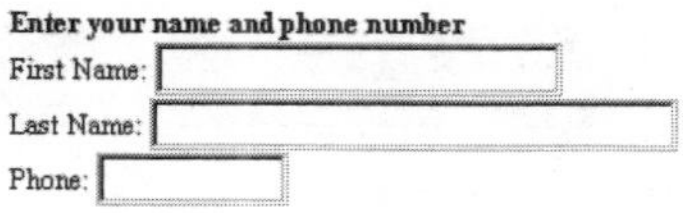

Figure 14.2

Look at the difference the <BR> tag makes!

Enter your name and phone number

First Name:

Last Name:

Phone:

Notice then, that the parts of a form (like the <INPUT> empty tag) work a lot like text in a regular HTML document. Even if you add returns while typing, they're still ignored by the browser. You need <BR> tags to create new lines.

Also notice the use of instructional text for these text boxes, which were put in boldface for the example. This is another important tenet of form design—using HTML emphasis tags to make things clear. Most of your forms will need instructions throughout, just like any paper-based form. It's a good idea to standardize your instructions, using bold or italic tags to make them stand out from your other text.

Horizontal Lines

Along that same line of thought, you should not only use instructional text but also break your form into smaller chunks by using the <HR> tag. Start with Listing 14.1, which uses <BR> and emphasis tags.

On the CD

Listing 14.1   *br_form.html*   Our Example so Far

```
<FORM>
<B>Enter your name and phone number</B><BR>
First Name: <INPUT TYPE="TEXT" NAME="first" SIZE="30"><BR>
Last Name: <INPUT TYPE="TEXT" NAME="last" SIZE="40"><BR>
Phone: <INPUT TYPE="TEXT" NAME="phone" SIZE="12"><BR>
<B>Enter your mailing address</B><BR>
Address: <INPUT TYPE="TEXT" NAME="address" SIZE="50"><BR>
City: <INPUT TYPE="TEXT" NAME="city" SIZE="25">
State: <INPUT TYPE="TEXT" NAME="state" SIZE="2">
```

continues

Listing 14.1 Continued

```
Zip: <INPUT TYPE="TEXT" NAME="zip" SIZE="7"><BR>
<B>Enter your email address</B><BR>
Email: <INPUT TYPE="TEXT" NAME="email" SIZE="45"><BR>
<B>Enter your comments below:</B><BR>
<TEXTAREA NAME="comments" ROWS="5" COLS="40">
Dear BigCorp,
</TEXTAREA>
</FORM>
```

Viewed in a browser, this form is easier for the user to understand, with instructions in bold and textboxes where you'd expect them (see fig. 14.3).

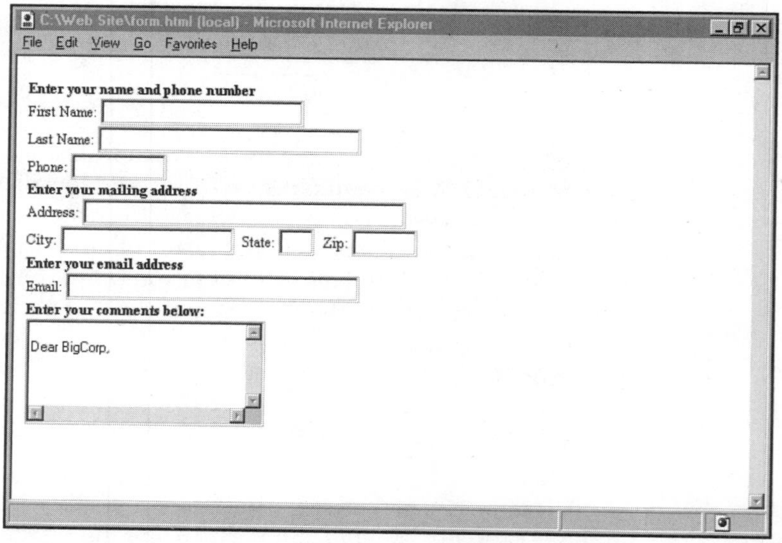

Figure 14.3

Adding "chunks" to the previous example.

But there's still more you can do. By placing <HR> tags in your form, you make it clear that new instructions are coming up or that the form has reached the next logical chunk of entry. The <HR> tag simply makes it easier to look at as it guides the user through the different parts of the form. In Listing 14.2, you add <HR> tags at the logical breaks.

Listing 14.2   _hr_form.html_   Adding _<HR>_ to the Form

```
<FORM>
<B>Enter your name and phone number</B><BR>
First Name: <INPUT TYPE="TEXT" NAME="first" SIZE="30"><BR>
Last Name: <INPUT TYPE="TEXT" NAME="last" SIZE="40"><BR>
Phone: <INPUT TYPE="TEXT" NAME="phone" SIZE="12"><BR>
```

```
<HR>
<B>Enter your mailing address</B><BR>
Address: <INPUT TYPE="TEXT" NAME="address" SIZE="50"><BR>
City: <INPUT TYPE="TEXT" NAME="city" SIZE="25">
State: <INPUT TYPE="TEXT" NAME="state" SIZE="2">
Zip: <INPUT TYPE="TEXT" NAME="zip" SIZE="7"><BR>
<HR>
<B>Enter your email address</B><BR>
Email: <INPUT TYPE="TEXT" NAME="email" SIZE="45"><BR>
<HR>
<B>Enter your comments below:</B><BR>
<TEXTAREA NAME="comments" ROWS="5" COLS="40">
Dear BigCorp,
</TEXTAREA>
</FORM>
```

Unfortunately, the form is a little larger now (see fig. 14.4). But I don't think you've sacrificed the approachability by adding <HR> tags. Increasing the white space in a form is nearly as important as keeping it short enough so it isn't intimidating to users. I think you'll agree that each part of the form now just makes more sense.

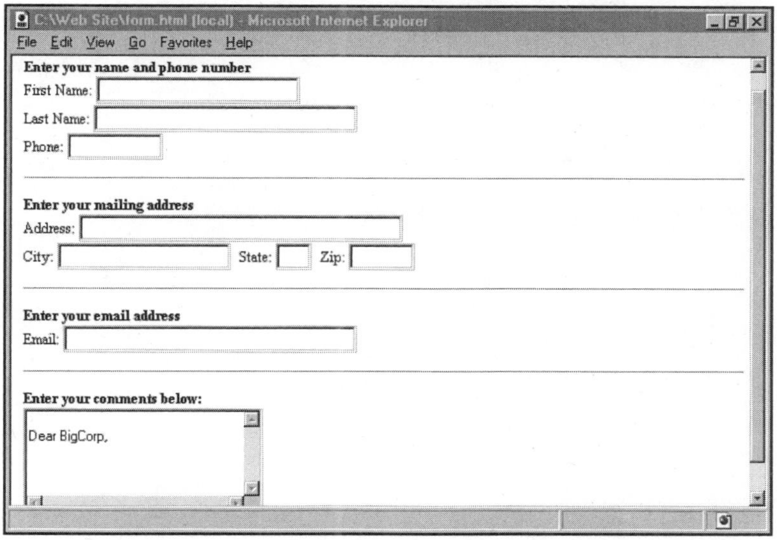

Figure 14.4

Adding <HR> tags to clearly define each new section of the form.

As you experiment with forms, you'll find that the larger the form—and the more diverse the types of information you're asking for—the more useful the <HR> tag becomes in guiding your user's eye to the appropriate spots.

Paragraph Tags

Paragraph tags are basically good for keeping form data together in smaller chunks. As always, paragraph tags will add space on either side of the text that they enclose. You don't always want to add `<HR>` tags just because your form needs some white space. For instance, here is a nice, short comment form:

```
<FORM>
<B>Who are you?</B><BR>
Name: <INPUT TYPE="TEXT" NAME="name" SIZE="50"><BR>
Email: <INPUT TYPE="TEXT" NAME="name" SIZE="50"><BR>
<HR>
<B>What product line do you wish to discuss?</B><BR>
Product: <SELECT NAME="product">
<OPTION SELECTED VALUE="sport"> Sporting Goods
<OPTION VALUE="home"> Home Furnishings
<OPTION VALUE="fashion"> Clothing/Fashions
<OPTION VALUE="electron"> Electronics
</SELECT><BR>
<HR>
<B>Okay, fire away!</B><BR>
<TEXTAREA NAME="comment" ROWS="5" COLS="40">
Dear BigCorp,
</TEXTAREA>
</FORM>
```

Again, this is fairly easy on the eyes. But the spacing isn't really great, and there are a lot of horizontal lines (see fig. 14.5).

Figure 14.5

Comment form without the `<P>` tag.

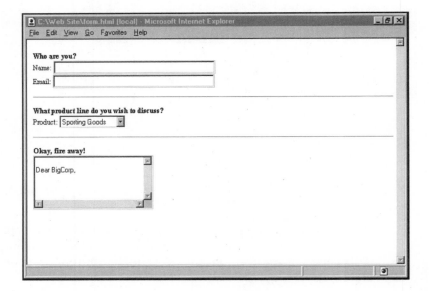

Let's look at this closely. Consider that second <HR> tag. Isn't that a little illogical? It seems that the user is supposed to select the product line that they'll be discussing in the comment form. The way it's set up, it isn't particularly clear that the <SELECT> menu and the comment <TEXTBOX> are related to one another.

Using paragraph tags, then, you can get the desired spacing between the <SELECT> and <TEXTAREA> elements, without the horizontal line that seems to break the two apart. You can also pad the rest of the form a bit to keep it nicely spaced from the horizontal lines that you *do* use. The key is adding <P> tags as in the following example:

```
<FORM>
<P>
<B>Who are you?</B><BR>
Name: <INPUT TYPE="TEXT" NAME="name" SIZE="50"><BR>
Email: <INPUT TYPE="TEXT" NAME="name" SIZE="50"><BR>
</P>
<HR>
<P>
<B>What product line do you wish to discuss?</B><BR>
Product: <SELECT NAME="product">
<OPTION SELECTED VALUE="sport"> Sporting Goods
<OPTION VALUE="home"> Home Furnishings
<OPTION VALUE="fashion"> Clothing/Fashions
<OPTION VALUE="electron"> Electronics
</SELECT><BR>
</P>
<P>
<B>Okay, fire away!</B><BR>
<TEXTAREA NAME="comment" ROWS="5" COLS="40">
Dear BigCorp,
</TEXTAREA>
</P>
</FORM>
```

Isn't that better (see fig. 14.6)? Now, the <SELECT> and <TEXTAREA> elements appear related to one another, but things aren't as crowded as they would be if you'd just used the <BR> tag. (Of course, the <P> tags don't have to be on lines by themselves in your HTML document.)

> **Tip:** Different browsers will interpret multiple <BR> tags in different ways, so it's best to use the <P> tag for sufficient spacing.

Figure 14.6

Better spacing and more conservative use of <HR> is possible when you include the paragraph tags.

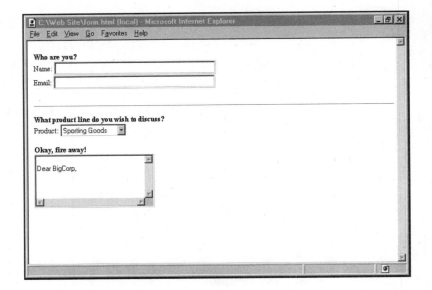

Example: Fix-A-Site

In this example, we'll start with a site that offers the bulk of the form elements you've learned, but none of the spacing and layout tips just discussed. It's just a plain little form. Then, let's go through it and change the way it looks to try to make it more intuitive and better looking.

Of course, there aren't any truly right answers when talking about aesthetics. By the end of this example, see if you agree with the changes made.

The HTML for your form is in Listing 14.3.

On the CD

Listing 14.3 *old_form.html* **Making a Form Look Better**

```
<BODY>
<H2>Customer Survey</H2>
<P>Please fill out the following form, including your personal informa-
tion, to help us better serve you. None of the addresses or other infor-
mation in these forms will be sold without your permission. Thank You!
</P>
<HR>
<FORM METHOD="POST" ACTION="http://www.fakecorp.com/cgi-bin/csurvey">
Enter your name and address:
Name: <INPUT TYPE="TEXT" NAME="name" SIZE="60">
Address: <INPUT TYPE="TEXT" NAME="address" SIZE="60">
City: <INPUT TYPE="TEXT" NAME="city" SIZE="25"> State: <INPUT TYPE="TEXT"
NAME="state" SIZE="2"> Zip: <INPUT TYPE="TEXT" NAME="zip" SIZE="5">
```

```
Phone: <INPUT TYPE="TEXT" NAME="city" SIZE="12">
Please check the type of computer you own:
<INPUT TYPE="CHECKBOX" NAME="pentium"> Pentium
<INPUT TYPE="CHECKBOX" NAME="486"> 486-series PC
<INPUT TYPE="CHECKBOX" NAME="386"> 386-series PC
<INPUT TYPE="CHECKBOX" NAME="mac"> Mac
<INPUT TYPE="CHECKBOX" NAME="win95"> Please check if your computer runs
Windows 95 What is your favorite way to shop for computer products
(choose one)?
<INPUT TYPE="RADIO" NAME="favorite" VALUE="mail"> Mail Order Catalog
<INPUT TYPE="RADIO" NAME="favorite" VALUE="local"> Local Computer Store
<INPUT TYPE="RADIO" NAME="favorite" VALUE="super"> Computer Superstore
<INPUT TYPE="RADIO" NAME="favorite" VALUE="net"> Internet/World Wide Web
Please enter any additional comments below:
<TEXTAREA NAME="comments" ROWS="5" COLS="70">
Enter comments here
</TEXTAREA>
Thanks for your input. Please click the Done button below to send us your
info or click Reset to clear the form.
<INPUT TYPE="RESET">
<INPUT TYPE="SUBMIT" VALUE="   Done   ">
</FORM>
</BODY>
```

See how this looks in a browser in figure 14.7.

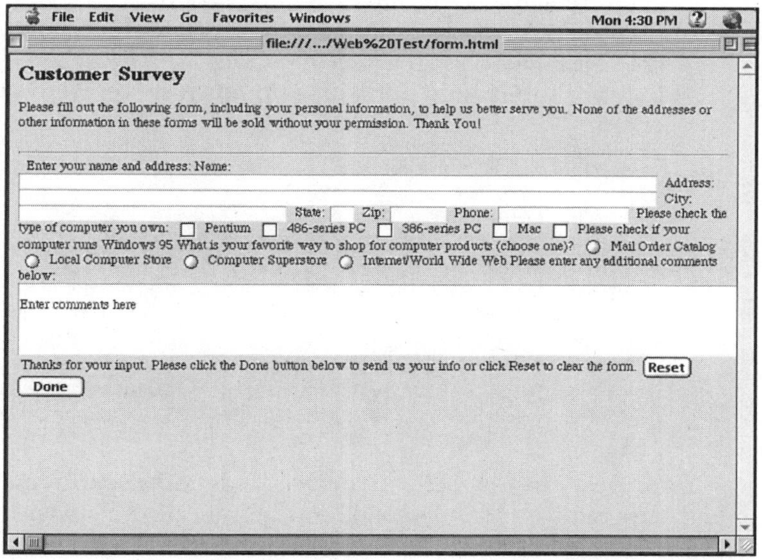

Figure 14.7

The initial attempt at the customer feedback form.

Now, let's pull this thing apart a bit and make some changes. It's a fairly logical organization, so you should be able to figure out what the chunks are. The first chunk is the address section, which currently looks like the following:

```
Enter your name and address:
Name: <INPUT TYPE="TEXT" NAME="name" SIZE="60">
Address: <INPUT TYPE="TEXT" NAME="address" SIZE="60">
City: <INPUT TYPE="TEXT" NAME="city" SIZE="25">
State: <INPUT TYPE="TEXT" NAME="state" SIZE="2">
Zip: <INPUT TYPE="TEXT" NAME="zip" SIZE="5">
Phone: <INPUT TYPE="TEXT" NAME="city" SIZE="12">
```

All this really needs is some HTML markup, some <BR> tags, a paragraph around it, and a horizontal line, shown in the following code:

```
<P>
<B>Enter your name and address:</B><BR>
Name: <INPUT TYPE="TEXT" NAME="name" SIZE="60"><BR>
Address: <INPUT TYPE="TEXT" NAME="address" SIZE="60"><BR>
City: <INPUT TYPE="TEXT" NAME="city" SIZE="25">
State: <INPUT TYPE="TEXT" NAME="state" SIZE="3" MAXLENGTH="2">
Zip: <INPUT TYPE="TEXT" NAME="zip" SIZE="5"><BR>
Phone: <INPUT TYPE="TEXT" NAME="city" SIZE="12"><BR>
</P>
<HR>
```

As discussed in Chapter 13, it's also a good idea to set the size of your textbox a little larger than the MAXLENGTH. In this case, though, you've only changed the MAXLENGTH of state since you want to allow users to enter more than the allotted characters in other textboxes (hence, no MAXLENGTH value).

Your next chunk is the computer-related questions. It might seem like two chunks, but let's use the idea of putting them in the same section of the form, since they are similar and don't take up much space. Here's the original code for this chunk:

```
Please check the type of computer you own:
<INPUT TYPE="CHECKBOX" NAME="pentium"> Pentium
<INPUT TYPE="CHECKBOX" NAME="486"> 486-series PC
<INPUT TYPE="CHECKBOX" NAME="386"> 386-series PC
<INPUT TYPE="CHECKBOX" NAME="mac"> Mac
<INPUT TYPE="CHECKBOX" NAME="win95"> Please check if your computer runs
Windows 95 What is your favorite way to shop for computer products
(choose one)?
<INPUT TYPE="RADIO" NAME="favorite" VALUE="mail"> Mail Order Catalog
<INPUT TYPE="RADIO" NAME="favorite" VALUE="local"> Local Computer Store
<INPUT TYPE="RADIO" NAME="favorite" VALUE="super"> Computer Superstore
<INPUT TYPE="RADIO" NAME="favorite" VALUE="net"> Internet/World Wide Web
```

How can you fix this? You need to be more specific about where the checkboxes and radio buttons end and how they are allowed to wrap with the browser screen (using <BR>). Plus, you should separate the three questions with <P> tags, like the following:

```
<P><B>Please check the type of computer(s) you own:</B><BR>
<INPUT TYPE="CHECKBOX" NAME="pentium"> Pentium
<INPUT TYPE="CHECKBOX" NAME="486"> 486-series PC
<INPUT TYPE="CHECKBOX" NAME="386"> 386-series PC
<INPUT TYPE="CHECKBOX" NAME="mac"> Mac<BR>
```

```
</P>
<P>
<INPUT TYPE="CHECKBOX" NAME="win95"> Please check if your computer runs
Windows 95
</P>
<P><B>What is your favorite way to shop for computer products (choose
one)?
</B><BR>
<INPUT TYPE="RADIO" NAME="favorite" VALUE="mail"> Mail Order Catalog<BR>
<INPUT TYPE="RADIO" NAME="favorite" VALUE="local"> Local Computer
Store<BR>
<INPUT TYPE="RADIO" NAME="favorite" VALUE="super"> Computer
Superstore<BR>
<INPUT TYPE="RADIO" NAME="favorite" VALUE="net"> Internet/World Wide
Web<BR>
</P>
<HR>
```

The three questions were separated into paragraphs, with an <HR> tag added at the bottom, since this would be one section. Also notice that the radio buttons all got <BR> tags, while we left the checkboxes. Why? Because it's always best to save space (by leaving the checkboxes on one line). But counting the characters in the descriptions of the radio buttons tells us that a single line of radio buttons would be well over 80 characters long—and that's likely to wrap oddly in the browser window.

The final two chunks currently look like this:

```
Please enter any additional comments below:
<TEXTAREA NAME="comments" ROWS="5" COLS="70">
Enter comments here
</TEXTAREA>
Thanks for your input. Please click the Done button below to send us your
info or click Reset to clear the form.
<INPUT TYPE="RESET">
<INPUT TYPE="SUBMIT" VALUE="   Done   ">
```

These chunks only need minor touch ups. Let's separate the control buttons from the comment window and add some formatting:

```
<P><B>Please enter any additional comments below:</B><BR>
<TEXTAREA NAME="comments" ROWS="5" COLS="70">
Enter comments here
</TEXTAREA>
<P>
<HR>
<P>Thanks for your input. Please click the Done button below to send us
your info or click Reset to clear the form.<P>
<INPUT TYPE="RESET"><BR>
<INPUT TYPE="SUBMIT" VALUE="   Done   "><BR>
<HR>
```

Then you close the form tags and you're done. By the way, that last little <HR> isn't really necessary—just my personal preference. And how does it look in a browser now? Take a look at figure 14.8.

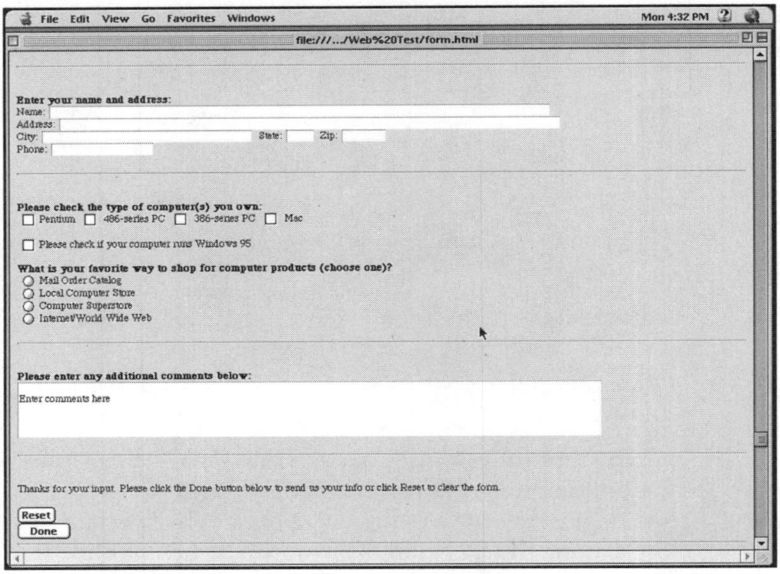

Figure 14.8

Our masterpiece of a customer service survey.

Other Tags for Form Formatting

So you've used <P>, <BR>, and <HR> tags for spacing things out and offering logical breaks for your forms. But what about other issues, like aligning form elements? You can turn to <PRE> tags and HTML list tags for that.

Using the *<PRE>* Tag

One of the most annoying parts of setting up a form so far has been the inability to line up textbox fields as they go down the page. For instance, whenever the Name: and Address: fields have been used in examples, they always look a little ragged.

The solution is the <PRE> tag. Because anything between the two tags uses the spacing and returns, this tag does two things. First, it allows you to line up your textboxes. Second, it eliminates the need for <BR> tags at the end of <INPUT> tags, since the browser will recognize your returns. The following is a ragged example:

```
Favorite Book: <INPUT TYPE="TEXT" NAME="book" SIZE="40"><BR>
Best Food: <INPUT TYPE="TEXT" NAME="food" SIZE="30"><BR>
Favorite Music Group: <INPUT TYPE="TEXT" NAME="music" SIZE="40"> <BR>
Personal Quote: <INPUT TYPE="TEXT" NAME="quote" SIZE="60"><BR>
```

Displayed (between <FORM> tags) in a browser, this looks like figure 14.9.

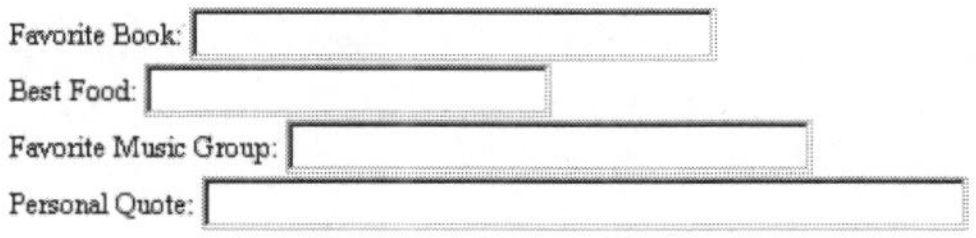

Figure 14.9

Ragged textboxes
in a form.

Favorite Book:	
Best Food:	
Favorite Music Group:	
Personal Quote:	

To improve this situation, you can put this HTML between <PRE> tags and format them yourself:

```
<PRE>
Favorite Book:          <INPUT TYPE="TEXT" NAME="book" SIZE="40">
Best Food:              <INPUT TYPE="TEXT" NAME="food" SIZE="30">
Favorite Music Group:   <INPUT TYPE="TEXT" NAME="music" SIZE="40">
Personal Quote:         <INPUT TYPE="TEXT" NAME="quote" SIZE="60">
</PRE>
```

Remember that you need to use spaces, not tabs, to create the space between the name of the box and the textbox itself. As before, you may need to play with the formatting a little to get things lined up like they are in figure 14.10.

> **Tip:** If you can, set your text editor to a monospaced font (like Courier) for editing text inside your <PRE> tags. Doing this will allow you to see exactly how <PRE> text will be displayed when viewed in a browser since <PRE> forces your browser to use a monospaced font.

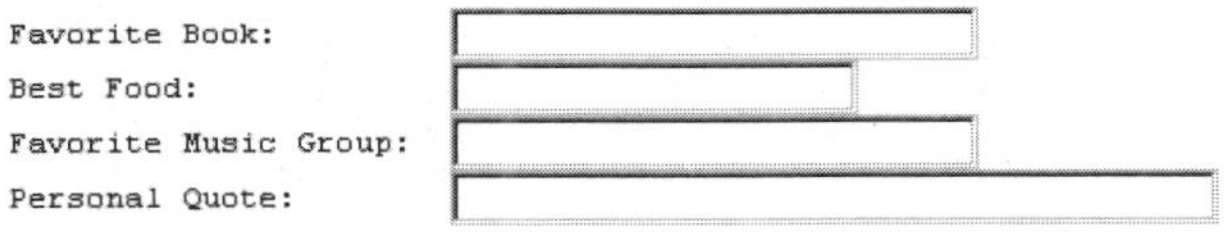

Figure 14.10

A much cleaner
looking form.

Favorite Book:	
Best Food:	
Favorite Music Group:	
Personal Quote:	

Using List Tags for Forms

The last little form design tricks you'll look at involve using the list tags—especially <OL>, <UL>, and <DL>—to create organization for your forms. Nearly any form element can be part of a list, and there are often good reasons to use them. Consider the following example:

```
<DL>
<DT> Please choose the type of pet you're interested in:
<DD> <INPUT TYPE="RADIO" NAME="pet" VALUE="dog"> Dog
<DD> <INPUT TYPE="RADIO" NAME="pet" VALUE="cat"> Cat
<DD> <INPUT TYPE="RADIO" NAME="pet" VALUE="fish"> Fish
<DD> <INPUT TYPE="RADIO" NAME="pet" VALUE="bird"> Bird
</DL>
```

You've used lists in this way before—to create indented lists or outline formats that help you communicate a little better. In this case, it also makes the form look a little better, too (see fig. 14.11).

Figure 14.11

Use list tags to spruce things up.

Please choose the type of pet you're interested in:
- ○ Dog
- ○ Cat
- ○ Fish
- ○ Bird

A great excuse for using the `<OL>` tag is to create form elements that are numbered for some reason. Since the `<LI>` tag for an ordered list enters a number, you can simply add form elements to create a numbered form, as in the following example:

```
Enter your guesses for the top three movies this week: <BR>
<OL>
<LI> <INPUT TYPE="TEXT" NAME="movie1" SIZE="40">
<LI> <INPUT TYPE="TEXT" NAME="movie2" SIZE="40">
<LI> <INPUT TYPE="TEXT" NAME="movie3" SIZE="40">
</OL>
```

Seen through a browser, each entry is numbered, eliminating the need for individual descriptive text (see fig. 14.12).

Figure 14.12

You can use an ordered list for your form.

Enter your guesses for the top three movies this week:

1. [   ]
2. [   ]
3. [   ]

Example: Customer Service Revisited

Let's see if you can do an even better job with the customer service form you created earlier in this chapter. Now, you have the opportunity to clean up some of those textboxes and other chunks. Listing 14.4 shows the example as it stands (recall that figure 14.8 showed this same form in a browser).

On the CD

Listing 14.4 *survey.html* **Customer Service Form**

```
<BODY>
<H2>Customer Survey</H2>
<P>Please fill out the following form, including your personal informa-
tion, to help us better serve you. None of the addresses or other infor-
mation in these forms will be sold without your permission. Thank You!
</P>
<HR>
<FORM METHOD="POST" ACTION="http://www.fakecorp.com/cgi-bin/csurvey">
<P>
<B>Enter your name and address:</B><BR>
Name: <INPUT TYPE="TEXT" NAME="name" SIZE="60"><BR>
```

```
Address: <INPUT TYPE="TEXT" NAME="address" SIZE="60"><BR>
City: <INPUT TYPE="TEXT" NAME="city" SIZE="25">
State: <INPUT TYPE="TEXT" NAME="state" SIZE="3" MAXLENGTH="2">
Zip: <INPUT TYPE="TEXT" NAME="zip" SIZE="5"><BR>
Phone: <INPUT TYPE="TEXT" NAME="city" SIZE="12"><BR>
</P>
<HR>
<P><B>Please check the type of computer(s) you own:</B><BR>
<INPUT TYPE="CHECKBOX" NAME="pentium"> Pentium
<INPUT TYPE="CHECKBOX" NAME="486"> 486-series PC
<INPUT TYPE="CHECKBOX" NAME="386"> 386-series PC
<INPUT TYPE="CHECKBOX" NAME="mac"> Mac<BR>
</P>
<P>
<INPUT TYPE="CHECKBOX" NAME="win95"> Please check if your computer runs
Windows 95
</P>
<P><B>What is your favorite way to shop for computer products (choose
one)?
</B><BR>
<INPUT TYPE="RADIO" NAME="favorite" VALUE="mail"> Mail Order Catalog<BR>
<INPUT TYPE="RADIO" NAME="favorite" VALUE="local"> Local Computer
Store<BR>
<INPUT TYPE="RADIO" NAME="favorite" VALUE="super"> Computer
Superstore<BR>
<INPUT TYPE="RADIO" NAME="favorite" VALUE="net"> Internet/World Wide
Web<BR>
</P>
<HR>
<P><B>Please enter any additional comments below:</B><BR>
<TEXTAREA NAME="comments" ROWS="5" COLS="70">
Enter comments here
</TEXTAREA>
<P>
<HR>
<P>Thanks for your input. Please click the Done button below to send us
your info or click Reset to clear the form.<P>
<INPUT TYPE="RESET"><BR>
<INPUT TYPE="SUBMIT" VALUE="   Done   "><BR>
<HR>
</FORM>
</BODY>
```

Clearly, the first chunk can benefit from the <PRE> tag so that you can line up those address lines. You might notice that because you're using the <PRE> tag, you no longer need the <BR> tag to end some of the lines, as in the following code:

```
<P>
<B>Enter your name and address:</B><BR>
<PRE>
Name:    <INPUT TYPE="TEXT" NAME="name" SIZE="60">
Address: <INPUT TYPE="TEXT" NAME="address" SIZE="60">
City:    <INPUT TYPE="TEXT" NAME="city" SIZE="25">
```

```
State:    <INPUT TYPE="TEXT" NAME="state" SIZE="3" MAXLENGTH="2">
Zip:      <INPUT TYPE="TEXT" NAME="zip" SIZE="5">
Phone:    <INPUT TYPE="TEXT" NAME="city" SIZE="12">
</PRE>
</P>
<HR>
```

What else can you do? Let's put the second chunk in list format. You can use a <DL> style list for the series of radio buttons. You probably shouldn't change the checkboxes since they're already formatted to appear on one line. The following code includes these changes:

```
<P><B>Please check the type of computer(s) you own:</B><BR>
<INPUT TYPE="CHECKBOX" NAME="pentium"> Pentium
<INPUT TYPE="CHECKBOX" NAME="486"> 486-series PC
<INPUT TYPE="CHECKBOX" NAME="386"> 386-series PC
<INPUT TYPE="CHECKBOX" NAME="mac"> Mac<BR>
</P>
<P>
<INPUT TYPE="CHECKBOX" NAME="win95"> Please check if your computer runs
Windows 95
</P>
<DL>
<DT><B>What is your favorite way to shop for computer products (choose
one)?
</B>
<DD><INPUT TYPE="RADIO" NAME="favorite" VALUE="mail"> Mail Order Catalog
<DD><INPUT TYPE="RADIO" NAME="favorite" VALUE="local"> Local Computer
Store
<DD><INPUT TYPE="RADIO" NAME="favorite" VALUE="super"> Computer
Superstore
<DD><INPUT TYPE="RADIO" NAME="favorite" VALUE="net"> Internet/World Wide
Web
</DL>
```

Notice that the <BR> tags at the end of each radio button entry are no longer required since each <DD> tag automatically appears on its own line.

The rest of the form can pretty much stand on its own. See how the whole thing looks in a browser in figure 14.13.

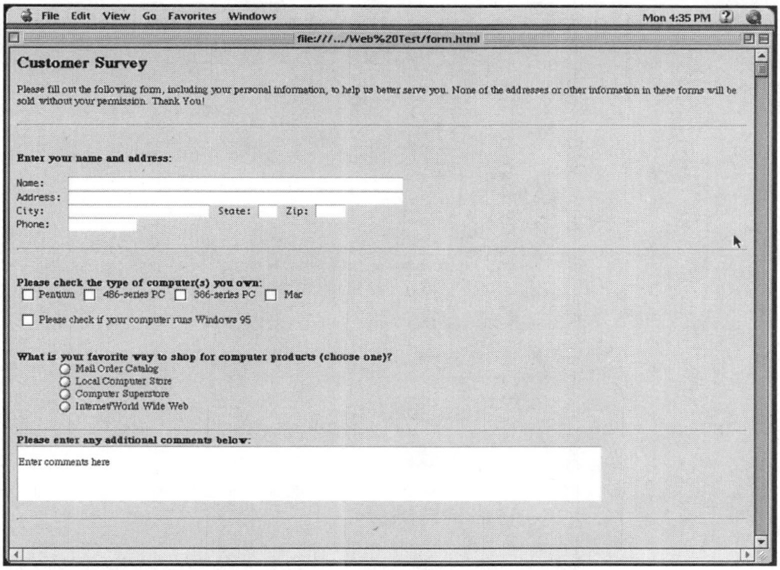

Figure 14.13

Our customer
service form,
now complete.

CGI-BIN Scripts and Dealing With Form Data

Before we're finished discussing HTML forms, we should touch on how data is passed to the Web server and how your script needs to be written to handle this data. First, you'd better start with a quick discussion of CGI-BIN scripts.

Using CGI-BIN Scripts

For the most part, CGI-BIN scripts are designed to receive values from your user and then create HTML code *programmatically* (or on-the-fly) by way of response. Scripts are most often used to handle form data but can also be used to add things like "hit" counters and *variable images* (different images that appear at different times). For instance, to add a counter to your page, you might have the following:

```
<IMG SRC="/cgi-bin/counter.pl">
```

This will cause the script counter.pl to be run and a value returned. The value will be the name of a graphics file, which will be used to display an odometer-style image, as in figure 14.4.

Figure 14.14

Adding a hit counter by calling a CGI-BIN script.

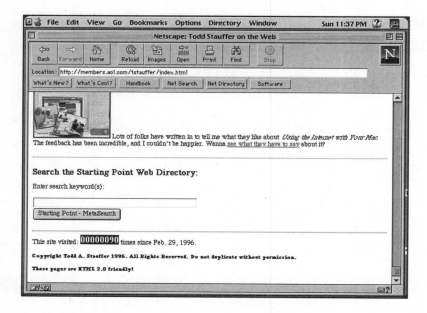

An URL to a script can be used just about anywhere you might use an URL to another document, a hypermedia file, or an image. In a hypertext link, for instance, you might use a script that chooses a "random" Web page to return, as in the following:

```
<A HREF="/cgi-bin/random.pl">Click me for a surprise Web page!</A>
```

Actually creating the scripts is a little beyond the scope of this book. Most of the time, CGI-BIN scripts are written in Perl, C, Visual Basic, or a scripting language like AppleScript. If you're a programmer, I'd recommend looking into a book that seriously discusses the ins and outs of CGI programming. Creating scripts can be complicated, but rewarding—especially if you have access to your Web server and aspire to be a Webmaster as well as an HTML designer.

> **Tip:** Look into Que's *Special Edition Using CGI* for an in-depth discussion of CGI scripts and programming.

In the case of forms, you've already seen that you call the CGI-BIN script in the <FORM> tag using the ACTION attribute. Once the script receives the data, it then needs to use that data to create an HTML "results" page, which is sent back to the browser.

Receiving Form Data

You may recall from Chapter 13 that there are two different METHODs to pass data to the script you've created to deal with it. The two methods, GET and POST, cause data to be sent in different ways.

The type of METHOD used to send the data is stored in an environment variable on the Web server called REQUEST_METHOD. The GET method simply appends your form data to the URL and sends it to the server. Most servers will then store this data in another environment variable called QUERY_STRING. This string is generally limited to less than one kilobyte of data (approximately 1,000 characters) which explains why it is becoming less popular.

The POST method causes the length of the data string to be stored in a variable called CONTENT_LENGTH, while the data itself is redirected to stdin (standard in). In effect, the data is made to appear to your script or program that it was typed into the server using a typical keyboard. Your script must then be designed to "parse" that input.

> **Tip:** I'd let a program do your parsing for you. `cgi-bin.pl` is the Perl library for this. Mac Web servers might use Parse CGI for AppleScript.

Generally speaking, programs that do this for you are already available. There are actually two steps to receiving the input: decoding and parsing. Data sent from your Web browser is encoded to avoid data loss—essentially by turning spaces into plus signs (+) and non-text characters (like !) into a percent sign (%) and a hexadecimal code.

Once you've worked through the decoding process, you're left with a text input that follows this format (where the ampersand simply separates each pairing of NAME and VALUE):

```
NAME1=VALUE1&NAME2=VALUE2&...
```

An example of this is:

```
ADDRESS=1234 MAIN ST&CITY=DALLAS&STATE=TX
```

and so on. If you're not using a parsing program or library (which, ideally, would allow you to simply reassign the VALUEs in this file to variables in your script), then your script will need to accept this data, strip the ampersands, and reassign the values to appropriate variables.

Your Script's Output

Output is much easier. Because stdout (standard out) is redirected to the HTML browser, you simply need to use print (Perl and other languages), lprint (C language), or similar commands that print directly to the screen (or terminal or console). You use the print command to output HTML codes, just as if you were using your text editor.

Here's a short snippet of a Perl script to do just that:

```
print "Content-type: text\html\n\n";
print "<HTML>\n<HEAD><TITLE>Response</TITLE></HEAD>\n"
print "<BODY>\n<H2>Success</H2>\n<P>Thank you for your submission<\P>\n"
print "<P>Click <A HREF="index.html">here</A> to go back <\P>\n</
BODY>\n</HTML>"
```

In a number of programming languages \n is the newline character, which simply feeds a Return to standard out. Otherwise, this should seem (and look) rather familiar (see fig. 14.15). It's just HTML!

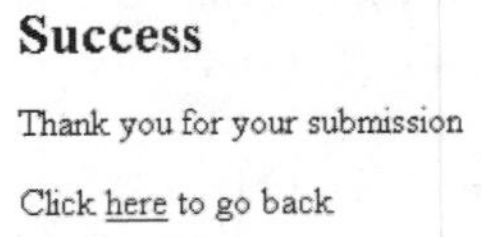

Figure 14.15

Results of the snippet of Perl scripting.

Success

Thank you for your submission

Click here to go back

Summary

Form design is something of an art and science—it's important that forms look good and be easy for the user to follow if they're going to be effective. There are some general rules you can follow for form design and, using other HTML commands you've learned previously, you can make your forms very easy to read. That, in turn, makes users more likely to use them.

It's also important for Web designers to have some idea how forms send their data to the Web server and associated script—even if they don't intend to create the scripts themselves. A designer with almost *any* programming experience will find it fairly easy to manage data-gathering scripts from their Web site.

Review Questions

1. Why is the <BR> tag more effective than the <P> tag for individual lines of forms?

2. Is it possible to use HTML tags (like <B> and <I>) within the confines of a <FORM> tag? What about just plain text?

3. What are "chunks" of form elements?

4. What do <P> tags offer you that help break up chunks of form elements? Why not just use multiple <BR> tags?

5. How can you get checkboxes and radio buttons to appear on a single line on your Web page?

6. What does MAXLENGTH do for <INPUT TYPE="TEXT"> style form elements? How is this error-checking?

7. What does the <PRE> tag allow you to do with forms? What do you "lose" by using the <PRE> tag?

8. What's the point in using a <DL> style list in a form? Why not use an <UL> list?

9. How can <OL> lists keep you from having to add descriptive text to each line of your form?

10. What METHOD of form data transfer is more popular? Why? Which is easier for programmers?

11. Why is it so simple to output HTML with a server-based script? What does the Web browser "act like?"

Review Exercises

1. Use <PRE> to make the following form easier to read:

```
<FORM METHOD="POST" ACTION="/cgi-bin/searcher">
Enter a Search phrase and a type of search (AND, OR, NOT).
Search phrase: <INPUT TYPE="TEXT" NAME="SearchFor" SIZE=38>
Type of search: <SELECT NAME="SearchType">
<OPTION SELECTED VALUE="and"> AND
<OPTION VALUE="or"> OR
<OPTION VALUE="not"> NOT
</SELECT>
<INPUT TYPE="submit" NAME="Submit" VALUE="Start the Search">
</FORM>
```

2. Create a form that allows the user to subscribe to a fictional magazine. Include different "chunks" for name and address, demographic information, and a credit card number. Also use layout and HTML emphasis to make it clear to the user what information is required and what information is optional.

3. If you understand how to program in Perl, C, or another CGI scripting language and you have access to your Web server (so you can place the script in the cgi-bin directory), create a script that accepts the value from the following simple form and outputs the appropriate HTML coded text:

```
<FORM METHOD="POST" ACTION="/cgi-bin/picker">
How would you like the next page to appear?<BR>
<SELECT NAME="Appear">
<OPTION SELECTED VALUE="bold"> bold
<OPTION VALUE="ital"> italics
<OPTION VALUE="list"> in an HTML list
</SELECT>
<INPUT TYPE="submit" NAME="Submit" VALUE="Create the Page">
</FORM>
```

Part IV

Page Layout and Formatting

## CHAPTER 15

Adding Tables to Your Documents

Many chapters ago you learned to use the <PRE> tag to create preformatted tables that align your data and text for easy reading. The HTML 3.0 table specification, however, takes you far beyond that. Tables are a great addition to any Web site—especially sites that need to offer a lot of information in an easy-to-read way. Unfortunately, tables can't be viewed by all browsers. So, you need to proceed with a little caution and consideration.

> **Note:** The current HTML 3.0 tables standard, in its entirety, isn't viewable by many browsers. In this chapter, everything discussed is part of the HTML 3.0 standard—but something less than the entire thing. Creating tables in this way will make your tables viewable in the widest number of browsers.

Creating a Table

Tables work a lot like HTML list tags, in that you must use the table container tag to hold together a group of tags that define each individual row. The main container is the <TABLE> tag, which uses enclosing tags for table rows (<TR>) and table data (<TD>). Most tables will also use an element for table headers (<TH>) which is generally used as the title text for rows and columns.

Tables take the following format:

```
<TABLE>
<CAPTION>Caption text for table</CAPTION>
<TR><TH>column1</TH><TH>column2</TH><TH>column3</TH>
<TR><TD>row1data1</TD><TD>row1data2</TD><TD>row1data3</TD>
<TR><TD>row2data1</TD><TD>row2data2</TD><TD>row2data3</TD>
...
</TABLE>
```

An example of a table using this format might be the following:

```
<TABLE>
<CAPTION>Team Members for 3-Person Basketball</CAPTION>
<TR><TH>Blue Team</TH><TH>Red Team</TH><TH>Green Team</TH>
<TR><TD>Mike R.</TD><TD>Leslie M.</TD><TD>Rick G.</TD>
<TR><TD>Julie M.</TD><TD>Walter R.</TD><TD>Dale W.</TD>
<TR><TD>Bill H.</TD><TD>Jenny Q.</TD><TD>Fred B.</TD>
</TABLE>
```

After you work with HTML list containers, it's fairly easy to make the jump to creating tables in HTML. You can see how this table looks in figure 15.1.

Figure 15.1

A simple table in HTML.

Team Members for 3-Person Basketball		
Blue Team	**Red Team**	**Green Team**
Mike R.	Leslie M.	Rick G.
Julie M.	Walter R.	Dale W.
Bill H.	Jenny Q.	Fred B.

The *<TABLE>* Tag

The <TABLE> tag is actually a rather complex creature, at least insofar as it can accept many different attributes. Some of the attributes are more useful than others, so let's look at the most useful of them as they currently stand:

♦ **ALIGN**. The ALIGN attribute is used to determine where the chart will appear relative to the browser window. Valid values are ALIGN=LEFT and ALIGN=RIGHT. As an added bonus, text will wrap around the table (if it's narrow enough) when the ALIGN=LEFT or ALIGN=RIGHT attributes are used.

♦ **WIDTH**. The WIDTH attribute sets the relative or absolute width of your table in the browser window. Values can be either percentages, as in WIDTH="50%", or absolute values. With absolute values, you must also include a suffix that defines the units used, as in px for pixels or in for inches (e.g., WIDTH="3.5in"). Absolute values for table widths are discouraged, though.

♦ **COLS**. The COLS attribute specifies the number of columns in your table, allowing the browser to draw the table as it downloads.

◆ **BORDER.** The BORDER attribute defines the width of the border surrounding the table. Default value is 1 (pixel).

◆ **CELLSPACING.** The CELLSPACING attribute tells the browser how much space to include between the walls of the table and between individual cells. (Value is a number in pixels.)

◆ **CELLPADDING.** The CELLPADDING attribute tells the browser how much space to give data elements away from the walls of the cell. (Value is a number in pixels.)

It is definitely not necessary to use all of these attributes for your table—in fact, the simple table example earlier didn't use any of them. Often, however, they will come in handy.

Example: Playing with Table Attributes

This is another fairly freeform example. Let's look at the difference between a plain table and a table embellished with a few attributes. Insert Listing 15.1 in a new HTML document.

On the CD

Listing 15.1 *badtable.html* **Creating a Plain Table**

```
<BODY>
<H2> BigCorp's Computer Systems </H2>
<P>We use only the highest quality components and software for all of our
Wintel computer systems. Plus, if you don't see a configuration you like,
call (or email) and let us know. We'll custom build to please!</P>
<TABLE>
<CAPTION>BigCorp's Computer Systems and Specifications</CAPTION>
<TR><TH>System 486</TH><TH>System 586</TH><TH>System 686</TH>
<TR><TD>486DX2-66 CPU</TD><TD>120 MHZ AMD586</TD><TD>200 Mhz Pentium
Pro</TD>
<TR><TD>8 MB RAM</TD><TD>16 MB RAM</TD><TD>16 MB RAM</TD>
<TR><TD>500 MB HD</TD><TD>1 GB HD</TD><TD>1.4 GB HD</TD>
<TR><TD>14.4 Modem</TD><TD>28.8 Modem</TD><TD>28.8 Modem</TD>
<TR><TD>desktop case</TD><TD>minitower case</TD><TD>tower case</TD>
<TR><TD>DOS/Win 3.1</TD><TD>Windows 95</TD><TD>Windows NT 4.0</TD>
</TABLE>
</BODY>
```

Now, take a quick glance at how this looks in a browser (see fig. 15.2).

Figure 15.2

A simple table, without attributes, can still be difficult to read.

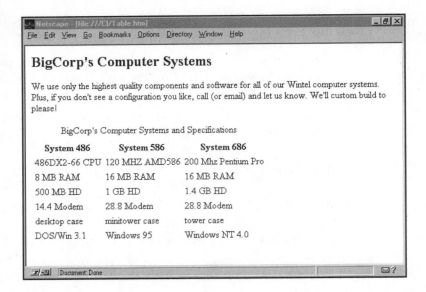

Last time we tried a simple table, it communicated its data well. But this one is fairly ineffective, with everything lined up so poorly. Using just the attributes only mentioned, though, you can change this table so that it looks better to the user and is easier to read.

All that needs to change is the first <TABLE> tag:

```
<TABLE BORDER ALIGN="LEFT" CELLSPACING="3" CELLPADDING="3">
```

That makes for a much nicer looking table, complete with borders and lines for cells, and a comfortable amount of spacing to separate cell data elements from one another (see fig. 15.3).

The rest of this example is up to you. Play with CELLSPACING and CELLPADDING without a border, for instance, or increase all values out of proportion. See the range of what's available, to help you choose how to format your tables in the future.

Figure 15.3

Look how nice the table looks with spacing and borders.

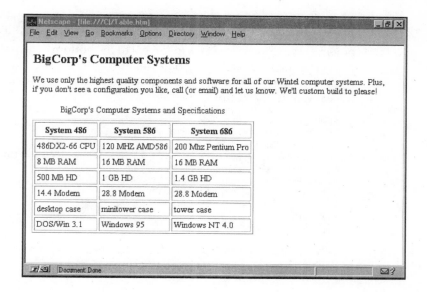

Captions, Table Headers, and Table Data

To round out your tables, you have the other basic tags to examine. You've already successfully used <CAPTION>, <TH>, and <TD>, but each has its own attributes and abilities that you need to know about.

<CAPTION>

The <CAPTION> tag is a container for reasons that may be obvious—it allows you to nest other HTML tags within the description. For instance:

```
<CAPTION><B>Table 3.1 from the book <I>Life in El Salvador</I></B></
CAPTION>
```

Just about any sort of markup tags are possible inside the <CAPTION> tags, although some—like list tags—wouldn't make much sense.

The <CAPTION> tag has one attribute, ALIGN. ALIGN="TOP" and ALIGN="BOTTOM" are encouraged. By default, text is also aligned to center (horizontally). By TOP and BOTTOM, I'm referring to the entire table; the caption will default to the top of the table if not otherwise specified. To align the caption to BOTTOM, for instance, enter the following:

```
<CAPTION ALIGN="BOTTOM">Table of Common Foods</CAPTION>
```

The <CAPTION> tag is commonly the first tag just inside the <TABLE> tag (although this placement is not required). Regardless of where you place the <CAPTION> tag, however, you must use ALIGN to force it to the bottom of the table. Otherwise, it will appear at the top, according to its default.

Let's create an entire table and use the ALIGN attribute to the <CAPTION> tag to force the caption to the bottom, like this:

```
<BODY>
<H3>Favorite Ice Cream Flavors</H2>
<TABLE BORDER>
<CAPTION ALIGN="BOTTOM">Data from the <I>New Jersey Times</I></CAPTION>
<TR><TH>Date</TH><TH>Chocolate</TH><TH>Vanilla</TH>
<TR><TH>1970</TH><TD>50%</TD><TD>50%</TD>
<TR><TH>1980</TH><TD>76%</TD><TD>24%</TD>
<TR><TH>1990</TH><TD>40%</TD><TD>60%</TD>
</TABLE>
</BODY>
```

When the browser interprets this table, it should place the caption at the bottom of the table, centered horizontally (see fig. 15.4).

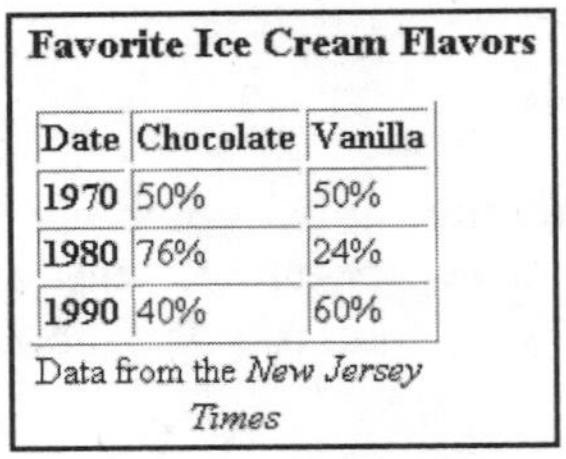
Favorite Ice Cream Flavors

Date	Chocolate	Vanilla
1970	50%	50%
1980	76%	24%
1990	40%	60%

Data from the *New Jersey Times*

Figure 15.4

You can align the caption to BOTTOM.

Table Rows

Table rows (<TR>) can accept one attribute you should concern yourself with—ALIGN. The ALIGN attribute is used to determine how text will appear (horizontally) in each of the rows data cells. For instance:

```
<TR ALIGN="CENTER"><TH>Date</TH><TH>Chocolate</TH><TH>Vanilla</TH>
<TR ALIGN="CENTER"><TH>1970</TH><TD>50%</TD><TD>50%</TD>
<TR ALIGN="CENTER"><TH>1980</TH><TD>76%</TD><TD>24%</TD>
<TR ALIGN="CENTER"><TH>1990</TH><TD>40%</TD><TD>60%</TD>
```

Here, I've added the ALIGN attribute (with a value of CENTER) to the rows in the previous example. Notice now that all cells center data horizontally (see fig. 15.5). This ALIGN attribute can also accept LEFT and RIGHT.

> **Note:** HTML 3.0 also supports another useful attribute, VALIGN, which accepts the values TOP, BOTTOM, and CENTER. Using this attribute, you can choose to align cells vertically as well as horizontally. Until they support VALIGN, non-HTML 3.0 browsers should ignore VALIGN. Unfortunately, those are currently the most popular browsers!

Figure 15.5

This uses the ALIGN attribute with <TR>. (Compare this to figure 15.4.)

Favorite Ice Cream Flavors		
Date	Chocolate	Vanilla
1970	50%	50%
1980	76%	24%
1990	40%	60%

Table Data and Rows

You've already used the <TH> and <TD> tags to include headers and data in your tables. You may have noticed that, essentially, the only difference between the two is that <TH> emphasizes (boldfaces) the text and <TD> does not. Now, technically, the <TH> is a tag that the browser interprets as a header and thus displays text in a way that's distinct from the <TD> tag. In practice, that generally means it's turned bold.

Aside from accepting nearly any type of HTML markup tags within them, both tags can accept four attributes (in most HTML versions). These are ALIGN, VALIGN, COLSPAN, and ROWSPAN. If you were to add all of these attributes, a typical <TH> (or <TD>) tag would be formatted like the following:

```
<TH ALIGN="direction" VALIGN="direction" COLSPAN="number"
ROWSPAN="italics">
```

ALIGN is used to align the data within the cell horizontally, accepting values of LEFT, RIGHT, and CENTER. Note that ALIGN is redundant when used with the ALIGN attribute of <TR>, unless it is used to override the <TR ALIGN=> setting.

VALIGN is used to align the data vertically within cells. Possible values are TOP, BOTTOM, and CENTER. COLSPAN and ROWSPAN are used to force a cell to span more than one column or row, respectively. An example of this might be:

```
<TABLE BORDER>
<TR><TH>Student</TH><TH>Test 1</TH><TH>Test 2</TH><TH>Average</TH>
<TR><TH>Mike M.</TH><TD>100</TD><TD>75</TD><TD ROWSPAN="3">N/A</TD>
<TR><TH>Susan T.</TH><TD>80</TD><TD>95</TD>
<TR><TH>Bill Y.</TH><TD COLSPAN="2">Dropped Course</TD>
</TABLE>
```

Viewed in a browser, the table looks like figure 15.6.

Figure 15.6

Using COLSPAN and ROWSPAN in a table.

Student	Test 1	Test 2	Average
Mike M.	100	75	N/A
Susan T.	80	95	
Bill Y.	Dropped Course		

Example: An Events Calendar

One interesting way to use a table is to create a calendar, which is possible with what we now know about attributes for tables and table elements. Let's create a calendar for November 1996. We'll also throw in some hypertext links that would (presumably) be used to discuss events planned for those days. Enter Listing 15.2 in a new HTML document.

On the CD

Listing 15.2 *calendar.html* **Using HTML Tables to Create a Calendar**

```
<BODY>
<H2>Coming Events</H2>
<P>Click any of the days highlighted in the calendar to read about the
event scheduled for that day.</P>
<TABLE BORDER WIDTH="75%">
<CAPTION>BigCorp's Calendar of Events - November 1996</CAPTION>
<TR ALIGN="CENTER"><TH>Sun</TH><TH>Mon</TH><TH>Tue</TH><TH>Wed</
TH><TH>Thu</TH>
<TH>Fri</TH><TH>Sat</TH>
<TR ALIGN="CENTER"><TD COLSPAN="5"> </TD><TD>1</TD><TD>2</TD>
<TR ALIGN="CENTER"><TD>3</TD><TD>4</TD><TD>5</TD><TD>6</TD><TD>7</
TD><TD>8</TD>
<TD>9</TD>
<TR ALIGN="CENTER"><TD>10</TD><TD><A
HREF="nov11.html">11</A></TD><TD>12</TD><TD>13</TD><TD><A
HREF="nov14.html">14</A></TD><TD>15</TD><TD>16</TD>
<TR ALIGN="CENTER"><TD><A HREF="nov17.html">17</A></TD><TD>18</
TD><TD>19</TD>
<TD><A HREF="nov20.html">20</A></TD><TD>21</TD><TD>22</TD><TD>23</TD>
<TR ALIGN="CENTER"><TD>24</TD><TD>25</TD><TD>26</TD><TD>28</TD><TD>29</
TD><TD>
30</TD><TD>31</TD>
</TABLE>
</BODY>
```

Notice the   in the <TD> tag that is defined with COLSPAN? That is an escape sequence for Web browsers that tells it "I want a non line-breaking space here." Without that, the extra-long cell won't be rendered correctly (with a complete border) because there's nothing in that cell. With it, this table looks like a calendar (see fig. 15.7).

Figure 15.7

Creating a
calendar with
HTML table tags.

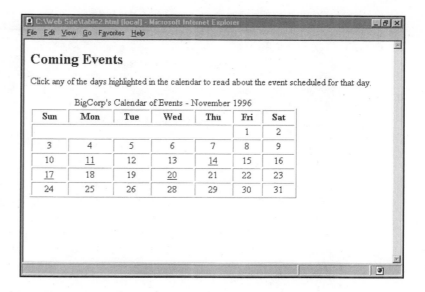

Example: Product Specifications

One thing that hasn't really been touched on so far is the possibility of including images in tables. It's definitely possible, and just about as easy as anything else you've done with tables.

In this example, let's create a product specifications table for a couple of our company's computer systems. With liberal use of the ALIGN and VALIGN attributes, this should come out looking rather pretty. Insert Listing 15.3 in a new HTML document.

Listing 15.3 *aligntbl.html* **Using *ALIGN* and *VALIGN* with Images in an HTML Table**

```
<BODY>
<H2>Product Specifications</H2>
<P>The following table will tell you a little more about our computer
systems. Clicking on the name of each system will tell you even more,
offering a full-size photo of the system and some suggestions on
peripherals.</P>
<HR>
<TABLE BORDER CELLSPACING="2" CELLPADDING="2">
<CAPTION>Our System Configurations</CAPTION>
<TR ALIGN="CENTER"><TH>Photo</TH><TH>Name</TH><TH>RAM</TH><TH>Hard
Drive</TH><TH>Video</TH><TH>Expansion</TH><TH>Case</TH>
<TR ALIGN="CENTER"><TD><IMG SRC="sml_6001.GIF"></TD><TD><A
HREF="6001.html">
System 6001-60</A></TD><TD>8 MB</TD><TD>500 MB</TD><TD>1 MB PCI</TD><TD>4
PCI
```

continues

247

Listing 15.3 Continued

```
Slots</TD><TD ROWSPAN="2">Desktop</TD>
<TR ALIGN="CENTER"><TD><IMG SRC="sml_7001.GIF"></TD><TD><A
HREF="7001.html">
System 7001-75</A></TD><TD>16 MB</TD><TD>1.0 GB</TD><TD>1 MB PCI
</TD><TD>5 PCI
Slots</TD>
<TR ALIGN="CENTER"><TD><IMG SRC="sml_8001.GIF"></TD><TD><A
HREF="8001.html">
System 8001-120</A></TD><TD>20 MB</TD><TD>1.6 GB</TD><TD>2 MB PCI
</TD><TD>5 PCI
Slots</TD><TD>Tower</TD>
</TABLE>
</BODY>
```

Graphics look very nice in tables, and they work well to enliven what would otherwise be drier, text-heavy information (like computer specs). I've offered up some creative uses of attributes in this example, but I think it was worth it (see fig. 15.8).

Figure 15.8

A very complete custom HTML table.

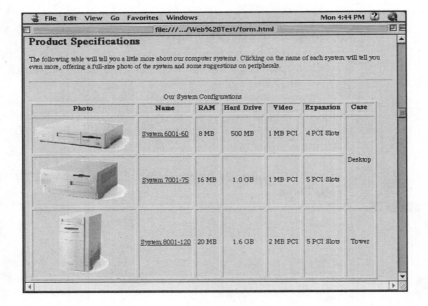

Summary

Tables are an incredible leap over the <PRE> tag for formatting HTML text. The basic tags, <TABLE>, <CAPTION>, <TR>, <TD>, and <TH>, give you everything you need to build an impressive, easy-to-read table for data elements.

Building on those tags, you can add formatting to rows, cells, and individual text. You can also add just about any conceivable type of HTML markup to your table data. You can even include graphics and hypertext links to take tables to a higher level.

Review Questions

1. Why doesn't this chapter discuss the entire HTML 3.0 tables standard?

2. Does the ALIGN attribute for <TABLE> allow text to wrap around the table?

3. What does the in stand for in the attribute definition WIDTH="3.5in" for the <TABLE> tag?

4. What's the different between the attributes CELLPADDING and CELLSPACING?

5. True or false. You must always define a value for the BORDER attribute to the <TABLE> tag.

6. If I had tmhe following example:

```
<TABLE>
<TR><TH>Soup</TH><TD>Chicken Noodle</TD>
<TR><TH>Salad</TH><TD>Tossed Green</TD>
<CAPTION>My favorite foods</CAPTION>
</TABLE>
```

where would the <CAPTION> text appear relative to the table?

7. Is it possible to ALIGN all of the data cells in a particular row with the <TR> tag?

8. What happens in the following example?

```
<TD>Ted David<BR>Mike Rogers<BR>Bill Howell</TD>
```

9. Which is used for horizontal alignment when used as an attribute to the <TD> tag, ALIGN or VALIGN?

10. What possible reason could there be to force a <TD ALIGN> tag definition to override a <TR ALIGN> tag?

Review Exercises

1. Create a caption, aligned to the bottom of the table, that includes an image. Does it work correctly?

2. Create a table that uses images as the column headers.

3. Create a table of "thumbnail" images, with an small image, description of the image, and the image's filename in each row. Make each image clickable, so that a larger image appears (on a new page) when the user clicks the thumbnail.

4. Create a table with no visible border (BORDER="0"). With this table, it's possible to lay out very intricate pages, with text and graphics aligned to the left or right of the page. Use the table to place a paragraph of text on the left side of the page and three clickable graphics on the right side. (Hint: Use ROWSPAN on the paragraph's cell.)

## CHAPTER 16

Images, Multimedia Objects, and Background Graphics

It is, perhaps, appropriate homage to the turbulent nature of HTML that the title of this chapter has changed three times now from conception to its final form. Initially conceived to discuss the elegant `<FIG>` tag of the HTML 3.0 specification, it seems that tag will be long in coming—if at all. At the same time, the `<IMG>` tag has been expanded somewhat to offer control over layout (in browsers that recognize it) and a new tag, `<INSERT>`, is making headway in the HTML world.

More Control with *<IMG>*

For the most part, today's graphical browsers seem to agree that the ALIGN attribute for the `<IMG>` tag is here to stay. As was discussed in Chapter 9, the `<IMG>` tag is useful for both graphical and non-graphical browsers because it allows for the text-only ALT attribute, which can explain your graphics to users who can't see them.

The ALIGN attribute allows more control over the display of the graphic and whether or not text will wrap around it. Its general format is the following:

```
<IMG SRC="URL" ALT="text description" ALIGN="Direction">
```

Appropriate values for the ALIGN attribute now include TOP, MIDDLE, BOTTOM, LEFT, and RIGHT. You may recall that TOP, MIDDLE, and BOTTOM were part of the HTML 2.0 specification discussed earlier. What's new, then, is just LEFT and RIGHT.

For all ALIGN attributes, the direction refers to where text will be displayed in relation to graphic image—and not the other way around. In essence, you're using the attribute to align text to the graphic—not aligning the graphic to anything in particular.

So why add LEFT and RIGHT? They offer options for wrapping text around an image. Consider the following example. Without the ALIGN attribute, you could render a graphic as the following:

```
<P>I just thought you might be interested in seeing this graphic I've
created for myself in PhotoShop. <IMG SRC="image1.gif" ALT="My Graphic">
I was actually a bit surprised at how easy it was to create. I'm not
artist, but there are enough filters and special effects in Photoshop
that it makes it possible for me to create something this professional
looking without being absolutely sure of what I'm doing!</P>
```

The following is the same example, except the ALIGN attribute is set to LEFT:

```
<P>I just thought you might be interested in seeing this graphic I've
created for myself in PhotoShop. <IMG SRC="image1.gif" ALT="My Graphic"
ALIGN="LEFT"> I was actually a bit surprised at how easy it was to
create. I'm not an artist, but there are enough filters and special
effects in Photoshop that it makes it possible for me to create something
this professional looking without being absolutely sure of what I'm
doing!</P>
```

Figure 16.1 shows you how these appear in a typical graphical browser. Interesting, isn't it?

Figure 16.1

Using the ALIGN attribute with the <IMG> tag.

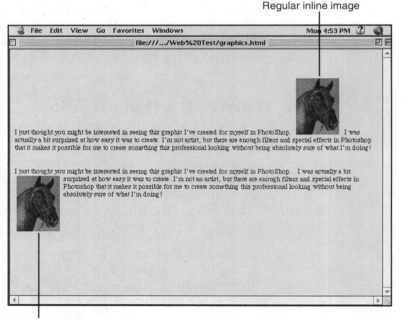

Regular inline image

Aligned to *LEFT*

As you can see, the ALIGN="LEFT" attribute forces this image to be displayed to the left of the text, and allows text to wrap above and below it on the page. Without it, the image is displayed *inline*. (When a graphic is displayed inline, it appears at the exact point in the text that the <IMG> tag appears.)

> **Tip:** Aligning to LEFT and RIGHT is most effective when embedded in a long paragraph of text in order to achieve a "text-wrap" feel.

Aligning to RIGHT works in a similar way:

```
<P>I just thought you might be interested in seeing this graphic I've
created for myself in PhotoShop. <IMG SRC="image1.gif" ALT="My Graphic"
ALIGN="RIGHT"> I was actually a bit surprised at how easy it was to
create. I'm not an artist, but there are enough filters and special
effects in Photoshop that it makes it possible for me to create something
this professional looking without being absolutely sure of what I'm
doing!</P>
```

The graphic is lined up with the right side border of the browser window, and is flexible with that window, so that dragging the window to make it larger or smaller would affect where the image would appear relative to the text (see fig. 16.2).

Figure 16.2

ALIGN to RIGHT.

253

Example: Magazine-Style Presentation

One of the nicer things about gaining this kind of control over your graphics is the options it gives you to present a long page of text in a way that's a little more pleasing to the eye—by breaking it up with graphics. This example is an article I've written for a local magazine. Notice also the advantage in putting this particular article in HTML form—you can add hypertext links when appropriate.

Start with a fresh HTML document (from your template) and enter something similar to Listing 16.1 between the <BODY> tags.

On the CD

Listing 16.1 *imgalign.html* **Using *ALIGN* for HTML Page Layout**

```
<BODY>
<IMG SRC="internet.gif" ALT="On the Internet" ALIGN="LEFT"> <IMG
SRC="todd.gif"
ALT="By Todd Stauffer" ALIGN="RIGHT">
<HR>
<H2>Figure Your IQ on the Web</H2>
<P>I was cruising along on the Web, engaged in one of my favorite
activities:plugging my name into search engines like Lycos and Infoseek.
My current favorite, <IMG SRC="alta.gif" ALT="Alta Vista Logo"
ALIGN="RIGHT"> Alta Vista (<A HREF="http://altavista.digital.com/">http:/
/altavista.digital.com/</A>),offers some great links to stuff that's
about me. (Just remember to put my name in quotes, like "Todd Stauffer"
in the searching text box. Or try your name...whatever.)</P>
<P>Somehow I came across a link to an IQ test in Europe. <IMG
SRC="iq.gif" ALT="I" graphic" ALIGN="LEFT"> With little sweat beads
forming on my fingertips, and errant thoughts clanging about the ego
parts of my psyche ("What if I'm stupid"), I plunged into the test,
trying to beat that 20-minute time limit.</P>
<P>I emerged from the test, clicked for my score and was pleasantly
shocked. "Wow," I thought. "That's high." But was it right? </P>
</BODY>
```

It's a little hit or miss, since some of how the graphics will display is based on the size of the browser window. Check it out in figure 16.3.

Figure 16.3

The ALIGN
example.

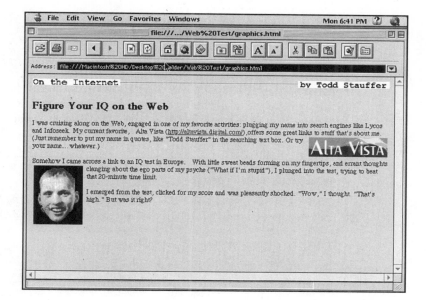

Inserting Multimedia Objects

One of the latest HTML 3.0 (or, at least, beyond HTML 2.0) initiatives has been the addition of a tag called the <INSERT> tag, which expands on the role of the <IMG> tag by allowing various different multimedia types to be displayed inline. As the bandwidth of connections to the Internet grows, and the technology for inline multimedia grows with it, more and more Web viewers will be capable of viewing inline animations, presentation graphics, movies, and more.

As of this writing, very few browsers support the <INSERT> tag. Unlike some other HTML initiatives, however, this specification has been written with much more involvement from industry leaders like Microsoft, Netscape, Spyglass, and Sun. So, I expect you'll see support for this tag very soon (probably by the time you're reading this) and might as well include it here now.

The *<INSERT>* Tag

This is not exactly the easiest tag to get your arms around. Like tables, the <INSERT> tag is a container for other tags that help define the element. But, somewhat unlike tables, most of those contained tags don't actually display anything.

> **Tip:** <INSERT> is a developing standard. Consult **http://www.w3.org/** for possible changes.

Let's take a look at a typical <INSERT> container:

```
<INSERT DATA="URL to multimedia file" TYPE="type of file">
Other Insert tags...
</INSERT>
```

Already, there are a couple of things you're required to know. You need to know the filename of the multimedia file—or the appropriate URL if it's not in the current directory. You also need to know the MIME-style "type" of the data file. (See sidebar.)

MIME-Style Data Types

MIME (Multipurpose Internet Mail Extensions) data types are simply the standardized way that certain Internet programs can identify the type of ASCII and non-ASCII files that are being transferred to a client application. A very common example of this is the `text/html` MIME type.

The <INSERT> tag (and HTML in general) is not limited to the official MIME categories and types, hence we'll call them MIME-*style* data types. For the purposes of the <INSERT> tag, this is just a more reliable way to tell a Web browser what type of multimedia file to expect—more reliable, that is, than just the file's extension.

Some common MIME-style data types appear in Table 16.1. These and others are all useful for the <INSERT> tag.

Table 16.1   Some MIME-Style Data Types for the <INSERT> Tag

Type of File	MIME Equivalent
GIF	image/gif
JPEG	image/jpeg
AIFF sound	audio/aiff
WAV sound	audio/x-wav
QuickTime video	video/quicktime
AVI video	application/avi
Real Audio	application/x-pnrealaudio
Macromedia Director	application/x-director
OLE object	application/x-oleobject

MIME-style data types for newer multimedia formats (especially vendor-specific ones like Macromedia Director) will generally be in the form of `application/x-datatype`. More often than not, these are the types you'll use for the `<INSERT>` tag, since these are the data types used for browser plug-ins.

<INSERT>'s Attributes

Aside from DATA and TYPE, `<INSERT>` can also accept the attributes ALIGN, WIDTH, HEIGHT, and BORDER. Its format is as follows:

```
<INSERT ALIGN="direction">
```

ALIGN works much as it does with `<IMG>`. The values possible for ALIGN are shown in Table 16.2. Notice that some of these values (LEFT, CENTER, MIDDLE) cause `<INSERT>` to act as a separate object, while the others assume the inserted multimedia object is supposed to be inline with the text of the document. You may recall that this is almost identical to what you learned about `<IMG>` at the beginning of this chapter.

Table 16.2 Values for the *<INSERT ALIGN>* Attribute

Value	Acts as...	How Object is Aligned
LEFT	Object	With left border and allows text wrap
RIGHT	Object	With right border and allows text wrap
CENTER	Object	Between browser borders and allows text wrap
TEXTTOP	Inline	Top vertically aligned with top of text's font
MIDDLE	Inline	Middle vertically aligned with middle of text's font
BASELINE	Inline	Bottom vertically aligned with baseline of text
TEXTBOTTOM	Inline	Bottom vertically aligned with lowest point in text

WIDTH and HEIGHT accept numbers and unit suffixes (like px for pixels and in for inches). These two attributes are used to define the size of the object for faster downloading. Some browsers will also resize objects according to these attributes, so that you might expand a smaller inline movie's object with WIDTH and HEIGHT, for instance, to save on downloading time. WIDTH and HEIGHT take the following format:

```
<INSERT WIDTH="#units" WIDTH="#units">
```

The last parameter is BORDER, which has a default value of 1. The border will generally only appear when the entire <INSERT> object in enclosed in an anchor tag, as in the following example:

```
<A HREF="intro.html"><INSERT DATA="intro.moov" TYPE="video/quicktime"
ALIGN="LEFT" WIDTH="3in"
HEIGHT="2in" BORDER="2">
</INSERT></A>
```

At least it's not complicated, right?

Using *<PARAM>* and *<IMG>* with *<INSERT>*

Two of the most common tags you'll want to use with the <INSERT> tag are the <PARAM> and <IMG> tags. The <IMG> tag is used just as it has been elsewhere—except it's only displayed when the browser isn't able to deal with the type of multimedia file that the <INSERT> tag is trying to send. For instance, if you were sending a Macromedia Director multimedia file from your Web pages, but the receiving browser wasn't able to deal with it, the <INSERT> tag would substitute the <IMG> you'd specified instead.

The <PARAM> tag is used to offer additional parameters to the <INSERT> tag—information like how many times to play a movie clip. The <PARAM> tag takes elements NAME and VALUE, which work a little like they do for certain table tags. Unfortunately, each different type of multimedia file will require different NAME and VALUE values, so you'll have to seek those out from the creator of the particular object type you're wanting to send.

> **Tip:** Often enough, you won't need the <PARAM> tag if you simply want something to play inline once. Also, for more tips, remember that you can view the source of pages that successfully use a multimedia object in a way that's new to you.

Here's an example of the <PARAM> tag:

```
<INSERT DATA="ship.avi" TYPE="application/avi">
<PARAM NAME="loop" VALUE="infinite">
</INSERT>
```

The <IMG> tag is used within an <INSERT> definition in the same way that it is used elsewhere, except that the ALIGN attribute isn't really necessary since the <IMG> will only be used to directly replace the inserted multimedia object. You can add the <IMG> like this:

```
<INSERT DATA="ship.avi" TYPE="application/avi">
<PARAM NAME="loop" VALUE="infinite">
<IMG SRC="ship.gif" ALT="The Ship">
</INSERT>
```

Clearly, you'll often want the graphic to at least represent the multimedia file that can't be displayed (see fig. 16.4). Or, perhaps, you could cause a graphic to load that tells the user that he or she is missing out on something better.

Figure 16.4

The `<INSERT>` tag in action.

Background Graphics

Let's move on from something that's barely been implemented at all (`<INSERT>`) to something that's been implemented in many different ways—background graphics.

The HTML 3.0-compliant way to change the background into a graphic is to use the BACKGROUND attribute for the body tag, as in the following example (see fig. 16.5):

```
<BODY BACKGROUND="paper.gif">
```

Figure 16.5

A background graphic.

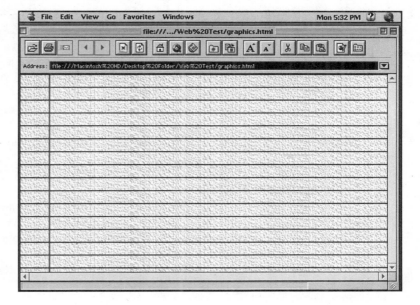

The HTML 3.0 standard (as it stands) has no other abilities to change colors of backgrounds or fonts, since HTML 3.0 will eventually rely on *style sheets* for Web page layout. As far as I know, nearly no current, popular browsers support style sheets. Plus, at the time of writing, the HTML 3.0 standard is no longer the primary concern of the W3C which, instead, is working on parts of the original standard which will now be formalized as separate standards (like tables and the <INSERT> tag).

What this means for you is if you use this HTML 3.0-compliant background graphic style, then you'll need to make sure you're not creating graphics that will offer a severe contrast with the text color used by the client browser, since there's no way for you to change the text color. This usually means you need to used light-colored (between tan and gray) background images. Netscape's more complete solution is discussed in Chapter 20.

Background Graphics: Size Matters

There's an interesting little paradox with background graphics. I've constantly told you that graphic files should be as small as possible to speed their downloading over the Internet. And, the same is true for background graphics, most of the time.

The exception is the fact that once a background graphic is downloaded to the Web browser, it's actually displayed a little quicker if it's *physically* bigger (e.g., three inches × four inches, instead of two inches × three inches). That's because the Web browser has to "tile" the image behind the Web page. The bigger the graphic, the fewer the tiles.

If you're using the same background graphic for *all* of your pages, then it's okay to send a file that's a little on the large size—both physically and in terms of kilobytes. Once the background is in the browser's cache, it will load rather quickly.

If you use a different background on every page, though, the cache effect won't help as much. In that case, you'll still want to keep your graphics fairly small.

Example: The HTML 3.0 Enhanced Graphics Page

Let's take what you've learned in this chapter and add some of these graphical, multimedia enhancements to a fairly standard Web page. We'll make this the About page for BigCorp, complete with an exciting multimedia logo, text wrapped around graphics, and a tasteful background graphic.

From your template, create a new document and add the text of Listing 16.2.

Listing 16.2 *graph30.html* **Enhancing a Page with HTML 3.0 Tags**

```
<BODY>
<BODY BACKGROUND="note_back.gif">
<INSERT DATA="logo.moov" TYPE="video/quicktime">
<IMG SRC="logo.gif" ALT="BigCorp">
</INSERT>
<H3>A little About Bigcorp</H3>
<H4><I>I sat on my father's knee, looking at his hands and knew I had to
make a better life...</I></H4>
<P>It was 100 years ago that Remmington Bigbucks, founder of BigCorp,
<IMG SRC="founder.gif" ALIGN="RIGHT" ALT="Mr. Big.">first uttered those
word to a local newspaper editor in Smallville, CT, where he first
started BigCorp. At that time, it was a small, privately held corpora-
tion, with fewer employees than it had banks trying to repossess the
single factory building. Remmington knew he needed something to save the
company, which was initially formed to promote the use of tin-can and
string-based telecommunications equipment, which seemed promising in the
face of the more expensive alternative being touted by the upstart,
American Telephone and Telegraph.</P>
<H4>Success is Sight</H4>
<P>One crisp Saturday morning Mr. BigCorp was running late for the office
<IMG SRC="pda.gif" ALIGN="LEFT" ALT="PDA">(he usually was, since he
relied on a wake-up call from his secretary and neighbor, Miss Goodbody,
but insisted on using a tin-can communications system at his bedside. The
rattling of the can as it crashed against the window was often not enough
of an irritant to awaken the reportedly near-comatose Mr. BigBucks) when
he was suddenly struck with an idea for attaching little bells to the
string that was strung between houses for his telephone system. It was at
that point that he realized that he didn't have ink well, feather and
parchment available to him. In a blazing moment of prophetic insight, he
invented the Personal Digital Assisant. Instantly realizing that was
futile, he conceived of the spiral-bound notepad.</P>
<P>From that moment, <IMG SRC="notepad.gif" ALIGN="RIGHT" IMG="The
Notepad"> Mr. BigBucks was headed for the Big Time with BigCorp. Profits
turned to company around, stock went souring and BigCorp was recognized
for it's unfailing strength and domination of the print communications
industry. Although he never realized his dreams of a PDA (in fact, he
never was really sure if he realized that he'd invented one at all) he
did single-handedly create the position of dictation secretary. His
improvements in tape recording mechanism (after an abortive attempt at a
reel-to-reel microrecorder) still affect the business world today.</P>
<HR>
<A HREF="index.html"><IMG SRC="left_arrow.gif" ALT="Back"></A>
</BODY>
```

The key to those ALIGNed images is to keep them relatively small, so that they are properly wrapped in text. A nice touch is to sprinkle small, transparent graphics to add interest to the text. You can see how this looks in figure 16.6.

Notice in the figure that you received the <IMG> part of the <INSERT> tag, not the QuickTime movie. This makes sense, of course, because no browser at the time of writing is capable of supporting the <INSERT> tag.

Figure 16.6

Some added graphical treats help a text-heavy page.

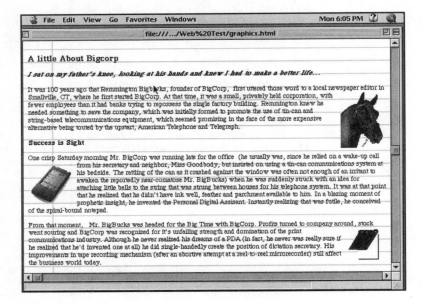

Summary

The turbulent world of HTML offers us a few different (and emerging) ways to add graphical interest to our pages. While these are bound to continue to change over the next few months and years, the tags in this chapter represent some of the latest changes.

The <IMG> tag discussed previously has recently been beefed up with two new ALIGN values, LEFT and RIGHT. Not only do these align graphics to the borders of the browser window, but they also allow text to wrap around the graphics.

The <INSERT> tag is a very new addition to HTML, designed to make it easier to add multimedia elements to Web pages. Once this tag is widely accepted, it will be much easier to view video, animations, presentations, and other multimedia file formats inline.

Finally, the HTML 3.0 way to add background graphics is generally supported by popular browsers, even if the implementation may be a bit incomplete. The key is to use background graphics that don't interfere with the text color of the user's browser, which is usually set to black by default.

Review Questions

1. Of the five values for the ALIGN attribute of the <IMG> tag, which are new to you in this chapter? (LEFT, TOP, BOTTOM, MIDDLE, RIGHT)

2. True or false. The ALIGN attribute for the <IMG> tag forces text to be aligned relative to the image.

3. What word describes the way that graphics are placed (relative to text) when the ALIGN attribute isn't used?

4. What does *MIME* stand for? Why are the TYPE values for the <INSERT> tag described as "MIME-style?"

5. If you enclose an <IMG> tag in an <INSERT> tag, when is it actually used by the browser?

6. Why isn't there a table of values for the NAME and VALUE attributes to the <INSERT> tag?

7. Is it possible to get away with not including the <PARAM> tag in your <INSERT> definition? Why or why not?

8. Why doesn't the HTML 3.0 specification offer more control over background and text color?

9. What colors should your background graphic be? Why?

Review Exercises

1. Use the ALIGN attribute with an image map graphic. Does it work correctly?

2. Again using ALIGN, test a small image and a long paragraph of text. Experiment a bit by placing the <IMG> tag at different points in the text. Does the image alignment vary with where you place the tag? Also try this experiment without the ALIGN attribute, to see how the <IMG> appears when it's an inline graphic.

3. Test your browser's support of the <INSERT> tag by using <INSERT> to add a QuickTime or AVI movie to an HTML document.

4. Create a "background-testing" page. Using thumbnail graphics, offer your user a choice of different background images. When they click one of the thumbnails, that link should load a page that uses the same graphic as a background for the page, so the user can "test" the background.

## CHAPTER 17

Client-Side Image Maps

Chapter 12, "Clickable Image Maps and Graphical Interfaces," discussed the use of image maps in interface design, and you found that creating these image maps made your Web sites more attractive and, often, more intuitive for users. The original, and now expired, HTML 3.0 working paper used the <FIG> tag to create something called a *client-side image map*. As mentioned before, it looks like the <FIG> tag may not ever make it in the HTML world. But client-side image maps will.

The current HTML 3.0-related draft has been offered for consideration by Spyglass, Inc. Fortunately, it agrees with the methods currently in use by Netscape and others—at least for the most part. Again, we'll try to take the least common denominator and come up with a specification that works for as many browsers as possible.

> **Note:** I'm basing this chapter on current drafts and market forces. Of course, the HTML 3.0 folks don't always agree with the market in general, and the "official" client-side image map specification may change. Keep a lookout at **http://www.w3.org/** just to be sure.

What's a Client-Side Image Map?

You've probably heard of *client/server* technology before, even if you weren't sure what it meant. Essentially, client/server describes the relationship between computers on the Internet (as well as elsewhere in computer networking). In most cases on the Web, for instance, the *server* is the Web server. The *client* is the Web browser program you use to access information on that server.

The image maps discussed in Chapter 12 were all server-side image maps, in that they required a special map server program to determine what coordinates matched up with what URLs. Instead of having your browser send an URL to the Web server, the map server program sent it.

Client-side image maps don't require a special map server to determine where the user clicked and what URL should be accessed. Instead, if properly marked-up by the Web designer, a client-side image map is interpreted by the browser itself, which simply loads the URL as if a regular hypertext link were clicked. This clearly requires a client-side aware browser like Netscape Navigator, MS Internet Explorer, NCSA Mosaic, or a Spyglass, Inc. product.

Advantages of Client-Side Image Maps

It may seem a bit redundant to talk about two different styles of image map creation in separate chapters of the book. You've already learned one, so why not stick to it?

If I wrote this book next year, I'd probably only cover client-side image maps. They're that much of an improvement. Unfortunately, as you'll see later is this chapter, the relative youth of the client-side concept can force you, at this point, to use both types of image maps on your Web sites.

But the inherent advantages in using client-side image maps are considerable. First, they do away with the need for extra files and programs on the Web server, which should be a great relief to non-programming Web designers. Client-side maps are just more HTML markup—and no `CGI-BIN` programming.

Related to that is the control that client-side maps offer you. As a designer, you're not forced to deal with your Web administrator to offer image maps to your users. If you don't think that's a big deal, try putting a server-side map on a Web page that's served by one of the major online services (like AOL's member pages).

Finally, client-side maps don't require a Web server—or the HTTP protocol—at all. In fact, they don't even have to be on the Internet. It will become more and more common to see non-Web applications for HTML in the future (like CD-ROM based HTML archives) where a Web server isn't part of the picture. With client-side maps, you don't need a server to create an interface.

Tip: As with most HTML extensions, you'll want to warn users when certain browsers are required to access features on your site.

Determining Your Hot Zones

This chapter assumes you've read about image maps in Chapter 12, "Clickable Image Maps and Graphical Interfaces." Client-side maps and the server-side maps discussed in Chapter 12 are very similar.

What you need to start with for your client-side maps is an appropriate graphic. Although client-side maps don't require a map definition file, using a map editing program (like MapEdit for Windows/UNIX or WebMap for Mac) is a sneaky way to come up with the information you do need for your client-side map.

Using your map editor, you can create hot zones (the clickable "shapes" that work as hyperlinks) that you'd like to use for your map (see fig. 17.1). If you need instructions for this, refer to Chapter 12. When you've created your hot zones for a particular graphic, save your map definition file. You now have the information you need to create a client-side map.

Figure 17.1

Creating hot zones
for a map
definition file.

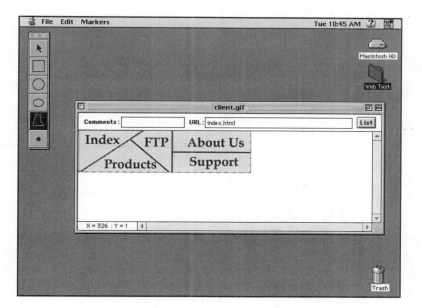

Example: Creating a Map Definition File

You've done this once already in Chapter 12, but how about doing it again, with some attention paid to the specifics of client-side maps? There are basically two things to remember about client-side maps:

♦ **Uncomplicate your hot zones.** You won't be using this map definition file directly—you'll be using it as a guide to create hot zones in your HTML document. So, you're best off if all of your shapes and coordinates make sense to you just by looking at them in the definition file. How can you do this? Keep them simple.

◆ **Determine the coordinates of your entire graphic**. Client-side maps don't have a default like server-side maps do, so you'll need to know the coordinates of your entire graphic to create your own default.

For this example, create a map definition file for the graphic you want to use as a client-side image map. Do your best to use simple shapes for your hot zones. Also remember to create a hot zone that covers the whole graphic. When you're done, you'll have a map definition file like the one shown in figure 17.2. Print this file out or save it somewhere where you can get at it. You'll use this as a reference when you create the client-side map.

Figure 17.2

Keeping the map definition file simple.

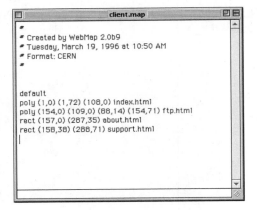

```
#
# Created by WebMap 2.0b9
# Tuesday, March 19, 1996 at 10:50 AM
# Format: CERN
#


default
poly (1,0) (1,72) (108,0) index.html
poly (154,0) (109,0) (88,14) (154,71) ftp.html
rect (157,0) (287,35) about.html
rect (158,38) (288,71) support.html
```

Adding a Client-Side Map to Your Web Page

Client-side maps require two different sections of code—the <IMG> tag and a new tag, the <MAP> container. <MAP> acts much like a map definition file does, except that it is part of the HTML document. You created the map definition file in the last section to help you with this new tag.

The *<IMG>* Tag

Let's look at the <IMG> tag first. In order to create a client-side image map, you need to add the new attribute USEMAP, as follows:

```
<IMG SRC="map_name.gif" USEMAP="#section_name">
```

Notice that USEMAP accepts a section-style hyperlink. That's how you can store the map definition information in the same HTML document. Here's an example:

```
<IMG SRC="mymap.gif" USEMAP="#mymap">
```

That's all you need in order to display the image and tell the browser that this is a client-side image map. Now, however, you need to create the definition that the browser will use for that map.

The *<MAP>* Tag

The <MAP> tag is a container tag that is referenced using a section-style NAME attribute. Inside the <MAP> container, you use the <AREA> tag to define each hot zone for the client-side map. Here's how it works:

```
<MAP NAME="section_name">
<AREA SHAPE="shape1" COORDS="coordinate numbers" HREF="URL">
<AREA SHAPE"shape2" COORDS="coordinate numbers" HREF="URL">
...
</MAP>
```

Notice that most of the information required for the <AREA> tag is available to you in your map definition file. See how easy this is going to be? Based on the map definition file you create in a map editing program, you can come up with a complete client-side <MAP> like the following one:

```
<MAP NAME="mymap">
<AREA SHAPE="POLY" COORDS="1,0,1,72,108,0"" HREF="index.html">
<AREA SHAPE="POLY" COORDS="154,0,109,0,88,14,154,71"" HREF="ftp.html">
<AREA SHAPE="RECT" COORDS="157,0,287,35" HREF="about.html">
<AREA SHAPE="RECT" COORDS="158,38,288,71" HREF="support.html">
<AREA SHAPE="RECT" COORDS="0,0,288,71" HREF="help.html">
</MAP>
```

That last <AREA> tag is the one you're using to define your entire graphic. According to the client-side specification, the area defined first takes precedence when two areas overlap. So, if someone clicks in one of the first four hot zones, they'll be taken to the appropriate URL. If they miss a hot zone, though, they'll be taken to help.html, where you'll tell them how to use the map. That's all there is to it!

> **Note:** If you elect not to create your own default hot zone, client-side maps will automatically ignore clicks that fall outside of your other hot zones. This may frustrate users, but at least they won't be sent to URLs at random.

The *<AREA>* Tag

Before you see an example, I need to point out to you that the shapes for client-side hot zones differ a bit from those for server-side maps. There are only three basic shapes. (Remember this is when you use your map editing program to determine coordinates.) The SHAPE attribute is used to accept these values. The numbers are given to the COORD attribute. The three basic shapes are as follows:

◆ RECT—The rectangular hot zone requires four coordinates: the top left corner and the bottom right corner. An example would be 1,0,55,54 which places the left at pixel 1, the top at pixel 0, the right at 55, and the bottom at 54.

◆ CIRCLE—A circular zone requires three different coordinates: center-x, center-y, and a radius. An example might be 20,20,5, which would represent a circle with its center at 20,20 and a radius of 5 pixels.

◆ POLYGON—For a polygon, each vertex requires a pair of points as its definition. (This is nearly the same as is created by most map definition programs.) A COORD value of 1,2,55,56,1,99 would create a polygon (triangle) with a vertex at 1,2, one at 55,56, and a third at 1,99.

The HREF attribute is used to give the appropriate URL for each hot zone. If no URL is desired, then the attribute NOHREF can be used to make a particular hot zone useless.

Three different examples of <AREA> tags might be:

```
<AREA SHAPE="RECT" COORDS="0,0,49,49" HREF="about_me.html">

<AREA SHAPE="CIRCLE" COORDS="75,49,10" HREF="resume.html">

<AREA SHAPE="POLYGON" COORDS="50,0,65,0,80,10,65,20,50,20" NOHREF>
```

Example: Creating a Client-Side Button Bar

Let's pull this all together into an example. You can create a client-side version of the button bar you used as an image map in Chapter 12. Figure 17.3 shows that graphic again.

Figure 17.3

Button bar example.

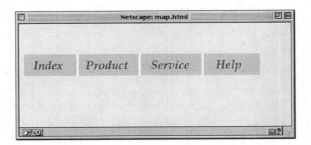

The first step is to use an image map editing application to create hot zones for the entire graphic. With a button bar, creating a default zone is up to you. If you think it's possible for your user to miss the other hot zones you define, and you want them to go to a specific page if they do, then create a hot zone for the entire graphic.

By necessity, all of the hot zones defined for the button bar will be rectangles. Figure 17.4 shows the map definition file to work with.

Figure 17.4

Map definition
information.

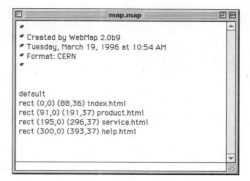

Now we'll start by creating a new HTML document that uses this graphic as a client-side image map (see Listing 17.1).

On the CD

Listing 17.1 *client_map.html* Inserting a Client-Side Image Map

```
<BODY>
<IMG SRC="menu.gif" USEMAP="#menu_map">
<H3> Welcome to My Home Page </H3>
<P> I'm just getting everything started, but you can use the button bar
above>to go to a couple of different places, like my <A HREF="news.html">
News Page</A>, my <A HREF="email.html">Email Tutorial</A> or to come back
to this Index. <B>Note: the above button bar requires a browser capable
of using client-side image maps.</B></P>
<MAP NAME="menu_map">
<AREA SHAPE="RECT" COORDS="0,0,88,37" HREF="index.html">
<AREA SHAPE="RECT" COORDS="91,0,191,37" HREF="product.html">
<AREA SHAPE="RECT" COORDS="195,0,296,37" HREF="service.html">
<AREA SHAPE="RECT" COORDS="300,0,393,37" HREF="help.html">
</MAP>
</BODY>
```

First of all, it's nice to see that your map definition information translates so nicely, isn't it? Second, notice that, even though the map definition file gives 36 as the bottom coordinate for your first hot zone, with client-side image maps you have the freedom to line that up with your others, and choose 37 instead. Most likely, you just clicked a pixel too high in the map editing program. Figure 17.5 shows the final product.

Figure 17.5

Notice that the
<MAP> data
doesn't appear
in the browser
window of the
client-side image
map.

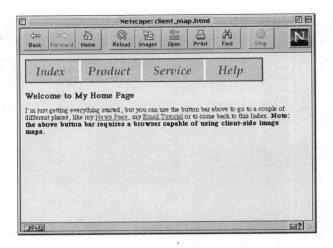

Total Image Maps

There are a few other things you can do with the <IMG> tag and client-side maps to make them more compatible and useful for all of your browsers. As more and more browsers support client-side maps, these suggestions may become less relevant. For now, though, it's important to at least consider these options.

Using Both Sides

The first tactic you can take will allow both types of image map—client-side and server-side—to coexist peacefully. If a browser is capable of offering client-side maps, it will choose that route. If not, it'll ignore the USEMAP attribute and consult the Web server for a map server program's help. The following example shows how it's done:

```
<A HREF="Map Definition URL">
<IMG SRC="map.gif" USEMAP="#name" ISMAP></A>
```

This is a basically a hybrid of the two systems. Any graphical browser—client-side savvy or not—can handle this image map. All you've got to do is set it up with both client-side data and a map definition file as described in Chapter 12. The following is an example:

```
<A HREF="http://www.fakecorp.com/cgi-bin/mymap.map">
<IMG SRC="mymap.gif" USEMAP="#map_data" ISMAP></A>
```

Adding Text Links

Another advantage of the client-side system is that it allows you to create individual links that display as text using the ALT attribute for the <AREA> tag. For a while, you'll probably still need to supply text links outside of your image map, since text-based browsers need to be updated to recognize the <AREA> tag, if only so that they can display the ALT text.

From an earlier example, you can add the ALT attribute like this:

```
<MAP NAME="menu_map">
<AREA SHAPE="RECT" COORDS="0,0,88,37" HREF="index.html" ALT="To Index">
<AREA SHAPE="RECT" COORDS="91,0,191,37" HREF="product.html" ALT="To
Products">
<AREA SHAPE="RECT" COORDS="195,0,296,37" HREF="service.html" ALT="To
Service">
<AREA SHAPE="RECT" COORDS="300,0,393,37" HREF="help.html" ALT="To Help">
</MAP>
```

Once this is fully supported by browsers, it should allow text-only viewers access to the client-side map's links.

The Clickable Image Fallback

Perhaps you want to offer a solution to browsers that can't accept client-side image maps, but don't have access to your Web server for offering a server-side map. In that case, you can make an image both a client-side map and a clickable graphic. Just assign the graphic as a whole to a link that explains that you're using a client-side map, like in the following example:

```
<A HREF="error_map.html">
<IMG SRC="mymap.gif" USEMAP="#map_data"></A>
```

In this example, if users click somewhere on the graphic, but their browser can't deal with client-side maps, they'll be taken to a page called error_map.html where you can explain the problem to them, and perhaps offer a series of clickable graphics or text links for them to use.

Example: A Complex, Complete Map

Let's take everything we've discussed and throw it together into a complete client-side image map—complete, that is, with some non-client-side failsafes. For this one, use a graphic that's a little more exciting and appealing for your intro page interface.

Start by creating the graphic. Be as wild as you want, but remember to keep the graphic itself fairly small (kilobyte wise) and remember that you want your client-side map hot zones to be relatively simple. Figure 17.6 shows the image.

Keep your hot zones basic geometric shapes and you won't be entering coordinates for the rest of your life. Now, use a map editing program to generate a map definition file, so you can get a basic feel for the coordinates you'll need to enter (see fig. 17.7).

Figure 17.6

A more complete Web interface for your client-side map.

Figure 17.7

The map definition file for your Web interface.

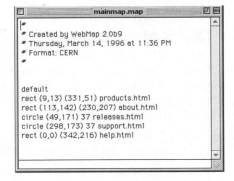

Finally, with the information in hand, you can enter the HTML in Listing 17.2 to activate this client-side map.

Listing 17.2   Activating the Client-Side Map with Failsafes

```
<BODY>
<A HREF="text_index.html">Click here for text menu</A><BR>
<HR>
<A HREF="http://www.fakecorp.com/cgi-bin/mainmap">
<IMG SRC="mainmap.gif" ISMAP USEMAP="#client_map"></A>
<HR>
<H3>Today's News:</H3>
<P>Read our latest <A HREF="releases.html">press releases</A> concerning
our Midwest exapansion.</P>
<P><B>Next week:</B> chat with the CEO! Tuesday at 9pm Eastern time, Mr.
Bigbucks is on IRC channel #bigchat on the Undernet.</P>
<HR>
<MAP NAME="client_map">
<AREA SHAPE="RECT" COORDS="9,13,331,51" HREF="products.html" ALT="To
Products">
```

```
<AREA SHAPE="RECT" COORDS="113,142,230,207" HREF="about.html" ALT="About
the Company">
<AREA SHAPE="CIRCLE" COORDS="49,171,37" HREF="releases.html" ALT="Press
Releases">
<AREA SHAPE="CIRCLE" COORDS="298,173,37" HREF="support.html" ALT="To
Support">
<AREA SHAPE="RECT" COORDS="0,0,342,216" HREF="help.html" ALT="To Help">
</MAP>
</BODY>
```

Clearly, an image map is a quick way to take up a lot of space on your Web page without a great deal of HTML and other text (see fig. 17.8). This page allows any graphical browser access to the image map, whether it chooses to process it as a client-side map or a server-side map. You've also defined a link at the top for a text-based menu that users can click if they're using a non-graphical browser, or if they don't want to wait for the image map to download.

Note: For the map definition file in figure 17.8 to work properly as a server-side map, you should delete the last rectangle (your client-side default) and assign `help.html` as the official default value in the definition file.

Figure 17.8

The intro page in action.

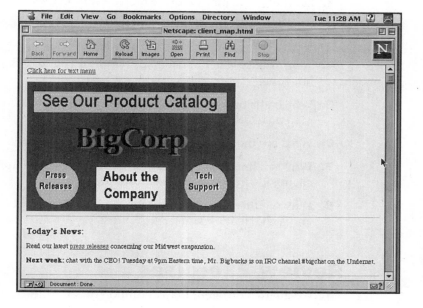

Summary

An emerging standard for HTML 3.0 allows you to create client-side image maps using the `<IMG>` tag and the USEMAP attribute. These client-side maps define hot zones within the HTML document, instead of relying on a special map server program.

Creating a client-side map can be made much easier if you use a map editing program to determine the appropriate coordinates for your particular graphic. With that information, you can create the `<MAP>` container element, which includes the information relevant to each hot zone.

You should keep the hot zone shapes fairly uncomplicated for client-side maps, since there are only three shapes to work with, and the hot zone coordinates have to be entered by hand. Past that, though, you have a very powerful tool with client-side image maps that eliminate the need for help from a Web server-based application.

Review Questions

1. What's the main different between a server-side image map and a client-side image map?

2. Do client-side maps require map definition files?

3. Why is it sometimes important to include HTML coding for both client-side and server-side maps for the same image?

4. True or false. Client-side maps required you to define your own default hot zone.

5. Which attribute to the `<IMG>` tag is used to create a link to the client-side map data? What tag is used to contain that data?

6. What are the three shapes for client-side hot zones?

7. Why is it important for text-based browsers to be updated to recognize the client-side image map specification?

8. Why would it be advantageous to make an image both a "clickable" image and a client-side map?

Review Exercises

1. Create two different map definition files for the same graphic, and then compare them. Are the coordinates the exact same? If not, what are the most appropriate coordinates?

2. Create a client-side map with overlapping hot zones (as defined in your <MAP> container). Test it in a browser. Notice how the order of your <AREA> tags really matter to your client-side map?

3. Using a fairly simple graphic, create a client-side image map without the help of a map definition file from a map editing program. Just use simple shapes and try to estimate the appropriate coordinates for hot zones.

## CHAPTER 18

Other HTML 3.0 Proposals

Although the HTML 3.0 standard as a whole has been "tabled" by the W3C, it looks like bits and pieces of it will continue to trickle out as parts of the standard are agreed upon. This can only be helped by the increased participation of the major Internet software vendors in the W3C's standardization process.

While everything from the 1995 HTML 3.0 draft won't make it, there are probably a few HTML 3.0 specifications that will be widely accepted by popular Web browsers. HTML needs a good way for folks to offer math functions on their Web pages, without resorting to clipping images from screenshots of other programs. Also in the works is the banner element, which has some similarity to Netscape's frame tags. Finally, you'll take a quick look at how HTML style sheets will most likely work and, hopefully, give designers complete control over the way a Web page displays.

> **Note:** Again, you're working with a lot of theory in this chapter (and it's going to be tough to show you screen shots, since so few browsers exist that comply with HTML 3.0). If you'd like to skip ahead to something more concrete, feel free. But, as the standard emerges, hopefully this chapter will have more relevance. Of course, HTML could always change dramatically from what is being laid out here. Your best bet is to check **http://www.w3.org/** for developments.

HTML Math

At the time of writing, it's a bit tough to pin down exactly what the future holds for HTML 3.0 math functions. It seems certain that a nice chunk of HTML designers would appreciate the ability to create math functions in their HTML code (instead or resorting to images of complex math); but the HTML 3.0 standard has expired, and no other math-related proposals have appeared. What there is of the math functions is sketchy, but this section should give you a feel for how things *might* work.

The HTML 3.0 specification introduces a new tag, <MATH>, which is a container tag that supports various other tags and HTML *shortrefs* (shortcuts for some <MATH> tags) to help you create mathematical formulae. The <MATH> tag works something like the following:

```
<MATH>math formula/markup</MATH>
```

The actual tags used for creating <MATH> formulae are still a little scarce, since the standard isn't exactly universally accepting. Let's look at some of the more basic tags.

Math Tags

Among the math tags that you can put your fingers on now are the <SUB>, <SUP>, <BOX>, and <OVER> tags. These tags can go a long way to represent most algebraic and some calculus-level formulae, although the list is by no means exhaustive.

> **Note:** I haven't seen shortrefs used much elsewhere in HTML design, but they're quite common in the HTML math specifications. Shortrefs are just shorthand references for common HTML tags.

Also, all of these but <OVER> are container tags. <SUB> and <SUP> turn text into subscripts and superscript, respectively. The shortref for <SUB> is the underscore (_), while the shortref for <SUP> is the caret (^). An example of these would be the following:

```
<MATH>A<SUB>2</SUB>=45<SUP>3</SUP></MATH>
```

Or, it could be the following, using the shortrefs:

```
<MATH>A_2_=45^3^</MATH>
```

Unfortunately, none of the popular browsers I have available to test can render these <MATH> tags. I'm using a slightly more obscure browser called UdiWWW for Windows (available on the Web at **http://www.uni-ulm.de/~richter/udiwww/ index.htm**) to view these HTML 3.0 specific <MATH> elements in figure 18.1.

Figure 18.1

<MATH> rendering in future browsers.

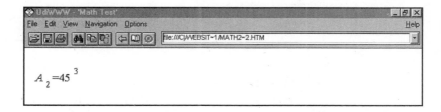

The <BOX> tag is used for invisible brackets, delimiters, and integral signs, and to suggest that something is going to be placed *over* something else. The <OVER> tag does the actual placing, so that the following:

```
<MATH><BOX>f(x)<OVER>1+x</BOX></MATH>
```

would put f(x) over 1+x. I'm not sure that the <BOX> element is really necessary at this point, but I imagine, just like good parenthesis in any mathematical equation, <BOX> can't hurt (unless you use it in the wrong part of your equation). The following is an example where <BOX> is mandatory:

```
<MATH>&int;_a_^b^<BOX>f(x)<OVER>1+x</BOX> dx</MATH>
```

The shortref for <BOX> is {, and for </BOX>, it's }. So, you could enter the above example as the following:

```
<MATH>&int;_a_^b^{f(x)<OVER>1+x} dx</MATH>
```

which is almost easy to look at (unless you had my experiences with calculus in college). To see what all this might look like in a browser, glance at figure 18.2.

Note: Notice the &int symbol at the beginning of the example formula? That's the *ISO entity*, or special character code for an integration symbol. Other symbols relevant for math include < (less-than sign) and > (greater-than sign). For more on ISO entities, consult the Web page **http://www.uni-passau.de/~ramsch/ iso8859-1.html**.

Figure 18.2

Integration with
HTML 3.0-style
math tags.

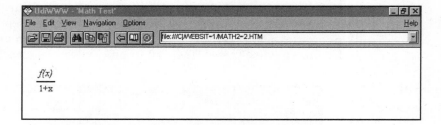

Other Math Tags

Other math tags are available in the HTML 3.0 standard that perform more specific tasks. These <VEC>, <BAR>, <DOT>, <DDOT>, <HAT>, and <TILDE> tags are container tags designed to affect certain variable names or parts of a formula by placing a particular symbol over the enclosed character or text. Respectively, they add a vector, bar, dot, double-dot, hat, or tilde above the enclosed text.

An example might be the following:

```
<MATH><HAT>O</HAT> = <DOT>A</DOT></MATH>
```

which would render in a browser similar to figure 18.3.

Figure 18.3

Viewing other
math tags in
UdiWWW.

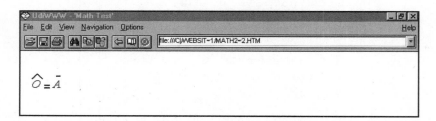

Two other tags allow you to create roots in your formulae: <SQRT> and <ROOT>. Both are container tags, and <ROOT> includes an empty tag, <OF>, that allows you to define the radix of the root function. The following:

```
<SQRT>1 + x</SQRT>
```

and

```
<ROOT>3<OF>1 + x</ROOT>
```

are both possible between <MATH> tags, forcing the browser to render these with a root bracket in the appropriate place, as in the following example (see fig. 18.4):

```
<MATH><SUP>1</SUP><ABOVE>5 + 3</ABOVE></MATH>
```

Figure 18.4

Using the `<SQRT>` *and* `<ROOT>` tags.

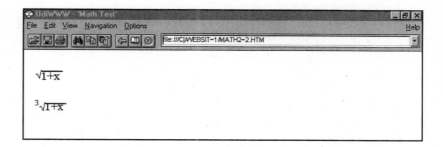

The final tag is the `<TEXT>` tag, which simply allows you to add regular text within a `<MATH>` container. It's often combined with the `<SUP>` or `<SUB>` tags (and `<ABOVE>` or `<BELOW>`) to allow you to describe variables or formula elements, like the following:

```
<MATH>1<OVER><TEXT>The sum of all x's</TEXT></MATH>
```

The Banner Element

If you're familiar with Netscape's frames concept at all, then the `<BANNER>` tag of the HTML 3.0 standard is something you might find interesting. Essentially, the `<BANNER>` container is used to fix a portion of your HTML page so that it doesn't scroll with the rest of the document. This gives you the ability to put a corporate logo, for instance, or navigation buttons (even an image map) in a portion of the screen that won't move, even if the rest of the document extends past the viewable page.

The question is, will `<BANNER>` live on? No popular browsers that I'm aware of support the tag, and it may be too similar to Netscape's frames to survive, since frames can also be used elsewhere on the page and they can access different URLs (effectively dividing a page to display more than one Web site at a time). Check **http://www.w3.org/** and elsewhere before incorporating the `<BANNER>` element into your pages.

If you accidentally memorize how to use the `<BANNER>` tag, and it turns out not to be supported—well, I can hardly blame you, because it's not a terribly complicated tag. It follows the format:

```
<BODY>
<BANNER>
banner text and HTML markup
</BANNER>
rest of HTML page
</BODY>
```

The `<BANNER>` tag is fairly straightforward. An example of the `<BANNER>` tag is the following:

```
<BANNER>
<IMG SRC="logo.gif">
</BANNER>
<H2>Computer Technical Support</H2>
<P>The following are some of the companies that offer tech support on
the Web:</P>
<UL>
<LI> Compaq
<LI> IBM
<LI> Apple
<LI> Packard Bell
<LI> HP

<LI> NEC
<LI> Compudyne
<LI> Toshiba
<LI> Sony
</UL>
```

Once you have enough information on the page to cause it to scroll, you'll see that the banner section doesn't scroll along with the rest of the text.

Document-Defined Style Sheets

The age-old debate in the HTML world (okay, so the debate's a year-and-a-half old) is the push and pull between designers who want control over the display of their pages and the standard-bearers who want the widest possible audience for Web pages. Up until now, it's been something of a stand-off, with companies like Netscape adding non-standard HTML-like references to their browsers' capabilities, while the standards organizations have ignored or repudiated those attempts.

The new world order of HTML standard creation may have finally changed that a bit. The W3C now comprises representatives of both camps—both the HTML standard-creators and the strongest corporate players in Web creation tools. So, the two philosophies have begun to merge, and style sheets seem to be one of their answers.

Put simply, a style sheet is a designer-suggested mechanism for the layout of a page. The magic of style sheets is that they can become almost infinitely complicated from the standpoint of the designer. You can decide minute details like character spacing, color, font families, and other desktop publishing-type decisions. At the same time, however, not rendering these decisions is up to the individual user and browser, so that minimal information is lost, and the majority of browsers can view your information from whatever platform they choose.

Let's take a cursory look at style sheets. Although part of the now-expired HTML 3.0 standard, the current thinking in style sheets is about three weeks old as of this writing. Will it change? I can almost guarantee it. I'll try to pick the parts that seemed destined to remain intact.

> **Note:** There are at least four different ways to start adding style sheets to your Web documents in the current working draft. In fact, style sheets are considerably more complicated than nearly any other aspect of HTML. Why? It's my belief that this is laying the groundwork for more advanced programs to make the leap into HTML design. Right now, the power of most desktop publishing programs is lost on Web design. In a few years, as the style sheet standards formalize and come into practice, I believe you'll begin to see fewer people using text editors for Web creation, and more professional-level page layout programs being brought to the game.

The *<STYLE>* Tag

It seems to me that the <STYLE> tag is the easiest to understand when it comes to style sheets in HTML, and I'd like to talk about it first. You're in the <HEAD> section of your document now, and you'll use the <STYLE> container to define some of the style elements you want to add to our Web page. The basic format is the following:

```
<HEAD>
<TITLE>Doc title</TITLE>
<STYLE TYPE="MIME type">
HTML tag.class {special formatting}
...
<SPAN> {special formatting}
</STYLE>
</HEAD>
```

Looks like this will require some explaining. For your purposes, the TYPE attribute of the <STYLE> tag will always accept the MIME type text/css. That stands for the *cascading style sheets (CSS)* standard for Web style, and it is basically just a standard that defines what sort of things you can do to text, images, and background on your Web page. It defines the special formatting codes you'll use within your <STYLE> definition.

HTML tag refers to any of the HTML you've learned thus far. Nearly all of them can be given a .class which creates a unique instance of this particular tag. When that class is specified in the body portion of your document, the special formatting will be used for that particular instance of the HTML tag.

Let's look at an example:

```
<HEAD>
<TITLE>My Styled Page</TITLE>
<STYLE TYPE="text/css">
  H1.italic { font-style: italic }
  P.red_caps { color: red; font-style: small-caps }
</STYLE>
</HEAD>
```

Now, with these style definitions, you've created new classes of the familiar `<H1>` and `<P>` tags named `italic` and `red_caps`, respectively. When you want these special instances to occur in our HTML document, use the CLASS attribute to the standard HTML tag. Therefore, the following would create the special cases for our HTML tags within the document itself:

```
<H1 CLASS="italic">This header is italicized</H1>
<P CLASS="red_caps">This text should be in red, and all small-caps.</P>
```

> **Tip:** Class names are completely of your choosing. Keep them short and descriptive and avoid spaces (use the underscore if necessary). Also avoid common HTML words and tag names, just for clarity.

Notice that the original pseudo-code example offered another new tag, the `<SPAN>` tag. `<SPAN>` is basically a designer-defined tag that allows you to create a special case for emphasizing certain text in your document. It works just like the `<EM>` tag except for one small detail—it has no HTML 2.0 counterpart. So, browsers that don't recognize style sheets won't interpret the `<SPAN>` element in any way. If you used a pre-existing tag, other browsers would only see half of your formatting.

Consider this example. In the `<HEAD>` section, you define `<SPAN>`:

```
<STYLE TYPE="text/css">
  SPAN { font-style: small-caps }
</STYLE>
```

Now, in the body of your document, you can do the following:

```
<P><SPAN>Welcome to</SPAN> my home page on the Web. I'm glad you could
find the time to drop by and see what we've got going today.</P>
```

In a style sheet-capable browser, you'll see small caps used for an attractive, printed-style introduction to your paragraph. In older browsers, the text is unaffected.

The CSS Style Sheet Definition

Having seen how certain style elements can be defined for your Web page, you might be interested in learning all of the different style changes you can make to your documents. There are two things you should recognize about this.

First of all, the CSS style sheet definition is only one of infinite possible style sheet definitions. That means that anyone can create a style sheet definition, give it a MIME name like `text/bob`, and create a browser that includes all of the programming required to render the elements of that style sheet. This can get very tedious to learn and design by hand, which is part of the fodder for my argument that style sheets are the beginning of the end of simple (unassisted) HTML layout.

Fortunately for you, the W3C (along with the corporations behind popular browsers) have just announced at the time of writing that the CSS will be the first standard for style sheets. That, at least, gives you common ground to work with when you set out to design Web pages for the general public. And, of course, the magic of style sheets is that if a browser can't use them, it won't. No basic information is lost.

The second major point is this: the current working draft of the CSS style sheet definition is over 40 pages long—and it's basically full of possible style properties. That means things go much deeper than { color: red } in CSS. I'll touch on some of the high points, but if you get very deep into style sheets, you'll want to consult **http://www.w3.org/pub/WWW/TR/WD-css1.html** for the latest CSS Level 1 developments and changes.

Table 18.1 offers some of the more likely CSS defined style properties and their possible values or value types.

Table 18.1   CSS-defined Style Properties

Property	Value	Example(s)
font-family	name of font	Helvetica, Serif, Symbol
font-size	number/percentage	12pt, +1, 120%
font-weight	number/strength	+1, light, medium, extra bold
font-style	name of style	italic, small caps, small caps italic
font	combination of above	12pt Serif medium small caps
color	word/hex number	red, green, blue, FF00FF
background	color/blend/file	paper.gif, red, black/white
word-spacing	number+units	1pt, 4em, 1in
text-spacing	number+units	3pt, 0.1em, +1
text-decoration	word	underline, line through, box, blink
vertical-align	word/percentage	baseline, sup, sub, top, middle, 50%
text-align	word	left, right, center, justify
text-indent	number/percentage	1in, 5%, 3em
margin	number	0.5in, 2em
list-style	word/URL	disc, circle, square, lower alpha
white-space	pre/normal	pre, normal

You can probably figure out what most of these do, but I want to point out something about a few of them.

The FONT property is basically a shorthand reference for the four properties that precede it in the table. You can simple use any of the related values for FONT, effectively describing its entire appearance in one tag. With any font tag, you probably want to be as generic with font names (like Helvetica or Courier) as possible, since the user's browser will have to decide what that font name's closest counterpart is on the user's system.

The possible values for COLOR include black, red, white, green, blue, yellow, brown, gray, orange, and purple. You can also add "light" or "dark" to any of these colors. Also, remember that you're acting on a particular tag (most of the time) and that color most often refers to text color. It can be used with any text-related tag, like <BLOCKQUOTE>, as in the following example:

```
<STYLE TYPE="text/css">
  BLOCKQUOTE.helv_red { font-family: helvetica; color: red }
</STYLE>
```

And, you'd call it just like any other CLASS of an HTML tag:

```
<BLOCKQUOTE CLASS="helv_red">Blockquote class</BLOCKQUOTE>
```

The properties VERTICAL-ALIGN and TEXT-ALIGN give Web designers the much-desired control over centering and justifying text in a document.

The BACKGROUND property is most often used in conjunction with the <BODY> tag, although you can technically change the background of nearly element. The background can be a color, two colors (blended in the background), or a URL to a graphic file. You can also include both color and file, so that a background color is used if the file isn't found. Here's an example:

```
<HEAD>
<TITLE>Background Page</TITLE>
<STYLE TYPE="text/css">
  BODY.back { background: "http://www.fakecorp.com/back.gif" white/blue }
</STYLE>
<HEAD>
<BODY CLASS="back">
```

Example: Incorporating a Style Sheet

For the most part, a style sheet should be secondary to the communicative nature of your text and graphics. Ideally, this is a page that would work for both HTML 2.0 users and users with style sheet-capable browsers. Let's put together a small style sheet and HTML page.

Save a new HTML document from your template and enter Listing 18.1.

On the CD

Listing 18.1 *style1.html* **Creating a Style Sheet**

```
<HTML>
<HEAD>
<TITLE>Style Sheet Example</TITLE>
<STYLE TYPE="text/css">
 BODY.back {background: "paper.gif" white}
 H2.ital {text-style: italic}
 H3.center {text-align: center}
 P.center {text-align: center}

 SPAN {font: 14pt sanserif small-caps; color: blue}
</STYLE>
</HEAD>
<BODY CLASS="back">
<H1>About BigCorp</H1>
<H2 CLASS="ital">Taking Over the World, One Step at a Time</H2>
<HR>
<H3 CLASS="center">About our Company</H3>
<P CLASS="center">
<SPAN>"Domination of the world</SPAN> is only the first step,"were the
immortal words of BigCorp founder, Mr. Bigbucks. "If it were that simple,
I would have a much better golf game."</P>
<P>But that's hardly the extent of BigBuck's ambition. From humble
starts,he's taken on the textiles, electronics, automotive, computer and
political-graft indsutries with a "kill-or-at-least-maim" attitude.</P>
</BODY>
</HTML>
```

Once you've got that entered, you meet up with the second half of the example. Now I just want you to load the page and see what parts (if any) of the style sheet your browser is capable of displaying. Depending on how quickly browsers begin to incorporate style sheets, a more mainstream browser (like Netscape Navigator or MS Internet Explorer) may display this page just as completely.

To view the page, use the Open File command in your browser. Then check to see how your page looks.

External Style Sheets and Other Style Sheet Tags

Let's talk a little more about some of the other new elements you can use, and how you can use a single style sheet for more than one page on your site. To use an external style sheet, you need to drop back to the <LINK> tag which was first discussed in Chapter 10.

The *<LINK>* Tag

In this case, <LINK> will serve a more specific purpose for your Web page than it has in previous discussions. Using the REL attribute for the <LINK> tag, you can add the STYLE elements from the linked page to the current page. Predefined style classes can then be used in the current HTML markup.

This version of the <LINK> tag works like this:

```
<LINK TITLE="link_doc_title" REL=stylesheet HREF="URL" TYPE="text/css">
```

The TYPE can accept any style sheet type you might be interested in using—we're sticking with CSS. The TITLE should be the same as the remote file's title and the HREF URL needs to be an URL to the document that includes the <STYLE> definition that you also want to use for the current page. An example might be:

```
<LINK TITLE="MY STYLE" REL=stylesheet HREF="my.style" TYPE="text/css">
```

So what type of file are you linking to? If you prefer, you can simply link to a common HTML file that defines the style for your Web site. Even your index page can serve as this common style page, if it includes a <STYLE> definition.

Or, you can create a document that includes nothing but a <STYLE> container and style page definitions. HTML and head/body tags aren't required since the <LINK> tag is essentially "replaced" in the current document with the <STYLE> information. And the <LINK> tag is already in the appropriate place for that <STYLE> information— between the <HEAD> tags.

Style Overrides

With either a <LINK> tag or a <STYLE> tag defined in the head of your document, you can use not only the currently defined classes for creating styles, but also overrides to change the style of nearly any HTML tag. How does this work? It's similar to defining style classes, but you instead use the STYLE attribute with any legal HTML tag. The following is an example:

```
<P STYLE="text align: center"> This paragraph is centered, even if it
doesn't have a CLASS defined that centers text.</P>
The following text is <EM STYLE="color: blue">blue and emphasized</EM>.
<OL STYLE="list-style: lower-roman">
<LI> Each list element
<LI> Is numbered with lowercase
<LI> Roman numerals
</OL>
```

You can see where the flexibility of style sheets is almost getting out of control. Although you can call these *overrides* for your current style sheet, the truth is that you can use these STYLE-attributed HTML tags anytime that you want to—as long as you've defined the text/css type through a <STYLE> or <LINK> tag in the head of your document. So, if you'd prefer to generate your style elements on-the-fly, you can define a <LINK> or empty <STYLE> tag that does little more than define the TYPE as text/css.

Divisions and the *ALIGN* Attribute

The style sheet standard also creates another tag, the <DIV> (division) tag, that allows you to assign attributes to a particular part of your document. <DIV> is a container tag that applies different styles to anything, including images, placed between the two tags. Ultimately, it gives the designer another level of organization for your Web page. If you think of a <DIV> as one level below the <BODY> tag, you're on the right track.

The <DIV> tag works like this:

```
<DIV CLASS="class_name" ALIGN="direction">
...HTML markup...
</DIV>
```

Notice that the <DIV> tag can accept the same CLASS attribute that most other HTML tags can take when used with a style sheet. This allows you to create a division of your HTML pages that accepts particular style properties. In addition, the <DIV> tag can take the attribute ALIGN, which can accept LEFT, CENTER, RIGHT, or JUSTIFY.

> **Note:** Many browsers began accepting the <DIV> tag and ALIGN attribute early in the original HTML 3.0 draft's lifespan. This is the most appropriate way to center a page or portion of the page. When possible, use this tag instead of the Netscape-specific <CENTER> tag. (More on that in Chapter 19.)

Let's take a look at the <DIV> tag in action:

```
<DIV ALIGN="CENTER">
<IMG SRC="XJ906.GIF">
<H3>The XJ906 Mega-Notebook</H3>
<P>We can't be more proud of our latest addition to our notebook line-up,
the XJ906. Available with a number of processors (all daughterboard
upgradable) and many memory configurations (up to 64 MB) the most impres-
sive aspect of the XJ906 has to be its cutting-edge approach to multime-
dia.</P>
<UL>
<LI>6x CD-ROM (internal, sliding-tray)
<LI>2 PCCard 2.0 slots
<LI>16-bit stereo sound and built-in speakers
<LI>Hardware MPEG support
<LI>NTSC Video In/Out Ports
<LI>Available docking station
</UL>
</DIV>
<H5>Copyright 1996.</H5>
```

Here, finally, is an HTML 3.0 tag you can view in the most popular browsers (see fig. 18.5). You can use the <DIV> tag with style sheets in the following example.

Figure 18.5

The `<DIV>` tag centers items in Netscape Navigator.

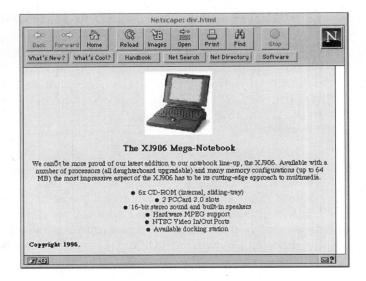

Example: Styles and the *<DIV>* Tag

Let's incorporate everything you've learned so far about style sheets and the `<DIV>` tag. You'll still define a minimal style sheet in the head of your document, but you'll use overrides for the bulk of the text. You'll also use the `<DIV>` tag to apply styles and global alignment.

Create a new HTML document based on your template, then enter something similar to Listing 18.2.

Listing 18.2 *style2.html* **Using the *<DIV>* Tag With Styles**

```
<HTML>
<HEAD>
<TITLE>Advance Style Sheets</TITLE>
<STYLE TYPE="text/css">
 H2.mycaps {font-style: small-caps}
 BODY.back {background: "paper.gif" white/light blue}
 SPAN {font-style: small-caps}
</STYLE>
</HEAD>
<BODY CLASS="back">
<H1 STYLE="text-align: center"> Micheal T. Williamson </H1>
<H2 CLASS="mycaps">Objective</H2>
<DIV ALIGN="CENTER">
<P STYLE="font: 14pt italics">I'm interested in a management-level
position with an exceptional graphics design/Internet firm. I'm looking
for a growth position that takes advantages of my writing, computer and
graphic design skills.</P>
```

```
</DIV>
<H2 CLASS="mycaps">Skills</H2>
<DIV STYLE="margin: 1.5in">
<UL STYLE="list-style: square">
<LI><B>Writer.</B> Skilled as a technical and product copy writer, with
education in English, technical writing, creative writing and advertising
copy writing. Experience includes work with successful PR firms and
advertising firms.
<LI><B>Technology.</B> A Master's Degree in Management Information
Systems has given me the background in computing that allows me a great
understanding of the magic behind the machines. A relentless effort to
stay "current" has me reading 5-10 periodicals a week related to the
industry.
<LI><B>Internet.</B> The emphasis in the last few years on the Internet
played to some skills I developed in pursuit of my Master's degree,
including experience with some of the earliest implementations of HTML.
Since that time I've been responsible for the development of five major
HTML projects, including the original BigCorp site in 1994.
</UL>
</DIV>
</BODY>
</HTML>
```

You get the idea. You can notice two things from this listing, both related to the style sheets and <DIV> tags discussed in this chapter. First, they are both very flexible and offer unprecedented control over page layout. Second, they can really fill up an HTML document fast. It may be best to define a style sheet and use the CLASS attribute whenever possible. Overrides for every element can be overkill—but, then again, there's a lot you can do to make you pages better looking.

Summary

A number of HTML 3.0 proposals are currently fighting for survival in the W3C and other places where HTML standards are created. With the demise of the original HTML 3.0 standard, current HTML 3.0 level components are being standardized one at a time. So, the future of math tags, the banner element, and style sheets are still up in the air.

Math tags will most likely be implemented because they fill a need in the HTML world for a convenient way to represent mathematical formulae without requiring the designer to use images created by other programs. The banner element might not be so lucky, since it has a lot in common with the frames tags proposed by Netscape.

Style sheets do look like they'll survive, but they'll also be somewhat complicated to implement. At their most basic, they offer designers unprecedented control over the look of their Web pages. At their most complicated, they'll probably require sophisticated applications (along the same lines as desktop publishing programs) for precision layout.

Review Questions

1. What are shortrefs?

2. The `<BOX>` tag is the HTML equivalent of what mathematical symbols?

3. True or false. HTML math tags are used to solve math problems in HTML documents.

4. What does `&int;` represent?

5. What would `<TILDE>e</TILDE>` look like?

6. Is the `<BANNER>` tag used to scroll text and graphics across the top of a page?

7. What are style sheets for? What makes them a fairly new concept in HTML design?

8. What does "CSS" stand for? What is it, and what makes it different from the HTML style sheet standard?

9. How do you define a style sheet "class?" How are classes used?

10. Why is the `<SPAN>` tag different from other HTML tags? Why is it similar to the `<DIV>` tag?

11. Consider this property definition: `{ background: white/blue }`. What will this background look like?

12. Why would you want to use the `<LINK>` tag instead of the `<STYLE>` tag to define a style sheet?

13. What Netscape HTML tag can be replaced in most cases with the `<DIV>` tag?

Review Exercises

1. Use math tags to represent the formula: `5 > 4 <= 4`.

2. Using math tags, create a formula that divides a fraction by a whole number.

3. What would `<ROOT>4<OF>2 * w</ROOT>` look like?

4. Using client-side image maps from Chapter 17, use the `<BANNER>` tag to keep a client-side map fixed at the top of your Web page.

5. Create a style sheet that renders the `<H2>` tag in a blue Sans Serif font in all caps. Also force that tag to align to the right side of the browser. Create a `<P>` tag that "justifies" Serif, black text. Use just these two tags and the appropriate style sheet elements to generate an "official" looking report.

6. In the above example, add a `<H1>` level title to the report, but don't use style sheet classes or overrides.

## CHAPTER 19

Netscape HTML

If you've been on the Web for any amount of time at all, chances are you've come across a page or site that suggests that its pages are "best viewed in Netscape Navigator" or something similar. Since the Netscape 1.1 version in mid-1995, the Netscape Navigator Web browser has been capable of supporting "extensions" to the HTML standard language. Extensions are essentially HTML-like commands that were originally only viewable by Navigator users.

Whether or not that was a good business decision is still being played out in the industry, although Netscape is clearly a dominant force among Web technology companies. What you should be more concerned with here in this chapter is whether or not you should use these special features—commonly called *Netscapisms*.

Should You Use Netscapisms?

For your purposes here, I'm going to describe Netscapisms as HTML-like extensions that run counter to the theories and guidelines that govern development of the HTML standard. For instance, the tables standard that you worked with in Chapter 15 owes a great deal to Netscape's early implementation of tables. That's not a Netscapism. The <BLINK> tag (to create blinking text) and the <CENTER> tag are Netscapisms, because they don't have any proposed counterpart in the HTML standard—and, perhaps more importantly, they are tags with no function but aesthetics.

Whether or not you use these Netscapisms in your Web pages is completely up to you. I'll try to refrain from value judgments, although I must say the <BLINK> tag is annoying! Aside from that, though, I'll just leave you with the following thoughts:

♦ **Netscape-only tags should go hand-in-hand with a "Netscape-only" warning**. Tell your users when you've used tags that can only be viewed in Netscape—or any other browsers. In fact, you should probably tell users you're using HTML 3.0 tags or MS Internet Explorer commands, as well.

♦ **Consider creating alternate pages**. It's not overwhelmingly difficult to create two versions of your site: an HTML 2.0 compliant site and a site with Netscape or HTML 3.0 additions. You can also create a "front door" that allows users to choose which they would prefer to view.

> **Tip:** You might want to make your HTML 2.0 site a low-graphics site, too, so that lower bandwidth users can choose that one over your highly-graphical Netscape-only site.

♦ **Use HTML 3.0 whenever reasonable**. It's difficult to keep up with the HTML 3.0 standard, which is why many people just keep listening to Netscape. But, when you have the opportunity (e.g., using `<DIV ALIGN="CENTER">` versus `<CENTER>`), use the "standard" tag.

♦ **Make sure you don't lose information**. Frankly, most Netscapisms do very little to communicate information; they, instead, format it a bit more attractively. If you do use Netscapisms, make sure you're not using them in a way that means your other users are missing out on something important.

Centering, Blinking, and Background Tags

You've seen tags very similar to these. Once the HTML style sheet standard has been universally accepted, it'll be time to put these guys to sleep. Each one has a style sheet alternative and, for centering and backgrounds, there are similar HTML 3.0 alternatives that have been rolled into the most popular browsers. Many browsers will still support Netscape-style centering and backgrounds (for backward compatibility, and to catch up to Netscape); but, if it seems style sheets are finally in vogue, switch over and ignore these.

The `<CENTER>` tag is used to center just about anything—graphics or text—in the browser windows. It works like this:

```
<CENTER>
...HTML markup...
</CENTER>
```

It's a container tag that works just about like the `<DIV ALIGN="CENTER">` tag, except that the `<CENTER>` tag can't do anything else, while the `<DIV>` tag is useful for style sheets. An example of `<CENTER>` would be the following:

```
<CENTER>
<IMG SRC="logo.gif">
<P>If you're ready to visit BigCorp, click <A HREF="main.html">here
</A>.</P>
</CENTER>
```

This looks like figure 19.1 in a browser.

Figure 19.1

Using the
<CENTER> tag
in Netscape
Navigator.

`<BLINK>` works in much the same way. As a tag, it's designed to make text more annoying by forcing a cursor-style reverse field to blink on and off on top of words contained by this tag. The following is an example:

```
<BLINK>Real Hot Sale Item!</BLINK>
```

Unfortunately, I can't show it to you in a browser, since a picture in this book can't show you the blinking. Too bad, huh?

Background and Foreground Colors

Netscape uses a different formula (different from the style sheet method) for adding colors to the background of your pages. Using the BGCOLOR attribute for the <BODY> tag, you create a background color by specifying a 6-digit hexadecimal number. This attribute takes the following format:

```
<BODY BGCOLOR=#rrggbb>
...HTML document...
</BODY>
```

The *rrggbb* number represents the two-digit hexadecimal number for red, green, and blue values of the color you want added to the background of your document. An example of this is the following which would turn the background of your page black:

```
<BODY BGCOLOR="#000000"
```

Similarly, FFFFFF would be a white background, FF0000 would be red, 00FF00 would be green, and so on.

> **Note:** Here's a quick refresher in hex numbers. Hexadecimal means base-16, as opposed to base-10 (normal counting numbers), so each column in a hex number represents a multiple of 16, not ten. The right-most column (we called it the "one's place" in grade school) needs single-digit numbers past nine in order to allow us to represent hex numbers.
>
> Unfortunately, our numbering system doesn't have single digits past nine. (Ten, which is past nine, is a two-digit number in base-10.) So, we use letters—the first six of the alphabet. An *F* in the right-most column represents the value 15, and an *F* in the 16's place represents 240 (15×16). So, the hex number FF is equal to 255 (240+15).

Once you've changed the background colors in your document, you may need to change the foreground (text) colors to make them readable. The default for most graphical browsers is black text, aside from hypertext links. If you change your background color so that it's also black, you'll have a communications problem.

> **Tip:** There are a number of pages on the Web to help you pick Netscape colors for backgrounds and links. Try **http://www.bga.com/~rlp/dwp/palette/palette.html** and **http://www.echonyc.com/~xixax/Mediarama/hex.html** to start.

To change the text color in Netscape HTML, you use the TEXT attribute to the <BODY> tag, which takes the following format:

```
<BODY TEXT="#rrggbb">
...HTML document...
</BODY>
```

In this code, *rrggbb* represents another series of three two-digit hex numbers. An example appropriate for the black background would be the following which would turn the text white:

```
<BODY TEXT="#FFFFFF">
```

It's also possible to change the colors used to represent hypertext links in Netscape HTML, using three different attributes: LINK, VLINK, and ALINK. These represent an unvisited link, a visited link, and an active link, respectively.

To change these, you'd use the following format:

```
<BODY LINK="#rrggbb" VLINK="#rrggbb" ALINK="#rrggbb">
...HTML document...
</BODY>
```

Once again, the numbers are three two-digit hex numbers that represent the red, green, and blue values of the desired color. The default values are blue for LINK, purple for VLINK, and red for ALINK. These values may also be overridden by the user if they've set different colors in Netscape's General Preferences dialog box.

> **Note:** How can you see an "active" link? If you notice, a link turns a different color right after you've clicked it—basically, just so you know you've been successful in selecting it. The ALINK value is also the color of a hypermedia link while the file is downloaded to the user's computer.

Example: Netscape Colors and Alignment

Let's use some of the Netscapisms to create a page in the best Netscape-only tradition. You can create a new page complete with a background color, foreground color, new colors for links, and some centering. You might even use the blink tag.

Save a new HTML document from your template and enter something similar to Listing 19.1.

On the CD

Listing 19.1 *door.html* **Adding Color and Alignment to Netscape Pages**

```
<BODY BGCOLOR=#000000 TEXT=#FFFFFF LINK="5555FF" VLINK="00FF00"
ALINK="FF5555">
<CENTER>
<H2><BLINK>Welcome!</BLINK></H2>
<P>I'm glad you could make it to the labyrinth of terror! We pride
ourselves here on the darker side of the Web with using some of the most
hideous and amazing colors, textures and HTML extensions ever conceived of.
```

continues

299

Listing 19.1   Continued

```
If you're interesting in entering the labyrinth, click
<A HREF="net_home.html">here</A>. If you're wondering what all the fuss
is about, and everything looks pretty normal to you, then you're probably
better off viewing our <A HREF="2_home.html">HTML 2.0</A> pages.</P>
<HR>
<H3><BLINK>Be Very Afraid!!!</BLINK></H3>
</CENTER>
</BODY>
```

Clicking one of the links (even though it probably won't actually work for you unless you change the example's URLs) should allow you to see the different link colors. Hopefully, it will be light blue before you click it, light red as you're clicking it, and bright green after it's been visited. Otherwise, the page should look something like figure 19.2, aside from the blinking.

Figure 19.2

An outrageous page as viewed through Netscape.

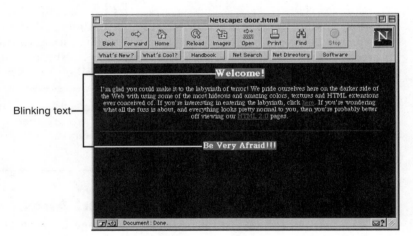

Blinking text

Manipulating Text with Netscape HTML

Again, the point of many Netscape commands is to directly affect the appearance of text. Outside of style sheets, this is something that HTML tries to avoid doing, preferring to leave the manipulation to the individual browser. But Netscape, in catering to appearance-motivated designers, lets you make those decisions for yourself. Not all of these tags are going to make it in any HTML 3.0 specifications, so if you find you must use them, I suggest warning your users that Netscape-compatibility is required.

<NOBR> and *<WBR>*

The <NOBR> tag won't allow text to wrap when it meets with the end of the browser screen. This is occasionally useful, especially in situations where your user might be confused by a line wrap. This is a container tag that accepts text and markup between its tags. Its format is as follows:

```
<NOBR>test and markup</NOBR>
```

Now, this doesn't necessarily mean that users will need to scroll their browser window in order to see the text—in many cases, they'll just need to expand the browser window. (Or, make it considerably smaller to force the entire length of <NOBR> text to the next line.) This might be useful for addresses, programming code, a line of numbers, or similar text. The following is an example:

```
<NOBR>1234 Main Street * St. Louis, MO  *  29000</NOBR>
```

The <WBR> tag is used in conjunction with the <NOBR> container for creating a line break when you know *exactly* where you want one to occur (if it needs to be broken by the edge of the Navigator window). It can also be used outside of the confines of the <NOBR> tag to let Netscape know where it's okay to break up a particularly long word.

<WBR> doesn't usurp the responsibilities of
—it's only a suggestion. If Netscape needs to break a line of text (or a particularly long word), then it will do so. If it doesn't need to break at the <WBR>, it won't. An example would be:

```
<P>When I move this Web site the new address will be
http://www.fakecorp.com<WBR>/main/mperry/public/index.html. Look for a
hyperlink soon!</P>
```

Since Netscape Navigator would interpret that address as one word, it allows you to suggest where it should be broken if the address would otherwise overlap the browser window.

> **Note:** For lines that always break where you want them to, the <PRE> tag is still your best bet (e.g., lines of poetry). The <BR> tag might work well, too, if you're not trying to line things up visually.

The *<FONT>* and *<BASEFONT>* Tags

Another ability unique to Netscape HTML (outside of style sheets) is specific control over the size of fonts. The general HTML theory is to allow a browser to decide what fonts will be larger than others, although it's safe to assume, for instance, that graphical browsers will render <H1> text larger than <H2>, etc.

Netscape, however, offers up the <FONT> and <BASEFONT> tags, which take the SIZE attribute to change the size of browser fonts, regardless of the tags used. <BASEFONT> changes the font size for an entire document relative to the default. <FONT> can then be used to set individual font sizes within the document. They're formatted like this:

```
<BASEFONT SIZE="number">
<FONT SIZE="(+/-) number">
```

You'll want to use an incremental number (for example, +2) for the SIZE attribute to the <FONT> tag when you're using the <BASEFONT> tag to set the default. The <FONT> tag can be used just about anywhere in regular text. For instance:

```
<BASEFONT SIZE="4">
<P>We're having a S<FONT SIZE="+1">A<FONT SIZE="+2">L<FONT
SIZE="+3">A<FONT SIZE="+4">BRA<FONT SIZE="+3">T<FONT SIZE="+2">I<FONT
SIZE="+1">O<FONT SIZE="+0">N!</P>
```

You can use <FONT> as often as you'd like. Just remember that as a general rule, the more you use it, the more annoying it is (see fig. 19.3).

Figure 19.3

Overuse of the <FONT> tag.

We're having a SALABRATIon!

Example: Putting Fonts in Their Place

Let's see what Netscape's control over fonts and other interface elements allows you to accomplish on a Web page. Start with a new document from your template and enter Listing 19.2.

On the CD

Listing 19.2 *font.html* **Using the *<FONT>* Tag**

```
<BODY>
<BASEFONT SIZE="4">
<H2>In the interest of science...</H2>
<P>It's been my experience lately that, in studying the concept
ASTRIOANGLANGIUM<WBR>POROPHATE as dilligently as I have, I've caused
quite a stir in the scientific world. I must say that I've been surprised
at how quickly the entire concept of lower-being brain transplant into
humanoids has caused the world in general to take up arms against me,
although I, frankly, cannot conceive of a rational explanation for it. It
seems that trainable, workable, intelligent humanoids would make the
perfect servants, virtually eliminating the need to keep regular humans
alive. That saves precious natural resources. I would, of course, be left
alive to rule this world.<P>
<P>I can only guess that the outcry is a result of my closely-guarded
formula. I now release it to the world:</P>
<NOBR><FONT SIZE="+2">X + (W*T) ^ 2 / 567.34cd_constant -
(T * X^.4) / ROOT(Wy + Xy) * 70%(Ry * Ty - Rf) = Secret Formula
Answer<FONT SIZE="+0"></WOBR>
<P>Go ye, then, and attempt to duplicate my work. I will destroy all of
you with my brilliance!</P>
</BODY>
```

It might be a bit disturbing to come across this page in real life, but let's see how it renders in Netscape (see fig. 19.4). Notice the use of <WBR> in the completely made up scientific jargon word, to suggest to Netscape where it would be okay to break that word. We've also used NOBR to keep the math formula from breaking.

> **Note:** Just to avoid confusion, the above example does *not* attempt to use HTML 3.0 math tags to render the math formula.

Figure 19.4

Font manipulation with Netscape tags.

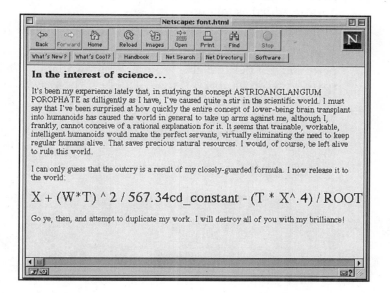

Plus, as an added bonus, the basefont comes across as a little too big—just to give it that mad scientist feeling.

Netscape Attributes for HTML Tags

Most of the Netscape additions that have been discussed thus far have been new tags, but Netscape also works its magic through attributes that can be added to existing HTML tags. In general, these attributes simply give you more visual control over an existing HTML tag by allowing you to choose width, height, and other special characteristics.

The *<HR>* Tag

This tag generally returns a horizontal rule in HTML, and it still does in Netscape, but Netscape-specific attributes give you more control over the appearance of the rule.

By default, the <HR> tag displays as a shaded, engraved-looking line. Thanks to Netscape, you can change this with the SIZE, WIDTH, ALIGN, and NOSHADE attributes. They're added as follows:

```
<HR SIZE="number" WIDTH="number/percentage" ALIGN="direction" NOSHADE>
```

The numbers for SIZE and WIDTH are in pixels, while WIDTH can also accept a percentage of the available browser window that you'd like to see using the <HR> span. ALIGN can accept LEFT, RIGHT, or CENTER. The NOSHADE attribute stands on its own. Let's look at a few examples:

```
<HR SIZE="5">
<HR WIDTH="75%" ALIGN="CENTER">
<HR NOSHADE>
```

In Netscape Navigator, these horizontal rules look like figure 19.5.

Figure 19.5

Netscape's attributes for <HR> in action.

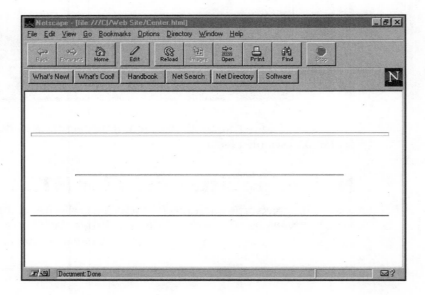

HTML Lists

Here's another cosmetic change that Netscape allows you to make with attributes to standard HTML 2.0 tags. The attribute TYPE can be used to change the type of bullet or number used by an <OL> or <UL> HTML list. It takes the following format:

```
<OL TYPE="number style">
<UL TYPE="bullet style">
```

For ordered lists, the TYPE value can be *A* for capital letters, *a* for lowercase letters, *I* for large roman numerals, or *i* for small roman numerals. For UL lists, the possibilities are DISC, CIRCLE, or SQUARE.

Within lists, the <LI> element can accept the attribute VALUE, which allows you to renumber lists as you go along. An example might be a list that you'd like to start with the number five:

```
<OL>
<LI VALUE="5"> Item numbered 5
<LI> Item numbered 6
<LI> Item numbered 7
</OL>
```

Used in conjunction with the TYPE attribute for the <OL> tag, the VALUE attribute would also allow you to start with different alphabetic or roman characters, such as with the following:

```
<OL TYPE="A">
<LI VALUE="5"> Item E
<LI> Item F
<LI> Item G
<LI VALUE="1"> Item A
<LI> Item B
</OL>
```

As shown in this example (results are shown in figure 19.6), you can even change the numbering / lettering values within the list, and it will pick up the counting from there.

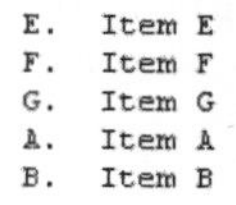

Figure 19.6

Renumbering lists with Netscape attributes.

```
E.   Item E
F.   Item F
G.   Item G
A.   Item A
B.   Item B
```

The *<IMG>* Tag

The <IMG> tag wins the prize for being the most heavily attributed by Netscape (at least currently). You can add the attributes ALIGN, WIDTH, HEIGHT, BORDER, VSPACE, and HSPACE to <IMG>, all of which enhance the appearance of the graphics in your Web documents.

Actually, the ALIGN attribute itself isn't new to you—it's available in both HTML 2.0 and 3.0. Netscape does have the following additional values for it, though, which can be used to more precisely align graphics and text:

♦ TEXTTOP. Aligns graphics to the top of a line of text. This is as opposed to the TOP value, which aligns the graphic to the top of the line (which could include another graphic, and hence be much higher).

♦ ABSMIDDLE. Aligns the image with the absolute middle of the current line of text.

♦ BASELINE. Aligns the image with the baseline value of the current line of text.

♦ ABSBOTTOM. Aligns the graphic with the absolute bottom of the current line of text. (Absolute bottom means it takes into consideration the descending letters in the line of text, like *y*, *g*, *q*, etc.)

You may notice that Netscape's added values are used to align the image to the text, which runs counter to our understanding of the ALIGN attribute up until now. For that reason, among others, I recommend sticking to either the HTML 2.0 or 3.0 specification for <IMG ALIGN>. Not only is the HTML version consistent, but, in most cases, these Netscape values are just overkill.

WIDTH and HEIGHT generally appear together, as in the following format:

```
<IMG SRC="URL" WIDTH="number" HEIGHT="number">
```

Both *number* placeholders are the desired dimensions of the graphic file. This is useful for the following two reasons:

♦ It allows Netscape to create space for the graphic without rendering it first, which speeds the display of the page.

♦ It allows you to resize the graphic to a desired width and height.

> **Tip:** Resizing graphics in this way doesn't change the size of the graphic file or the time it takes to download it. For best speed, use a graphics application to create thumbnails instead of the HEIGHT and WIDTH attributes.

To change the size of the border (or to add one to graphics that aren't also hyperlinks), you can use the BORDER attribute. This attribute also accepts a number in pixels, so that the following example results in a rather thick border around the image, as shown in figure 19.7:

```
<IMG SRC="image.gif" BORDER="10">
```

Figure 19.7

The BORDER attribute.

Finally, remember that using the LEFT and RIGHT values for ALIGN (which are available in Netscape as well as in HTML 3.0) causes your image to change from an inline image to a "floating" image. Netscape offers the attributes VSPACE and HSPACE to add additional space around a floating image, so that text doesn't press up against the image. These attributes take the following format where *number* is in pixels:

```
<IMG SRC="URL" ALIGN="LEFT/RIGHT" VSPACE="number" HSPACE="number">
```

The VSPACE number "pads" the image above and below, while HSPACE adds white space to the left and right.

Example: Netscape Attributes at Work

This example will concentrate on the added attributes and attribute values in Netscape HTML. You can do some interesting things with lists, horizontal rules, and images.

First, create a new document from your template and enter Listing 19.3.

Listing 19.3   Netscape Attributes to Common HTML Tags

```
<BODY>
<CENTER>
<H2>About My Family</H2>
</CENTER>
<H3>Me -- Richard Thompson</H3>
<IMG SRC="doomed.gif" ALIGN="RIGHT" HSPACE="4" VSPACE="4">
<P>Hi, I'm Richard and I'm 12 years old. I like to play baseball, hang
out, listen to music and play with my best friends Bill and Mike. I guess
school is okay, but I have more fun at the Y, where I'm on the
Sidekickers soccer team, which won second place last year at the city
tourney. I'm into computers and video games, and I spend a lot of time on
the Web. My favorite game right now is Doomed, like in the picture.</P>
<H3>Dad -- Robert Thompson</H3>
<HR SIZE="3" WIDTH="50%" ALIGN="CENTER">
<P>My Dad, Bob, works at BigCorp Inc. as a Sales Manager. Basically what
he sells is computer stuff, although he doesn't really do it so much
unless the customers are really big serious ones like Ford or GM or
something. He travels a lot, but he brings me home cool computer stuff,
too. He takes off for vacations in the summer mostly, and last summer we
went fishing in Oklahoma. I didn't think there was much reason to go to
OK, but the fishing was cool, and we stayed in a little cabin that didn't
have phones or TV.</P>
```

continues

Listing 19.3 Continued

```
<HR SIZE="3" WIDTH="50%" ALIGN="CENTER">
<H3>Sister -- Julie Thompson</H3>
<P>My sister isn't really a whole lot like me in that she is a brat. I
think we'd get along better if it wasn't for this list.<BR>
List about Julie:<BR>
<UL TYPE="SQUARE">
<LI> She's a dork
<LI> She's not good at sharing
<LI> She keeps saying that Rusty is her dog, but he's not cause she's too
young
<LI> She doesn't understand anything about cars
<LI> She doesn't throw a baseball very far
</UL>
Of course there's other stuff, but I don't want to drag her through it on
the Web.</P>
<HR SIZE="3" WIDTH="50%" ALIGN="CENTER">
<H3>This page looks coolest in <A HREF="http://www.netscape.com/
">Netscape Navigator</A>.</H3>
</BODY>
```

Some of Netscape's added attributes are useful, but this is essentially a page you could create with HTML 3.0 standard elements. That's not to say that Netscape isn't good for tweaking the appearance of your page, though (see fig. 19.8).

Client-Pull Tags and Attributes

Client-pull is another concept that began with Netscape, but should catch on with other browsers (Microsoft Internet Explorer already supports it). The client-pull tag and attributes allow you to automatically load another HTML page after a prede-termined amount of time. You can also use these tags to reload, or "refresh," the same HTML document over and over.

The client-pull concept introduces you to the <META> tag, which is used in the head of your document. For client-pull, the <META> tag takes the attributes HTTP-EQUIV and CONTENT. Client-pull follows this format:

```
<HEAD>
<META HTTP-EQUIV="REFRESH" CONTENT="seconds; URL="new URL">
</HEAD>
```

Unfortunately, this is a little messy compared to most HTML tags, so we'll have to wade through it. The HTTP-EQUIV attribute always takes the value REFRESH in client-pull; it only loads a new document if the CONTENT attribute includes an URL. Otherwise, it refreshes (reloads) the current document.

Figure. 19.8

Your Netscape-
enhanced
example.

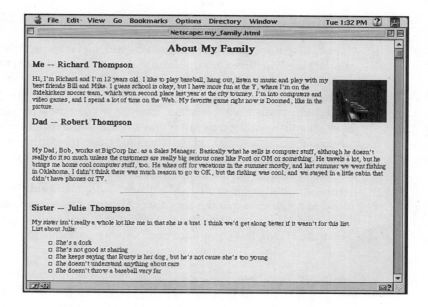

The CONTENT attribute accepts a number for the amount of time you want the browser to wait before the next page is loaded (or the current page is refreshed). Then it accepts a colon and the statement URL=, followed by a valid URL for the page that should be loaded automatically.

Here's an example that just refreshes the current page after waiting ten seconds:

```
<HEAD>
<META HTTP-EQUIV="REFRESH" CONTENT="10">
</HEAD>
```

And, in this example, we'll use client-pull to load a new page after waiting 15 seconds:

```
<HEAD>
<META HTTP-EQUIV="REFRESH" CONTENT="15; URL="http://www.fakecorp.com/
index.html">
</HEAD>
```

One of the best uses for client-pull is as part of a "front door" page to your site. You can assume that a user's browser that accepts the client-pull commands is also capable of rendering Netscape-specific commands. Users with browsers that don't recognize client-pull can click another link on the page to allow them to view regular HTML 2.0 pages.

Summary

Netscapisms are, as defined in this chapter, Netscape-specific HTML codes that go against the "no direct manipulation" theory of standard HTML. These HTML-like tags allow you to directly control things like font size, text alignment, and image alignment.

In some cases, these Netscape ideas have been incorporated into HTML 3.0 level specifications—although not always in the same exact way. When possible, you should use the "official" HTML tags for these functions. Style sheets described in Chapter 18 are especially effective replacements for many of the Netscapisms.

When you do decide to use a Netscape-specific tag, you should be careful that you warn your users of such. Many users will not be able to view those tags, so you need to make sure that the tags are not being used to communicate something that will be lost on others. If this is the case, it may even be in your best interest to create separate HTML 2.0-compliant and Netscape-specific sites.

Review Questions

1. What is the HTML 3.0 substitute for Netscape's <CENTER> tag?

2. What do the six-digit numbers used for Netscape background colors represent? What numbering system is this?

3. What is the ALINK attribute to the <BODY> tag used to set?

4. What, according to the text, is the most annoying tag ever conceived?

5. Does the <WBR> tag require the <NOBR> tag? Does it do the same exact thing that <BR> does?

6. True or false. Setting the BASEFONT value to something other than one changes the size of all fonts in the document?

7. Does the SIZE attribute for <FONT> require either a plus (+) or minus (–) sign?

8. True or false. The NOSHADE attribute for the <HR> tag accepts a percentage as its value.

9. Can you change numbering and bullet styles in the middle of lists?

10. What attributes to the <IMG> tag are used to add extra space between the image and text.

11. What attribute and attribute values create a floating image when used with the <IMG> tag?

Review Exercises

1. Create an HTML style sheet based alternative to the <BLINK> tag.

2. Translate the following numbers to hexadecimal: 1, 35, 256.

3. Using the text from a poem or song, render a verse three different ways, using the <PRE> tag, using <BR> to end each line, and using the <NOBR> and <WBR>. What is the difference between each?

4. Take the words "Catch a Wave" and using the SIZE attribute with the <FONT> tag, make the C very large and each letter smaller until you get to the *e*, which should be the smallest letter.

5. Create a horizontal line that's three pixels high, takes up 50 percent of the browser window, and is right justified.

6. Use the different attributes for list tags to create a full-fledged outline, using large roman numerals for the main headings, capital letters for the second level, regular numbers for the third level, and lowercase letters for the forth level.

7. Using client-pull, create a "front door" page that automatically loads a Netscape-specific index page for browsers compatible with client-pull. The page should also include a link to HTML 2.0 pages for browsers that don't recognize client-pull.

## CHAPTER 20

Netscape Frames

One of the most exciting Netscape-only additions to HTML recently has been the frames specification. Although submitted to the W3C, frames, for now, remain almost exclusively Netscape-only. (Keep watching the W3C to see when that may change. Even if it remains a Netscape standard, more browsers should begin supporting frames.)

> **Note:** Late in the writing of this book, Microsoft announced that Internet Explorer 3.0 had begun alpha testing, and that it would support the Netscape frames specification. Other browsers are sure to follow.

Frames aren't overwhelmingly difficult to add to your pages, although they do require a slight shift in thought. Although they seem similar to tables at first, frames are considerably more powerful. So much so, in fact, that frames can even divide your Web page so that it is accessing more than one URL at a time.

The Idea Behind Netscape Frames

Netscape frames are basically another way you can create a unique interface for your Web site. By dividing the page into different parts—each of which can be updated separately—there becomes a number of different interface elements you can offer. Even a simple use of the frame specification lets you add interface graphics or a corporate logo to a site, while the rest of your page scrolls beneath it (see fig. 20.1).

Figure 20.1

A simple frames
interface.

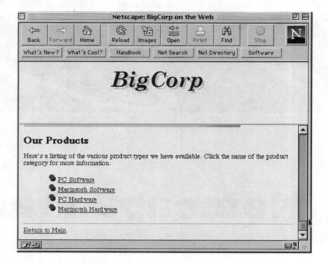

Using frames in this way takes you one step closer to the ideal Web interface, because it makes it as intuitive and universal as possible. Frames are ideal for the following:

♦ **Table of Contents (TOC)**. By placing the TOC in a "column" on your Web page, people can click around your site or your documentation pages without being forced to constantly move "back" to the contents page. Instead, users simply click a new content level in the static frame.

♦ **Fixed interface elements**. As mentioned previously, you can force clickable graphics, logos, and other information to stay in one fixed portion of the screen, while the rest of your document scrolls in another frame.

♦ **Better forms and results**. Frames also enable you to create a form in one frame and offer results in another frame. This is something we're beginning to see extensively with Web search pages (look to fig. 20.2). With the search text box always available, you're free to change search phrases or pinpoint your search more quickly, without moving back in the hierarchy of the Web pages.

Creating Frames

Probably most unique among the HTML-style tags so far is the <FRAMESET> tag. This container is required for frames-style pages—but it also replaces the <BODY> tag completely on these pages. When you use frames then, you're committed to using them completely—you can't just add frames to part of your page. On a typical page, <FRAMESET> is added like this:

```
<HTML>
<HEAD>
...HEAD markup...
</HEAD>
<FRAMESET>
...Frames and other HTML markup...
</FRAMESET>
</HTML>
```

The `<FRAMESET>` tag can accept two attributes: ROWS and COLS. Both attributes accept either numerical values (size in pixels), percentages, or a combination of both. The value * can also be used to suggest that a particular row or column should take up the rest of the page. The number of rows or columns is suggested by the number of values you give the attribute. These attributes take the following format:

```
<FRAMESET ROWS="numbers,percentages,*" COLS="numbers,percentages, *">
```

An example like the following would create two rows: one 50 pixels long and another row that took up the rest of the page:

```
<FRAMESET ROWS="50,*">
```

(This would be useful for a page that displays a fixed map or graphic at the top.) The following example would create a Web interface with two columns: one on the leftmost 25 percent of the screen and one on the other 75 percent:

```
<FRAMESET COLS="25%,75%">
```

This would be a good way to set up a documentation (or FAQ) site, that offered contents in the first frame and actual text and examples in the second, larger frame. Each `<FRAMESET>` statement will work with one attribute or the other. That means you can only create a frameset with either rows or columns. In order to create rows within columns (or vice-versa), you can nest `<FRAMESET>` statements. For instance, the following will create a page with two columns:

```
<FRAMESET COLS="25%,75%">
   <FRAMESET ROWS="50%,50%">
   </FRAMESET>
   <FRAMESET ROWS="10%,90%">
   </FRAMESET>
</FRAMESET>
```

The first column will be divided into two rows that take up 50 percent of that column a piece. The second column will be divided into two rows, the first taking ten percent and the second taking the rest of that column. Although this doesn't display anything in and of itself, it creates logical breaks in the page that look like figure 20.2. You'll come back to nesting `<FRAMESET>` tags as you develop more advanced frame interfaces in this chapter.

Figure 20.2

The logical breaks
created by nested
<FRAMESET>
tags.

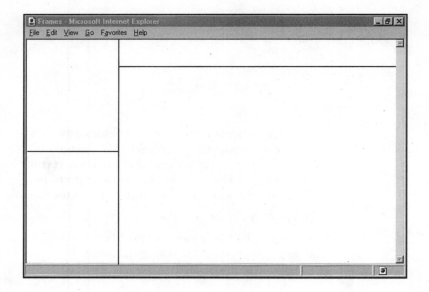

The *<FRAME>* Tag

The <FRAME> tag is used within the <FRAMESET> container to determine what will actually appear in a particular frame. Each <FRAME> tag is an empty tag—and it's not unlike the <LI> tags you add to HTML lists. It's simply there, within the <FRAMESET> container, to determine what URL or name is associated with the particular frame it defines. It takes the following format:

```
<FRAMESET COLS/ROWS="numbers">
<FRAME SRC="URL">
...
</FRAMESET>
```

The SRC attribute is used to tell the frame what URL should be loaded in that frame. For instance, the following would create two frame rows—one that loaded the URL index.html at the top of the Web page and one that loaded the URL help.html at the bottom of the page (see fig. 20.3):

```
<FRAMESET ROWS="50%,50%">
<FRAME SRC="index.html">
<FRAME SRC="help.html">
</FRAMESET>
```

Figure 20.3

The <FRAME> tag assigns URLs to each frame window.

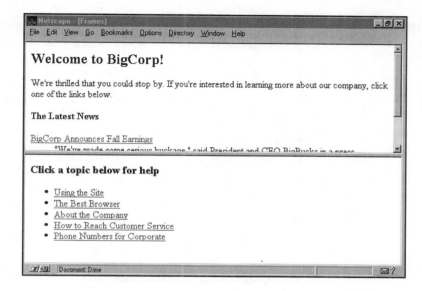

By using the <FRAME> tag, you create what's known as a *frame window*. Each window corresponds to a "row" or "column" definition in the <FRAMESET> tag, but nothing is drawn or displayed until an appropriate <FRAME> tag is used to define each individual window.

Example: A Simple Frame Document

You'll essentially create the same document that was shown in the previous figure, but you should feel free to play with the numbers a bit to see how different percentages and even different attributes to <FRAMESET> changes how the page displays. Enter Listing 20.1 in your text editor.

On the CD

Listing 20.1 *smpframe.html* Simple Frame Document

```
<HTML>
<HEAD>
<TITLE>Frame Example</TITLE>
</HEAD>
<FRAMESET ROWS="25%,75%">
<FRAME SRC="menu.html">
<FRAME SRC="help.html">
</FRAMESET>
</HTML>
```

While you're at it, you also need to create some files to put in those frames. If you have some HTML documents hanging around, you can rename menu.html and help.html to any HTML file you'd like to load. For this example, any HTML document names will work (see fig. 20.4).

Figure 20.4

Loading separate
HTML documents
into a frame-based
page.

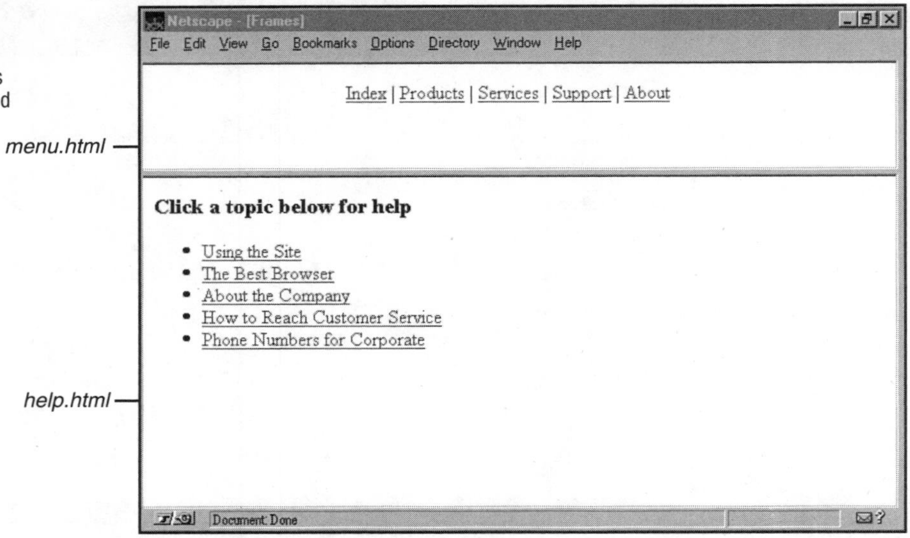

menu.html —

help.html —

If you'd like to experiment further, try changing the <FRAMESET> tag in Listing 20.1
to the following:

```
<FRAMESET COLS="25%,75%">
```

Or, change the percentages to see how that affects your layout.

Attributes for *<FRAME>*

Aside from SRC, the <FRAME> tag can accept the attributes NAME, MARGINWIDTH, MARGINHEIGHT,
SCROLLING, and NORESIZE. All of these but NAME are appearance-oriented. Let's deal
with them first and come back to NAME in a moment.

MARGINWIDTH and MARGINHEIGHT are used to control the right/left margins and the
top/bottom margins of the text and graphics within a frame, respectively. Each
takes a numerical value in pixels. For example:

```
<FRAME SRC="text.html" MARGINWIDTH="5" MARGINHEIGHT="5">
```

This creates a five pixel border between the contents of text.html and the frame
edges.

SCROLLING can accept the values yes, no, and auto and is used to determine whether
or not scroll bars will appear in the frame window. The default value is auto, and this
is probably the best to use in most cases. Since users have all different screen
resolutions and available browser window space, even short documents will
sometimes need to be scrolled.

The NORESIZE attribute doesn't require a value assignment, and is used to keep the
user from resizing a frame window. (Frame windows can be resized by dragging
the frame with the mouse in the viewer window.)

An example of SCROLLING and NORESIZE would be:

```
<FRAME SRC="text.html" SCROLLING="yes" NORESIZE>
```

The *<NOFRAMES>* Tag

This container tag is used to contain HTML markup intended for browsers that do
not support the frames specification. Text and HTML tags inside the <NOFRAMES>
container are ignored by frames-capable browsers. All others should generally
ignore the other frames tags (which they won't recognize), but display the text in
between the <NOFRAMES> tags. The following is an example:

```
<FRAMESET ROWS="25%,75%">
<FRAME SRC="menu.html">
<FRAME SRC="index.html">
<NOFRAMES>
<P>This page requires a Frames capable browser to view. If you'd prefer,
you can access our <a href="2_index.html">HTML 2.0 compliant pages</a>
to view this information without the frames interface.</P>
</NOFRAMES>
</FRAMESET>
```

Example: Frames and No Frames

Now we'll create another example, this time using the attributes and additional tags
you've seen since the last example. Create a new HTML document and enter Listing
20.2 (use your own HTML document names for <FRAME SRC> if desired).

On the CD

Listing 20.2 *frames2.html* **Frames and No Frames**

```
<HTML>
<HEAD>
<TTLE>Frames Example #2</TITLE>
</HEAD>
<FRAMESET COLS="25%,75%">
<NOFRAMES>
<P>If you are seeing this message, then your browser isn't capable of
viewing Frames. Please access our <A HREF="2_index.html">HTML 2.0 compli-
ant</A> Web pages.</P>
<P>If you like, you can go directly to these pages in our site:
<UL>
<LI><A HREF="products.html">Product pages</A>
<LI><A HREF="support.html">Support pages</A>
<LI><A HREF="help.html">Help page</A>
</UL>
</NOFRAMES>
```

continues

Listing 20.2 Continued

```
<FRAME SRC="index.html" MARGINWIDTH="5" MARGINHEIGHT="2" SCROLLING="no">
<FRAME SRC="info.html" MARGINWIDTH="5" MARGINHEIGHT="2" NORESIZE>
</FRAMESET>
</HTML>
```

Notice that you've used the attribute NORESIZE with the <FRAME> tags for the second column. What's interesting about this is that it forces the first column to also be non-resizable, since the columns share a common frame border (see fig. 20.5). This is the case with any <FRAME> tag.

Figure 20.5

The <FRAME> and <NOFRAME> tags in action.

This frame border can't be resized

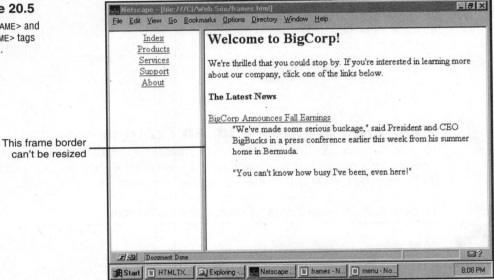

Experiment with different values for the <FRAME> attributes and see what makes a big difference in terms of margins, scrolling, and resizing. Also, if you have access to a browser that isn't frames-capable, load the page and see how the <NOFRAMES> markup looks (see fig. 20.6).

Figure 20.6

The <NOFRAMES>
HTML message.

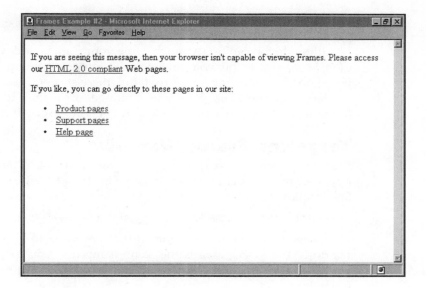

Targeting Frame Windows

So far, you've seen that frame windows offer you the ability to load URLs independent of one another, so that you can present two (or more) different HTML pages in the same browser window. But what good is this to you? In many cases, it may be useful to offer multiple documents at once.

For instance, with what you know now, you could use frames to add a button bar image map to the top of every HTML page you create. But that would get tedious—each link would have to point to a new frame document that would then load the button bar and the next document.

But what if you could just leave the button bar in the top frame window and load a new document in the other window? You can do just that, if you know a little about *targeting.*

The *NAME* Attribute

First, you need to name your frame windows—at least, you have to name the windows you might want to change. This is accomplished with the NAME attribute to the <FRAME> tag, which takes the following format:

```
<FRAME SRC="original URL" NAME="window_name">
```

This shouldn't look too foreign to you, as it's a little like the way that the NAME attribute works for <A NAME> links. Once the frame window has a distinct name, you can access it directly from other frame windows. An example of this is the following:

```
<FRAME SRC="index.html" NAME="main_viewer">
```

Although you can pretty much name your frame window anything you want, there is one restriction: you can't start the name with an underscore character (_). If you do, the name will be ignored. But, there's a good reason for that.

The underscore is used to signal a number of "magic" target names. You'll get to those after you learn how to target regular browser windows.

Targeting Frame Windows

With your frame successfully named, you're ready to target the name with a hypertext link. This is accomplished with the TARGET attribute to a typical <A> anchor tag. It follows this format:

```
<A HREF="new_URL" TARGET="window_name">link text</A>
```

The *new_URL* is the new document that you want to have appear in the frame window. The *window_name* is the same name that you used to name the frame windows with the NAME attribute to the <FRAME> tag. An example would be the following:

```
<A HREF="products.html" TARGET="main_viewer">View Products</A>
```

Example: A Reason to Use Frames

Now, you finally have a good excuse for using frames. Let's create a document with two frames (in rows). In the top frame, you can put a quick HTML menu of possibilities. In the second frame, put most of the information from your Web site. That's where you'll display the actual pages you've created. The top frame will just be for static controls.

This will take two different listings, and both need to be complete Web documents (see Listings 20.3 and 20.4).

On the CD

Listing 20.3 *control2.html* **Links for the Top Frame**

```
<HTML>
<HEAD>
<TITLE>Controls</TITLE>
</HEAD>
<BODY>
<DIV ALIGN="CENTER">
<A HREF="index.html" TARGET="big_window">Index Page</A> ¦
<A HREF="products.html" TARGET="big_window">Products</A> ¦
<A HREF="service.html" TARGET="big_window">Customer Service</A> ¦
<A HREF="support.html" TARGET="big_window">Tech Support</A> ¦
<A HREF="about.html" TARGET="big_window">About Us</A>
</DIV>
</BODY>
</HTML>
```

That's the control document (save it as `control2.html`). Now, you'll create the main frame document that will contain both this control document (at the top) and whatever other documents it feels like tossing at the other frame, called `big_window`.

Listing 20.4 *frames.html* **The Frames Document**

```
<HTML>
<HEAD>
<TITLE>BigCorp World</TITLE>
</HEAD>
<FRAMESET ROWS="10%,90%">
<FRAME SRC="controls.html" SCROLLING="no" NORESIZE>
<FRAME SRC="index.html" NAME="big_window">
</FRAMESET>
</HTML>
```

Save the second file as `frames.html`—that's the one you'll load in your browser window. Notice that you've told the second frame (the one named `big_window`) to load `index.html` initially. While an empty frame is possible, you generally don't want to do that—things work better with a default page in every frame. You've also chosen certain attributes for the first frame. That's just personal preference, but I'd rather have my viewer resize their browser window to see all of the controls, so I won't allow that window to scroll.

> **Tip:** Whenever possible, view your pages to make sure they're not abnormally wide or that you're forcing users to scroll constantly to read your pages.

Figure 20.7

Up top, it's always `control2.html`; but below, it's an ever-changing URL.

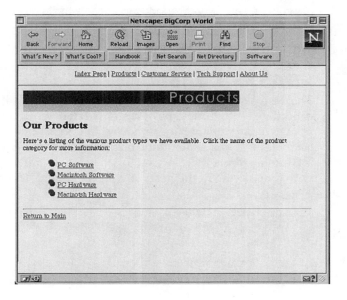

Finally, you can load `frames.html` in Netscape (see fig. 20.7). If all goes well, you should be able to click the menu items in the top frame, and change the content in the bottom one!

Advanced Targeting

Other link-related tags have been updated to accept a TARGET attribute along with the anchor tag. For instance, client-side image maps have their AREA tag updated to accept a target window, so that an area defined to access a certain link loads that page into the target. This is the format:

```
<AREA SHAPE="shape" COORDS="numbers" HREF="URL" TARGET="window_name">
```

Likewise, you can add a TARGET attribute to the <FORM> tag. Remember that it's the <FORM> container tag that tells the browser the URL for the script that is required to process the form data. In that same tag, you can also specify a target window for the results that are received from the server. If you want users to be able to use your form repeatedly (to allow them to generate different results), you can leave both the form and the results in separate frames. This attribute takes the following format:

```
<FORM ACTION="Script_URL" TARGET="window_name">
```

> **Note:** Just in case you're wondering why you haven't learned about these attributes before (like in the client-map and target chapters), it's because they don't necessarily exist. That is, a browser has to be specifically programmed to add these attributes to older tags. If a browser is programmed to deal with frames (and it happens to follow this early Netscape specification), then the browser programmers will add support for these tags. In other browsers, they'll (hopefully) just be ignored.

<BASE> Targets

The last example you went through (Listing 20.4) would have been a great candidate for this one type of target. What if you want the majority of your links to point to a particular frame window? In the early example, you created a file called `control2.html` that had nothing but hypertext links. Each one of those links required a TARGET attribute that pointed to the `big_window`. You could have made that easier with a <BASE> tag in the head of your document. Use this format:

```
<HEAD>
<BASE TARGET="window_name">
</HEAD>
```

A good example of this for the previous example would be:

```
<BASE TARGET="big_window">
```

You don't have to specify the target window in each individual anchor in an HTML document that has this tag in its head. Now all links will default to the target defined in the <BASE> tag.

> **Note:** If you *do* use TARGET attributes, they will override the <BASE> tag for that particular link.

"Magic" Targets

Here's why you can't name frame windows with something that starts with an underscore. The "magic" target names all start with an underscore, which signals to the browser that they should treat this link extra special. The following are some examples:

♦ **TARGET="_blank"**—The URL specified in this link will always be loaded in a new blank browser window.

♦ **TARGET="_self"**—This is used for overriding a <BASE> tag, and forcing a link to load in the same window that it's clicked in.

♦ **TARGET="_parent"**—This causes the document to load in the current window's parent—generally, the frame window immediately preceding in the <FRAMESET> definition. If no parent exists, it acts like "_self".

♦ **TARGET="_top"**—The document is loaded in the topmost frame of the current browser window.

Basically, these magic targets are designed to let you break out of the current <FRAMESET> structure in some way. Experiment with them to see how you can move around to different windows.

Thoughts on Using Frames

I personally have two problems with the frame interface, and both of them revolve around those browser control buttons that one gets used to after a few years of working on the Web.

First, using a frame-based document as an interface for your Web site makes the Back and Forward buttons on the user's Web browser program nearly useless. As far as the browser is concerned, no completely new pages have been loaded. So, if you click Back, you'll go to the site you visited before you loaded the frames document—no matter how long or far you've been surfing *inside* the frames.

The answer to this is simple. Take special care that you're providing your user with enough controls to move around in your Web site. If you're using a specific frame window for controls, remember to give your user as many links in that window as possible. Let them go directly to the main pages of your site and never bury a user five or six pages deep without giving them an easy way back.

The second problem is related. If you've ever spent any time accessing a site that uses a frames interface, you'll notice that the URL reported by the browser doesn't ever change. If you used a document called `frames.html` for instance, then the URL will reflect that for the entire time that a user accesses your site.

This many not seem like a problem, except that it defeats the bookmark option of many browsers and makes it impossible to cut-and-paste URLs into other applications (at least currently). The solution is simple—put the URL for each page somewhere in the document, perhaps somewhere close to the bottom of the page in a smaller font (use `<H5>` or `<H6>`). Hopefully, browsers will implement more elegant solutions in the near future. In fact, Netscape's Atlas version (in beta testing at the time of writing) is rumored to be an answer to some of these issues.

The Elegant Frame Interface

Now I'm not a huge fan of using a great number of frames, although I've seen some snazzy implementation of three or four frames on a page. Let's use three different frame windows. One will hold a client-side graphic for your site, one will offer a "table of contents" page, and one will display the actual information for your site.

You'll need a fixed window for the client-side map and two dynamic windows. One will load the parts of the table of contents, and one will load the information pages. Use Listing 20.5 for the client-side map.

On the CD

Listing 20.5 *control3.html* **HTML for a Client-Side Map**

```
<HTML>
<HEAD>
<TITLE>Control Map</TITLE>
<BASE TARGET="toc_window">
</HEAD>
<BODY>
<DIV ALIGN="CENTER">
<IMG SRC="control.gif" USEMAP="#control">
</DIV>
<MAP NAME="control">
<AREA SHAPE="rect" COORDS="0,0,61,22" HREF="index_toc.html">
<AREA SHAPE="rect" COORDS="62,0,146,22" HREF="prod_toc.html">
<AREA SHAPE="rect" COORDS="146,0,222,22" HREF="serv_toc.html">
<AREA SHAPE="rect" COORDS="222,0,296,22" HREF="supp_toc.html">
<AREA SHAPE="rect" COORDS="296,0,359,23" HREF="about_toc.html">
</MAP>
</BODY>
</HTML>
```

Notice that this graphic isn't designed to change the main window. It's going to change the documents that show up in your table of contents window. Each of the TOC documents should be a simple HTML list of links that shows the branch that the users have traveled down. For instance, let's create the document `serv_toc.html` (see Listing 20.6).

On the CD

Listing 20.6 *serv_toc.html* **A Sample TOC Document**

```
<HTML>
<HEAD>
<TITLE>Service Contents</TITLE>
<BASE TARGET="main_window">
</HEAD>
<BODY>
<UL>
   <LI><A HREF="products.html">Main Products Page</A>
   <UL>
       <LI><A HREF="software.html">Software</A>
       <LI><A HREF="hardware.html">Hardware</A>
       <LI><A HREF="furniture.html">Furniture</A>
       <LI><A HREF="access.html">Accessories</A>
   </UL>
</UL>
</BODY>
</HTML>
```

See what I'm getting at here? The image map will change these controls, and then these links will change the main frame window. It gives a nice, easy interface to the whole site. Now let's create the frames page which we'll call `main.html` (see Listing 20.7).

On the CD

Listing 20.7 *main.html* **The Main Frames Interface**

```
<HTML>
<HEAD>
<TITLE>BigCorp on the Web</TITLE>
</HEAD>
<FRAMESET ROWS="15%,85%">
<FRAME SRC="controls.html" SCROLLING="no" NORESIZE>
   <FRAMESET COLS="30%,70%">
   <FRAME SRC="index_toc.html" NAME="toc_window" MARGINWIDTH="3"
    MARGINHEIGHT="3">
   <FRAME SRC="index.html" NAME="main_window" MARGINWIDTH="3"
    MARGINHEIGHT="3">
   </FRAMESET>
</FRAMESET>
</HTML>
```

This one doesn't take up much space. Here's what you've done. The first <FRAMESET> created two rows—one for image map and one for the rest of the page. In that bottom row, you used another <FRAMESET> to create two columns within that row. The smaller is for the table of contents pages. In the other frame window, you put all of the main HTML documents. Get it? Look at figure 20.8 to see how the whole thing looks in Netscape.

> **Note:** For this example to work well, you may need to create some other files like `index_toc.html`, or rename files to work in your main window.

Figure 20.8

A three-way interface is attractive, but it can be tough to manage.

TOC pages ——

Main HTML documents ——

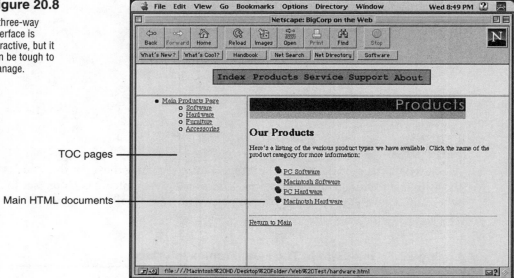

Summary

Netscape frames are an elegant, if currently Netscape-specific, way to load multiple Web pages in a single browser window. Creating frames requires a few new tags, including the <FRAMESET> container and the <FRAME> empty tag. <FRAMESET> containers can be nested to create columns within rows for multiple frame windows on a single page.

Dealing with frames also introduces the concept of "targeting," which means naming frame windows and using the attribute TARGET to point anchor tags toward the named window. With targeting, however, comes the power of frames. With these two concepts, you can create detailed, elegant interfaces for your Web pages that really help you get a lot of information across quickly.

Review Questions

1. What makes <FRAMESET> unique among the tags you've learned so far?

2. True or false. A single <FRAMESET> can create either rows or columns for your page, but not both.

3. What does this page look like in a browser?

```
<HTML>
<HEAD>
<TITLE>Test</TITLE>
</HEAD>
<FRAMESET COLS="25%, 75%">
<FRAMESET ROWS="100%">
</FRAMESET>
<FRAMSET ROWS="50%, *">
</FRAMESET>
</FRAMESET>
</HTML>
```

4. What's the default setting for the SCROLLING attribute to the <FRAME> tag?

5. Why does text in between <NOFRAMES> appear in non-frame browsers, but not in frame-capable browsers?

6. What is the one rule for naming frame windows with the NAME attribute to the <FRAME> tag?

7. Aside from the anchor tag, what two other tags can accept the TARGET attribute?

8. Why does using the <BASE TARGET> tag and attribute make targeting frame windows easier?

9. True or false. "Magic" targets are shortcuts for more complicated TARGET statements.

10. What two problems do frames cause for your user?

Review Exercises

1. Use the `<BASE>` tag for the following:

```
<BODY>
<UL>
<LI> <A HREF="index.html" TARGET="main_window">Index</A>
<LI> <A HREF="feedback.html" TARGET="main_window">Feedback</A>
<LI> <A HREF="survey.html" TARGET="main_window">Survey</A>
</UL>
</BODY>
```

2. Create a frames document with two frames—one for a fixed image map interface and the other to act as a target for the pages of a Web site. Create the image map so that it targets the main frame window with new pages from the site.

3. Now, put the client-side image map at the bottom ten percent of the page, with the Web site pages targeted at the top.

4. Using clickable graphics, create an interface in a frame window along the left side of your page. On the right side, display the pages that are loaded by the form buttons. Make sure each clickable graphic appears below the one before it.

## CHAPTER 21

Internet Explorer Extensions

Not to be outdone by Netscape and others, Microsoft Internet Explorer adds a number of HTML-type tags and attributes that further enhance your ability to layout and customize your pages. It's difficult to say which browser offers support for more off-the-wall extensions—it basically depends on who's come out with the most recent version. There's a browser war on, and you can bet that standard HTML features won't be moving fast enough for Microsoft and Netscape.

In fact, at the time of this writing, Microsoft had just released an alpha (developers-only) version of Internet Explorer 3.0, which promises to support Netscape-style frames, the HTML 3.0 <INSERT> tag, and HTML 3.0 style sheets. All of these have been discussed in earlier chapters, but it's significant to note that a major force in the industry has decided to support these tags. (Of course, I can't make any guarantees concerning the final Internet Explorer 3.0 product.)

> **Note:** Using the extensions in this chapter probably warrants a "best viewed in Internet Explorer" or similar line of text on your page. But how can you tell if an extension is Internet Explorer only? You can track changes to Internet Explorer's HTML support, including tags created by Microsoft, at **http://www.microsoft.com/ie/author/htmlspec/html_toc.htm** on the Web.

Backgrounds and Fonts

Internet Explorer (IE) adds a number of extensions to the <BODY> tag, generally to affect the appearance of the background itself. IE also adds support for background sounds (sounds that are played by the browser as the page loads).

The BGPROPERTIES attribute can be used in conjunction with BACKGROUND specified by HTML 3.0. In IE-compatible browsers, this forces the background to work like a "watermark," which Microsoft defines as a background graphic that doesn't scroll. The only value for BGPROPERTIES is "fixed." The following is an example:

```
<BODY BACKGROUND="PATTERN.GIF" BGPROPERTIES="fixed">
```

As always, <BODY> is a container tag, so you'll need a </BODY> tag at then end of your HTML markup for this page.

The <BODY> tag can accept two other attributes in IE-compatible browsers: LEFTMARGIN and TOPMARGIN. Each of these accepts a value in pixels, specifying the amount of white space between the left and top sides of the browser window (respectively) and your text or graphics. For example:

```
<BODY LEFTMARGIN="30" TOPMARGIN="30">
```

<BGSOUND>

If you'd like your page to play a sound as the page loads into your user's browser, you can add that capability with the <BGSOUND> tag. You'll generally want to put it near the top of the <BODY> section of your HTML document, but that's only for your benefit—it'll load as it's recognized by the browser.

The <BGSOUND> tag is an empty tag that accepts two attributes: SRC and LOOP. SRC is used to specify the sound file that you want played. LOOP determines how many times you want the sound played, and can have a number for a value or the word "infinite" for constant playing. <BGSOUND> takes the following format:

```
<BGSOUND SRC="URL" LOOP="number/infinite">
```

An example of this might be:

```
<BGSOUND SRC="intro.au" LOOP="2">
```

In IE, the sound file can be a sound sample (.au or .wav files) or a MIDI (.mid or .midi) format sound file. Other browsers, if they support <BGSOUND>, may vary in their ability to play certain types of sounds.

> **Tip:** Be careful with LOOP="infinite". A constantly repeated sound, especially a system sound, might confuse your user into thinking there's something wrong with his or her computer. (Or it may just annoy your user.)

Font Color and Typeface

IE adds two attributes to Netscape's <FONT> tag: COLOR and FACE. Actually, you may remember that you were able to change the overall text color in Netscape. In IE, you can change the color for a single word (or even individual letters, if you've got a lot of time on your hands).

> **Note:** Unless everyone in the world has switched to IE by the time you read this, recognize that clever use of color and font faces can communicate something that is lost on other HTML users. When possible, use either the HTML style sheet or standard HTML markup to change font appearance and emphasize text.

To change the color of a font in the middle of your document's text, use the <FONT> container with the COLOR attribute, like this:

```
<FONT COLOR="#rrggbb/color name">new color text</FONT>
```

The COLOR attribute can accept either three two-digit hex numbers to describe a color, or a color name itself. For example, both of the following result in red text:

```
<FONT COLOR="#FF0000">This is red text</FONT>
```

```
<FONT COLOR="Red">This is also red text</FONT>
```

The FACE attribute can be used to change the actual typeface used in the IE browser window. Because different systems can offer different fonts, this attribute allows you to offer a list of font names. Each name will be tried in succession until a matching font name is found. The FACE attribute takes the following format:

```
<FONT FACE="name, name2, name3,...">
```

Look at the following example:

```
<FONT FACE="Arial, Helvetica, Times Roman">
```

Your browser will attempt to use the font Arial, and then fall back to Helvetica and Times Roman until it finds a font match on the user's computer system. If none of the fonts are found, a default font is used.

Example: A Study in Absurdity

Without being too coy here (and letting on that I'm not terribly fond of these IE tags), I'd like to create an example that not only makes use of these tags, but overuses them. One of the biggest problems with these IE tags is that they are so browser-specific that you can get yourself in trouble. Let's create a page that, when loaded in your copy of IE, will make you want to immediately unload it.

> **Note:** If you want to download a copy of IE, you can get it from **http://www.microsoft.com/ie/ie.htm**. There's no UNIX version (just various Windows versions and one for Macs) which is probably a good thing. If you're like me, you'd have a hard time trying to figure out what font names to use in UNIX for the <FONT FACE> tag.

To start, create a new HTML document and enter Listing 21.1.

On the CD

Listing 21.1 *ie_ext.html* Fonts, Sounds, and Background with IE Extensions

```
<BODY BACKGROUND="logo.gif" BGPROPERTIES="fixed">
<BGSOUND SRC="beep.wav" LOOP="infinite">
<H2><FONT FACE="Script, Times">Welcome <FONT COLOR="blue">to <FONT
COLOR="green">BigCorp!</H2>
<P> <FONT COLOR="#FF00FF" FACE="Arial, Helvetica">If you've got Internet
Explorer, then you're probably having the experience of your life. There's
<FONT COLOR="red">nothing wrong with your system<FONT COLOR="#FF00FF">,
We've just added a little noise to help make your stay more pleasant!</P>
<HR>
<P> <FONT FACE="Courier, Courier New" COLOR="blue"> Click below if you're
ready to go somewhere else within our site!<BR> <UL>
<LI>Head over to our <A HREF="products.html">Product pages</A>
<LI>Learn <FONT COLOR="red">a little more <A HREF="about.html">About
BigCorp</A>
<LI>Need some help? Try <A HREF='support.html'>Tech Support</A>
<LI><FONT FACE="Times, Times Roman">Wanna buy something?
<A HREF="service.html">Customer Service</A> is a click away.
</UL>
</P>
</BODY>
```

Take a look at figure 20.1 for an example screenshot of this listing, but a graphic can't do it justice. To truly experience this, you'll need to load it in your own copy of Internet Explorer. Also, change beep.wav to any other annoying sound you happen to have lying around and are able to copy to the same directory as your HTML document.

Figure 21.1

This page is a poster-child for conservative use of IE HTML extensions.

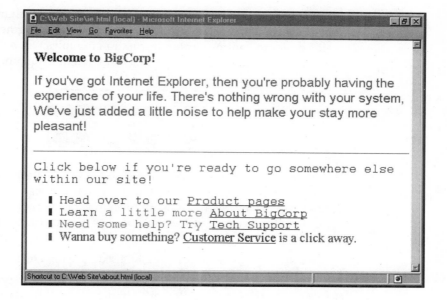

IE Extensions for Tables

Internet Explorer fully implements the HTML 3.0 standard for tables (described in Chapter 15), with some additional attributes, again targeted to users that would prefer to have more control over the appearance of the table. I personally like these extensions a little more than the others we've seen from IE. Why? Because the table standard is already geared directly to the graphical browser community. These additions make them even more attractive, without to much effort. Other browsers will probably support these extensions quickly.

Most interesting is the BGCOLOR attribute, which can be used to change the background color of rows or columns. The BGCOLOR attribute accepts three two-digit hex numbers or a color name and works with the <TABLE>, <TR>, and <TD> tags (see Listing 21.2).

Listing 21.2   IE Table Extensions

```
<TABLE BORDER="1" CELLSPACING="2" CELLPADDING="2">
<TR><TH>JOB</TH><TH>MONDAY</TH><TH>TUESDAY</TH><TH>WEDNESDAY</TH>
<TR BGCOLOR="#000022"><TH>Clean</TH><TD>Mike</TD><TD>Bill</TD><TD>Sue</TD>
<TR><TH>Cook</TH><TD>Sue</TD><TD>Mike</TD><TD>Bill</TD>
<TR BGCOLOR="#000022"><TH>Wash</TH><TD>Bill</TD><TD>Sue</TD><TD>Mike</TD>
</TABLE>
```

As you can see in figure 21.2, you can do more than just change the background color of tables for aesthetic reasons. As accountants and engineers have known for years, it's easier to communicate information in tables when you're able to shade different rows to make it clear what data is related to what other data and headers.

Figure 21.2

Using color in
IE tables.

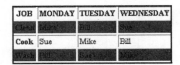

The other attributes, BORDERCOLOR and BORDERLIGHT, are used to change the color of the border in IE tables. They must be used with the BORDER attribute to the <TABLE> tag (or the <TR> or <TD> tag if you want to change border colors in mid-table). Both accept either three two-digit hex numbers or a color name. The following is an example:

```
<TABLE BORDER="3" BORDERCOLOR="blue" BORDERLIGHT="lightblue">
```

The BORDERCOLOR value affects the top portion of IE's 3D style table border. The BORDERLIGHT value changes the "lower" (shadow) part of IE's border. Basically, these values just let you toy with the 3D effect on IE table borders. Listing 21.3 shows another example using the above line of code.

Listing 21.3 Border Colors with IE Tables

```
<TABLE BORDER="1" CELLSPACING="2" CELLPADDING="2" BORDERCOLOR="blue"
BORDERLIGHT="lightblue">
<TR><TH>JOB</TH><TH>MONDAY</TH><TH>TUESDAY</TH><TH>WEDNESDAY</TH>
<TR><TH>Clean</TH><TD>Mike</TD><TD>Bill</TD><TD>Sue</TD>
<TR><TH>Cook</TH><TD>Sue</TD><TD>Mike</TD><TD>Bill</TD>
<TR><TH>Wash</TH><TD>Bill</TD><TD>Sue</TD><TD>Mike</TD>
</TABLE>
```

IE Extensions to *<IMG>*

Chapter 16 discussed the <INSERT> tag, designed for adding inline multimedia objects to your Web pages. IE has it's own version, which will probably be de-emphasized as <INSERT> becomes more widely accepted. It is possible, with IE-specific attributes, to add an inline video clip or VRML world with extensions to the <IMG> tag.

> **Note:** I'd suggest using the `<INSERT>` tag instead of these extensions to the `<IMG>` tag as `<INSERT>` becomes more popular. Check with the W3C, Netscape, and Microsoft IE Web sites to get a feel for whether or not popular browsers are supporting `<INSERT>`.

DYNSRC and *CONTROLS*

IE accepts the attribute DYNSRC along with an URL to indicate the video clip you want displayed by the user's browser. You can also include a SRC attribute for `<IMG>`, thus allowing it to display a standard graphic file for browsers that don't support DYNSRC. These attributes take the following format:

```
<IMG SRC="graphic URL" DYNSRC="video URL">
```

Currently, the *video URL* needs to be a `.avi` video file. The *graphic URL* can be any typically accepted graphic format, like GIF or JPEG. An example would be the following:

```
<IMG SRC="earth.gif" DYNSRC="earth.avi">
```

In addition, `<IMG>` will also accept the attribute CONTROLS, which displays a set of video controls under a video clip, if present. CONTROLS, then, requires that the DYNSRC attribute also be present. For example:

```
<IMG SRC="moon.gif" DYNSRC="moon.avi" CONTROLS>
```

In Internet Explorer, this adds video controls to the inline clip, as shown in figure 21.3.

Figure 21.3

An inline `.avi` file in IE.

LOOP and *START*

Two other attributes for `<IMG>` also affect the way your video clip will play—LOOP and START. LOOP allows you to choose the number of times that the video will play once started. START allows you to decide how it will be started.

LOOP accepts either a number or the value "infinite." For instance, in the following example, the video will play three times in a row once it is started:

```
<IMG SRC="earth.gif" DYNSRC="earth.avi" LOOP="3">
```

To start the video clip, you can use the START attribute. This takes either FILEOPEN or MOUSEOVER as its value. FILEOPEN instructs the video to begin when the page is loaded. MOUSEOVER starts the video when the user moves the mouse pointer over it. The following example will start the video clip when the mouse pointer is moved over it by the user, and play the video three times in a row:

```
<IMG SRC="earth.gif" DYNSRC="earth.avi LOOP="3" START="MOUSEOVER">
```

Summary

Not to be left out of the race, Microsoft's Internet Explorer adds HTML-like extensions much like Netscape. Also, like Netscape, many of these tags are designed to enhance designers' control over the page, or to increase their ability to deal with new multimedia technology.

With IE, this means more control over font faces, font colors, background colors, table border colors, and the addition of tags to support background sounds. Extensions to the <IMG> tag also allow you to play certain video files "inline"—that is, without a helper application.

Review Questions

1. Which of the following is not an attribute for the <BODY> tag: BGPROPERTIES, BGSOUND, LEFTMARGIN, RIGHTMARGIN. Which of the four is an actual tag?

2. What type of sound files can be used as a background sound?

3. Aside from a color name, what else can the COLOR attribute to the <FONT> tag accept as a value?

4. How often can you change the color or the font in an IE document?

5. What is the LOOP attribute used for with background sounds?

6. With what HTML table tags can the BGCOLOR attribute be use?

7. What tag will eventually be substituted for the combination of the <IMG> tag and the DYNSRC attribute in IE?

8. How is it possible to start a IE video clip by pointing the mouse at it?

Review Exercises

1. Create a page that plays a background sound three times, while displaying a background image as a watermark.

2. Change the colors in each letter of the word *Congratulations* using IE HTML extensions.

3. Change the font of each letter in the word *Welcome* using IE HTML extensions.

4. Using tables HTML tags, create a table that puts squares of different colors on the page, but without any table lines or borders.

5. Using a border, force the border lines to disappear into the background color of an HTML table.

6. Add an AVI video clip to your page, and have it play twice as the page loads, without showing controls.

Part V

Internet Programming and Advanced Web Technologies

## CHAPTER 22

Using Java and JavaScript

We should start this chapter by making a distinction between Java and JavaScript. Java is an object-oriented, compiled (at runtime), full-fledged programming language in the spirit of C++. It is designed for the more advanced programmer, with its strength being the ability to run in a "virtual machine" that can be created by a Web browser. Java, then, is similar to the programming languages used to build full-fledged applications that can be run on PCs, Macs, and UNIX machines. It's well-suited for the Internet, but not necessarily exclusive to the Web.

JavaScript, on the other hand, is a less complex, interpreted scripting language similar to AppleScript, Visual Basic Scripting, and similar languages. JavaScript is similar in some ways to Java, but it doesn't require the programmer to understand or implement the complicated object-oriented syntax or worry about programming issues like variable typing and object hierarchies.

In fact, Java and JavaScript are different enough that you can think of them with different titles depending on your ability. It's convenient to think of creating programs in Java as *programming*, and you can call creating scripts in JavaScript *authoring*.

> **Note:** Java programming is outside of the scope of this book. (I'd suggest *Java by Example* or *Special Edition Using Java* from Que.) In this chapter, you'll learn about adding Java programs to your HTML pages, and then look at the basics of JavaScript authoring.

Adding Java Applications to Your Web Pages

There are two basic ways to add Java *applets* (programs) to your Web pages. The first is an HTML-like extension that Netscape and other companies rolled into their browsers as the Java language first became popular. For a while, at least, this will be the preferred way of adding applets. The other method, based on the HTML 3.0 suggested <INSERT> tag, is still under discussion at the time of writing but should eventually replace the more proprietary <APPLET> tag.

The *<APPLET>* Tag

This first method adds the HTML-like tag <APPLET> container tag. Along with the <APPLET> tag is the <PARAM> tag, used to offer certain parameters to the browser concerning the applet (like the speed at which something should display, initialize, and so on). <APPLET> accepts the attributes CODE, CODEBASE, HEIGHT, and WIDTH.

An <APPLET> tag follows the general format:

```
<APPLET CODEBASE="applet_path_URL" CODE="appletFile.class" WIDTH="number"
HEIGHT="number">
<PARAM NAME="attributeName" VALUE="string/number">
...
Alt HTML text for non-Java browsers
</APPLET>
```

CODEBASE is the path (in URL form) to the directory on your server containing the Java applet. CODE takes the name of the applet. This file always ends in .class, to suggest that it's a compiled Java class. CODE should always be just the filename since CODEBASE is used to find the path to the Java applet.

> **Tip:** Notice that CODEBASE and CODE work together to create a complete URL. So, for a relative URL, CODEBASE isn't required if the applet is in the same directory as the Web page.

The WIDTH and HEIGHT attributes accept the number in pixels for the Java applet on your Web page.

An example of the first line of <APPLET> would be the following:

```
<APPLET CODEBASE="http://www.fakecorp.com/applets/" CODE="clock.class"
HEIGHT="300" WIDTH="300">
```

<PARAM> is a bit easier to use than it may seem. It essentially creates a variable, assigns a value, and passes it to the Java applet. The applet must be written to

understand the parameter's name and value. NAME is used to create the parameter's name; it should be expected by the applet. VALUE is used to assign the value to that particular parameter. It could be a number, bit of text, or even a command that causes the applet to work in a particular way.

> **Note:** Understanding the <PARAM> tag might enable you to use freeware/ shareware Java applets on your own pages. By passing your own parameters to general purpose applets, you may find them useful for your particular Web site.

A simple <PARAM> tag is the following:

```
<PARAM NAME="Speed" VALUE="5">
```

In this case, the Java applet will have to recognize and know what to do with a variable named Speed with a value of 5.

The alternative HTML code in the <APPLET> container allows you to offer HTML text to browsers that aren't Java-enabled. A Java-aware browser will ignore the markup (and display the applet window instead), while non-Java browsers will ignore everything but the markup. So an example would be the following:

```
<APPLET CODE="counter.class" HEIGHT="20" WIDTH="20">
<P>You need a <I>Java-aware</I> browser to see this counter!</P>
</APPLET>
```

This will display the text, instead of the applet, when it encounters a browser that doesn't support Java.

The *<INSERT>* Tag

As you may remember from Chapter 16, the <INSERT> tag is the current thinking by the W3C for adding inline multimedia elements to Web pages. In fact, it's designed to work for Java applets as well, as most browsers work with applets in a way similar to inline video and animations.

The basic format for the <INSERT> tag (as it regards Java applets) is as follows:

```
<INSERT CLASSID="Java:filename.class"
        CODE="URL/filename.class"
        WIDTH="number"
        HEIGHT="number"
        ALIGN="direction">
<PARAM NAME="name" VALUE="number/string">
<IMG SRC="URL" ALT="text">
</INSERT>
```

For the most part, this works a lot like the <APPLET> tag, except that it does away with the CODEBASE tag, instead requiring that you use a full URL for the CODE attribute. (This makes more sense in terms of the HTML conventions you've learned in the past.) The CLASSID is a MIME type name, which is required for all <INSERT> tags. HEIGHT and WIDTH are just numbers that represent pixels for the applet window on your Web page. ALIGN works as it does for other <INSERT> elements.

The <PARAM> tag for <INSERT> elements is essentially the same as the <PARAM> tag you used previously for the <APPLET> tag. Your Java applet will still need to recognize and deal with the incoming data. The <IMG> tag, as with other <INSERT> elements, allows you to add the URL to an image that can display in browsers that aren't Java-enabled.

An example might be:

```
<INSERT CLASSID="Java:counter.class"
        CODE="http://www.fakecorp.com/applets/counter.class"
        WIDTH="20"
        HEIGHT="20"
        ALIGN="LEFT">
<PARAM NAME="Speed" VALUE="5">
<IMG SRC="nojava.gif" ALT="This applet requires a Java-enabled browser">
</INSERT>
```

Example: Adding Java Applets

This example is designed to do two things: reinforce the ways you can add Java applets to your Web pages, and test your browser for Java capabilities. If your browser supports Java, it'll be interesting to see which method it prefers for adding Java applets.

To begin, create a new HTML page and add the code in Listing 22.1.

On the CD

Listing 22.1 *addjava.html* **Adding Java Applets to a Web Page**

```
<BODY>
<H3>This applet has been added using the APPLET tag:</H3>
<APPLET CODE="Clock2.class" HEIGHT="150" WIDTH="150">
{<P>You need a <I>Java-aware</I> browser to see this clock!</P>}
</APPLET>
<HR>
<H3>This applet was added using the <INSERT> tag:</H3>
<INSERT CLASSID="Java:Clock2.class"
        CODE="Clock2.class"
        WIDTH="150"
        HEIGHT="150"
        ALIGN="LEFT">
<IMG SRC="no_work.gif" ALT="Looks like Insert doesn't work!">
</INSERT>
</BODY>
```

On the CD

Save this file as `clock.html`. To get this to work correctly, you'll need a Java applet. You can use an applet written by Rachel Gollub of Sun Microsystems, `clock2.class` which is available on the included CD-ROM. Make sure it's in the same directory as `clock.html`. Then load the page in your browser to test it (see fig. 22.1).

Figure 22.1

Here's what works and what doesn't in my copy of Netscape Navigator (Mac 2.0 Java beta).

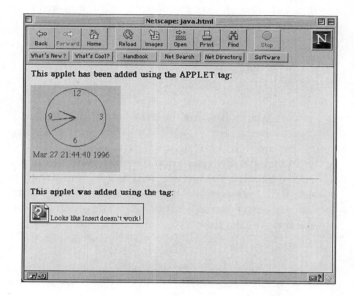

Creating JavaScript Programs

Now let's move on to JavaScript, the smaller Java-like scripting language available in Netscape Navigator and other programs. Unlike Java, JavaScript programs are generally written right in HTML pages. You'll start with how to add JavaScript code to a Web page and then look at how these programs are created.

The *<SCRIPT>* Tag

The `<SCRIPT>` tag is used to add JavaScript commands to your HTML pages. `<SCRIPT>` is a container tag that can accept the attribute LANGUAGE, which allows you to specify the scripting language used (JavaScript is generally the default). Here's how it works:

```
<SCRIPT LANGUAGE="lang_name">
script code
</SCRIPT>
```

Remember that LANGUAGE is optional—you probably won't need to use it while authoring JavaScript, but it can't hurt.

Hiding Code

While it's possible that old browsers (those that don't recognize JavaScript) will just skip over the <SCRIPT> tag, it's also possible that the browser will attempt to interpret your script commands or other text as HTML markup. To keep this from happening, you can embed the script commands in HTML comments. You might try something using the HTML comment tags like the following:

```
<SCRIPT>
<!--
script commands
-->
</SCRIPT>
```

This works fine for the non-Java browser. Unfortunately, the JavaScript will choke when it sees -->, since it will try to interpret that as scripting code. So you need to comment the comment.

In fact, it's always a good idea to create comments within your script that allow you to document what you're doing in your programming. Unfortunately, you've just told Java-enabled browsers that HTML comments (between <SCRIPT> tags) contain active script commands. So how can you add comments for the benefit of the script? Like this:

```
<SCRIPT>
<!--
script command     // One-line comment
...script commands...
/* Unlimited-length comments must be
ended with */
// comment to end hiding -->
</SCRIPT>
```

Looks like you can fill a decent-sized page with nothing but comments, eh? Notice that you've solved the HTML comment problem with a single-line JavaScript comment. Single-line comments start with two forward slashes and must physically fit on a single line with a return at the end. Multi-line comments can be enclosed in between an opening comment element (/*) and a closing comment element (*/).

Example: Hello World

Although you haven't learned how to do anything with a script yet, I'll throw one quick command at you for the purpose of getting your first JavaScript page to work. It's document.write, and it's something called a *method* in JavaScript. It's basically a variable that does something automatically. In this case, it prints text to your Web page.

Create a new HTML document and enter Listing 22.2.

On the CD

Listing 22.2 *hiworld.html* "Hello World" JavaScript Document

```
<HTML>
<HEAD>
<TITLE>Hello World JavaScript Example</TITLE>
</HEAD>
<BODY>
<H3>The following text is script generated:</H3>
<SCRIPT LANGUAGE="JavaScript">
<!--
/* Our script only requires
one quick statement! */
document.write("Hello World!") // Prints words to Web document
// end hiding-->
</SCRIPT>
</BODY>
</HTML>
```

Save this document, and then load it in the browser of your choice. If your browser is capable of dealing with JavaScript, then your output should look something like figure 22.2. If it's not, then you'll just see the header text.

Tip: If your browser can't see the JavaScript example, I suggest getting the latest copy of Netscape Navigator for testing your work in this chapter.

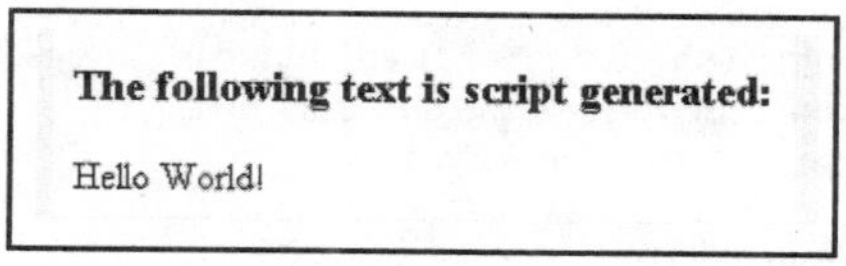

Figure 22.2

Your first JavaScript program.

> **The following text is script generated:**
>
> Hello World!

Functions

The basic building block of a script in JavaScript is the *function*. A function is basically a "mini-program." Functions start by being "passed" a particular value; they work with that value to make something else happen and then "return" a new value to the body of your program.

In JavaScript, there are two times you need to work with functions. First, you need to declare the function. This means that you're defining how the function will work. The browser, when it loads a page, will make note of the different functions that you may use in your script.

The second step is to call the function in the body of your script. Generally, your script will be just a series of function calls. There isn't a whole lot of calculating done in the body of your script. You send a value out to a function to be computed and then receive the results back in the body of your script.

Declaring Your Functions

A good rule, although it's not necessary, is to declare your functions in the head of your document. The function declaration needs to appear between <SCRIPT> tags, but you can have more than one set of <SCRIPT> tags in an HTML document. A single set of <SCRIPT> tags doesn't necessarily define an entire script—it just sets script elements apart from other HTML tags. Function declarations look like the following:

```
<SCRIPT>
<!--
  function function_name(value_name) {
  ...function code...
  return (new_value)
}
// end hiding -->
</SCRIPT>
```

The *value_name* for the function is just the variable name that you assign to the passed value for the duration of the function. When the body of your JavaScript document calls this function, it will generally send along a value. When that value gets to the function, it needs a name. If the function is designed to perform simple math, for instance, you might call the passed value old_num.

Also, notice that the entire calculating part of the function is between braces. An example of a function declaration might be the following:

```
<SCRIPT>
<!--
  function get_square(old_num) {
  new_num = (old_num * old_num)
  return (new_num)
}
// end hiding -->
</SCRIPT>
```

In the example, you've created a function called get_square which accepts a value, names it old_num, and then squares that value and assigns it to a variable named new_num. At least, that's what the function is supposed to do. It won't do it yet, because this is just a declaration. It doesn't even know what actual values to work with until you call the function.

Calling a Function

You call the function from the body of your script, which is generally in the body of the document. It doesn't really matter where you declare functions (although, as mentioned, it's best to declare them between the <HEAD> tags), but it is best to put the function calls of your script close to the parts of your document where they're needed (this will become more obvious as you work with JavaScript). A function call is basically formatted like the following (and always appears between <SCRIPT> tags):

```
function_name(value);
```

In this function call, the `function_name` should be the same function name that you used in the function declaration, while the `value` can be anything you want to pass to the function. In the previous example, this `value` was to be renamed `old_num` and then squared. So it would make sense to put a number in the parentheses of that particular function call. In fact, you can put almost anything in the parentheses—a variable name, an actual number, or a string of text—as long as the function is designed to accept such a value. For instance, the `get_square` function will work equally well if you use:

```
number = 5;
num_squared = get_square (number);
```

or

```
num_squared = get_square (5);
```

By the way, if something looks strange to you here, it might be the way I'm naming variable names—especially if the last time you did any programming was a number of years ago. The following would work just as easily:

```
x = 5;
y = get_square (x);
```

Does that make you more comfortable?

Remember, though, that you should be passing a value that the function expects. If you pass a string of text to a function designed to perform math functions, you won't get anything useful.

Notice also that, in the previous three examples, the function is on the right side of an *assignment*, represented by the equal sign. This may take a little leap of thought, but JavaScript does two things with function calls. First, the call is used to pass a value to the function. Then, when the function returns a value, it "takes the place" of the original function call.

Look at the following example:

```
num_squared = get_square (5);
```

After the math of the `get_square` function is completed and the value is returned, the entire function call (`get_square (5)`) is given a value of 25. This, in turn, is assigned to the variable `num_squared`.

Example: Calling All Declarations

You know enough now to build a fairly simply little script. You'll use `document.write` again, with a function declaration and a function call. In this script, you'll do some simple math and track the results in your browser window.

Create a new HTML document and enter Listing 22.3.

On the CD

Listing 22.3 *simpmath.html* **Using JavaScript for Simple Math**

```
<HTML>
<HEAD>
<TITLE>Simple Math</TITLE>
<SCRIPT>
<!--
  function simple_math(num) {
  document.write("The call passed ",num," to the function.<BR>");
  new_num = num * 2;          // multiple the value by 2
  document.write(num, " * 2 equals ",new_num,"<BR>");
  return new_num;             // return new_num to the function call
}
// end hiding -->
</SCRIPT>
</HEAD>
<BODY>
<H3>Let's watch some simple math:</H3>
<SCRIPT>
<!--
  x = 5;
  document.write("The starting number is ",x,"<BR>");
  new_x = simple_math(x);
  document.write("The function returned the number ",new_x,"<BR>");
// end hiding -->
</SCRIPT>
</BODY>
</HTML>
```

And that's pretty much it. Notice that document.write lets you track the progress of your number as it moves from the function call through the function itself and back down to the main part of your script. You can see this working by focusing on the order of the output in figure 22.3.

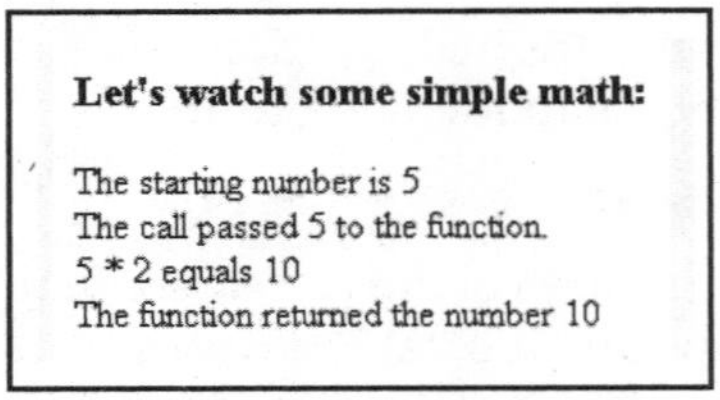

Figure 22.3

The results of your script.

> **Let's watch some simple math:**
>
> The starting number is 5
> The call passed 5 to the function.
> 5 * 2 equals 10
> The function returned the number 10

Handling Events

Well, you've created a complete script, but it can't do much. That's because the strength of JavaScript, more than anything else, is in *event handling*. That is, it's best at responding to something a user does on your page. This is generally done in response to some HTML tag. Here's the basic format for an event handler:

```
<TAG event_handler="JavaScript code">
```

`<TAG>` can be just about any form or hyperlink tag. Most other tags don't have the ability to accept input from the user. The *event_handler* is the browser's code for some action by the user. The *JavaScript code* will most often be a function call.

For instance, you could use an input textbox to send data to a function you've written, as with the following code:

```
<INPUT TYPE="text" NAME="number" SIZE="4">
<INPUT TYPE="button" NAME="Calculate" onClick="result =
compute(this.form.number.value)">
```

In this example, you're responding to the event created when the user clicks the input button. When that happens, the value `this.form.number.value` is sent to a function called `compute`. Notice that the variable `this.form.number.value` is JavaScript's object-oriented way of storing the value of the textbox named `number` in the first statement.

Returning Values

Let's dig a little deeper into how the object-oriented storage thing works. Your average object is usually just a bunch of grouped variables. For instance, a typical browser has a JavaScript object called `this`, which (in our example) means "variables for this page." Within `this` is a subcategory called `form` which means "the form variables." So the name `this.form` is basically where "the form variables for this page" are stored.

> **Note:** Actually, `this` is a special keyword in JavaScript, used to refer to the current object. In the case of our example, the current object is, in fact, where the "variables for the page" are stored. We'll discuss the correct use of `this` a bit more in Chapter 23, "JavaScript Objects and Functions."

When you use the NAME attribute to an `<INPUT>` tag, you're creating another variable within this object. For instance, `NAME="mynumber"` creates `this.form.mynumber`. The value of this variable is stored at `this.form.mynumber.value`.

Let's look at that last example again:

```
<INPUT TYPE="text" NAME="number" SIZE="4">
<INPUT TYPE="button" NAME="Calculate" onClick="result =
compute(this.form.number.value)">
```

Now, the neat trick here is that you don't necessarily have to pass the specific value to a function in order to use it. All you need to do is send the name of the object that you want the function to concentrate on. That way, it can deal with more than one value from that object.

Consider this. You've just gathered `this.form.number.value` from the textbox. Now you want to send that to a function. You can make the function call like this:

```
<INPUT TYPE="button" NAME="Calculate" onClick="result =
compute(this.form)">
```

You've also cleverly designed the function to work with this value. So your function will look something like the following:

```
function compute(form) {
  new_number = form.number.value;
  new_number = new_number * 2;
  return (new_number);
}
```

The function received what's known as a *pointer* to the object responsible for storing information about this page. Once the function has its hands on that pointer (which the function calls `form`), it's able to access data within that function by using the object variable scheme, as in `form.number.value`. Get it?

But this gets even cooler. If the function knows the pointer to the data storage object, then it can also create new variables within that object. So you can change a few more things:

```
<INPUT TYPE="text" NAME="number" SIZE="4">
<INPUT TYPE="button" NAME="Calculate" Value="Click Me"
onClick="compute(this.form)">
<INPUT TYPE="text" NAME="result" SIZE="8">
```

Now (in the second line), you're just telling the browser to run the `compute()` function when the Calculate button is clicked. But you're not assigning the function to a value. So how do you get an answer for your user? By using the object pointer. Here's the new function:

```
function compute(form) {
  new_number = form.number.value;
  form.result.value = new_number * 2;
  return;
}
```

In line three of the function declaration, notice the new variable `form.result.value`. What happens now is the function call sets the function in motion and passes it the object pointer. The function creates its own new variable within the object, called `result`, and gives it a new value. When the function returns, the next line of script is activated. That line is:

```
<INPUT TYPE="text" NAME="result" SIZE="8">
```

Notice the NAME. Since there's already a value assigned to this NAME, that value will be displayed in the textbox (just as if it were default text). In your case, it happens to be the answer (see fig. 22.4). Here's the complete code again:

```
<HTML>
<HEAD>
<TITLE>Compute A Number</TITLE>
<SCRIPT>
<!--
function compute(form) {
  new_number = form.number.value;
  form.result.value = new_number * 2;
  return;
}
// -->
</HEAD>
<BODY>
<INPUT TYPE="text" NAME="number" SIZE="4">
<INPUT TYPE="button" NAME="Calculate" Value="Click Me"
onClick="compute(this.form)">
<INPUT TYPE="text" NAME="result" SIZE="8">
</BODY>
</HTML>
```

Figure 22.4

Your textbox
script, complete
with a result.

Possible Events

There are a number of different events that a typical browser will recognize, and for which you can write handlers. Even the simplest handler should call a function you've declared previously and then elegantly return to that point in the Web document. Table 22.1 shows you some of the events for which there are associated handlers (according the Netscape Navigator's documentation).

Table 22.1   Events and Their Event Handlers

Event	Means...	Event Handler
blur	User moves input focus from form box	onBlur
click	User clicks form element or link	onClick

continues

Table 22.1   Continued

Event	Means...	Event Handler
change	User changes a form value	onChange
focus	User gives a form box input focus	onFocus
load	User loads the page in the Navigator	onLoad
mouseover	User moves mouse over a link	onMouseOver
select	User selects form input field	onSelect
submit	User submits a form	onSubmit
unload	User exits the page	onUnload

You can probably figure out what most of these do from the table. And it should also make you realize how scriptable your Web page really is. You can create alert dialog boxes, for instance, that tell your user that a particular field is required—or that it needs to be filled with a certain number of characters. You can even say "Goodbye" to users as they leave your page, perhaps displaying a phone number of other useful (albeit intrusive) information.

Example: Event Handling, Part One

Let's start with the simple event I just mentioned—creating an alert to say goodbye. As an added bonus, you'll learn how to create an alert box, which is simply a dialog box that requires your user to click OK to clear the box.

You may want to use an HTML document you've created previously. Any document will do. Add Listing 22.4 to the head and body of your page.

On the CD

Listing 22.4   *events1.html*   Handling a Simple Event

```
<HTML>
<HEAD>
<TITLE>Saying Goodbye</TITLE>
<SCRIPT>
<!--
  function goodbye () {
  alert("For more information about BigCorp products\nPlease call
  1-800-BIG-CORP");
  return;
  }
// end hiding -->
</SCRIPT>
</HEAD>
```

```
<BODY>
<A HREF="http://www.netscape.com/" onClick="goodbye()">Click here to
leave.</A>
</BODY>
</HTML>
```

I've re-introduced something else too (you originally saw it with form processing and CGI scripts in Chapter 14). It's the newline character \n which allows you to add a newline in the middle of a text string that's to be written to the browser or another interface element.

It is possible to have eliminated the function goodbye with a simple line of script like the following:

```
onUnload="alert('For more information about BigCorp products\nPlease call
1-800-BIG-CORP')"
```

Notice that this forces you to use the single quote character for the alert text. If you prefer to script this way, that's okay. But realize that it's generally considered poor programming technique since it includes actual calculations in the interior of your HTML code. For best results, you want to separate the calculations into functions, which should all be stored in the head of your document. Either way, it should look something like figure 22.5.

Figure 22.5

Before the current link is followed, this alert will appear.

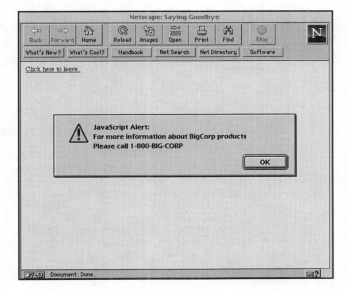

Example: Event Handling, Part Two

Now let's use event handling for something a little more complex and perhaps more useful. One of the best uses of event handling seems to be for verifying form data. You can use JavaScript to hand off your data object pointer to a function, which can then take a close look at what your user has entered and determine if it's correct.

We'll try it for a ZIP code. You're simply going to make sure that the user has entered five numbers. Enter Listing 22.5 in a new HTML document.

On the CD

Listing 22.5 *events2.html* Verifying Form Data with JavaScript

```html
<HTML>
<HEAD>
<TITLE>Data Checking</TITLE>
<SCRIPT>
<!--
  function zip_check (form) {
  zip_str = form.Zip.value;
  if (zip_str == "") {
    alert("Please enter a five digit number for your Zip code");
    return;
    }
  if (zip_str.length != 5) {
    alert ("Your Zip code entry should be 5 digits");
    return;
    }
  return;
  }
// end hiding -->
</SCRIPT>
</HEAD>
<BODY>
<H3>Please fill out the following form:</H3>
<FORM ACTION="http://www.fakecorp.com/cgi-bin/address_form">
<PRE>
Name:     <INPUT TYPE="TEXT" SIZE="50" NAME="Name">
Address:  <INPUT TYPE="TEXT" SIZE="60" NAME="Address">
City:     <INPUT TYPE="TEXT" SIZE="30" NAME="City">
State:    <INPUT TYPE="TEXT" SIZE="2" NAME="State">
Zip:      <INPUT TYPE="TEXT" SIZE="5" NAME="Zip"
          onChange = "zip_check(this.form)">
Email:    <INPUT TYPE="TEXT" SIZE="40" Name="Email">
<INPUT TYPE="SUBMIT" VALUE="Send it" onClick = "zip_check(this.form)">
</FORM>
</BODY>
</HTML>
```

This event handling script checks an entry in the Zip box, using the `onChange` handler to determine when the user has moved on from Zip's textbox (either by pressing Tab or clicking in another textbox with the mouse). Notice that it's a good idea to place the Zip textbox before the E-mail box since the user could just click the Submit button and skip past your error check.

Also, by adding the `onClick` event to the Submit button, you're able to catch them if they happen to skip the Zip box completely. Now you've double-checked their entry.

I've also cheated and introduced another new method. In the function declarations, you may have noticed the following line:

```
if (zip_str.length != 5) {
```

variable`.length` is a method that allows you to determine the length of any variable in JavaScript. Since JavaScript does no variable typing (it doesn't explicitly require you to say "this is a number" or "this is text"), then any variable can be treated as a string. In this case, even though the ZIP code could be interpreted as a number, `zip_str.length` tells you how many characters long it is.

The above snippet could be said "if the length of `zip_str` does not equal 5, then...." Notice that `!=` is the "does not equal" comparison. Similarly, `==` is the "does equal" comparison. Look at the following snippet from the braces function declaration:

```
if (zip_str == "") {
```

This could be read as "if `zip_str` equals nothing, then...." If the condition (`zip_str == ""`) is true, then the code specified by the braces is performed.

> **Tip:** Be very careful that you use `==` for comparisons and `=` for assignments. If you've accidentally used (`zip_str = ""`), that means "make `zip_str` equal nothing." You've made it so that the condition is always true since it's an assignment.

You'll learn more about conditions and JavaScript methods in the next chapter. For now, let's just see this script in action, in figure 22.6.

Figure 22.6

Error checking
with JavaScript.

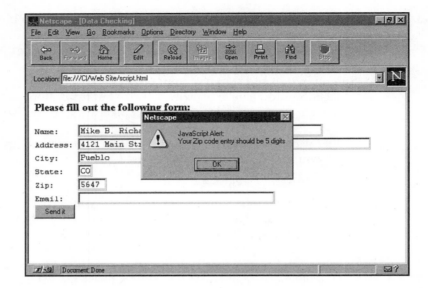

Summary

Java and JavaScript are distinct entities—Java being a sophisticated full-fledged programming language while JavaScript is a smaller, easier-to-grasp scripting language.

There are two ways to add Java applets to your Web pages. The first, using the <APPLET> tag, is currently more pervasive. The second is the <INSERT> tag, HTML 3.0's all-purpose tag for adding multimedia and applet files to HTML documents.

JavaScript can be added directly to your HTML pages, fitting between <SCRIPT> tags. Script code should be hidden between HTML comment tags, to keep it from being interpreted by non-JavaScript browsers.

There are two basic parts to any JavaScript script: the function definitions and the function calls. Function definitions should be in the head of your HTML document, while function calls can appear anywhere you want in the <BODY> of your document. Function calls can also appear as event handlers in certain HTML tags. One of the strengths of JavaScript is error checking for HTML forms.

Getting serious about JavaScript authoring requires an understanding of the object-oriented methods used to store variables related to your page. You can then pass pointers to these data objects to your functions, which allow you to work with more than one variable at once, creating scripts that accomplish more.

Review Questions

1. Which of the tags, <APPLET> or <INSERT>, is the Netscape-specific way to add Java applets?

2. Can Java applets be stored in the same directory as your HTML pages?

3. What is the <PARAM> tag used for with <APPLET> and <INSERT>?

4. What attribute can the <SCRIPT> tag accept?

5. What do you call the type of JavaScript command that document.write represents?

6. In the following function declaration, where does the value for number come from?

```
function add_two (number) {
```

7. What's wrong with the following script?

```
<SCRIPT LANGUAGE="JavaScript">
<!--
document.write("Hi!")
-->
</SCRIPT>
```

8. What is the purpose of an event handler? What's an event?

9. True or false. If a function call sends the value this.form, then the function declaration must call the value form, as in calculate (form).

10. What is the full object-hierarchy style name for the value created by <INPUT NAME="city">?

11. Why is a blur event called a blur event?

12. What method can be used to determine the length of a variable string?

Review Exercises

1. Write a JavaScript script (and the HTML page) that asks for the user's name and then tells the user how many characters are in his/her name.

2. Write a script and page that shows an alert box when the user clicks an anchor link.

3. Now, write a script that pops up an alert when the user clicks the link, but doesn't move him or her to a new HTML document or part of an HTML document. (For instance, clicking the word *hypertext* brings up an alert with the definition of hypertext.)

4. Write a script that pops up an alert when the user touches a graphic with the mouse pointer. (Hint: make it a clickable graphic. Suggestion: use a picture of a person and make the alert say "Stop touching me, I'm ticklish," or something similar.)

5. Write a script that determines whether or not a number entered in a textbox is "798."

## CHAPTER 23

JavaScript Objects and Functions

In the last chapter, you learned enough JavaScript to accomplish some pretty impressive things, like error checking on forms, creating alert messages, and performing simple functions like math. In this chapter, you get a little deeper into how JavaScript and Netscape Navigator store values for scripting. Then you learn how you can use this knowledge to do even more sophisticated things with JavaScript.

> **Note:** This chapter assumes you have some experience with computer programming languages. JavaScript is a fairly simple scripting language for the "initiated," but this chapter may be less than useful if you've had no exposure to programming or script authoring concepts.

The JavaScript Object Model

An object, for the purposes of this discussion, is basically a collection of properties. Often, these properties are variables, but they can also be functions or JavaScript methods. Properties within objects are accessed using the following notation:

```
objectName.propertyName
```

For instance, if you created an object called `myComputer`, you might have properties called `diskspace`, `monitor`, and `cdspeed`. You could assign values to those properties like this:

```
myComputer.diskspace = "2.4 GB"
myComputer.monitor = "17-inch VGA"
myComputer.cdspeed = "6x"
```

What we've basically done is assign values to variables that happen to all be associated with one another since they're part of my computer (and myComputer). So you could pass this object to a function using the following function call:

```
<SCRIPT>
printSpec (myComputer);
</SCRIPT>
```

And then use the pointer to that object to access each of the individual variables:

```
<SCRIPT>
function printSpec (computer) {
    document.write ("Disk space = " + computer.diskspace + "<BR>">);
    document.write ("Monitor = " + computer.monitor + "<BR>");
    document.write ("CD Speed = " + computer.cdspeed + "<BR>");
    return;
    }
</SCRIPT>
```

Methods

Methods, then, are basically functions associated with objects. For instance, one of the methods we've used quite a bit is document.write, which is really just a function provided by JavaScript that allows you to write HTML code to the current document.

Notice, then that write is the function, and document is the associated object. Netscape Navigator and other JavaScript browsers define certain basic objects, like document, that are designed to make it easier for you to deal with the document or window in question. You'll learn about some of those standard objects later in this chapter.

You can even create your own methods by simply assigning a function name to an object variable, following this format:

```
object.methodname = function_name
```

Creating New Objects

You may remember that you used the keyword this for an object reference in the last chapter. JavaScript offers you the special keyword this, which acts as a placeholder. It's used to represent the current object involved in a function call. An example is the following:

```
<FORM NAME="MyForm">
<INPUT TYPE="Text" NAME="first" onClick="check(this)">
</FORM>
```

This sends a pointer to the current object to the function check. In this case, the actual object is document.myform.first, but the keyword this can be used here since it's clear what the current object is.

That's part of how you create your own objects. It's done in two steps. First, you need to define a function that outlines the basic object you'd like to create. This is your own personal object definition for this new type of object.

For instance, if you wanted to create a data object that could be used to describe a person, you might use the following function:

```
function person(name, height, weight, age) {
    this.name = name;
    this.height = height;
    this.weight = weight;
    this.age = age;
    }
```

Notice the use of this. In the case of this example here, this refers to the object that's being created by another keyword, new. Using new is the second step in creating your new object. The following is an example:

```
debbie = new person("Debbie", 5.5, 130, 27) ;
```

The keyword new creates a new object. It also tells the object-creating function person that the name of this new object will be debbie. So when the function is called, debbie will replace this and the assignment will work like this:

```
debbie.name = "Debbie";
debbie.height = 5.5;
debbie.weight = 130;
debbie.age = 27;
```

Of course, you won't see any of this happen. But it's now possible for you to access this data just like a regular object, as in the following:

```
document.write("Debbie's age is: ",debbie.age);
```

Example: Creating New Objects and Methods

In this example, you'll create a script that not only creates a new object but creates a method within that object. The object will be designed to hold data concerning a user's purchase. The method will be designed to generate a total of what is owed. You can use HTML form tags to allow the user to enter the information.

You start out by defining all of your functions in the head of the document and then creating the form in the body. Create a new HTML document and enter Listing 23.1.

On the CD

Listing 23.1 *method.html* **Creating Objects and Methods**

```html
<HTML>
<HEAD>
<TITLE>Customer Purchases</TITLE>
<SCRIPT>
<!--
function customer (val1, val2, val3) {
    this.item1 = val1;
    this.item2 = val2;
    this.item3 = val3;
    this.getsum = getsum;
    }

function getsum (form) {
    var total = 0
    total = this.item1 + this.item2 + this.item3;
    form.Sum.value = total;
}
// -->
</SCRIPT>
</HEAD>
<BODY>
<H3> The amount of each puchase is: </H3>
<PRE>
Purchase 1:    $5
Purchase 2:    $10
Purchase 3:    $12
</PRE>
<SCRIPT>
<!--
cust1 = new customer (5, 10, 12);
// -->
</SCRIPT>
<FORM NAME="form1">
<INPUT TYPE="BUTTON" NAME="Total" VALUE="Get Total" onClick="cust1.getsum
(this.form)">
<INPUT TYPE="TEXT" NAME="Sum" SIZE="12">
</FORM>
</BODY>
</HTML>
```

Notice first that the function that defines the object, called customer, uses the keyword this to reference its individual properties. When the new object is created, it's called cust1 and the new keyword passes that name to the object creator. So, in the onClick statement, you can then call the object's properties using cust1, as in cust1.item1 or cust1.getsum.

In fact, cust1.getsum is a special case—it's the method you're creating in this example. All you have to do is assign the function getsum as a property of your object and then you can call it using object notation, as in cust1.getsum (this.form). Notice that the function getsum() is designed to accept a pointer to form data. See figure 23.1 for an example of how this will look in a browser.

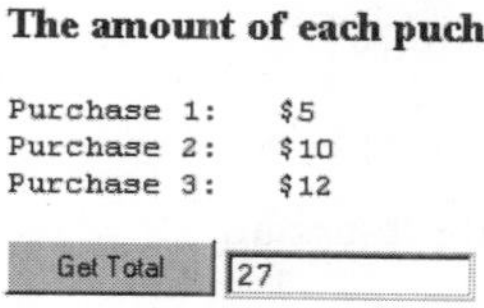

Figure 23.1

Your object and method example.

The amount of each puchase is:

```
Purchase 1:    $5
Purchase 2:    $10
Purchase 3:    $12
```

| Get Total | 27 |

JavaScript Statements

If you have any experience with programming languages, you'll be familiar with JavaScript's small set of statements. JavaScript includes the conditional statement if...else and the loop statements for, while, break, and continue. You'll also get to know some of the associated JavaScript operators.

> **Tip:** Remember that, in most cases, you'll use these statements in functions. These are the commands in JavaScript you'll use to actually process data.

The key to many of these statements is called the *condition*, which is simply a bit of JavaScript code that needs to be evaluated before your script decides what to do next. So before you look at JavaScript statements, let's look at the conditions and operators that JavaScript recognizes.

Comparison Operators and Conditions

Conditions are generally enclosed in parentheses, and they are always a small snippet of code that is designed to evaluate as true or false. For instance, the following is a conditional statement:

```
(x == 1)
```

If x does equal 1, then this condition is valid.

And this is why it's important to recognize and use the correct operators for conditions. For instance, an assignment always evaluates to true, so that the following condition:

```
(errorLevel = 1)
```

is always true since it's an assignment. Although it may seem to make sense to use an equal sign in this instance, you actually need to use the comparison operator == for this condition. (See Table 23.1 for a listing of the comparison operators.)

Table 23.1 Comparison Operators in JavaScript

Operator	Meaning	Example	Is True When...
==	equals	x == y	x equals y
!=	not equal	x != y	x is not equal to y
>	greater than	x > y	x is greater than y
<	less than	x < y	x is less than y
>=	greater than or equal to	x >= y	x is greater than or equal to y
<=	less than or equal to	x <= y	x is less than or equal to y

So you have a number of different ways to create conditions by using comparisons. Realize, too, that conditions are not necessarily limited to numerical expressions. For instance, look at the following:

```
(carName != "Ford")
```

This will return the value false if the variable carName has the value of the string Ford.

Boolean Operators

The other operators common to conditional statements are the boolean operators. In English, these operators are AND, OR, and NOT. In JavaScript, AND is &&, OR is ¦¦, and NOT is !. An example of a condition is the following:

```
((x == 5) && (y == 6))
```

This condition evaluates to true only if each individual comparison is true. If either comparison is false—or both comparisons are false—the entire conditional statement is false.

On the other hand, the following conditional statement uses the OR operator:

```
((x == 5) ¦¦ (y == 6))
```

In this case, if either of the conditions is true, then the entire statement is true. The statement is only false if both of the conditions are false.

Finally, the NOT operator changes the result of an expression, so that assuming x == 5, you can create the following conditional:

```
(!(x == 5))
```

NOT simply reverses the result of the conditional statement. In this example, the entire condition is false since (x == 5) is true, and the NOT operator reverses that.

if...else

So how do you put these conditional statements and operators to use? JavaScript offers the `if...else` conditional statement as a way to create either/or situations in your script. The basic construct is as follows:

```
if (condition) {
  script statements }
else {
  other statements }
```

The `condition` can be any JavaScript that evaluates to either true or false. The statements can be any valid JavaScript statements. For example:

```
if (x == 1) {
  document.write("X equals 1!");
  return;
  }
  else {
  x = x + 1;
  }
```

The `else` and related statements are not required if you simply want the `if` statements to be skipped and the rest of the function executed. An example might be:

```
if (errorLevel == 1) {
  return (false);
  }
```

In this case, if the condition is false (e.g., `errorLevel` does not equal 1), then the rest of the function executes. If it is true, then the function ends.

Loop Statements

The next two statement types are used to create loops—script elements that repeat until a condition is met. These loop statements are FOR and WHILE.

A FOR loop follows the basic construct:

```
for (initial_assignment; condition; increment) {
    JavaScript statements
    }
```

You'll generally start a FOR loop by initializing your "counter" variable. Then you'll evaluate the counter to see if it's reached a certain level. If it hasn't, then the loop will perform the enclosed statements and increment your counter. If the counter has reached your predetermined value, then the FOR loop ends. For example:

```
for (x=0; x<10; x=x+1) {
    y = 2 * x;
    document.write ("Two times ",x," equals ",y,"<BR>");
    }
```

You start by initializing a counter variable (x=1) and then evaluating the counter in a conditional statement (x<10). If the condition is true, then the loop will perform the enclosed scripting. Then it will increment the counter—in this case, add 1 to it. When the counter reaches 10 in your example, the loop will end.

The WHILE loop is similar to the FOR loop, except that it offers a little more freedom. WHILE is used for a great variety of conditions. The basic construct is as follows:

```
while (condition) {
  JavaScript statements
  }
```

As long as the condition evaluates to true, the loop will continue. An example is the following:

```
x = 0;
while (x <= 5) {
   x = x +1;
   document.write (X now equals ",x,"<BR>")
   }
```

As long as the condition remains true, the WHILE statement will continue to evaluate. In fact, the risk with WHILE statements is that they can be infinite if the expression never evaluates to false. A common mistake is the following:

```
while (x=5) {
  x = x +1;
  document.write (X now equals ",x,"<BR>")
  }
```

The condition is actually an assignment, so it will always evaluate to true. In this example, the loop would continue indefinitely, and the output would always be X now equals 6.

BREAK and CONTINUE

Two other keywords, BREAK and CONTINUE, can be used in FOR or WHILE loops to change the way the loop operates when certain conditions occur. Notice that both of these are generally used with an if statement.

An example of BREAK is:

```
for (x=0; x < 10; x=x+1) {
   z = 35;
   y = z / x;
   if (y == 7)
      break;
   }
```

BREAK will terminate the loop when encountered. In this example then, the loop is terminated when x is equal to 5 since 35 divided by 5 is 7. When the condition (y == 7) evaluates to true, the loop stops and you move on to the next script element.

CONTINUE is basically used to skip a particular increment. For instance:

```
while (x < 10) {
    x = x +1;
    if (x == 5)
        continue;
    y = y + x;
    }
```

In this case, when the condition (x == 5) evaluates to true, the CONTINUE statement will cause the loop to move directly back to the WHILE statement, thus skipping over the last line (y = y + x). When the condition is false, the last line will execute normally.

Increments and Decrements

So far, you've seen me using statements like x = x + 1 in many of these examples to increment the values in your loop statements. JavaScript allows you to do this in other ways, using *unary* operators. A unary operator is an operator that requires only one operand, as in the unary increment operator:

```
x++
```

In fact, you can increment with either x++ or ++x. The difference is when the increment occurs, for instance, if x equals 2:

```
y = x++
```

y will be assigned the value 2, then x will be incremented to 3. In the following example, though:

```
y = ++x
```

x will first be incremented to 3, then y will be assigned 3. This is especially significant in loop statements. Where x++ would work in past examples, it should be noted that the following will actually increment x before performing the rest of the script elements:

```
for (x=0; x < 5; ++x) {
    y = x;
    }
```

In this case, the first assignment to y would actually have a value of 1, instead of 0.

Decrementing works the same way, with both x-- and --x as possibilities. Both work similarly to x = x - 1, except that --x will decrease before being assigned or used in a loop statement.

It is also possible to assign variables at the same time you increment or decrement. Generally, you would do this with an expression like the following:

```
x = x + y
```

However, this is also possible with the unary operators += and -=. For instance, the previous example could be written as:

```
x += y
```

Similarly, the following two expressions yield the same result:

```
y = y - 2
y -= 2
```

Examples: Looping and Conditions

Let's create an example that incorporates the statements and operators you've seen thus far. In this example, the user enters a number on the page. If the number is within a certain range, it is accepted and you move on. If not, then the user is given an alert and asked to enter a new number.

The number will then increment or decrement until it reaches ten. As it does so, it will print results to a text area on the screen. The user will see the progress as the script counts toward ten.

Create a new HTML page and enter Listing 23.2.

On the CD

Listing 23.2 *condition.html* **Increment or Decrement with Results**

```
<HTML>
<HEAD>
<TITLE>Looping and Conditions Script</TITLE>
<SCRIPT>
<!--
  function countTen (user_num, form) {
      if ((user_num < 0) || (user_num > 20)) {
        alert("Please enter a number between 0 and 20.");
        return;
    }
    while (user_num != 10) {
        if (user_num < 10) {
            addition = "Adding 1...value is now " + (++user_num) + "\r\n";
            form.results.value += addition;
        }
        else {
            subtraction = "Subtracting 1...value is now " + (--user_num) +
              "\r";
            form.results.value += subtraction;
        }
    }
    return;
}
```

```
// -->
</SCRIPT>
</HEAD>
<BODY>
<H3> Please enter a number between 0 and 20 </H3>
<FORM NAME="form1">
Your Number: <INPUT TYPE="TEXT" NAME="number" SIZE="3">
<INPUT TYPE="Button" VALUE="Submit Number" onClick="countTen
(this.form.number.value, this.form)">
<HR>
<H4> The result: </H4>
<TEXTAREA NAME="results" COLS="60" ROWS="10"></TEXTAREA><BR>
<INPUT TYPE="RESET" VALUE="Clear Form">
</FORM>
</BODY>
</HTML>
```

This may take some wading through, but it works—and it should eventually make sense.

Starting in the body of the document, the form requests a number from the user. When the user enters that number and clicks the Submit button, that number's value and a pointer to the form object are sent to the function declaration.

The first if statement determines whether or not the number is between 0 and 20. If it isn't, an alert is shown and the user is asked to enter another number. If it is between 0 and 20, you move on to the WHILE statement.

The WHILE statement will only loop until the value of your number reaches ten. If the value is not currently ten, then the if...then statement will determine whether or not you need to increment or decrement the number to move it toward ten. It then prints the statement, incrementing or decrementing the number while, at the same time, adding the text string to the form's results property.

When the function returns, there's a new value for the TEXTAREA named results. So those strings are printed, and you can see what the script did to move the original number toward ten (see fig. 23.2).

Note: This example introduces two miscellaneous scripting ideas. First, notice that you can use an addition sign (+) to piece together a string. "You and " + "me" results in the string "You and me". Also notice the carriage return character \r\n. This carriage return varies from platform to platform. In Windows, use \r\n; UNIX and Macs use \n. (When you have to choose one, the Windows style works best.) In Chapter 30, "HTML Examples," you'll look at slightly more complicated examples that format correctly on all platforms.

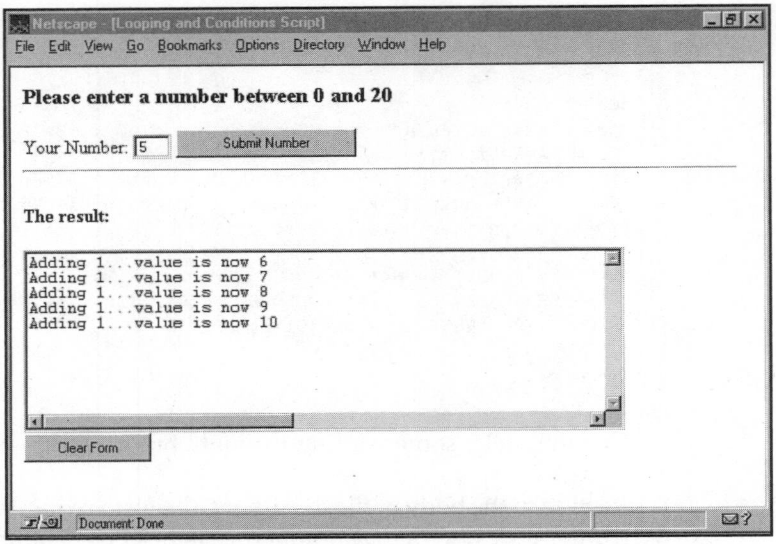

Figure 23.2

The results of the looping and conditions example.

Built-in Objects

In authoring scripts, there are a number of things you're likely to do over and over again. Instead of forcing you to write your own functions and create your own objects to achieve this, JavaScript includes some of these often used calls in the language itself. The built-in objects tend to store useful values or offer convenient methods. The functions usually perform some fairly intensive calculating that you'll often need to use.

The String Object

We'll talk about two major built-in objects available to you in JavaScript. The first is the string object, which helps you manipulate your strings. The math object holds certain constant values for you to use in your script and methods that make it a little easier to perform some mathematical functions.

The first object, the string object, is interesting if only for the fact that you don't actually have to use the notation string.*property* to use it. In fact, any string you create is a string object. You can create a string as simply as this:

```
mystring = "Here's a string"
```

The string variable mystring can now be treated as a string object. For instance, to get a value for the length of a string object, you can use the following assignment:

```
stringlen = mystring.length
```

When you create a string (and JavaScript makes it a string object), the value of its length is stored in the property length. It also associates certain methods with the object, like toUpperCase. You could change a string to all uppercase letters with the following line:

```
mystring = mystring.toUpperCase
```

If the string had the value Here is a string, this assignment changes it to HERE IS A STRING. Table 23.2 shows some of the other methods available with string objects.

Table 23.2 Methods for JavaScript String Objects

Method	Works...	Example
anchor	between <A NAME=> tags	mystring.anchor (section_name)
big	between <BIG> tags	mystring.big()
blink	between <BLINK> tags	mystring.blink()
bold	between <B> tags	mystring.bold()
charAt	by choosing single letter at index	mystring.charAt(2)
fixed	between <TT> tags	mystring.fixed()
fontcolor	between <FONT COLOR=> tags	mystring.fontcolor("red")
fontsize	between <FONT SIZE=> tags	mystring.fontsize(2)
indexOf	by finding index of certain letter	mystring.indexOf("w")
italics	between <I> tags	mystring.italics()
lastIndexOf	by finding occurrence before indexOf	mystring.lastIndexOf ("w")
link	between <A HREF=> tags	mystring.link ("http:// www.com")
small	between <SMALL> tags	mystring.small()
strike	between <STRIKE> tags	mystring.strike()
sub	between <SUB> tags	mystring.sub()
substring	by choosing part of a string	mystring.substring (0,7)

continues

Table 23.2 Continued

Method	Works...	Example
sup	between <SUP> tags	mystring.sup()
toLowerCase	by changing string to lowercase	mystring.toLowerCase()
toUpperCase	by chaging string to uppercase	mystring.toUpperCase()

Most of these methods should be fairly self-explanatory—they allow you to use the method to create and print text as if it were between HTML tags. For instance, the following two script lines have the same results:

```
document.write("<BIG>" + mystring + "</BIG>");
document.write(mystring.big);
```

Some of the other tags take some explaining—especially those that deal with indexes. Every string is "indexed" from left to right, starting with the value 0. So in the following string, the characters are indexed according to the numbers that appear under them:

```
Howdy, boy
0123456789
```

In this case, using the method howdystring.charAt(4) would return the value y. You could also use the method howdystring.indexOf("y"), which would return the value 4.

Example: Talking Decimals

Let's see how this string stuff can be useful. What you'll do is a little bit of math involving decimal numbers, known to programmers as "floats" because they include a floating decimal point. The problem is, when you use dollars and cents decimals, you can get in trouble with JavaScript because it tends to return as many decimal places as possible. This is actually a bug (of sorts) in certain Netscape versions, and it may be changed some time in the future. In the meantime, you'll need to use these string methods to display things correctly.

Create a new HTML page and enter Listing 23.3.

On the CD

Listing 23.3 *strings.html* **Numbers as Strings in JavaScript**

```
<HTML>
<HEAD>
<TITLE> Doin' Decimals </TITLE>
<SCRIPT>
<!--
  function sumValues (val1, val2, val3, form) {
    sum = val1 + val2 + val3;
    form.total.value = sum;
    return;
    }
  function findPoint (form) {
    tot = form.total.value;
    var point_idx = tot.indexOf(".");
    form.results.value = tot.substring (0,point_idx+3);
    return;
    }
// -->
</SCRIPT>
</HEAD>
<BODY>
<H3> The Sum of Your Purchases is:</H3>
<SCRIPT>
<!--
var pur1 = 4.95;
var pur2 = 10.95;
var pur3 = 12.50;
// -->
</SCRIPT>
<FORM>
<INPUT TYPE="Button" VALUE="Click to Compute" onCLICK="sumValues
(pur1, pur2, pur3, this.form)"><BR>
<INPUT TYPE="Text" NAME="total" SIZE="10"><BR>
<INPUT TYPE="Button" VALUE="Click to Cut" onClick="findPoint
(this.form)"><BR>
<INPUT TYPE="Text" NAME="results" SIZE="10"><BR>
</FORM>
</BODY>
</HTML>
```

There are two things to notice here. First, when you use the substring method, you need to add 3 to the index of the decimal point since the values for substring tell the method where to start (e.g., index 0) and how far to go (e.g., point_idx + 3). For example:

```
mystring.substring (0, 7)
```

This doesn't mean "get all the characters and index 0 through index 7." What it really means is "get 7 characters, starting with index 0." So since it's counting from zero, it will stop gathering characters at `index 6`.

Number two is simple: there's a problem with this script. It doesn't round the value. In fact, using exactly the numbers in this example, the total cheats you of nearly a full cent (see fig. 23.3). Use this exact script for a million transactions and you have the potential to loose $10,000! You'll look at rounding in the next example.

Figure 23.3

Taking a substring of a calculated value.

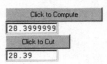

The Sum of Your Purchases is:

The Math Object

The math object basically just holds some useful constants and methods for use in mathematical calculations. The math objects properties are mathematical constants like E, PI, and LOG10E (log, base 10, of E). You can use these by simply adding the name as math's property, as in the following example:

```
var pi_value = Math.PI;
area = Math.PI*(r*r);
```

Table 23.3 shows you the various properties for PI.

Table 23.3 Properties for the Math Object

Property	Value
.PI	Pi (approx. 3.1416)
.E	e, Euler's constant (approx. 2.718)
.LN2	natural log of 2 (approx. 0.693)
.LN10	natural log of 10 (approx. 2.302)
.LOG10E	base 10 log of e (approx. 0.434)
.SQRT1_2	square root of 1/2 (approx. 0.707)
.SQRT2	square root of 2 (approx. 1.414)

The math object's methods are called like any other methods. For instance, the arc sine of a variable can be found by using the following:

```
Math.asin(your_num);
```

Table 23.4 shows the methods for the math object.

Table 23.4 Methods for the Math Object

Method	Result	Format
.abs	absolute value	Math.abs (*number*)
.acos	arc cosine (in radians)	Math.acos (*number*)
.asin	arc sine (in radians)	Math.asin (*number*)
.atan	arc tangent (in rads)	Math.atan (*number*)
.cos	cosine	Math.cos (*num_radians*)
.sin	sine	Math.sin (*num_radians*)
.tan	tangent	Math.tan (*num_radians*)
.ceil	least integer >= num	Math.ceil (*number*)
.floor	greatest int <= number	Math.floor (*number*)
.exp	e to power of number	Math.exp (*number*)
.log	natural log of number	Math.log (*number*)
.pow	base to exponent power	Math.pow (*base, exponent*)
.max	greater of two numbers	Math.max (*num, num*)
.min	lesser of two numbers	Math.min (*num, num*)
.round	round to nearest int	Math.round (*number*)
.sqrt	square root of number	Math.sqrt (*number*)

Example: Rounding for Dollars

With the newly learned Math.round method, maybe you can get that last example to round dollars correctly. Create a new HTML document and enter Listing 23.4 (or make changes on the last example, using Save As to change the name).

On the CD

Listing 23.4 *rounded.html* **Rounding Decimal Numbers in JavaScript**

```
<HTML>
<HEAD>
<TITLE> Rounding for Dollars </TITLE>
```

continues

Listing 23.4 Continued

```
<SCRIPT>
<!--
 function sumValues (val1, val2, val3, form) {
   sum = Math.round ((val1 + val2 + val3)*100);
   form.total.value = sum * .01;
   return;
   }
 function roundTotal (form) {
   var tot = form.total.value;
   var sub_total = Math.round (tot * 100);
   tot_str = "" + sub_total;
   var point_idx = tot.indexOf(".");
   result_str = "";
   y = 0;
   x = 0;
   while (x <= (point_idx+2)) {
      if (x == point_idx && y == 0) {
          result_str += ".";
          y = 1;
      }
      else {
          result_str += tot_str.charAt(x);
          x++;
       }
    }
   form.results.value = result_str;
   // form.results.value = totstr.substring (0,point_idx+3);
   return;
   }
// -->
</SCRIPT>
</HEAD>
<BODY>
<H3> The Sum of Your Purchases is:</H3>
<SCRIPT>
<!--
var pur1 = 4.96;
var pur2 = 11.13;
var pur3 = 13.15;
// -->
</SCRIPT>
<FORM>
<INPUT TYPE="Button" VALUE="Click to Compute" onCLICK="sumValues
(pur1, pur2, pur3, this.form)"><BR>
<INPUT TYPE="Text" NAME="total" SIZE="10"><BR>
<INPUT TYPE="Button" VALUE="Click to Round" onClick="roundTotal
(this.form)"><BR>
<INPUT TYPE="Text" NAME="results" SIZE="10"><BR>
</FORM>
</BODY>
</HTML>
```

JavaScript does weird things with math, so it's difficult to make this work exactly right. Here's my logic. Your values are passed to `sumValues` like before, and the same answer appears in the first textbox. (This is already weird because adding numbers shouldn't give you this odd answer. Unfortunately, this is the kind of trouble you run into with decimal math on computers.)

When you click the second button, the form is sent to `roundTotal`, and a subtotal is generated by multiplying the total by 100 and rounding (remember, `Math.round` rounds to the nearest integer). The subtotal is turned into a string, and then the `while` loop is implemented to find the right place for the decimal point and replaced in the rounded number. Why not just multiply by .01? Good idea, except you'd get a weird floating point number again—and you'd have to start over again!

Take special notice that the following line turns `tot_str` into a string variable with the value `sub_total`:

```
tot_str = "" + sub_total;
```

The alternative is the following:

```
tot_str = sub_total;
```

This assignment would make `tot_str` a numerical variable, which wouldn't work in the subsequent `while` loop. Figure 23.4 shows the whole thing in action.

Figure 23.4

Finally, you've done some rounding.

The Sum of Your Purchases is:

Thoughts on JavaScript

Although JavaScript is a fairly easy language, it still can become very involved, and there's no way you can cover the entire thing in a few chapters. If you'd like to learn more about JavaScript, I'd suggest starting with the *JavaScript Authoring Guide* by Netscape Corporation at **http://home.netscape.com/eng/mozilla/3.0/handbook/javascript/index.html**. If you don't have any programming experience, you might be better off picking up a book designed to teach you JavaScript from the ground up. Both *Special Edition Using JavaScript* and *JavaScript By Example* are excellent titles from Que.

JavaScript is a very powerful way to make your Web site client-side, in that it allows you to actually compute and process without the help of a Web server and special handling (like that required for CGI-BIN scripts). Even more powerful for this are full-fledged Java applets, and you may be able to find some of those that will help you do what you want on your page without much programming at all.

Summary

Once you get deeper into the JavaScript object model, you can start to see a number of easier ways to accomplish advanced scripting issues. Objects can have both properties (variables) and methods (functions) associated with them. The ability to store a number of associated values and function calls in one object makes it easier to group data and work with calculation in JavaScript.

JavaScript also includes a number of keywords and statements for creating if...else and looping statements. Using these takes some understanding of the comparison operators used in JavaScript, as well as a look at the assignment operators. These operators, which can be either binary or unary, can be used to increment, decrement, multiply, assign, and compare values or strings.

Loops can then be used to calculate something a number of times until a condition changes. You can also use the BREAK or CONTINUE statements to perform special commands when a certain condition within a loop is encountered.

JavaScript includes some of its own built-in objects, including those for math and strings. Both have properties and methods associated with them that make many common calculations easier.

Review Questions

1. How can you assign the property at_bats (with a value of 25) to the object player2? (Assume the object already exists.)

2. If document is an object, what is write in document.write?

3. What is substituted for the keyword this in an object definition when a new object is created?

4. True or false. To assign a new method to an existing object requires the new keyword.

5. What's the difference between (x == 1) and (x = 1)? Which of these always evaluates to true?

6. What happens if you don't include an else statement with an if condition and the if condition is false?

7. Consider the following:

```
for (x=0; x<5; ++x) {
    y = x;
}
```

The first time this loop executes, what is the value of y?

8. In the following example, what is the final value for y?

```
for (x=0; x<5; x++) {
  if (x == 4)
    continue;
  y += x;
}
```

9. How can you piece two strings together?

10. What `string` method would you use to create a link to a new HTML document?

Review Exercises

1. Create a new object function called `player` that creates the properties `name`, `hits`, `strikeouts`, `atbats`, and `homeruns`.

2. Add a method to the above object definition that computes the batter's batting average (`hits`/`atbats`). (Baseball enthusiasts will please excuse the crudity of this model.)

3. Write a script that defines a new `player` object and outputs the batter's average in a form textbox.

4. Write a script that defines a new player object and allows the user to enter the `name`, `hits`, `strikeouts`, `atbats`, and `homeruns` values in a text form. Then compute the average and print the player's name and stats to a form textarea.

> **Note:** There's something you need to know for this example. The built-in function `parseInt` (*string_variable*, `10`) can be used to change a string to an integer. The parameters for this function are the name of the string variable and the base numbering system you want to use (i.e., ten for base-10 or decimal numbers). This is an important step because form values are always strings.

## CHAPTER 24

Understanding VRML and Creating VRML Objects

Virtual Reality Modeling Language, or VRML, isn't technically HTML at all, but the two are close cousins. Born out of a desire for a more "human" interface to the Web, VRML is a readable, ASCII-based description language for creating 3D interfaces to the World Wide Web. Eventually, the point is to be able to create rich multimedia 3D worlds for you to explore via the Web, perhaps offering something useful in the process. That really hasn't happened yet, but VRML is definitely the next level of "cool" on the Web.

VRML Standards

VRML is still in its infancy, as the 1.0 standard was only fully completed in the spring of 1995. As I write, version 1.1 is waiting in the wings while version 2.0 is being held out as the next great leap. Currently, VRML 2.0 may not even be based on the same basic file format as VRML 1.0. Better, smaller, faster technology has already overtaken the old standard.

Currently, VRML 1.0 has only limited support for things like "walk through" interfaces. Right now, it's basically a way to render 3D polygons in a way that may or may not seem somewhat realistic (see fig. 24.1). It does have the ability to embed hyperlinks in objects, though, and VRML "worlds" are fairly easy to create with nothing more than a text editor. So, we'll try our hands at it.

Note: It may be wishful thinking, but VRML documents are generally called "worlds," perhaps because the word "document" seems rather two-dimensional. A single ASCII listing can be used to create a world, however.

Figure 24.1

A VRML world on the Web.

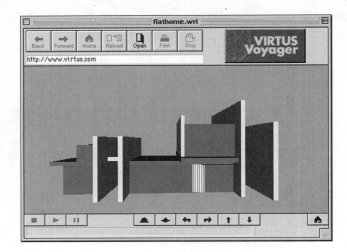

What happens in the future remains to be seen. More than likely, VRML will move quickly toward a standard that requires sophisticated programs to render objects. The VRML 2.0 standard, only recently decided, will incorporate more advanced commands and an optional binary file format from Apple's QuickTime VR technology. Perhaps some backward compatibility will remain, but I wouldn't count on it. Unlike HTML documents, which are largely made up of text, VRML worlds are almost completely graphical. The ability for normal human beings to continue to render them seems unlikely. For now, though, you can.

The Past and Future of VRML

VRML was first conceived in the spring of 1994 at the first WWW Conference in Geneva. With the ambition of having a specification by the fall, an existing Web-friendly 3D file format was sought. It was found in the Open Inventor ASCII file format from Silicon Graphics (SGI). VRML 1.0 went on to become a subset of this file format, with extensions for the purposes of adding hyperlink abilities.

In May 1995, the third and final draft of VRML 1.0 was completed, and work was begun by interested Web developers and applications developers to add VRML functionality to Web browsers, plug-ins, and authoring/rendering solutions.

With the growth in popularity, VRML 2.0 was sought to fill some of the gaping holes in VRML 1.0, like sound support, interaction with objects, and the ability to create "solid" objects that can't be walked through.

In late March of 1996, it was announced that the Moving Worlds proposal from SGI, including the last minute addition of binary file technology in the form of Apple Computer's 3DMF file format, would be the basis of the standard. While not exactly backward-compatible with VRML 1.0, programs should be created to make changing 1.0 documents to 2.0 fairly straightforward.

While hopefully not overwhelmingly more complex, there's also a good chance that VRML 2.0 will be beyond the scope of typical Web authors who will instead rely on VRML 2.0 3D authoring utilities. This will be especially true when using the 3DMF file format, which is a binary (non-ASCII) file format.

How VRML Works on the Web

Plug-ins are being developed for browsers that allow the user to view VRML worlds as inline images, but this too is a young industry. Currently, there is no standard way to embed VRML worlds in Web pages, so plug-ins use their own HTML extensions. This will perhaps be changed by the HTML 3.0 level <INSERT> tag.

VRML Worlds as Hypermedia

Generally, VRML worlds are simply another hypermedia link, used to call a file of MIME type x-world/x-vrml with the file extension .wrl for "world." The following hypermedia link is an example of a link to a VRML world:

```
<A HREF="http://www.fakecorp.com/worlds/support.wrl">Enter Virtual
Support</A>
```

The VRML world would then be loaded into a helper application designed to give the user access to the VRML world, including controls for manipulating the VRML graphics in 3D (see fig. 24.2). Double-clicking different objects will generally send a command back to the browser, which can then move on to another URL.

In general, VRML browsers are configured as helper applications that recognize the x-world/x-vrml MIME type and are loaded whenever a link to a .wrl file is clicked. The VRML browser can then pass links back to the Web browser, so that new worlds (or Web pages) can be loaded when items in the VRML world are selected.

Figure 24.2

A VRML 1.0 world gives you some of the sensations of moving around in a video game.

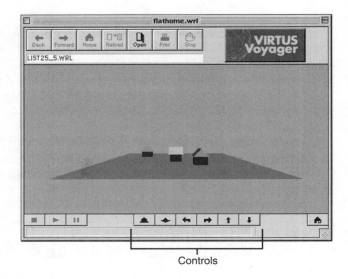

Controls

Servers for VRML

Generally speaking, VRML doesn't require much interaction from your server. Currently, there really aren't any VRML specific servers, although this may change if downloading VRML "streams" becomes popular. (Streams are "just-in-time" downloads that display information as it's sent, like the popular RealAudio radio feeds, for instance.)

One common problem with VRML worlds is that not all servers are set up for the correct MIME type yet, which means users often receive text of VRML worlds instead of a multimedia file that automatically launches a helper or plug-in. If you have this problem with your server, ask your server administrator to set up the x-world/x-vrml MIME type for filename extension .wrl. Once they do that, you should have little trouble making your VRML worlds available on your Web site.

VRML Concepts

As I've said, it's possible to create a VRML world with nothing more than a text editor and some know-how. VRML can get rather complicated, but you can start out with the basics and see how far you can get into Virtual Reality before you throw your hands up.

The Basic Page

In your text editor, you'll need to start out with a new text file. Type the following as the first line of your document:

```
#VRML 1.0 ascii
```

This tells VRML browsers what format you're using. (Later standards will have a different first line.)

> **Note:** Most of the VRML browsers I've encountered are case-sensitive about this first line. Enter it exactly as above.

You can also use the # sign to begin comments in your VRML document. For instance, the following is a comment that will be ignored by the VRML browser, but useful to you and others as documentation of your VRML commands:

```
# This is the left front leg of the chair
```

Coordinates and Distances

The other thing you need to do with VRML is switch over to a 3D way of thinking. Many VRML objects and commands have coordinates, which include X, Y, and Z components, usually in that order. On your screen, X is left and right, Y is up and down, and Z is from the back of your head to the back of the monitor.

These directions are also in positive and negative numbers from a point directly in the middle of the screen or, at least, from the active part of the VRML's display (see fig. 24.3.). Left is negative from center, down is negative, and into the monitor is negative.

Distances in VRML are measured in meters, while angles are given in radians. While VRML objects aren't actually rendered in meters (you'd have trouble fitting them on a computer monitor), this is a relative measurement. It allows something the size of .01 meters, for instance, to be a pencil, while something the size of 1 meter might be a table top.

Radians are the angle (e.g., 45 degrees) divided by 180, times Pi (approximately 3.14). Most browsers will accept best guess radians, so multiplying by 3.14 for Pi is acceptable.

> **Note:** Remember radians? (Hey, I had to look them up.) To get the radians of an angle in degrees, divide the degrees by 180, and then multiply by Pi. For instance, a 360 degree angle, divided by 180 is 2. 2 times Pi gives you the answer—about 6.28 radians.

Figure 24.3

How coordinates work in VRML.

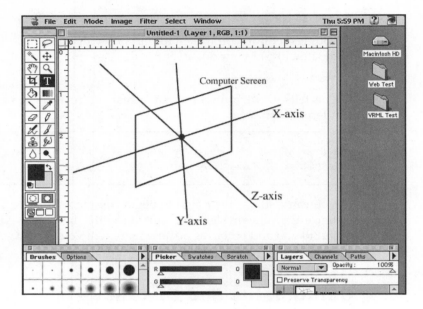

Example One: Starting Out

Just a short and sweet example. Starting with a new text document, enter Listing 24.1.

Listing 24.1 *template.wrl* **Creating your VRML Template**

```
#VRML V1.0 ascii
#
#Comments about this
#world go here.
#
```

Don't forget to save it as your template. No big deal, right? Remember, though, that you're dealing with something other than the HTML page. This is a completely different format, with a different template, different commands, and a different extension.

Nodes

The basic building block of a VRML world is called a *node*. Nodes can do a number of different things, including creating shapes, moving shapes, describing colors and textures, and creating hyperlinks. Nodes can be used together to achieve different effects—in fact, they very commonly are.

Curly brackets are used (as in JavaScript and many programming languages) to represent the beginning and end of a node. The pattern is similar to the following:

```
Cube {
    shape properties
    }
```

A node like this might create a sphere, cone, cylinder, or other shape. The shape will be white (without color description) and centered on the screen. In order to change those characteristics, it's necessary to use nodes together, somewhat like the following:

```
Transform {
    transformation properties
    }
    Cube {
        shape properties
        }
```

Using the various properties for `Transform`, the cube created can be moved in three dimensions, rotated, and scaled. In fact, every node that follows this `Transform` node will be affected unless a `Separator` node is used to enclose the `Transform` and shape nodes. For instance:

```
Separator {
 Transform {
    transformation properties
    }
    Cube {
        shape properties
        }
    }
more VRML
```

What's important here to notice is that both nodes are required to create the shape and change its position in the VRML world. On its own, the shape node would simply create a basic shape. The `Transform` node is designed to affect other nodes, and creates nothing on the screen by itself. The `Separator` node is used to separate these two cooperating nodes from others in the VRML document.

VRML Primitives

Let's begin the discussion of VRML nodes with the primitives, which are simply the basic geometric shapes you can use to create 3D worlds. These include spheres, cylinders, cones, cubes, and text. You'll quickly look at how to create each of these, then you'll figure out how to move them around in our virtual world.

Most primitives follow the basic format of the following:

```
primitive_name {
    properties
    }
```

Spacing is unimportant, but braces are required around the shape's properties.

The Sphere

Probably the easiest shape to create in VRML is a sphere. All you really need to know is what you want the radius to be in meters (well, *virtual* meters). This is done with curly brackets. The primitive name is Sphere and the property name is radius, so an example would be:

```
Sphere {radius 3}
```

That's it. In a properly-formatted VRML document (with the information in Listing 24.1), this single command would create a sphere in a VRML world (see fig. 24.4).

Figure 24.4

Our first, rather primitive, sphere.

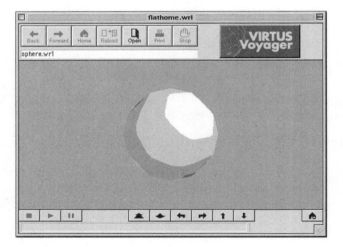

Cylinders and Cones

Some other one-line primitives are cylinders and cones. Both take the property height, but a cylinder and a cone handle their radius differently. These shapes can also take the property parts, which is used to determine which parts of the shape will be rendered. The general format for Cylinder is the following:

```
Cylinder {
    parts part_names
    height size
    radius size
    }
```

The *part_names* can be SIDES, TOP, BOTTOM, or ALL, depending on how you want the cylinder to appear. An example for a cylinder could be the following:

```
Cylinder { height 4 radius .5 }
```

Notice that ALL is always the default for parts so it isn't necessary when you want to render the entire shape. This example creates a cylinder about four meters high and one meter in diameter (see fig. 24.5). Probably perfect for the columns outside of a virtual house. At the same time, a cylinder like the following might be correctly sized and rendered for an eight-ounce drinking glass:

```
Cylinder {
    height .15
    radius .04
    }
```

Figure 24.5

A sample cylinder.

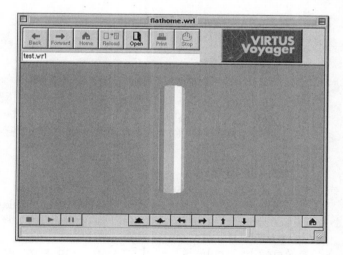

Notice that spacing isn't important, but when you have more than one or two properties, it's probably best to space them out for the sake of clarity.
The cone primitive requires a radius for its base, and a height. Since the radius of a cone changes consistently from bottom to top, you use the property bottomRadius:

```
Cone { height 15 bottomRadius 10 }
```

This one might make a good approximation of a pine tree outside of your virtual mountain cabin (see fig. 24.6).

Figure 24.6

A sample cone.

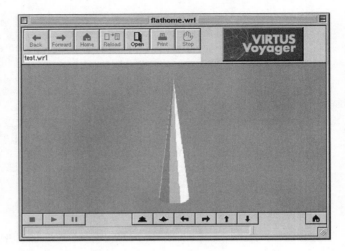

On the other hand, you might use the following:

```
Cone {
    parts SIDES
    height .10
    bottomRadius .02
    }
```

This could easily represent an ice cream cone (albeit upside down for now). The parts property for cones accepts the values SIDES, BOTTOM, or ALL.

The Cube

Perhaps more appropriately called the "cuboid," the cube primitive can have unequal sides, making it more or less a 3D rectangular shape. It's also probably the most useful shape, if for no other reason than the fact that you'll generally want to use it as the floor in your virtual world.

Actually, a cube is useful for representing many different things, from appliances and furniture to buildings and ceilings. Since you can stretch the cube in 3D, you have limitless possibilities—as long as you don't mind jagged edges.

The basic format for a cube is the following:

```
Cube {
  width size
  height size
  depth size
}
```

When initially rendered, the `width` is in the X axis, the `height` is in the Y axis, and `depth` is in the Z access. An example might be the following:

```
Cube {
   width 1
   height 1
   depth 1
   }
```

This one actually is a cube, a meter on each side. It might be good to represent a nice-sized shipping box.

An example that meets the challenge of being a virtual room's "floor" would be the following:

```
Cube {
   width 20
   height .01
   depth 25
      }
```

This is just about the right size for a reasonably dimensioned den or family room—maybe even a master suite. You can see it extending out into the distance in figure 24.7.

Figure 24.7

A virtual floor.

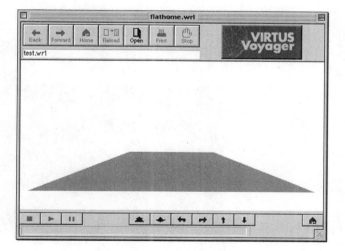

AsciiText

The final primitive accepts a string value of ASCII text and writes it to the screen—`AsciiText`. You can choose values for the spacing, justification (alignment), and width of the string, if you want to confine it to a particular size. The basic format is the following:

```
AsciiText {
    string "Text"
    spacing number
    justification DIRECTION
    width size
    }
```

You enter the text you want to use between the quotation marks. spacing is used to determine the distance between lines when you include more than one string statement.

The justification property takes the values LEFT, CENTER, and RIGHT, and aligns the text relative to the point where x=0 (the center of the screen). LEFT, for instance, causes the string to end at x=0; RIGHT causes the text to begin at x=0.

The width property is often set to zero (which is also the default), but can be used to cause your text to conform to a certain width. The following is an example of AsciiText:

```
AsciiText {
    string "A long, long time ago,"
    spacing 2
    justification CENTER
    }
```

Figure 24.8 shows how this text looks in a VRML browser.

Figure 24.8

AsciiText in
your virtual world.

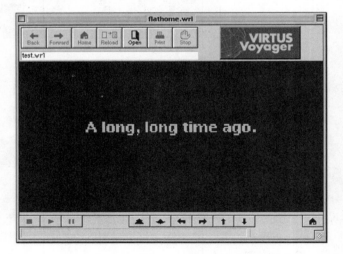

Example: Occupying the Same Space

With what you know now about primitives, you can create some fairly interesting shapes—but you can't do much about where they appear in your virtual world. You'll look into that next. For now, let's see what it's like when you put two shapes in the same world.

Enter Listing 24.2 in a new VRML document.

Listing 24.2 *twoshape.wrl* **Two Shapes in the Same Space**

On the CD

```
#VRML V1.0 ascii
#
#Two shapes in
#one space
#
Sphere { radius 2.5}

Cube {
   width 20
   height .02
   depth 20
   }
```

(Don't forget to save the file with a .wrl extension.) When you load this file into your VRML browser, you should notice that the two have the same point of origin, and are trying to occupy the same space. Things are a bit difficult to puzzle out, since both are the same color, but if you pan up or down slightly, you should be able to see how the two shapes seem fused (see fig. 24.9). From certain perspectives, the sphere is a bump on the road—or perhaps a lone mountain!

Figure 24.9

Are two shapes
better than one?

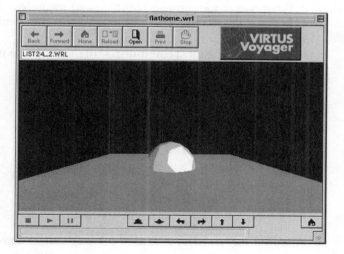

Moving Your Primitives Around

Here, you'll move on to using nodes that move your primitives around in the VRML world. You're using a node called Transform, which is designed to affect the location, rotation, and scale of the objects that come after it.

The basic format is:

```
Transform {
   translation X-distance Y-distance Z-distance
   rotation X-axis Y-axis Z-axis Angle
   scaleFactor X-factor Y-factor Z-factor
   }
Primitive to move/rotate/scale
```

Just to keep this from seeming too intimidating, let's quickly look at an example:

```
Transform {
   translation 2 2 0
   rotation 0 1 0 3.14
   scaleFactor 1 1 1
   }
```

translation

The `translation` property is responsible for actually moving the object in VRML space, and it uses a basic 3D vector to do that. This vector can be seen as a 3D description of how the object should be moved from the point of origin. Consider this part of the last example:

```
translation 2 2 0
```

Whatever shape comes after this `Transform` node will be moved two meters to the right (+2 in the X axis), two meters up (+2 in the Y axis), and will stay at the same distance near/far (0 in the Z axis).

Since this is the most common use of the `Transform` node, it's perfectly reasonable to have a node like this:

```
Transform {translation -2 0 -5}
```

rotation

The `rotation` property allows you to choose which axis you would like to rotate the shape around, and then lets you enter an angle (in radians) for that rotation. Look at the following example:

```
Transform {rotation 0 1 0 1.57}
```

I've chosen to rotate the shape 90 degrees around its Y axis. This would be akin to "spinning" the shape, since the Y axis can be seen as a line from the top of the screen to the bottom of it. Here's another example:

```
Transform {rotation 1 0 0 3.14}
```

This rotates any associated shapes 180 degrees around the X axis. This would be "flipping" the shape. The X axis runs from left to right across the screen, so rotating a shape around the X axis 180 degrees would turn the shape "upside-down."

scaleFactor

The `scaleFactor` property very simply allows you to choose a factor by which a shape can be sized in each access, as in the following example:

```
Transform {scaleFactor 1 4 -2}
```

This would keep any subsequent shapes the same size in the X axis, make the shape larger by a factor of four in the Y axis, and make it smaller by a factor of two in the Z axis.

The *Separator* Node

Of course, the `Transform` node does nothing on its own. But it will now affect any primitives that occur after it until it is separated from the rest of the document with a separator node.

The separator node is very simple. An example would be as follows:

```
Separator {
    Transform {
        translation 2 2 0
        rotation 0 1 0 3.14
        scaleFactor 1 1 1
    }
    Cylinder{}
}
Cube{}
```

Using the `Separator` node in this way, the `Transform` node will affect only the default cylinder you've created. The cube, which is defined outside of the separator, will not be affected by the `Transform` node. Instead of moving, the cube will appear centered in the screen, like the primitives you created earlier in the chapter.

Example: Moving and Flipping

Using everything you've learned up until now, let's create a scoop of ice cream and an ice cream cone—except that they'll be appropriate for someone with the same sized neck as, say, King Kong.

You'll use the sphere and cone primitives to create the basic shapes and the `Transform` node to move those shapes around. On top of that, you'll need `Separator` nodes to transform the shapes individually. Let's also make the shapes a little larger than life so they're easier to see.

Create a new VRML document and enter Listing 24.3.

Listing 24.3 *moving.wrl* **Moving and Flipping Primitives in the VRML World**

```
#VRML V1.0 ascii
#
# Moving and flipping
# VRML primitives
#
Separator {
   Transform {
      translation -1 0 0
      rotation 1 0 0 3.14
   }
   Cone {
      height .75
      bottomRadius .12
   }
}
Separator {
   Transform {
      translation 0 0 -1
   }
   Sphere {radius .5}
}
```

Each of the shapes has an associated `Transform` node that is enclosed with it in a `Separator` node. In the first `Separator` node, you're creating a `Transform` node that moves the shape two meters to the left and "flips" it 180 degrees. You then create the cone primitive, which is 1/2 of a meter in height and about .24 meters in diameter at its bottom. (Of course, flipping it makes the bottom the top, at least insofar as this is supposed to represent an ice cream cone.)

The second `Separator` node uses `Transform` to move the primitive two meters to the right and two meters behind the center point of the screen. Then it creates a sphere with a diameter of .4 meters, which hopefully will make it about the right size for Kong's ice cream appetite (see fig. 24.10).

Figure 24.10

A heckuva lot of virtual calories.

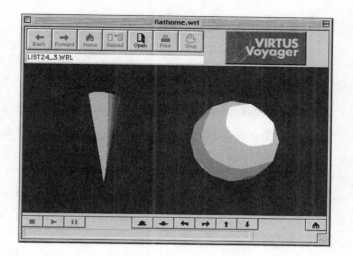

Summary

VRML is more of a cousin to HTML than part of the specification. In some ways it is similar—it's text-based and can be used to navigate the Web. In many ways, it is very different, including the fact that it is basically graphical and 3D. New standards are emerging that may eventually make it difficult for non-programmers to create VRML worlds without special applications.

For now, though, you can create documents that are properly formatted for VRML, and then enter the correct nodes to create various primitive shapes. On their own, primitives appear at the 0,0,0 point in your browser, and will overlap one another when rendered together.

To get past this, you use another node, Transform, to move objects around in the virtual world. Transform is designed to affect every object that comes after it though, so you run into similar overlapping problems unless you use the Separator node.

The Separator node allows you to "nest" nodes within it, thus separating those nodes from the rest of the VRML description. So, a Transform node can be made to affect only the primitive that is in the same Separator.

Review Questions

1. What is the most likely reason for the VRML 2.0 specification to require special programs for creating aspect of your VRML world?

2. What is the MIME type and file extension for VRML worlds?

3. Why is it advisable to create a new template for VRML documents?

4. What is 180 degrees expressed in radians? 90 degrees?

5. You've seen that sphere {} will create a shape, in spite of the fact that it has no properties. Will cube {} create a shape in a VRML browser?

6. Which primitive is the only one to use the bottomRadius property?

7. True or false. Justifying an AsciiText string to the RIGHT will cause the string to end at X=0.

8. Which property for Transform can be used to change the size of a given primitive?

9. How will the following cylinder appear in a VRML browser?

```
Transform {rotation 0 1 0 3.14}
cylinder {}
```

10. True or false. You can nest Separator nodes within one another.

Review Exercises

1. Create a sphere with a radius of five and one with a radius of ten. Without using the Transform node, see if it's possible to view both in your browser.

2. Create a sphere and a cylinder that, when viewed from certain angles in a VRML browser, approximates a planet with rings (like Saturn).

3. Use the Cone, Cylinder, and Transform nodes to create a shape that approximates a pine tree, completely with a trunk.

4. Move the "ice cream scoop" in Listing 24.3 so that it's on top of the "ice cream cone" you created.

## CHAPTER 25

Creating VRML Worlds

In Chapter 25, you learned about creating, placing, and manipulating primitives in VRML. In this chapter, you'll take that knowledge and build on it to create more convincing VRML worlds. Aside from appearance and color issues, you'll look deeper into how to create efficient VRML worlds, and how to add hyperlinks that make them useful for maneuvering on the World Wide Web.

Primitive Appearances

You have two basic alternatives for creating different effects and appearances on primitives in VRML: the Material and Texture2 nodes. Material is used to control the colors assigned to the shapes. Texture2 is used to add graphics files as textures to your shapes.

The *Material* Node

The Material node accepts a number of basic properties: diffuseColor, ambientColor, emissiveColor, specularColor, shininess, and transparency. All of the numbers involved have values from zero to one. The following is the format:

```
Material {
    diffuseColor red_num green_num blue_num
    ambientColor red_num green_num blue_num
    emissiveColor red_num green_num blue_num
    specularColor red_num green_num blue_num
    shininess number
    transparency number
}
```

The first four properties accept values for each of the red, green, and blue channels for the color desired. The values can be any decimal between zero and one (although using a decimal past the "hundredths" place, like .507, is fairly useless).

Most important among the color values is probably diffuseColor, which is essentially the basic color of your primitive. The value ambientColor is sometimes described as "how dark the color is" and it's generally a slightly darker version of the same color as diffuseColor. Look at the following example:

```
Material {
    diffuseColor 0 0 1
    ambientColor 0 0 .8
    }
```

This sets the basic color to blue, with a slightly darker blue used for the ambientColor. The emissiveColor property determines what color your shape will be as it fades into the background. Generally, you'll want this to be darker—meaning you use a smaller number.

The property specularColor is used to represent the color of light bouncing off of the shape. Depending on how surreal your world is, you'll probably want this to be a white/yellowish color. An example of both these properties is the following:

```
Material {
    diffuseColor 0 1 0
    emissiveColor 0 .2 0
    specularColor .8 .6 .8
    }
```

This basically translates to "bright" green in the foreground and darker green in the background, with a yellow/white (with hints of green) as the "light-bouncing" color.

> **Note:** Remember with these red, green, and blue values that as you approach one with all values, you get closer to white. 0,0,0 is black. Everything in between is a spectrum—each color is at its "brightest" at one while the other colors remain zero.

The last two Material properties are simply levels from zero to one. Both are fairly self-explanatory. shininess suggests how much light bounces off the object; transparency affects how solid the material appears. The default value for shininess is 0.2 (a little shiny); default for transparency is 0, or completely solid.

Example: Adding a Little Color

Let's work a little with the last example from Chapter 24, adding a little color to your ice cream cone for Kong. Notice that the Material node affects all other shapes in a particular Separator.

Create a new VRML document (or add the `Material` nodes to your work from last chapter), save it with a `.wrl` extension, and then enter Listing 25.1.

On the CD

Listing 25.1 *color.wrl* **Changing the Colors of VRML Objects**

```
#VRML V1.0 ascii
#
# Moving and flipping
# VRML primitives

Separator {
   Transform {
      translation 0 0 0
      rotation 1 0 0 3.14
   }
   Material {
      ambientColor .6 .4 .2
      diffuseColor .7 .5 .3
      emissiveColor .6 .4 .2

   }
   Cone {
      height .5
      bottomRadius .12
   }
}
Separator {
   Transform {
      translation 0 .25 0
   }
   Material {
      ambientColor .9 .9 .8
      diffuseColor 1 1 .5
      shininess .9

   }
   Sphere {radius .20}
}
```

The best advice for the red, green, and blue (RGB) values is simply to experiment with them until you get what you feel is close to the color you wanted. If you have a graphics program available to you, you might use its color palette to try different RGB levels to achieve the desired colors, then test them in your VRML browser.

In the example, I'm basically going for a light-brown cone and a yellowish sphere, which is meant to suggest a sugar cone and vanilla ice cream. I've also altered the translation values to try to line the ice cream up on top of the cone (so you can see the contrast). It loses something in this screenshot, but figure 25.1 will give you an idea of how this looks.

Figure 25.1

Kong's cone in color. (The picture is black and white, not the cone.)

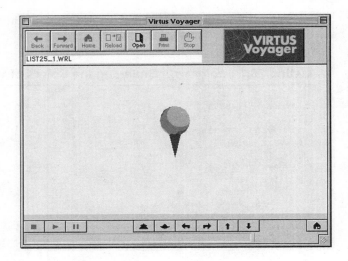

The *Texture2* Node

The basic point of the Texture2 node is to allow you to wrap a graphic around a primitive. (And no, I don't know what happened to Texture1.) Texture2 takes the properties filename, wrapS, and wrapT. The basic format is the following:

```
Texture2 {
    filename "image URL"
    wrapS REPEAT/CLAMP
    wrapT REPEAT/CLAMP
}
```

Now, honestly, there's a lot more to the wrapS and wrapT, but it's rather confusing to me. Here's the scoop: many browsers tend to implement Texture2 in only the most basic ways. If your browser happens to support these two properties, then setting wrapS and wrapT to CLAMP forces just one instance of your graphic to be pasted on the primitive. Using REPEAT for both will tile the graphic all over the primitive. An example of this is as follows:

```
Texture2 {
    filename "earth.gif"
    wrapS CLAMP
    wrapT CLAMP
    }
```

REPEAT is the default value for both, so there's no need to include the properties if you want the image to tile onto your primitive.

Example: Covering Up Primitives

Here's a good example of how images will cover different primitives. Just about any graphics file will do—just make sure you have it in the same directory as the VRML file. Create a new .wrl file and enter Listing 25.2.

Listing 25.2 *texture.wrl* **Adding Textures to VRML Objects**

```
#VRML V1.0 ascii
#
#adding Texture
#to VRML primitives
#

Separator {
    Separator {
        Texture2 {
            filename "wood.gif"
            wrapS CLAMP
            wrapT CLAMP
        }
        Translation { translation -3.5 0 0 }
        Sphere { }
    }
    Separator {
        Texture2 { filename "wood.gif" }
        Translation { translation -1.25 0 0 }
        Cone { }
    }
    Separator {
        Texture2 { filename "wood.gif" }
        Translation { translation 1 0 0 }
        Cylinder { }
    }
    Separator {
        Texture2 { filename "wood.gif" }
        Translation { translation 3.5 0 0 }
        Cube { }
    }
}
```

Use whatever graphics file you'd like in place of wood.gif. You're probably better off with a texture, but it can be just about as much fun with the picture of a cartoon character or politician. In fact, you can make your VRML world look a little like some of the popular movies that have included VR by creating a flat cube for the face and pasting a graphic to it using the CLAMP values.

I'd also recommend that you experiment with different values, graphics, and primitives using this example.

Adding Hyperlinks in VRML

Links in VRML just require another node, the WWWAnchor node. This one accepts two basic properties, name and description as in the following example:

```
WWWAnchor {
   name "URL"
   description "Alternate text"
   }
```

The WWWAnchor node works a lot like a Separator node in that it actually includes the primitive and whatever descriptive nodes you've used to affect that node. An example might be:

```
WWWAnchor {
   name "http://www.fakecorp.com/worlds/world2.wrl"
    description "Into the next world"
   Separator {
        Texture2 { filename "wood.gif" }
        Translation { translation -1.25 0 0 }
        Cone { }
   }
}
```

The name property can accept any sort of URL, whether it's another VRML world, a regular HTML document, or a hypermedia link. The description text is similar to ALT text for the <IMG> tag. Some VRML browsers will allow the ALT text to pop-up on-screen to help the user decide if this is a useful link for them.

Example: Linking in Your VRML World

In this example, you'll create some basic primitives and see how different links react when clicked in your VRML world. Create a new VRML document and enter Listing 25.3.

On the CD

Listing 25.3 *links.wrl* **Creating HTML Links for Your VRML Objects**

```
#VRML V1.0 ascii
#
#adding links
#to VRML primitives
#
```

```
WWWAnchor {
    name "index.html" #A regular HTML page
     description "To Our Index Page"
    Separator {
        Translation { translation -3.5 0 0 }
        Sphere { }
    }
}
WWWAnchor {
    name "demo.moov" #A hypermedia link
     description "See the Presentation (QT 1.4mb)"
    Separator {
        Translation { translation -1.25 0 0 }
        Cone { }
    }
}
WWWAnchor {
    name "office.wrl" #Another VRML world
     description "Move to the Office"
    Separator {
        Translation { translation 1.25 0 0 }
        Cylinder { }
    }
}
```

You'll probably want to change the names of the different files (in the links) above so you can use files hanging around on your hard drive (make sure they're all in the same directory as your VRML document). You should also experiment with different types of files to see how things are loaded and passed between the HTML browser, the VRML browser, and other helper applications.

> **Note:** Some VRML browsers download the `.wrl` file to the user's hard drive and then access it from there. That means that relative links in the `.wrl` file will break, since the links will now be "relative" to the user's hard drive. For this reason, it's a good idea to use absolute URLs (even for your texture images) if you add VRML worlds to a real Web site.

Back in your VRML world, things really haven't changed much. In some browsers, primitives will be highlighted when they're clickable. In others (like mine), you'll just get a slightly different cursor (see fig. 25.2).

Figure 25.2

The cursor will change from this arrow to a crosshair for links.

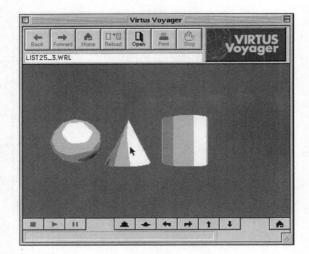

More Fun with Shapes

So far, you've been dealing with the built-in primitives of VRML, and you've completely passed over the possibility of creating your own shapes. Is it possible? Sure. But it'll take some thinking. It's also possible, and timesaving, to use special commands to give your shapes "nicknames" for referring to shapes you can create. The advantage is that it then takes one line of VRML code to create another one!

More Nodes: *Coordinate3* and *IndexedFaceSet*

Creating your own shapes takes two steps, and two different nodes. The first node, Coordinate3, is used to layout the coordinates for your new shape. This doesn't actually create anything in the VRML world. It's more of a template for the next node, IndexedFaceSet. Using this second node, you actually draw the faces of your shape by specifying the points for each.

> **Tip:** Draw your object in as close to 3D as possible (or make it in clay or origami), and label the points (starting with zero). This will help you create it in VRML.

The Coordinate3 node is used with the point property in the following format:

```
Coordinate3 {
  point [
      x1-coord y1-coord z1-coord, #point 0
      x2-coord y2-coord z2-coord, #point 1
      ...,
  ]
}
```

Each coordinate for your shape requires an X, Y, and Z coordinate. This creates a point in your VRML world. Get enough points together, and you'll have a shape. But you won't be able to see anything.

The next step is to add the IndexedFaceSet node. The order in which you assign points in the Coordinate3 node is noticed by VRML, and you can use that to determine what points make up each "side" of your shape. The number -1 is used to tell IndexedFaceSet that you're done with that side. IndexedFaceSet uses the property coordIndex for the listing of sides, as in the following format:

```
IndexedFaceSet {
  coordIndex [
      point_num, point_num, point_num, -1, #side1
      point_num, point_num, point_num, -1, #side2
      ...
  ]
}
```

You should probably also consider that not every side necessarily has three points—in fact, many won't. That's why you use -1 to represent the end of a shape. Depending on your mood and the number of advanced degrees in mathematics you have, the sides of your shapes could have many, many points to connect.

Example: Up on the House Top

Here's a shape you might want to use in your VRML world—a rooftop. It takes six points and five sides to create this particular rooftop. Fortunately, you can limit the number of dimensions and triangular hypotenuses you're working with.

Figure 25.3 shows you a sketch of the rooftop, including the coordinates you'll use. It doesn't look like it, but the bottom points of this roof all sit at the same Y coordinate. It's tilted to show 3D on this 2D page.

Actually, it's not that bad, is it? Architects could learn from the symmetry of your rooftop. Now look again and see which sides you're going to need to draw with the IndexedFaceSet node. Figure 25.4 shows those sides.

Figure 25.3

Here's your shape and the coordinates for each point.

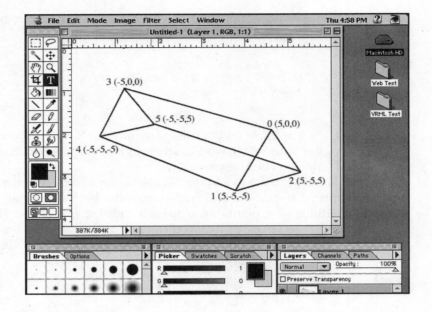

Figure 25.4

Here's your shape with the sides you need to draw

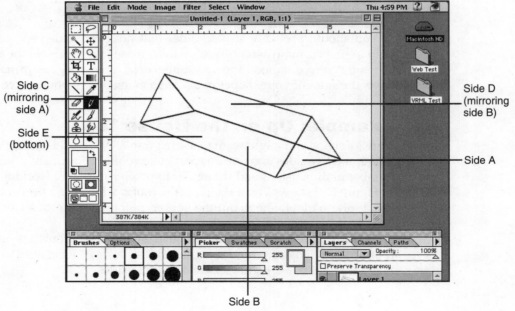

Now, armed with all this information, you're ready to code this roof! Create a new VRML document and enter Listing 25.4.

Listing 25.4   *rooftop.wrl*   Creating the Rooftop Shape

```
#VRML V1.0 ascii
#
#Creating our own
#rooftop shape
#

Separator {

  Coordinate3 {
    point [
      5  0  0,        #0
      5 -5 -5,        #1
      5 -5  5,        #2
     -5  0  0,        #3
     -5 -5 -5,        #4
     -5 -5  5,        #5
    ]
  }

  IndexedFaceSet {
    coordIndex [
      0, 1, 2, -1,        #Side A
      0, 1, 4, 3, -1,     #Side B
      3, 4, 5, -1,        #Side C
      0, 2, 5, 3, -1,     #Side D
      5, 2, 1, 4, -1,     #Side E
    ]
  }
}
```

Notice in `IndexedFaceSet` that you're able to create the different sides required for this shape—both the triangles for the ends and the four-pointed rectangles for the slopes (and bottom) of the roof. You can see this roof in figure 25.5.

Figure 25.5

The rooftop, complete.

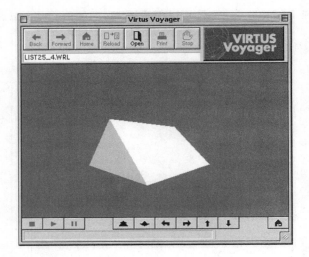

Instancing

One of the major concerns with VRML worlds, especially as their popularity begins to grow, is the size of the world files. Currently, low bandwidth connections make using large VRML worlds more of a "cool toy" than a reasonable alternative to HTML. Higher bandwidth may change that in a future, and it's reasonably easy to see a time when VRML will make navigating the Web very interesting.

VRML itself addresses this problem with file size by noticing that many of the shapes you'll use to create your world happen to be rather similar to one another. You might want to create a world, for instance, with a number of houses in it. Creating a complete house every time can be a little intimidating for the designer, as well as expensive in terms of file size. (Look how much code it took just to create the rooftop!) So, VRML gives you something called *instancing*.

This is a little like creating an object in JavaScript and similar programming/scripting languages. Basically, you just assign a "nickname" to a particular node or group of nodes. When you want to use that node again, you just type the keyword USE, followed by the nickname, as in the following example:

```
DEF beach_ball Sphere { radius .5 }

USE beach_ball
```

This is a simple example, but notice how powerful this ability is. Now, instead of using all of the code back in Listing 25.4 to create another rooftop, you could use the DEF keyword to create a nickname for the entire process—like my_roof—and you could duplicate them to your hearts' content.

DEF needs to be used with a node, but that node needn't stand on its own. You can easily assign a DEF name to a Separator node, which could encompass an entire defined "object" in your world. You can even assign DEF to non-drawing nodes, as in the following example:

```
DEF make_red Material {
    ambientColor .9 0 0
    diffuseColor 1 0 0
    emissiveColor .9 0 0
  }
```

Now the command USE make_red can be used as a one-line statement to add red to subsequent nodes within your VRML world.

Example: A VRML Neighborhood

Using instancing, you can take your rooftop, add a house for it, instance the house, and create a complete neighborhood in short order. Create a new VRML world document and enter Listing 25.5.

On the CD

Listing 25.5   *nbr_hood.wrl*   Using DEF for Cloning

```
#VRML V1.0 ascii
#
#Creating our own
#neighborhood
#

Transform {                    #move whole world away and below 1
    translation 0 -1 -50
}

Separator {                    #create the ground
   Material {
      ambientColor 0 .9 0
      diffuseColor 0 1 0
      emissiveColor 0 .5 0
   }
   Cube {
      height .01
      width 100
      depth 100
   }
}

DEF my_house Separator {    #define this as a my_house instance
```

continues

Listing 25.5   Continued

```
  Material {                    #add color to main house
     ambientColor 0 0 .9
     diffuseColor 0 0 1
     emissiveColor 0 0 .5
  }

Separator {                     #move cube up above ground
    Transform {
        translation 0 2.5 0
    }

  Cube {                        #create house
     height 5
     width 8
     depth 8
  }
}

  Material {                    #add color to roof
     ambientColor .4 .9 .4
     diffuseColor .5 1 .5
     emissiveColor .5 .5 .5
  }

  Coordinate3 {                 #create roof points
     point [
       5 10 0,        #0
       5 5 -5,        #1
       5 5 5,         #2
      -5 10 0,        #3
      -5 5 -5,        #4
      -5 5 5,         #5
    ]
  }

  IndexedFaceSet {              #draw sections of roof
     coordIndex [
       0, 1, 2, -1,      #Side A
       0, 1, 4, 3, -1,   #Side B
       3, 4, 5, -1,      #Side C
       0, 2, 5, 3, -1,   #Side D
       5, 2, 1, 4, -1,   #Side E
     ]
  }
}                               #bracket ends this DEF instance

Separator {                     #new house
  Transform {
     translation 15 0 15
     rotation 0 1 0 1.57
  }
```

```
    USE my_house
}

Separator {                        #another new house
    Transform {
        translation -25 0 -25
        rotation 0 1 0 1.57
    }
    USE my_house
}
```

So you define an instance for the entire house, and then simply type the
USE command to add another instance of it. Of course, they're all the same color, but
at least you can use Transform to put the house in another part of your world and
rotate it.

If you did want to change the colors of your house, you'd probably want to break
out the parts of my_house, perhaps creating my_roof and my_house so you could use
different Material nodes for each. Of course, you could always have different DEF
statements for Material, so that eventually USE had houses like the following:

```
Separator {
USE make_red
USE my_roof
USE make_green
USE my_house
}
```

That creates an entire house in four lines! Plus, once you get a glimpse of your
little VRML neighborhood, you'll probably want to figure out how to change house
colors quickly (see fig. 25.6).

Figure 25.6

Here's your, uh,
smurfy little
village.

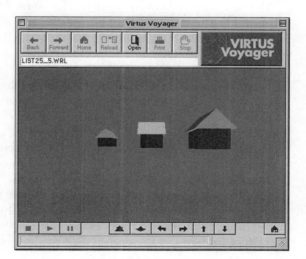

More VRML

Like our discussion of JavaScript, there's a lot more to VRML that can't be covered in this book. But, you've got a great start. For more VRML info, check out the following Web sites:

- Pioneer Joel:

    http://honors.uhc.asu.edu/~joel/vrml/

- Silicon Graphics' VRML 2.0 site:

    http://webspace.sgi.com/moving-worlds/

- Pete's Easy VRML Tutorial:

    http://www.mwc.edu/~pclark/vrmltut.html

- Macmillan's VRML Foundry

    http://www.mcp.com/general/foundry/

- Cindy Reed's VRML Textures:

    http://www.ywd.com/cindy/texture.html

Summary

After you've learned to create the basic shapes in VRML, you can move on to making things feel more like a "world." Using the nodes `Material` and `Texture2`, for instance, you can add color, images, and light properties to your shapes.

The next step is to make your world useful for the Web—so you need to add hyperlinks. The `WWWAnchor` can be used to make any primitive or other shape a hyperlink to just about anything: another VRML world, an HTML document, or even a hypermedia file.

You can also create your own shapes. Using the `Coordinate3` and `IndexedFaceSet` nodes, you can tell your VRML browser where the coordinates for your shape are—and then you can use those points to tell the browser where to draw the sides of your shape. These two may be among the most powerful nodes for serious VRML world creators.

Instancing, however, is easily the most powerful node for the lazy creator. Not to mention that it's good for low bandwidth connections to your VRML world. With instancing, you can create "nicknames" for your VRML objects—even from something as big as a house—and create another like it with a one-line command.

There's more to it than that, and the end of this chapter details some Web sites for learning more about VRML. Hopefully, you've got a good enough start to have some fun, though.

Review Questions

1. Choose the one that would create a darker color:

```
Material {diffuseColor .9 0 0}
Material {diffuseColor .1 0 0}
```

2. What RGB color are you working with in question 1?

3. What's the major difference between REPEAT and CLAMP? Which one do you never actually need to type?

4. Why would it be best to use absolute URLs for the following:

```
Texture2 { filename "URL" }?
```

5. What other VRML node works a lot like WWWAnchor?

6. What's wrong with the following?

```
WWWAnchor {
    name "http://www.fakecorp.com/index.html"
    description "Back to Index"
    Material {diffuseColor 0 0 .5}
      }
```

7. For what is the –1 in the coordIndex property of IndexedFaceSet used?

8. In the following:

```
Coordinate3 {
    point [
      0 1 -1
      5 1 -1
      5 -1 -1
      0 -1 -1
    ]
}
```

What is the point number assigned to {5 -1 -1}?

9. True or false. You can create an instance of the Transform node.

10. When you create the primitive sphere {} and view it in a browser, where (virtually) are you in relation to the sphere?

Review Exercises

1. Using any series of primitives or world you've created, use the Transform node to move the entire world away from the opening point-of-view.

2. Using the rooftop you created in Listing 25.5, create a rooftop with different colors for each (or at least a few) of the sides.

3. Change Listing 25.5 so that you can choose different colors or textures for each house and roof you create.

4. Change Listing 25.5 so that each house becomes a clickable hyperlink. Also, use the AsciiText node from Chapter 24 to add a label to each house.

## CHAPTER 26

Adding Portable Documents to Web Sites

One of the things I've mentioned over and over about HTML and the Web in general is the lack of control you, as a Web designer, ultimately have over your own page. Even with Netscape extensions, IE extensions, HTML 3.0 style sheets, and other extensions, you still only have control when your pages are viewed in compatible browsers. While Netscape and Internet Explorer alone make up a sizable part of the browser market, there's no way to guarantee that everyone will see your site in the same exact way.

For most people, and in most cases, that's not a problem. But consider this example. What if you were setting up a Web page for the IRS? With the complex, computer-readable forms that the IRS has to distribute to tax payers, HTML just wouldn't be able to cut it. For the answer to this example—and any others where forms, newsletters, instruction sheets, legal documents, or any other published material needs to be delivered completely intact—we must turn to portable document formats.

What Are Portable Documents?

Portable Document Format is actually a file format (like GIF or MPEG) created and used by the Adobe Acrobat system. The Acrobat system is probably the most widely known (and Internet pervasive) method for distributing portable documents. Based on Adobe's PostScript technology, certain Adobe products are capable of generating PDF files, which can then be viewed by Web helper applications and plug-ins (see fig. 26.1).

Figure 26.1

Viewing an Adobe PDF file.

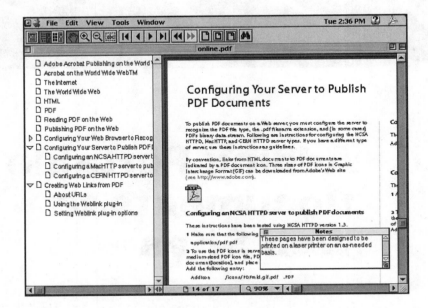

In more general terms, portable documents refer to any sort of technology that allows you to distribute documents intact to users, without relying on the "machine-dependent" nature of HTML. In other words, these are documents that can be viewed by the user, but only in one way—they cannot be reformatted to fit the needs of the user's Web browsing program or machine.

Although more sophisticated than this, you can almost think of portable documents as just big graphics files. Most of these documents don't allow the user to alter them in any way, although some, like Envoy (formerly WordPerfect Envoy), allow you to annotate these documents with little electronic "sticky notes." You can't change the original documents, but you can add comments that appear on top of the document.

So what qualifies as a portable document? Well, among others, Adobe Acrobat, Envoy, Common Ground, RTF files, Microsoft Word DOC files, and even ASCII text files. Each offers various advantages and tradeoffs, but all (with the exception of ASCII) also offer the ability to control the display of your text to a greater degree than you can with HTML.

Adding PDFs To Your Web Site

The good news is, Adobe distributes Acrobat Reader for free. The bad news is, you have to pay a decent amount of money for the products that create Acrobat files, like Adobe Exchange. These products help you create, lay out, and save your files as .pdf format files. They can then be added to your Web site for downloading by interested users.

> **Tip:** To find out more about Acrobat products, visit **http://www.adobe.com/**.

Adding an Acrobat file to your Web page takes nothing more than a hypermedia link with the appropriate extension. For instance:

```
Here are Adobe's <A HREF="online.pdf"> Tips for Adding Acrobat Files to
Web Sites</A> in Acrobat format.
```

When clicked, this link will cause the browser to download the PDF document to the user's hard drive. If the user's browser is properly configured, the document will be loaded into Adobe's Acrobat reader, as in figure 26.2.

Figure 26.2

Adobe's Acrobat Reader.

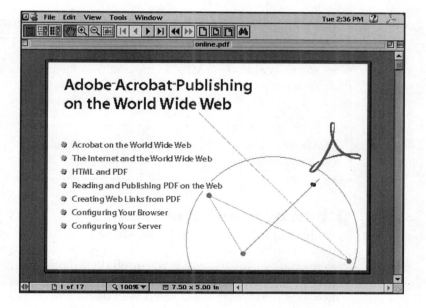

MIME Type

In order for the browser to accept these files, however, it needs to have the Adobe Acrobat reader set up properly as a helper application. In Netscape Navigator, for instance, this is accomplished through the Helpers tab in Netscape's General Preferences. Add a new document type with the MIME type of application/pdf with the extension .pdf (see fig. 26.3).

Figure 26.3

You can add the Adobe Acrobat reader as a helper in Netscape Navigator.

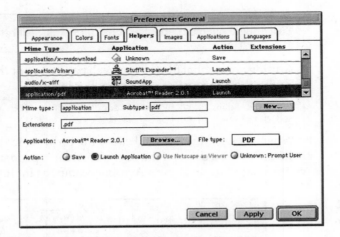

In addition, this same MIME type and file extension may need to be added to your Web server as recognized file types. Otherwise, your files may not always be correctly downloaded and fed to the helper application by your user's browser.

> **Note:** Adobe Acrobat files can also be viewed directly in the Netscape browser window with help from the Adobe Amber plug-in for Netscape.

Other Acrobatic Moves

In addition to slick text and graphics, Adobe Acrobat products (both the reader and creator programs) can accept plug-in programs to increase their abilities. The Weblink plug-in, for instance, gives Adobe PDF files the ability to embed hyperlinks within them. When clicked by the user, the link is fed back to the Web browser, which then retrieves the associated Web document or multimedia file. Much like VRML, this gives a file format other than HTML the ability to access URLs (see fig. 26.4).

Figure 26.4

Accessing hyperlinks in PDF documents.

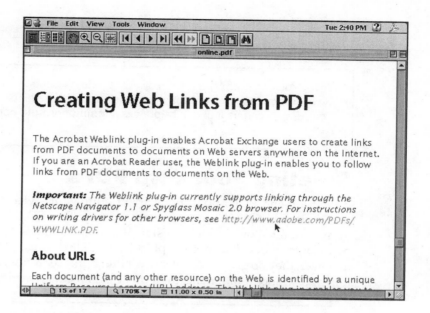

Other plug-ins give Acrobat the ability to play inline movies, animations, sounds, and other multimedia files in a way that's similar to newer plug-in technology for Web browsers.

> **Note:** The plug-ins discussed here are for the Adobe Acrobat program itself—not for Netscape Navigator or another Web browser.

Other PDF Formats

Other commercially available PDF creators and readers include Envoy and Common Ground Digital Paper. Both offer free readers that can be added as helper applications in Web browsers.

To serve Envoy documents from your Web site, make sure your server is capable of recognizing files with the MIME-type `application/x-evy` and the extension `.evy`. Adding them to your Web pages is as easy as PDFs. For example:

```
<A HREF="demo.evy">Our Demo Envoy portable document.</A>
```

For Common Ground Digital Paper, the MIME type is `application/x-dp` and the file extension is `.dp`. They can be added to Web documents just like Envoy and PDF files, as in the following:

```
<A HREF="form.dp">Please download the Digital Paper formatted form for
printing.</a>
```

> **Note:** You can download the Envoy viewer and Netscape plug-ins from **http://www.twcorp.com/viewer.htm**. Information and viewers for Common Ground Digital Paper can be found at **http://www.commonground.com/index.html**.

Creating Your Own PDFs

If the high-end PDF applications aren't quite your style, you can still use other programs you have hanging around as substitute PDF files. Most of these file formats don't allow for the inclusion of graphics and don't give you much control over fonts, while the more sophisticated PDF formats do. At the same time, however, they do give you control over things like centering, text size, hard returns, font appearance (bold, italic, underlined), and similar attributes.

> **Note:** PDF formats are designed to appear exactly the same on different computer platforms. These makeshift PDFs (like MS Word documents discussed below) will generally have slight differences from platform to platform and version to version.

For instance, Microsoft Word documents are an easy way to distribute documents on the Web, as Word tend to be one of the most popular word processors, and most other word processors can read Word's DOC files.

But even if a user's word processor can't read DOC files, Microsoft offers a free Word document viewer for Windows users. The Word Viewer is designed to do just that—allow your users to view and print Word documents. Without Word or another word processor, they can't do any editing. But they can view and print your pre-formatted form (see fig. 26.5).

> **Tip:** The Word viewer can be downloaded from **http://www.microsoft.com**. You might want to let your users know this if you offer Word documents for downloading.

Figure 26.5

Using the
Microsoft Word
Viewer.

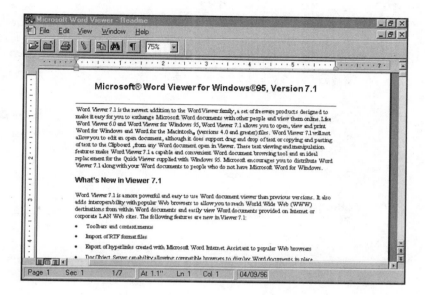

Creating the Word Document

Fortunately, there's nothing special you need to do to create a Word document for viewing on the Internet. The only requirement is that you use Microsoft Word to create the documents (or a word processor that can save in Microsoft Word for Windows 2.0 and above or Word for Mac 4.0 and above formats). Save the file with a .doc extension just as Windows and DOS users normally would.

> **Tip:** Windows 95 users can use WordPad to create, view, and edit Word documents.

Then, you can make it available as a hyperlink on your Web site, just as with any other multimedia file, as in the following example:

```
Download the file in <A HREF="file.doc> MS Word format </A>.
```

Using Rich Text Format

Another interesting way to distribute formatted documents on the Web is by using the Rich Text Format (RTF). RTF is a Microsoft file format that's designed to be more sophisticated than plain ASCII text, but less proprietary and complicated than word processing document types. Most word processors can create, view, print, and save documents in this format.

To make RTF format files available on your Web site, first save your document in your word processor as an RTF file with the extension .rtf. From there, all you have to do is include it in a hypertext link, like in the following:

```
<A HREF="myfile.rtf">Here's a copy of my special RTF file.</A>
```

Example: Creating a Portable Word File

If you have Microsoft Word, WordPad, or any word processor available that can save files in MS Word for Windows 2.0 or above format, then enter Listing 26.1 in a new Word document.

Listing 26.1   A Portable MS Word File

```
Printable Order Form

The following information is required to complete your order in as timely
a fashion as possible.

First Name:
Last Name:
Street Address:
City:
State:
Zip:
Daytime Phone Number:
Evening Phone Number:
Credit Card Number:
Expiration Date:

Signature:

If you prefer, please enclose a check for $43.95US ($39.95 and $4.00
shipping).

Please mail this order form to:

BigCorp
Attn: Order Processing
001 Tallest Building
Metropolis, USA 10001

Copyright 1996 BigCorp. Please allow 4-6 weeks delivery.
```

Now, Microsoft Word or your word processor offers you the freedom to alter this form with font size, emphasis, and even centering. For instance, I'm going to center the title of this page, make it slightly bigger than the rest of the form, and bold it. I'm also going to boldface the "most required" information on the form, so that users see what's most important. I'll make the small print at the bottom of the page even smaller (see fig. 26.6).

> **Tip:** Use common fonts (like Times, Courier, Helvetica) when creating these documents, so that nearly any MS Word user can view them just as you create them.

Figure 26.6

My new "portable" MS Word form.

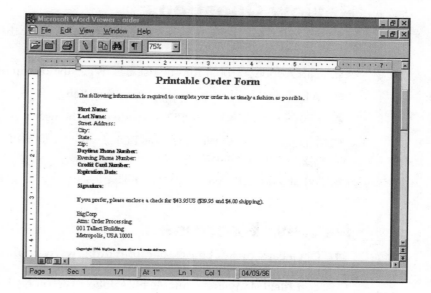

Summary

In some instances, HTML simply doesn't give you enough control over the documents you distribute on the Web. Whether you simply want your "corporate image" to remain intact or if you need to transmit format-dependent forms for official use, you can use portable documents when HTML won't work.

Adobe Acrobat is easily the most popular PDF format, and adding these documents to your Web pages is as simple as creating a hypermedia link. Acrobat files can be read with the free Acrobat viewer program for most computer platforms. If you include Acrobat or any other formats, like Envoy or Common Ground Digital Paper, you'll need to correctly set the MIME type for your server. You'll also want to point your user to the correct Web site for downloading the appropriate viewer software.

The "poor man's" portable document format might just be MS Word files, or even Rich Text Format (RTF) files. Both of these formats are widely supported by Microsoft and other word processing products. Microsoft even offers a Word Viewer program free on the Web. While control is not as rich as with true PDFs, these are good, inexpensive substitutes for documents that are still more reliably rendered than HTML.

Review Questions

1. True or false. PDFs give you increased control over the physical appearance of your documents.

2. Can Adobe Acrobat files be used as hypertext documents?

3. Which PDF is the most popular on the Web?

4. In most cases, how are PDFs handled by the user's Web browser?

5. To use Microsoft Word files as PDFs, what version of Word should you save your documents in?

6. What's the difference between RTF files and ASCII files?

Review Exercises

1. Get a copy of Adobe Acrobat from **http://www.adobe.com** and configure it as a helper application for your Web browser. Now, download and view a `.pdf` file. (Many are available on Adobe's Web site.)

2. Add an Adobe `.pdf` file to your Web site, and then download it (over the Internet) with your browser. Does it load properly into the Acrobat helper application?

3. Create a Word document for distribution on your Web site, then download it over the Internet. If possible, use a different computer to download the Word document and view it in Word or the Word viewer. Does it look any different?

Part VI

HTML Editors and Tools

CHAPTER 27

Creating HTML Documents with Netscape Gold

Up until now, all of the HTML page creation you've done has been with a standard text editor and a Web browser for viewing. But that isn't the only way to go. In this chapter and the next few chapters, you'll learn about some of the programs that are now making it possible for you to create HTML documents without resorting to hand entering tags. While some of these products are still developing, they're at least a great way to create basic sites, which you can hand edit later.

In this chapter, you'll learn specifically about Netscape Gold, the special edition of Netscape Navigator that includes the Netscape Editor. This editor allows you to create HTML documents in a what-you-see-is-what-you-get (WYSIWYG) environment.

Note: Netscape Gold is actually a commercial product available from Netscape Corporation. Netscape offers a shareware "try and buy" deal or (sometimes) a free beta test version of Netscape Gold for general downloading. You might want to visit **http://www.netscape.com/** to see what's currently available.

Why Edit By Hand at All?

I wouldn't be surprised if you were wondering why I bothered to write an entire book about editing HTML by hand when tools like Netscape Gold exist. Well, In my defense, I've got some answers to that.

First, without a pretty solid knowledge of how HTML works, using many HTML editors, especially Netscape Gold, could get you into some trouble. Netscape is particularly bad about giving you options in its menu and button bar without making it clear what standard they adhere to. Netscape extensions are rolled right in with HTML 2.0 and HTML 3.0 level tags and attributes.

Also, many editors, Gold included, don't offer complete support for all of the tags and HTML constructs you might want to use. The Gold editor has no easy way to create HTML tables, for instance, and only a few nods to creating frames.

While it's true that editing basic HTML in these editors can be easier and more convenient than using a plain text editor, I feel like you should know what you're doing, and what's happening behind the scenes. Having read this book, you know how HTML and extension tags work. If Netscape Gold (or others) makes that easier, fine.

Chances are you'll still need to get your hands dirty with HTML to make your pages great.

Editing HTML With Netscape Gold

To begin the Netscape Gold HTML Editor, simply choose File, New, Blank. What appears next is the Netscape Gold HTML Editor (see fig. 27.1). From here, you can simply begin typing your HTML document.

Tip: Choosing From Template or From Wizard in the New Document menu gives you access to templates and walk-throughs designed by Netscape to make Web document creation easier.

The Netscape Gold Editor is really designed to be used much like a standard word processor. Notice that the toolbar across the top gives you the option of making text bold, italic, or teletype; choosing different font sizes; and even inserting images and creating hyperlink anchors by simply pressing buttons. Using just the toolbar, it's simple to create a basic HTML page.

For instance, to create a header for your page, enter the text for the header, like the following:

```
Welcome to my Page
```

Figure 27.1

The WYSIWYG HTML Editor in Netscape Gold.

Bold icon Italics icon Teletype icon

Pull-down for headers and other tags

Document window

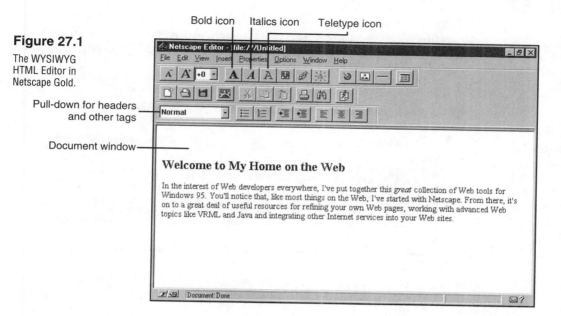

Then, highlight the text by dragging the mouse pointer from one end to the other. Now, using the pull-down menu in the Editor's toolbar, change the text from Normal to Heading 2, or another heading level. The text will change in the editor window to suggest the new "look" of your text (see fig. 27.2).

Figure 27.2

HTML "markup" in Navigator Gold.

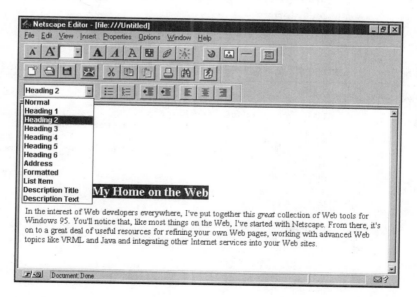

Of course, like a good word processor, you could also choose to change the text to a heading level first and then type. For instance, use that same pull-down menu to change the appearance to Heading 6. Now, back in the Netscape Editor window, type some text like:

```
Copyright 1996. Do not duplicate without permission.
```

Notice that it comes out looking just as if it were between <H6> tags (see fig. 27.3).

Figure 27.3

Changing the HTML types before typing.

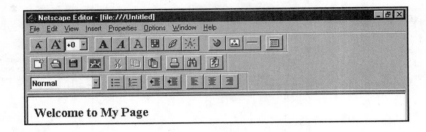

Welcome to My Page

In fact, that's exactly what Netscape Gold is doing—it's putting your text between HTML tags. To prove it, let's try the following example.

Example: Checking Under the Hood

In this example, you'll create a simple HTML document in the Netscape Gold Editor. Then, you'll take a look at it with your trusty text editor (like Notepad). You'll see that all Netscape Gold is really doing is basic HTML markup—it just has a fancy interface.

Enter Listing 27.1 in the Netscape Gold Editor.

On the CD

Listing 27.1 *goldtest.html* **A Sample Netscape Gold Document**

```
Products
All of our products here at BigCorp are designed with the consumer in
mind. It's more important to us that you be happy with our products and
services than it is that we make a profit. If we can make money, so much
the better, but we like to think of ourselves as a charitable organiza-
tion.
The following is a list of our more popular product lines:
Fine Jewelry
Luxury Automobiles
Cruises and Exotic Vacations
Deforestation Services
Chemical Pollutants
Indoor Mall Construction
```

With that entered, there's some formatting you should do. For instance, highlight the word "Product" and change it to a heading (perhaps Heading 2) with the pull-down menu in the Editor button bar. Then, as your heart desires, change text in the document to bold, italics, or teletype using the appropriate buttons. Then, choose File, Save to save the document as goldtest.htm. Now is when you see Netscape Gold's secret.

Using WordPad or a similar text editor, open the document goldtest.htm. Anything look familiar (see fig. 27.4)? Again, this is just regular HTML markup.

Figure 27.4

Netscape Gold just creates standard HTML documents.

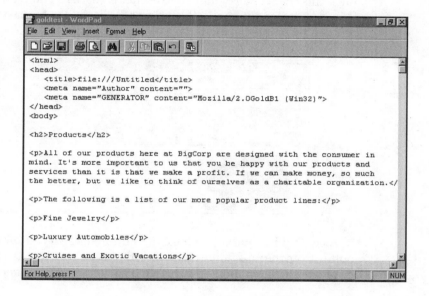

> **Note:** Notice something else about this document? It doesn't quite follow all of the conventions that you've set up for HTML documents in this book. Most documents created by the Gold Editor and others will have slight variations in the way they use HTML tags, especially where the standard itself allows for some flexibility. This isn't necessarily bad, although I believe the way you've learned it in this book is the most complete and elegant. If you disagree with the HTML layout created by a special editor, here's your chance to change it. Just edit away in Notepad!

Creating HTML List Items

The convenience of the Gold Editor doesn't really stop with basic HTML markup, either. One of the typical HTML elements you may want to add to your documents is an HTML list. This is done in two steps, and you can go about it a number of ways. Start by entering the text from the previous example:

```
Fine Jewelry
Luxury Automobiles
Cruises and Exotic Vacations
Deforestation Services
Chemical Pollutants
Indoor Mall Construction
```

Now, highlight all of the above items using the mouse. When you've got them all selected, choose List Item from the pull-down menu you used earlier for heading tags. This changes all of the text to list items, just as if you'd typed them after the list item tags. It also automatically encloses the list in <UL> tags, so that the items appear with bullet points next to them (see fig. 27.5).

Figure 27.5

Creating lists in the Gold Editor.

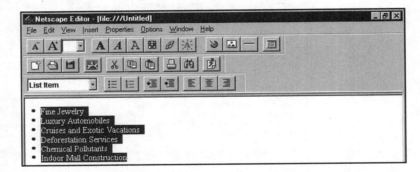

As with other markup in the Gold Editor, it's also possible to select the list item option from the pull-down menu first, then type your text. All the text you enter will be of type list item until you change it back to normal or another tag type.

Changing List Types

Once you have all of your text entered as list items, changing the type of list (ordered or unordered) is only a menu item away. Open the Properties menu and choose Text. The Properties dialog box appears. Then click the Paragraph tab (see fig. 27.6).

Changing the list type is simple. In the Additional style drop-down list box, choose List. Then, in the section marked List, choose a Style for the list and a Bullet or Number style if appropriate. Click OK and you've got yourself a new list type!

> **Note:** Notice that this dialog box allows you to use Netscape-specific HTML extensions for bullet types and numbering schemes. If you elect to use these, realize that not all of your users will be able to see them.

Figure 27.6

The Properties dialog box with the paragraph tab open.

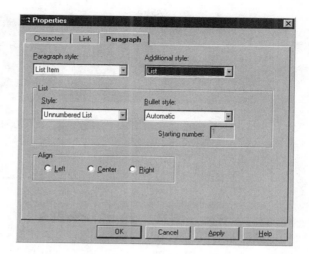

Creating Definition Lists

Definition lists work only slightly different than our other list types. Starting with the same sample text, let's change it to a definition list:

```
Fine Jewelry
Luxury Automobiles
Cruises and Exotic Vacations
Deforestation Services
Chemical Pollutants
Indoor Mall Construction
```

It's okay if you still have this text in the form of another list. Simply select all of the above text and use the pull-down menu to change it from normal or list item text to description title (DT) text. Now this text is treated as if it's <DT> text between <DL> (definition list) tags. So far so good.

> **Note:** For some reason, Netscape has decided to call HTML definition lists (DL), terms (DT), and definitions (DD) "description lists," "description titles," and "description text," respectively. I guess that makes some sense, but I've never heard those names before either. Don't let them confuse you.

The next step is to add text between each <DT> line. Just use the Return key to create a space between the list items, and type the text you want to define as your description text (DD). Then, select that text with the mouse and use the pull-down menu to change it to DD text. It's that simple (see fig. 27.7).

Figure 27.7

Creating a
definition list.

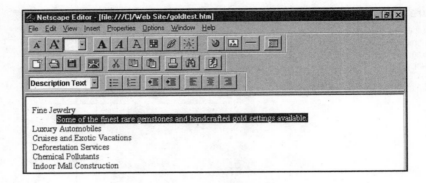

Inserting *
* and *<HR>*

This one isn't quite as obvious from the outset. It's clear that Netscape Gold creates new <P> paragraph tags whenever you simply hit Return in the Editor window (except when <P> is inappropriate, as with list elements). But how do you create a <BR> tag?

Just press Shift+Return on your keyboard. That's all there is to it. For instance, try entering the following:

```
How do I love thee?
```

Press Shift+Return, and then enter the following

```
Let me count the ways.
```

Were you to view this in Notepad or WordPad, you'd see that the <BR> tag has been inserted where you hit Shift+Return. If you only use the Return key, then Netscape will use the <P> tag instead.

Inserting an <HR> tag is even easier. Simply place the cursor at the point in the document where you'd like the horizontal ruler to appear, then select Insert, Horizontal Line from the menu. Your line is then inserted in the document.

To change the style of your horizontal line, select it in the Editor window, and then choose Properties, Horizontal Line. In the Horizontal Lines Properties dialog box that appears, you can change the dimensions, alignment, and shading for the line. Click OK when you're done, and the line will change in the Editor window.

> **Note:** Again, these <HR> properties are Netscape-specific. If you change <HR> properties, realize that not all your users will be able to view the modified line.

Hyperlinks, Images, and Head Elements

Of course, the Gold Editor allows you to add both hyperlinks and images to your documents. Both are accomplished through commands in the Insert menu. You can also create clickable images rather easily. And, while you can designate a graphic as an image map, there is currently no way to use the USEMAP attribute to create client-side image maps in the Gold Editor. (You can always manually edit files created otherwise in the Gold Editor.)

Adding Hyperlinks

Adding a typical hypermedia or hypertext link is just about as easy as regular markup in the Gold Editor. Simply highlight the text, choose Insert, Link from the menu, and you're presented with the Properties dialog box (see fig. 27.8). (You can also click the Make Link button on the button bar.) Make sure that the Link tab is selected. Now you can either enter the name of the URL to the linked document (or file) or you may use the Browse File button to find the file on your hard drive.

Note: If you're currently not working with files resident on the Web server, remember that you'll need the correct relative path to your files (once they're on the Web server) in this dialog box. So take special care when using the Browse File button.

Figure 27.8

The Properties dialog box.

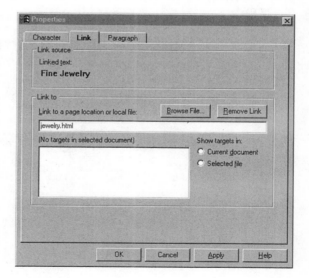

When you've completed entering the URL and clicked OK, the highlighted text will now act as a link in your Web document.

Adding Images

To add an image file to your document, place your cursor at the point in the editor where you would like the image to appear. Then, choose Insert, Image. (You can also click the Insert Image button on the button bar.) The Properties dialog box should appear with the Image tab selected. In this dialog box, enter the URL to the graphic that you want to include. Or, you can use the Browse button to find the file.

> **Note:** With images, using the Browse button actually causes the graphic file to be copied to the current directory. If this isn't what you want, check the Copy image to the document's location checkbox at the bottom of the dialog to turn this feature off. You should also enter absolute URLs in the Image file name field when using graphics already on the Web (or in specific directories on your own Web server).

Now, you have some more choices to make. First, you can use the Alignment section of the Properties dialog box to decide how text will be aligned relative to the graphic. Remember that only top, bottom, and middle are recognized in HTML 2.0. (Left and right are HTML 3.0 level standards.) In the Dimensions section, specify the height and width for the image. In the Space around image section, you can decide how much space to put between the image and surrounding text (see fig. 27.9).

Figure 27.9

The Properties dialog box with the Image tab open.

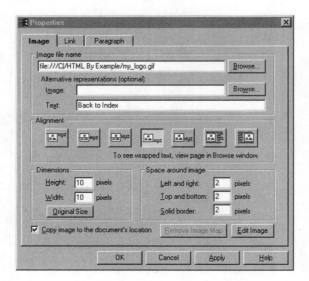

To cause this graphic to be a clickable image, click the Link tab and enter an URL in the Link to section. When you click OK, your graphic should appear in the document, and clicking it should cause it to appear to act as a clickable image (although your linked page won't load). To test this for sure, click the View in Browser button in the Gold Editor's button bar, and test the document in Navigator.

Editing the Head

The Gold Editor automatically adds <HEAD> and <BODY> tags to your document, but since you can't edit the HTML directly, the Editor gives you the opportunity in a dialog box. Choose Properties, Document. The Document Properties dialog box that appears allows you to enter various head properties (see fig. 27.10).

Figure 27.10

Adding information to the document's head.

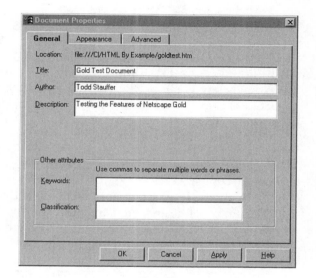

Notice that this dialog box uses a tabbed interface that will also allow you to add more advanced head elements as well as background images and document color information.

Example: Putting it All Together

Let's take the document you created in Listing 27.2 and add some of the things you've learned. Enter Listing 27.2 in the Netscape Gold editor—or use the document you created in the first example.

Listing 27.2   *gold2.html*   Advanced Editing in Netscape Gold

```
Products
All of our products here at BigCorp are designed with the consumer in
mind. It's more important to us that you be happy with our products and
```

continues

443

Listing 27.2 Continued

```
services than it is that we make a profit. If we can make money, so much
the better, but we like to think of ourselves as a charitable organiza-
tion. ·
The following is a list of our more popular product lines:
Fine Jewelry
Luxury Automobiles
Cruises and Exotic Vacations
Deforestation Services
Chemical Pollutants
Indoor Mall Construction
```

If you've already turned the product lines into list items, great. If not, highlight them all together, then choose List Item from the pull-down menu in the button bar.

Now, select each product line name individually and give each a hypertext link. Click the Link button in the button bar or choose Insert, Link from the menu. In the Links dialog box, enter an URL for your link, or click Browse to choose a local file. Click OK to change the text to a link.

Next, you'll enter a graphic (use anything handy). Find a good place in your document for it, andthen click the Image button or choose Insert, Image. In the Image tab of the Properties dialog box, give an URL or path for the image, or choose to Browse for the graphic file. If you'd like this image to be clickable, choose the Link tab and then enter an URL.

Finally, choose Properties, Document. In the Document Properties dialog, give your document a title and enter any other information you feel like giving (name, description, etc.). Click OK and, as far as this example is concerned, you're done. Try viewing it in the Netscape Browser (see fig. 27.11).

Figure 27.11

The final product in Navigator.

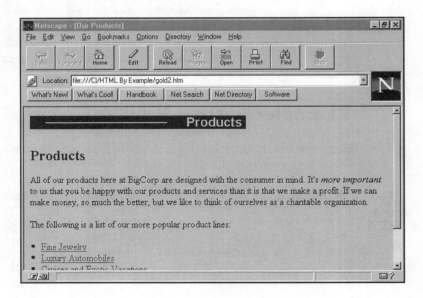

Summary

You've spent most of this book learning about raw HTML text—how to create Web documents using nothing more than a text editor. More and more programs are appearing, though, that try to make creating HTML documents easier and more friendly. Netscape Gold is one of those programs.

Creating basic HTML pages is fairly easy, since Netscape Gold features an Editor interface that's a lot like popular word processors. Bold, italics, teletype, and other text manipulation is easy. You can also create HTML lists, add horizontal rulers, and use the <BR> tags to end lines.

The heart of your Web site—hyperlinks and images—are easy enough in Netscape Gold as well. Gold doesn't have great support for image maps (and no client-side support), but the basics are easy enough. Plus, once you've created an HTML document in Netscape Gold, you can always open in a text editor for further enhancements.

Review Questions

1. Is it possible to change HTML styles in Netscape Gold before typing the text for a particular style?

2. To what other sort of computer application is Netscape Gold similar?

3. In what type of file does Netscape Gold save your HTML? Can you edit this with other programs?

4. True or false. Changing text to a list item in Netscape Gold automatically creates an HTML list.

5. What menu command allows you to change from an unordered to an ordered list type?

6. What does Netscape Gold call HTML definition lists?

7. Is there a menu command for
?

8. Why should you be careful when using the Browse button to create hypertext links?

9. How is the Browse button for images different from the Browse button for hyperlinks?

10. Can you type the Title of your document directly in the document window?

Review Exercises

1. Use Netscape Gold's definition lists and hyperlinks to create a page of book reviews. Clicking the book's name shows the user a graphic of the book. For instance, an entry might be the following:

```
HTML By Example
The best book ever written for learning HTML the right way.
```

2. Based on the example above, add another definition (DD) line that includes a link to order the book, the author's name, copyright information, and price. For instance:

```
HTML By Example
The best book ever written for learning HTML the right way.
Todd Stauffer, Copyright 1996, $34.99. Order this book.
```

3. Create a button bar interface using Netscape Gold. (No image map is necessary; just create a series of clickable images.)

4. Add client-pull abilities to your Web page using Netscape Gold.

## CHAPTER 28

Using Microsoft Internet Assistant

If your main HTML editor is Microsoft Word, or you have a copy of Microsoft Word and you've been using something else, you may really like Internet Assistant. Although Internet Assistant (IA) only offers basic support for HTML tags in your documents, that might not be so bad. Especially since there's nothing wrong with editing the rest of the document by hand.

> **Note:** Internet Assistant is a free add-on for Microsoft Word version 6.0 and above. A separate version is available for either Windows 3.1 or Windows 95. (A Mac version should also be available by the time you read this.) You can download them from Microsoft's Web site at **http://www.microsoft.com/**.

Internet Assistant actually adds two different elements to Microsoft Word. After installation, a few new menu items exist for your use, including Insert, Hyperlink. But Internet Assistant also adds the ability to view basic HTML documents from within Microsoft Word with the command File, Browse Web (see fig. 28.1).

Figure 28.1

The MS Word/
Internet Assistant
browser.

Basic Markup in Internet Assistant

Creating HTML documents in Internet Assistant isn't really much different from creating a typical Word document. The key is to use the HTML template. In Word, choose File, New. In the new document, select the HTML template for use with your new document. Then place your cursor and begin typing. You can use bold, italics, or underlining as you type.

You can also use the HTML style sheet definitions to help you change basic text to HTML markup. Consider the example, just typed directly into a new HTML-template Word document, like the following:

```
BigCorp's Customer Service Pages
```

To change this text from normal text to a Heading 2 (<H2>), select the text with the mouse in Word, and then pull down the style menu and select Heading 2. Word automatically formats the selected text to conform to the HTML standard for Heading 2. As an added bonus, you can see how it might look in a browser window (see fig. 28.2).

> **Tip:** As with Word templates in general, you can always select the style first, then type your text.

Figure 28.2

Changing text to
an HTML header.

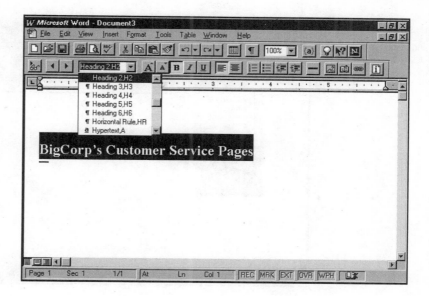

HTML Lists

Creating a list in Internet Assistant is pretty easy, too. For an ordered or unordered
list, all you need to do is enter the text for your list, hitting Enter after each. An
example might be:

```
Downloadable Support Files
Frequently Asked Questions
Send Us a Note
Toll-Free Numbers
```

The next step is to select the entire list with the mouse. With all of the above
highlighted, you can either select the appropriate list button in the buttonbar or
select the list type in the pull-down style menu. For instance, if you click the Bullet
List (UL) button in the button bar, you'll get something like what's shown in figure
28.3.

If you're interesting in indenting list items, like when creating an outline, the
Internet Assistant will let you do that, too. Use an unordered list like the following:

```
Section 1
Chapter 1
Part 1
Part 2
Chapter 2
```

Figure 28.3

Changing regular
text to a bulleted
list.

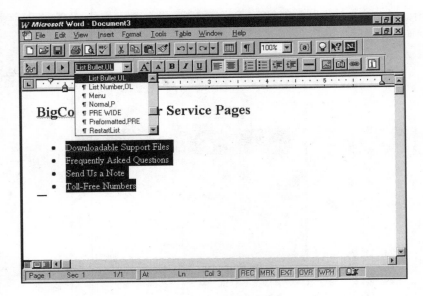

You can use the Internet Assistant button bar to move some of these over. First, you can select all of the text under Section 1 and click once on the Increase Indent button to move everything over once. You can also choose Format, Increase Indent. Select Part 1 and Part 2, or Chapter 1, and you can click the button once more to indent those, too (see fig. 28.4).

Figure 28.4

Indenting
(nesting) your
lists.

Decrease Indent button

Increase Indent button

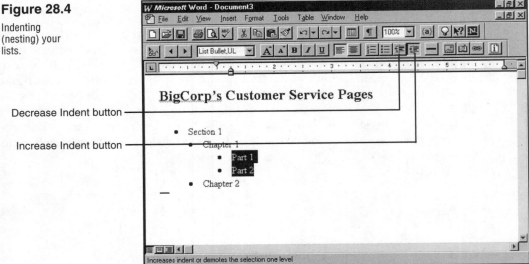

Definition Lists

Some HTML mark up in Internet Assistant requires that you follow special instructions, depending on the Windows version you're using. Internet Assistant 1.0 for Windows 3.1 handles definition lists differently from IA 2.0 for Windows 95. Start by typing the first word from your list, then press Tab and type the definition. You do this for your entire list, as in the following example:

```
Mr. Ted Smith           President, CEO. Ted's a huge Cubs fan, an avid
golfer,
father of three daughters and Carol's husband. He also works here.
Ms. Gina Miles          CFO. Gina enjoys hiking, mountain biking and
weekend lecturing. Also a Cubs fan, Gina enjoys attending the games with
her husband Mike.
Mr. Rick Felps          EVP, Marketing. Rick's passion is his '67 Mustang
Convertible, which he often drives to the lake on weekends for fishing
outings. Rich hates the Cubs, preferring the Phillies.
```

Now, by selecting the text and choosing the definition list (DL) option from the pull-down menu, the names will become definition terms (DT) and the descriptions become definitions (DD).

In Windows 95, things are a little more involved. Using the sample text, choose all of the text and make it a definition list using the pull-down menu. Then, select each element separately and make it either a definition item or definition, as appropriate. That will cause the definitions to standout from the definition terms (see fig. 28.5). You can also hit Return after each DT to place the definitions below their respective terms.

> **Tip:** You can also assign shortcuts to common HTML styles. Choose Format, Style to open the Style dialog box. Pick the correct style, choose Modify, and then select the Shortcut key. Then you just enter a keyboard combination for that style.

Notice that Internet Explorer's pull-down style menu will also let you create a <DL COMPACT> list. To do this, follow the appropriate procedure above, but choose definition compact instead of definition list.

Figure 28.5

Changing regular
text to DL terms
and definitions.

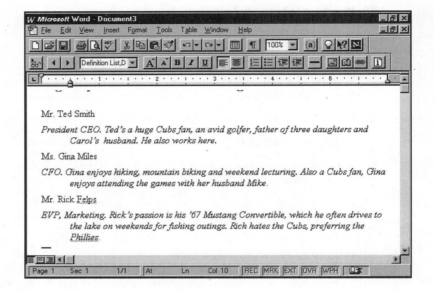

Saving Your HTML Document

Microsoft Word defaults to the HTML file format when you use the HTML template (in Internet Assistant) to create your document, so you can basically save your Web page in the same way that you might save a regular MS Word document.

With an HTML document active, choose File, Save. The Save As dialog box appears (see fig. 28.6). Give your file a name in the File name box. Make sure HTML Document is selected in the Save as type menu at the bottom of the dialog box. When you're finished, choose Save. Now you've got an HTML document for your Web site.

Figure 28.6

Saving your HTML
documents.

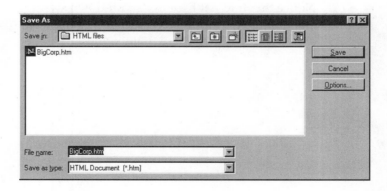

Example: Simple Markup With Internet Assistant

Let's create a simple page in Internet Explorer and use what you've learned so far to create a new HTML document. To begin, create a new Word file based on the HTML template. You may also want to save this file to give it a name. Then, just type Listing 28.1 (or something similar).

Listing 28.1   *iatest.htm*   **A Sample Page for Internet Assistant**

```
BigCorp's Customer Service Pages

To help you get the most out of our products, or just help if you're
having a problem, we've created the following Web pages with downloading
files, tips, tricks, fixes and answers to your questions. Just click any
link to get to that page.

Downloadable Support Files      Fixes, drivers, free stuff, utility
programs, documents and even a game or two written by our engineering and
tech support staffs. If you can't find it here, BigCorp hasn't written
it. (Or you'll have to buy it from us!)
Frequently Asked Questions      Listing of questions that our tech support
reps hear all the time. They're willing to answer them again, but that
just means they get frustrated and take more breaks.
Send Us a Note           Send email directly to the most prolific answer
guy on our support staff.
Toll-Free Numbers      Phone numbers for tech support, customer service,
and, for good measure, we've even thrown in our toll-free, 24 hour sales
numbers. Good of us, eh?
```

Now the trick is to turn this into a more interesting page. You can start with the heading by selecting the entire heading and changing it to a Heading 2 using the pull-down style menu.

In the descriptive text (first paragraph), there's nothing particularly special you need to do. You can always add bold and italic text where it seems appropriate by highlighting the text and clicking the buttons in the Word/Internet Assistant button bar. You could also experiment by turning the entire paragraph into blockquote text or other HTML mark up.

> **Tip:** The Horizontal Rule button—or the Insert, Horizontal Rule menu command—can be used to insert an <HR> line in your document.

In the next section, notice that I've used <TAB> to prepare it to be a definition list. Select the entire section of text and change it to a definition list, DL in the pull-down style menu. (In IA 2.0, you also need to select each element separately to assign it as a DT or DD.)

Now, save the file as an HTML document, along with the appropriate file extension. You're set. To view the document in Word's built-in browser, click the Switch to Browser button (far left on the second row of the button bar), or select View, Web Browse. It should look something like what's shown in figure 28.7.

> **Note:** You can also use the Preview in Browser button (the rightmost button on the first row of the button bar) to load the document directly into the default Windows 95 browser. Or, choose File, Preview in Browser. To work with your document as a plain text file, choose the View, HTML Source command. Word will close the HTML document (and HTML template) and re-open the file as a text file, complete with the tags and other markup.

Figure 28.7

Your example in Word's new built-in browser.

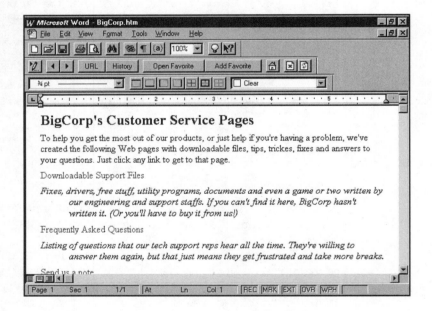

After you've viewed the document, you can switch back to edit mode by clicking the Switch to Browser button again, which has now changed to a pencil icon.

Links, Images, and Head Elements

Internet Assistant also gives you the ability to add the trappings of good Web pages, including hypertext links, images, and <HEAD> information. For the most part, you can do just about anything possible in HTML 2.0, and it's all fairly straightforward.

Hypertext Links

To insert a hypertext link, highlight that text and click the Hyperlink button, or choose Insert, Hyperlink. The Hyperlink dialog box opens allowing you to enter or edit text for the link and choose a local file or URL as the document (or multimedia file) this link references (see fig. 28.8). Enter or edit the text and choose a file. Click OK when finished and your hypertext link will appear in the document.

Figure 28.8

Creating hyper-text links.

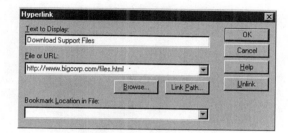

Bookmark Links

Word calls local HTML NAME anchors "bookmark" links, and allows you to create them with the help of Internet Assistant. Remember that NAME links have two different components: a calling link and a NAME anchor to which the link points.

You need to start by creating the bookmark link (NAME anchor). To do this, place the cursor where you want the bookmark anchor to be in the document. Then, you can click the Bookmark button on the button bar or choose Edit, Bookmark from the menu. In the Bookmark dialog box that appears, enter a name for this bookmark.

To create the calling link, use the same Hyperlink button or choose Insert, Hyperlink. After entering text for the link, choose the bookmark name from the pull-down menu at the bottom of the dialog box. Make sure it's selected, and then click OK.

Inserting an Image

Inserting an image in an Internet Assistant HTML document is similiar to inserting a hypertext link. Start by placing your cursor in the document where you'd like the image to appear. Next, click the Picture button or choose Insert, Picture. In the resulting dialog box, choose the name of an image. You can also enter ALT text for displaying instead of the graphic in text-based browsers.

To determine whether or not this image will be a server-side image map and how text will align to it, click the Options tab in the Picture dialog box (see fig. 28.9). Now you can choose the Image is a sensitive map option to add the ISMAP attribute and how you want the image aligned. (Remember that LEFT and RIGHT are not HTML 2.0 values.) Click OK in both dialog boxes and you've inserted your image.

Notice that you can also enter video clips with the Picture dialog box (click the Video tab). This uses Microsoft Explorer's proprietary tags for adding and playing AVI files.

Figure 28.9

Adding a picture with advanced settings.

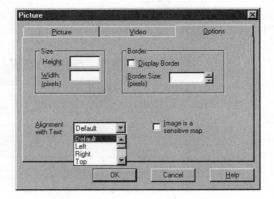

Editing <*HEAD*> Elements

Since Internet Assistant doesn't give you direct access to the HTML tags in your document, you'll need to use a special command for <HEAD> elements. On the button bar, click the Title button, or choose File, HTML Document Info. The HTML Document Head Information dialog box appears.

In this dialog box, enter the Title for your Web document. Click OK if that's all you need to add. If you need to add a Base address, click the Advanced button in this dialog box. Enter the URL in the HTML Document Head Info—Advanced field. You can also click the Is Index checkbox if you'd like this page to be an index.

To enter custom HTML text in the head of your document, click the Meta button (this isn't just for the <META> tag, as used for client-pull, but any <HEAD> tags). In the Insert HTML Markup textbox, you can enter any HTML code you'd like to have appear in the head of your document. When you're finished, click OK.

> **Note:** You can use a similar command to add your own tags within the body of your document. With the cursor placed at the point in your document where you want to enter the special tag, choose Insert, HTML Markup. In the Insert HTML Markup dialog box that appears, enter the special HTML markup and click OK.

Example: Finishing the Page

Now, let's take the page you created in the first example and add links, images, and a title. If you use the same document (complete with markup) that you used in the original example, that's great. If not, re-enter the text from Listing 28.1 and save it as `iatest2.htm`.

Let's start by adding an image to this page just before the heading. Place the cursor, and select the Picture button or choose Insert, Picture. The Picture dialog box should appear with the Picture tab open. In this dialog box, choose a graphic file. When you click OK, the picture will appear in your document. (You may want to press Return after the graphic to place the heading text on the next line.)

Now let's create the hypertext links for the definition terms. Highlight each term with the mouse (e.g., Downloadable Support Files) and click the Hyperlink button, or choose Insert, Hyperlink. Your text will appear in the Text to Display textbox. Now you can enter the file, URL, or bookmark to which this link should point.

Finally, let's give your document a title. Click the Title button or select File, HTML Document Info. In the dialog box, enter a title for this page and click OK. You're done. It should look something like figure 28.10 in Word's built-in browser.

Figure 28.10

Your example
page.

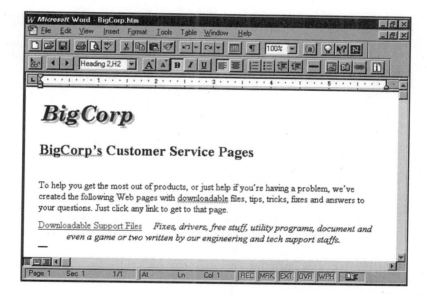

Adding Form Fields

To create a form and add your first form field, choose Insert, Form Field command. In the New Form dialog box that appears, you'll get a little bit of instruction for entering form elements. If you don't want to see this dialog every time you add forms to a new document, click the Don't Display This Message Again checkbox. Then click OK.

In the list of radio buttons that appears, choose a field type to add. (I'm starting with a text field.) Next stop is the Text Form Field dialog box, which allows you to name the element and set some basic characteristics (see fig. 28.11).

Figure 28.11

Adding a form field.

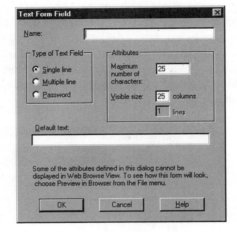

To add more fields, you can go straight to the Forms controls and click the type of field you want to add. Make sure you give each a unique name, just as if you were hand editing the form.

In order to get the form data to your form script, you need to set up the Submit button. When you've finished adding other script elements, click Submit in the Forms control window. In the Submit Button Form Field dialog box that appears, you can name the button, change the button's label (value), and enter an URL for the ACTION attribute (see fig. 28.12). You can also use the pop-up menu to choose the METHOD for sending form data.

Figure 28.12

Creating the
Submit button.

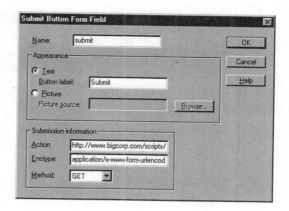

Example: A Simple Form

You can't do much of a listing here, since you're not dealing in much raw HMTL or text. Let's create a new document that includes just two form fields and a Submit button.

If you want to, you can start by jazzing the form up with a logo graphic. Then, underneath it, type something like the following:

```
Customer Service Form
Your name:
Your email:
```

Change the first line to a Heading 2 using the pull-down menu, but leave the other text as is. Place the cursor to the right of the second line and choose Insert, Form Field to create a form. Select Text from the Form Field menu and enter a name for this field in the Text Form Field dialog box.

Go through the same thing just to the right of the third line, except this time you can use the Forms controls to create the text field (use the top left button). Remember to name it something different, like "e-mail."

Back in the document, press Return after the second text field and click the Submit button in the Forms controls. In the Submit Button Form Field dialog box, name the button, give it a label, enter an URL for your ACTION, and choose a METHOD. Click OK and you're done. Figure 28.13 shows this form in Word's Web browsing mode.

Figure 28.13

Your form through
the MS Word
browser mode.

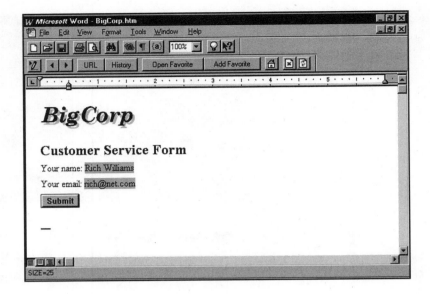

Summary

Internet Assistant is designed to add Web browsing and editing functionality to the Microsoft Word word processor. Downloading this free add-in adds two different components. One allows you to view HTML documents from within Word. The other adds an HTML template and special menu/button bar commands for creating and editing Web pages.

Basic HTML is about as simple as creating a regular Word document—just type text and apply styles. Generally speaking, everything can be done a couple of different ways. You can choose to click the Bold button, for example, or you can choose Style, Bold.

Creating lists is also fairly simple in Internet Assistant, although creating definition lists can be a little tricky. Hypertext links, images, and head elements are all added via menu items and dialog boxes. For NAME hypertext links, IA uses Word's bookmark system.

The key to IA is its ability to save files in HTML format. It's this "translator" that does the real work once you've created your page. By saving your document as an HTML file (the default when you use the HTML template), you're able to edit it in a text editor and display it on the Web.

Review Questions

1. Is Internet Assistant an application program? Where do you get it?

2. Is it possible to select an HTML style first, then type your text?

3. In what type of file does IA save your HTML? Can you edit this with other programs?

4. True or false. Indenting list items actually creates a "nested" list.

5. What command allows you to change from an unordered to an ordered list type?

6. What is the major difference between definition lists in IA 1.0 versus IA 2.0?

7. True or false. Since HTML documents are just ASCII text, it's acceptable to save your IA HTML document as "text only."

8. What is the HTML equivalent of Internet Assistant's bookmark link?

9. Which do you create first: the bookmark link or the calling link?

10. What element controls the SUBMIT and METHOD information for your form?

Review Exercises

1. Use Internet Assistant's definition lists and hyperlinks to create a page of book reviews. Clicking the book's name shows the user a graphic of the book. For instance, an entry might be:

```
HTML By Example     The best book ever written for learning
HTML the right way.
```

2. Based on this example, add another definition (DD) line that includes a link to order the book, the author's name, copyright info, and price. For instance:

```
HTML By Example     The best book ever written for learning
HTML the right way.
Todd Stauffer, Copyright 1996, $34.99. Order this book.
```

3. Create a text-based menu-bar using IA. For instance:

```
Index ¦ Product Pages ¦ Customer Service ¦ Feedback ¦ About Us
```

4. Add client-pull abilities to your Web page using Internet Assistant.

## CHAPTER 29

HTML with Adobe PageMill for Macintosh

Heralded as one of the first HTML editors to truly make a dent in the process of HTML creation, I have to admit that PageMill surprised me a bit. I stand pretty firm in the opinion that the only way to create the best HTML documents is with a text editor, but PageMill is beginning to change that. It's actually fun to use and impressively powerful.

That said, even PageMill has room to grow toward properly supporting and formatting HTML documents, and some advanced capabilities are still out of reach for PageMill users. You'll still end up editing some HTML by hand, but, fortunately, you can even do most of that directly in PageMill.

> **Note:** The other serious drawback to Adobe PageMill is the cost—currently about $100. That's more expensive than Netscape Gold, which includes a browser, mail interface, and newsgroup reader. Of course, Netscape Gold is also a Windows-only application (Mac version due mid-1996). PageMill is currently Mac-only, although its popularity has convinced Adobe to announce a future Windows version. A demo of PageMill is available from **http://www.adobe.com/Apps/ PageMill/pagedemo.html**.

Basic Markup in PageMill

Starting with a new document (choose File, New Page), entering basic text is as simple as typing characters in the document window. The PageMill interface doesn't really offer buttons for bold, italics, and so on, but these commands are readily available under the Style menu. In addition, most text styles follow the traditional Mac command-key shortcuts, so that ⌘+B will allow you to enter bold text, and ⌘+I lets you type subsequent text in italics. Table 29.1 shows the command key equivalents for common HTML text styles.

> **Tip:** Clicking the paper/pen icon (or the globe icon) in the top right corner switches PageMill between "edit" and "preview" mode.

Table 29.1   Command Key Shortcuts for HTML Tags

Keyboard Shortcut	HTML Equivalent	Meaning
Shift+⌘+P	plain text	Ends other pages
⌘+B	`<B>, </B>`	Bold
⌘+I	`<I>, </I>`	Italics
Shift+⌘+S	`<STRONG>, </STRONG>`	Strong emphasis
Shift+⌘+E	`<EM>, </EM>`	Emphasis
Shift+⌘+C	`<CITE>, </CITE>`	Citation
Shift+⌘+A	`<SAMPLE>, </SAMPLE>`	Sample
Shift+⌘+K	`<KEYBOARD>, </KEYBOARD>`	Keyboard
Shift+⌘+O	`<CODE>, </CODE>`	Code
Shift+⌘+V	`<VARIABLE>, </VARIABLE>`	Variable
Option+⌘+(1...6)	`<H1...6>, </H1...6>`	Heading level
Option+⌘+F	`<PRE>, </PRE>`	Preformatted text
Option+⌘+A	`<ADDRESS>, </ADDRESS>`	Address text
Option+⌘+P	`<P>, </P>`	Paragraph Text

There are two basic ways you can enter text in PageMill. Using the keyboard shortcuts or menu commands, you can apply an HTML tag, then type the text in that style. Or, you can select text that's already been typed and apply the style. For instance, if I type the following:

```
I cannot stress the importance of Point #1 enough.
```

In plain text, I can go back with the mouse and highlight importance then use either ⌘+I or the menu command Style, Italics to change the text to italic. Selecting Point #1, I could use Shift+⌘+S or Style, Strong to apply the HTML tag <STRONG> to that text (see fig. 29.1).

Figure 29.1

Applying text style HTML tags.

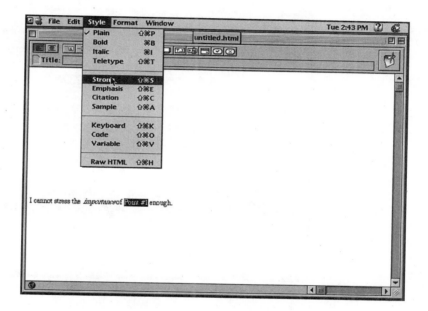

PageMill requires you to use the <P> key sequence or command more often than it should. Hitting Return after typing a heading, for instance, doesn't automatically change the text back to <P> style, although that might seem to make sense. Instead, it's necessary to use the paragraph menu command whenever you want to type plain text.

> **Tip:** If you ever feel "stuck" in a tag's particular format, try changing back to the <P> tag with the Option+⌘+P combination.

HTML Lists

Again it's possible to change to a list format, then type your entries. The easier way to do it, though, is to type each entry with a Return at the end, and then go back and change the style to a list style. For instance, try typing this "list" in plain text:

```
Baseball
Football
Hockey
Basketball
Tennis
```

Now, by highlighting the list and choosing a list style from the Format, List menu, we can quickly turn this regular text into an HTML list (see fig. 29.2).

Figure 29.2

Changing plain text to an HTML list.

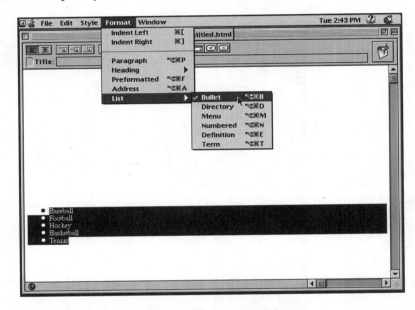

For hierarchical lists, you can select the list items that you'd prefer to see indented, then choose the command Format, Indent Right. This essentially nests a list within a list. If you again select the indented list items (or leave them still selected) and choose a new list style using the Format, Lists menu command, you have effectively nested a different type of list within the first one.

Definition Lists

Definition lists aren't remarkably different than other list types in PageMill, except that they take a bit more effort. Since nothing can be assumed about definition lists, you may need to select and change each line individually. For instance, enter the following plain text:

```
Baseball
Easily my favorite game, Baseball is still the American Pastime.
Football
My second favorite game, nothing gets me more pumped than a good NFL
game.
```

```
Hockey
Everybody gets in the playoffs, but I love watching it live.
Basketball
Not much of a pro fan, but I love the college sport.
Tennis
Of all these sports, this is the one I play the best. Never will make
pro, though.
```

To create the definition list, your best bet is probably to choose the entire listing and turn everything into a definition term with the menu command Format, List, Definition Term. This saves about half the work. The next step is to select each definition separately and apply the menu command Format, List, Definition.

If you prefer, of course, you can simply select each individual entry and give it the appropriate command for definition term or definition. Either way, it ends up looking like figure 29.3.

Figure 29.3

Creating a definition list for your HTML document in PageMill.

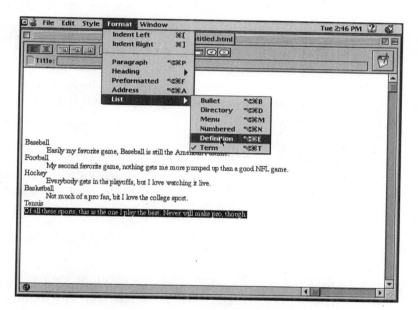

Inserting *<HR>*

There's pretty much just one way to enter a horizontal line in PageMill, and it's nothing more than pressing the button that looks like a line in PageMill's button bar. By example, you can type the lines:

```
Ending of first section.
Beginning of second section.
```

If you place the cursor (insertion point) at the beginning of the second line and press the Horizontal Line button in the button bar, you've got a line (see fig. 29.4).

Figure 29.4

Adding a horizontal line to your document.

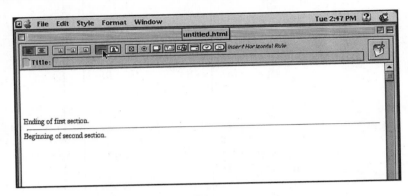

Links, Images, and Special HTML

PageMill has a very simple interface for adding hypertext links and images to your Web document. In addition, PageMill includes impressive tools for editing images and creating transparent GIFs, and even allows you to drag-and-drop graphics onto your document.

Adding Links

There are a few different ways you can add links to your pages. Probably the most common—manually entering the link—works like the following:

1. Select the text for the link.

2. With the text highlighted, click in the Link Address bar (just right of the globe at the bottom of the page).

3. Enter the URL for this link. Hit Return when you're finished.

By way of example, enter the following text in PageMill or select some text you've already entered:

```
Back to Index
```

Now, highlight the text with the mouse, and then click just to the right of the globe in the bottom left corner of the PageMill window. Enter an URL for this link. When you hit Return, your text should change to a hypertext link (different color and outlined) (see fig. 29.5).

> **Tip:** You can test local links by switching to "preview" mode and clicking the link. The local page will appear in a new PageMill window.

Figure 29.5

Adding links manually.

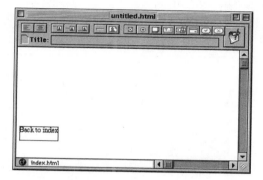

Another way to add links to your pages is by using drag-and-drop. Within PageMill, you can link to another page (if it's currently open in its own PageMill window) by dragging the small Page icon (next to the "title" text box at the top left of the PageMill window) to the document that you're currently editing. The link automatically appears with the title of the page as its text.

To use your own text, highlight it in the document you're editing, and then drag the other page's Page icon to your highlighted text.

You can also cut-and-paste links from one page to another. PageMill will alter the link to make it work for the current page.

Adding Images

Adding images is also very simple, although there's a lot you can do with an image once you've got it on the page.

The easiest way to add an image to your page is to drag-and-drop it from another PageMill page, the Scrapbook, the Finder, or any drag-and-drop enabled application (Adobe Photoshop, for instance). PageMill can handle images of type GIF, JPEG, or PICT (PICTs are automatically converted to GIFs).

To add a graphic using the filename, click the Insert Image button in the PageMill button bar. In the resulting dialog box, enter the filename for the image you want to insert, or choose it from the listing. When you've got it, click Open. PageMill will open the graphic at that point in your document.

Manipulating Images

PageMill also offers some advanced features for manipulating graphics once you have them on the page. Click once on the graphic and notice that the graphic is highlighted with a box and drag boxes. Click and hold on these drag boxes and you can resize the graphic (see fig. 29.6). You can also turn this graphic into a clickable image. With the image selected, just enter an URL in the Link Address bar at the bottom of the page.

Tip: As in many graphics applications, by holding down the Shift key before you select a drag box, you can resize the graphic proportionately.

Figure 29.6

Resizing and linking graphics in PageMill.

Drag box

Enter URL

Transparency and Client-Side Maps

If you'd like to turn this graphic into a transparent GIF, double-click the graphic. PageMill's GIF tools appear. Using the "magic wand," you can click the color in the graphic that you'd like to turn transparent (see fig. 29.7).

Tip: You can change a JPEG to a GIF by clicking the GIF button, since GIFs are required for transparency.

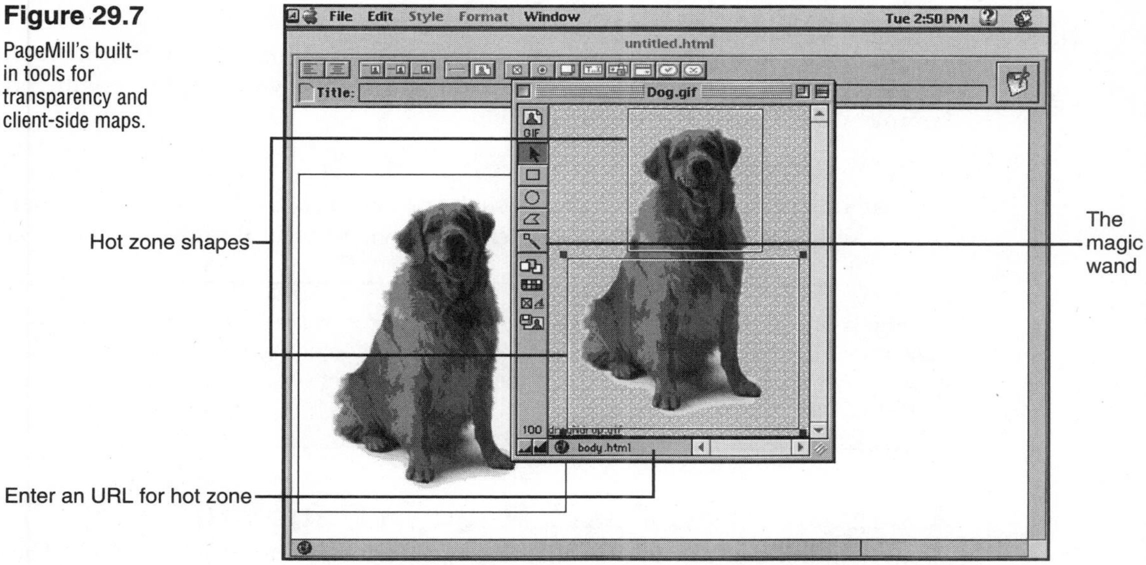

Figure 29.7

PageMill's built-in tools for transparency and client-side maps.

Hot zone shapes

The magic wand

Enter an URL for hot zone

What else can you do? How about creating a client-side image map? Click a shape tool and drag it over the graphic. You've just created a hot zone. You can enter an URL for this link at the bottom of the graphic window (click to the right of the globe) or you can drag the Page icon from another PageMill document onto the hot zone to create the link.

To create a "default" link, just click the entire graphic and give it an URL. The hot zones will override this default; clicking outside of the hot zones will cause the default to be used as the link.

When you're done with the graphic, click the close box. You'll be asked to save the graphic. Do so and you're done.

Actually, there's something else we need to do to create the client-side map. Back in the actual document, make sure the graphic is highlighted and then select Windows, Show Attributes Inspector. Now, click the Image button at the top of the Attributes Inspector window. Click the radio button under Behavior that's marked Map. Now you've got a client-side map!

Tip: You can test your client-side map in Preview mode if you've linked to local files.

Entering Unsupported HTML

Do you have a special tag you want to insert into the document? All you have to do is select the Style, Raw HTML command. Then type your HTML command, complete with brackets, like the following:

```
<SCRIPT>document.write("Howdy!")</SCRIPT>
```

That's all it takes. Notice that PageMill turns raw HTML a different color to help it stand out from the rest of the document. In Preview mode, the tags won't appear.

> **Note:** Of course, you can hand edit the HTML document all you want by saving it in PageMill and then re-opening it in SimpleText or another text editor. It's still plain text, and PageMill doesn't have commands for a lot of the advanced HTML you've learned in this book.

Example: The Basic Page in PageMill

This shouldn't take any time at all. Start by entering raw text into PageMill. Then we'll go back and clean it up, adding HTML emphasis and markup tags. Create a new document in PageMill and enter Listing 29.1.

On the CD

Listing 29.1 *pagemill.html* **PageMill's Basic Page**

```
Other Sites of Interest
We've included a number of other sites below that you might find inter-
esting if you use any of our products. We can't guarantee the accuracy or
usefulness of these sites, but they seem friendly enough.

Mike's Internet Stop
Finding Mr. Write
Left at the Fork
Toasting Your Toes
Horsing Around the Mountain
```

Now let's see how quickly we can make this an attractive page. Start by highlighting the first line and choose Format, Heading to change it to an appropriately-sized heading.

Next, add a horizontal line after the paragraph of text. Simply place the cursor in the blank space and click the horizontal line button on PageMill's button bar. (You may also want to add space on either side of the HR.)

Then choose the entire listing of sites and use the Format, List commands to change the list to a bullet-style (UL) HTML list. Finally, select each individual site name and assign it an URL for a hypertext link. I'd suggest trying both the manual and the drag-and-drop method to get a feel for both. When you're done, it ought to look something like figure 29.8.

Figure 29.8

The completed
PageMill example.

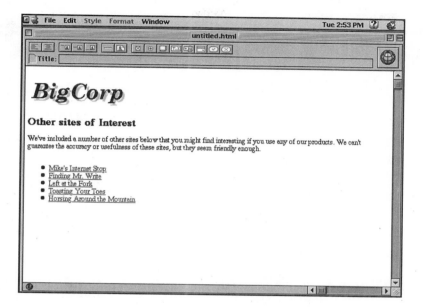

Creating Forms

PageMill makes form creation so easy that we might as well cover it here. There are basically two steps to creating your form. You start by using the button bar to create and paint the entry elements onto your screen. Next, you pull up the Attributes Inspector again and use it to assign names, sizes, and forms submitting information.

Laying Out the Form

Creating your form is basically point-and-click. Every time you click one of the form elements in the PageMill button bar, an associated form field appears on-screen. Create a new document and click some of those buttons. If you play with them a little, you'll notice that you can click an element once to highlight it, pick it up and drag it around on the page, and place it just about anywhere you want to—as long as it's legal under HTML rules.

> **Tip:** If you move the mouse pointer slowly over each button in the button bar, its name appears in the top right corner of the PageMill window.

For example, create three textboxes and a pop-up menu using the PageMill buttons. You might also want to create a Reset button, and you should definitely create a Submit button. After you've done that, you'll have a page that looks something like figure 29.9.

Figure 29.9

The raw elements for your HTML form.

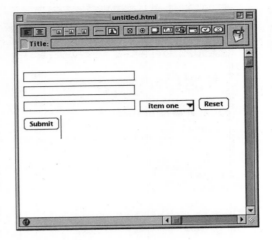

The first step is to insert a return between each element and line them up nicely down the left side of the screen. Then, enter some text to the left of each form field to describe it. Make the text boxes "Name," "E-Mail," "Web URL," and describe the pop-up as "Favorite HTML Editor."

Then, notice that you can double-click each textbox to enter default text. Do so if you want to. Also, double-click the pop-up. Click inside it and you can edit *all* of the choices. I'm going to put some popular HTML editors in mine (see fig. 29.10). You can even double-click the buttons to edit their values.

Figure 29.10

Adding names and values for the form elements.

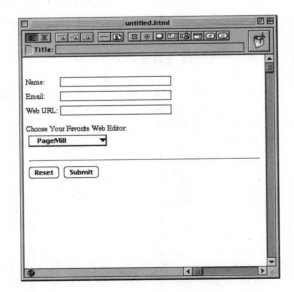

With all of this done, we turn to the Attributes Inspector. With the first textbox selected, click the rightmost button on the Inspector (the picture/forms button). It will change to show you the type of form element that's selected and give you a field to enter the name for this textbox. Click in the field, name the form element, and hit Return.

You'll need to do this for each of the form buttons. Notice that the pop-up menu gives you other FORM SELECT choices in the Inspector, like how many elements to display and whether or not more than one selection is possible. (In this example, I'm choosing to show one element at a time and to make only one selection possible.)

Finally, you need to set the form METHOD. This is done by clicking the leftmost button on the Inspector (the document button). In the ACTION field, enter the URL for your form-processing script (make sure you hit Return when you've finished). In the METHOD pop-up, you can choose GET or SEND for your form data. That's it—your form is ready (see fig. 29.11).

Figure 29.11

Browsing the form in the PageMill's Preview Mode.

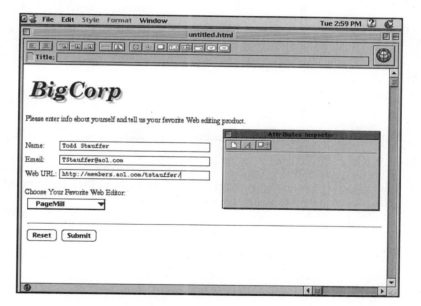

Document Info

Under that same document button in the Attribute Inspector, you may notice that you have control over some other document issues as well. To change any color in the dialog, just pull down its menu and choose Custom. You'll then be presented with a color wheel for choosing your color. When you've found the color you want, click OK. That color will take effect immediately.

If you want a background image, simply drag the image to the box marked Background Image in the Attribute Inspector. When the box is highlighted, drop the image on it. Suddenly, you've got a background (see fig. 29.12). To delete the background, click the tiny trash can icon.

Figure 29.12

Adding a background with drag-and-drop.

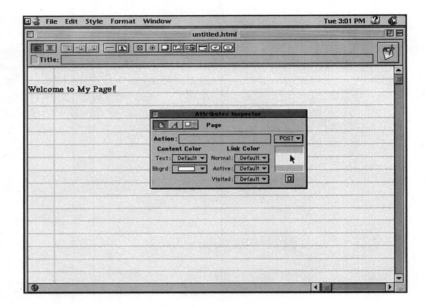

All you have left to do is add a title to the PageMill document. And, honestly, if you haven't figured out how to do this, I'm a little disappointed. (Actually, I missed it the first time around, too.)

Click the box next to the word "Title" under the PageMill button bar. Type your title. Hit enter. That's your title (see fig. 29.13). I'll enter:

```
Do You Like My Dog?
```

Pretty obvious, huh?

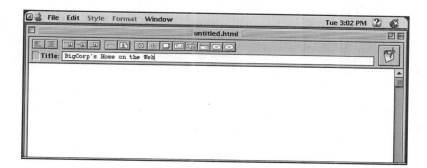

Figure 29.13

Entering a title for your HTML document.

Summary

In my personal opinion, PageMill is the best example of an application that really makes powerful HTML easier than hand editing. Unfortunately, even PageMill doesn't offer every HTML tag and construct we've learned in this book. But it's a good start, and you can always go back in with a text editor to change things.

Basic markup is easy, but, since the button bar doesn't offer many text-oriented options, I'd recommend you learn some of the keyboard shortcuts for bold, italic, paragraph, headings, and other tags. Applying list tags is just as easy, although you need to define DT and DD tags separately within definition lists.

PageMill's interface for creating links is a bit unique, but very easy and effective once you get used to it. Support for a number of different drag-and-drop options also makes working on a big, interconnected site much easier.

Perhaps PageMill's greatest strength is dealing with graphics. You can drag-and-drop graphics, add them by filename, and even edit them from within PageMill. Not to mention, PageMill makes creating client-side image maps actually fun. Big kudos for these extra features.

Finally, PageMill makes form creation very graphical and understandable. Although you'll still need to edit manually to add JavaScript and similar elements, the basic server-side form is a cakewalk to create.

Review Questions

1. Are menu commands the only way to access style elements like bold and italics in PageMill?

2. What should you do if you feel PageMill is "stuck" in a particular tag like a heading or list tag?

3. In creating a definition list, why is it helpful to choose an entire list and change its definition terms (DT), even if some of the elements are definitions (DD)?

4. What is the menu command for <HR> in PageMill?

5. Can you cut-and-paste a link from one page in PageMill to another?

6. What happens to PICT files when they are drag-and-dropped on PageMill documents?

7. What is the name of the tool used to create transparency in GIF files?

8. What are the three steps to creating a client-side image map?

9. What is "raw HTML"? Why does PageMill need a special command for this?

10. Where do you enter METHOD and ACTION information for forms in PageMill?

Review Exercises

1. Use PageMill, definition lists, and hyperlinks to create a page of book reviews. Clicking the book's name shows the user a graphic of the book. For instance, an entry might be:

```
HTML By Example
The best book ever written for learning HTML the right way.
```

2. Based on the example above, add another Definition (DD) line that includes a link to order the book, the author's name, copyright info, and price. For instance:

```
HTML By Example
The best book ever written for learning HTML the right way.
Todd Stauffer, Copyright 1996, $34.99. Order this book.
```

3. Create a button bar interface using PageMill. (No image map is necessary, just create a series of clickable images.)

4. Make a similar button bar, but use PageMill's built-in client-side image map creator.

5. Add Internet Explorer "background" sounds to a PageMill document.

6. Determine which type of centering (Netscape's <CENTER> tag or HTML's <DIV ALIGN="CENTER">) PageMill uses.

Part VII

HTML Examples

## CHAPTER 30

HTML Examples

Well, it's time to see if we can't apply just about everything you've learned to the world of the Web. This is also a wonderful opportunity to find a page that works well for the type of site you're trying to build. If you find a close match, you can get a headstart on your own site by copying the example from the included CD and altering it to fit your needs.

> **Note:** This is one chapter where the included CD can really help you out. If I've created a page that you think will work well for your site, just grab the HTML off the CD, change it to suit your needs, and toss it up on the World Wide Web. Hopefully, I've already done most of the work for you!

Back to Basics: Basic HTML 2.0 Pages

The beauty of designing HTML 2.0-compliant sites is that you never really have to worry about whether or not your users are happy, satisfied, and fully informed. Everyone, regardless of his or her browser, can see just about your entire site (except for text-based users who can't see your graphics). The downside is you don't get to do too much cool stuff.

For the typical personal Web site, though, HTML 2.0 is a great place to start designing. One of the most important rules to remember in HTML design is that your information is more important than the presentation. If using nothing but HTML 2.0—like basic text, lists, graphics, and even server-side maps—helps you update your pages quicker and keep things interesting, then you're doing better than the advanced Java programmer with nothing to say.

Let's see some examples of a "personal" Web site, perhaps useful for a home-based business or even just for fun. My examples are for a fictitious graphic designer named John Jones, who uses his site as both a business and a personal site. We'll create four basic pages—an index page, a personal biography, a business information page, and a resume page. These days, sometimes you tell people your life story with little more than an URL.

Example: The Personal Index Page

Since we're not talking about any major leaps of thought in HTML, I'll concentrate more on design issues with these personal pages. The keys to your index page will be an attractive presentation, while making it clear that things are dynamic on the page—you'll highlight your changes early. To create the index page, enter Listing 30.1 in your text editor.

On the CD

Listing 30.1 *index.html* **The Personal Index Page**

```
<HTML>
<HEAD>
<TITLE>John Jones on the Web</TITLE>
</HEAD>
<BODY>
<IMG SRC="johnlogo.gif" ALT="John Logo">
<H5>
<A HREF="index.html">Index</A> ¦ <A HREF="about.html">About John</A> ¦
<A HREF="contract.html">Business Info</A> ¦ <A
HREF="resume.html">Resume</A> ¦
<A HREF="feedback.html">Web Feedback</A>
</H5>
<HR>
<H2>Welcome to My Home on the Web!</H2>
<P>I'm <A HREF="about.html">John Jones</A>, and you've reached my home on
the Web. If you were looking to find me here, thanks for the thought. If
you're here by accident, well, maybe there's something interesting. Stay
a while.</P>
<HR>
<IMG SRC="news.gif"><BR>
<H3>What's News?</H3>
<P>I've finally gotten around to updating my <A HREF="macnet.html">Apple
QuickTime VR on the Net</A> pages. Those of you getting used to following
the news here will hopefully find everything you need.</P>
<P><A HREF="apple_pr1.html">Mac's Make it Big with VRML</A> Click for a
copy of Apple's PR on new QuickDraw 3D technology in the Web. To learn
more, check out
<A HREF="http://www.apple.com/">Apple's Web site</A>.</P>
<P><A HREF="ab_pics.html">Family Vacation Photos</A>! Just got back from
vacation in the Bahamas, and if you've never been you should check out
these photos. You can't beat the parasailing!</P>
```

```
<HR>
<IMG SRC="thesite.gif"><BR>
<H3>Stuff that John does that you may or may not find interesting...</H3>
<UL>
<LI> Magazine writer for <A HREF="http://www.netmag.com/">Net Mag</A> the
online Web graphics resource.
<LI>Freelance <A HREF="contract.html">Macintosh consultant</A> that you
can hire for <B>your own Web development</B> needs!
<DD>Just somebody's <A HREF="about.html">dad</A>.
</DL>
<HR>
<H3>Your Feedback on this Web Site...</H3>
<P><A HREF="feedback.html">Feedback</A> Lots of folks have written in to
tell me what they like about this site. The feedback has been incredible,
and I couldn't be happier. Keep it coming! If you've got something to
say, please
<A HREF="mailto:jjones@net.com">send mail</A></P>
<HR>
<H6>Copyright John Jones 1996. All Rights Reserved. Do not duplicate
without permission.</H6>
<H6>These pages are HTML 2.0 friendly!</H6>
</BODY>
</HTML>
```

Boring? I hope not. Let's call it "clean." This is a page that uses a couple of different ways to get around on the site, including a text menu at the top of the page and links throughout to relevant material. It also features site news right up front and some invitations to wander the site. Tasteful graphics and logical formatting let users get a feel for the site quickly, so they know they're not missing anything (see fig. 30.1).

Figure 30.1

An inviting, clean index page for a personal site.

483

Example: The Personal Biography

The next step is to create a biography page for John, complete with some interesting text and classy use of photos. Personal bios should probably be the most laid back part of the site; but it's important to remember that John is also using this as a business site—so it should probably be rather tasteful, too. Enter Listing 30.2 in your text editor.

On the CD

Listing 30.2 *about.html* **The Personal Bio Page**

```
<HTML>
<HEAD>
<TITLE>About John</TITLE>
</HEAD>
<BODY>
<IMG SRC="aboutlogo.gif" ALT="About John Logo">
<H5>
<A HREF="index.html">Index</A> ¦ <A HREF="about.html">About John</A> ¦
<A HREF="contract.html">Business Info</A> ¦ <A
HREF="resume.html">Resume</A> ¦
<A HREF="feedback.html">Web Feedback</A>
</H5>
<H3>A Little About Me...</H3>
<P>What is there to say about myself? I'm a graphic designer, a World
Wide Web addict and a <A HREF="ab_pics.html"> post-vacation dad</A> and
husband. I'm an incredible nut about Macintosh computers...
professionally. I play a lot of golf, a little tennis, and I do some
<A HREF="http://www.aescon.com/ski/">skiing</A>.
</P>
<P>I'm a graduate of <A HREF="http://www.unt.edu/">the University of
North Texas</A>.
My degree is in Fine Arts, with a minor in computer science. Since that
time I've worked in a number of positions as an artist, designer and senior
designer. I currently work in advertising as a Creative Manager.</P>
<P>I'm a nut about flying private airplanes, and recently completed the
requirement for my private license. Want to see
<A HREF="ab_solo.html">pictures</A> of me soloing? Now it looks like it's
a crap-shoot to see if the kids get through college before or after I buy
myself a plane!</P>
<HR>
<img src="business.gif" ALT="Business">
<H2>John's Contract Web Services</H2>
<H3><I>How Great Can It Look?</I></H3>
<P>I make every effort to make myself available at reasonable rates to
local businesses who have a serious need for a strong graphics designer.
```

```
With a background in advertising, public relations and editorial layout,
I'm the all-around solution for any business that needs something that
looks just right!
</P>
<P>My <A HREF="contract.html">sales pitch</A>, <A
HREF="resume.html">resume</A>
and <A HREF="contract.html#rates">freelance rate card</A> are available
here for your appraisal. If you'd like to get a hold of me to discuss a
project, you can do that by <A HREF="mailto:jjones@net.com">sending me
email</A> or call me during business hours at 214/555.4369.</P>
<HR>
<H6>Copyright John Jones 1996. All Rights Reserved. Do not duplicate
without permission.</H6>
<H6>These pages are HTML 2.0 friendly!</H6>
</BODY>
</HTML>
```

If there's anything this page shows, it's the importance of content over design. The point of this page is just to be friendly and talkative, while using HTML throughout to make the page presentable and approachable. Are people really interested in John's family photos? They probably are, and it's not so bad for business contacts to get to know you as a person. Take the space you need, but break up text with lines and small graphics (see fig. 30.2).

Figure 30.2

The About John page.

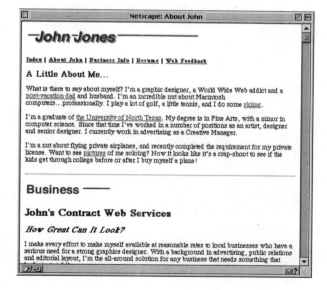

Also notice the consistency from page to page, like the text menu and logo at the top of the page. I'd suggest this same level of consistency for your pages, as well. It makes them more memorable and reminds people that all this great information is part of your site. You don't have to be dull on your pages, but I do suggest that you have a guiding design.

Example: Simple Business Pages

Perhaps this next page could be a little more graphically appealing, but I'm not a graphic artist—John is. What it does is communicate business information without being too overwhelmingly commercial. Are you going to generate a lot of leads on the Web? Not without investing a lot of time in your site and making an effort to distribute your URL. But, it's also a ready-made brochure for folks who are interested. Perhaps it'd be a good idea for John to put some designs online to serve as a Net-based portfolio—especially if he plans to work for people around the country (or world) via the Internet. Enter Listing 30.3 in your text editor to create the page.

On the CD

Listing 30.3 *contract.html* **Communicating Business Information on a Personal Site**

```
<HTML>
<HEAD>
<TITLE>Freelance Info and Rates</TITLE>
</HEAD>
<BODY>
<IMG SRC="contractlogo.gif" ALT="Freelance Logo">
<H5>
<A HREF="index.html">Index</A> ¦ <A HREF="about.html">About John</A> ¦
<A HREF="contract.html">Business Info</A> ¦ <A
HREF="resume.html">Resume</A> ¦
<A HREF="feedback.html">Web Feedback</A>
</H5>
<HR>
<H2>Shouldn't Your Business Literature Show Your Strengths?</H2>
<P>No matter what you may hear, there's only one way to be a great
salesperson.
<B>Believe in your product!</B> If you believe in your product, then
people will believe in you and your company. In order to make sure they
understand the depths of your faith, though, you need to catch their
eye!</P>
<UL>
<LI>Brochures and Sales Literature
<LI>Catalog Layout
<LI>Advertising/Promotional Layout
<LI>HTML and Web Site Development
<LI>Corporate Presentations
<LI>Public Relations Material
</UL>
```

```
<HR>
<A NAME="Rates">
<H2>Freelance/Contract Rates</H2>
<P>I'm willing to work both as a contractor and per piece. As is gener-
ally the case, any project is negotiable. Please contact me with full
details of the project. My office number is 214/555.4369. Or, feel free
to send me
<A HREF="mailto:jjones@net.com">email</A>.
</P>
<P>The following are my base rates for contract and per piece work:
<PRE>
Brochures and Sales Literature            $100-300 per page
Catalog Layout                            $65 an hour
Advertising/Promotional Layout            $100-300 per advertisement
HTML & Web Site Development               $65 an hour, $100-200 per page
Corporate Presentations                   $100 an hour
Public Relations Material                 $65 an hour
</PRE>
<H6>Copyright John Jones 1996. All Rights Reserved. Do not duplicate
without permission.</H6>
<H6>These pages are HTML 2.0 friendly!</H6>
</BODY>
</HTML>
```

Aside from the continued consistency, we've got two notable uses of HTML here. First, the use of a NAME anchor isn't even taken advantage of in the HTML on this page. But back in the personal biography, we did link to this part so that folks can get right to the rates if they want. Also, notice that the <PRE> tag works as a low-end HTML substitute for the table tags that you can't use (since you're doing this with only HTML 2.0 tags) (see fig. 30.3).

Figure 30.3

John's freelance info page.

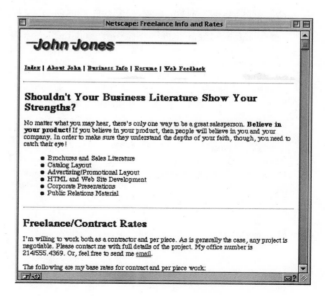

Example: John's Resume

Our next step is to add John's resume. I guess, by rule, a resume is a little dry, but perhaps that also adds to the professionalism. Again, a graphic designer should be a little more original with his/her resume than this—but it's a nice template for the rest of us (see Listing 30.4).

On the CD

Listing 30.4 *resume.html* **A Sample Resume in HTML**

```
<HTML>
<HEAD>
<TITLE>John's Resume Page</TITLE>
</HEAD>
</BODY>
<IMG SRC="resumelogo.gif" ALT="Resume Logo">
<H5>
<A HREF="index.html">Index</A> ¦ <A HREF="about.html">About John</A> ¦
<A HREF="contract.html">Business Info</A> ¦ <A
HREF="resume.html">Resume</A> ¦
<A HREF="feedback.html">Web Feedback</A>
</H5>
<HR>
<H2>John's Resume</H2>
<H3>EDUCATION</H3>
<B>University of North Texas </B> <I>Sept. 1984-May 1989</I>
Denton, Texas BA in Fine Arts, Minor in Computer Science.
<I>Cum Laude Honors, Dean's List, National Merit Scholar.</I>
<H3>SUMMARY OF QUALIFICATIONS</h3>
<UL>
<LI>Proven designer and layout artist strong background in computing.
<LI>Experience with creation and implementation of Hypertext Markup
Language (HTML)
<LI>Very familiar with Internet and online issues.
<LI>Constantly in touch with the computer industry through trade publica-
tions, on-line interaction and dealings with computer publishers and
industry contacts.
<LI>Solid team player and leader with experience and formal education in
business management.
</UL>
<H3>WORK EXPERIENCE</h3>
<P><B>BigCorp Advertising</B> (Dec. 1994-Present)<BR>
Dallas, TX<BR>
<I>Advertising Creating Manager</I><BR>
Manage staff of twenty-five designers, writers and support personnel in
the creation of all in-house advertising. Oversee the production of all
print and direct mail advertising, and responsible for managing input
from out-sourced advertising specialists.
```

```
</P>
<P><B>BigCorp Advertising</B> (Oct. 1989 - Dec.1992)<BR>
Dallas, TX<BR>
<I>Designer</I><BR>
Responsible for creating print advertising on Macintosh computers for a
variety of products and mediums. Contributed to multimedia projects, TV
design and in-store retail signage.
</P>
<P><B>Jones Designs</B> (Sep. 1988 - Present)<BR>
Dallas, TX<BR>
<I>Freelance Artist/Designer</I>
Accounts have included BigSoftDrink Co., FashionableClothes Inc, and
MajorProductionCompany Entertainment.
</P>
<H6>Copyright John Jones 1996. All Rights Reserved. Do not duplicate
without permission.</H6>
<H6>These pages are HTML 2.0 friendly!</H6>
</BODY>
</HTML>
```

Again, there's good continuity and clean design (see fig. 30.4). Can't ask for much more than that.

Figure 30.4

John's resume.

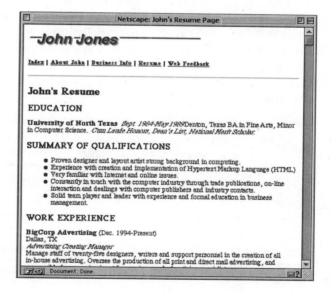

I think you can see where I'm going with this. The strongest point is this: you can do a lot with an HTML 2.0 site, and working just in 2.0 makes sure your documents are available to the widest audience possible. Keep your site newsworthy, interesting, consistent, and personal, and you'll succeed with your small site.

BigCorp's Client-Side Site

In this section, you'll start by walking through the creation of a large Web site—you guessed it, BigCorp's—in an effort to apply most of the tags, extensions, programming, and theory you've learned throughout this book. I'll try to point out the major issues in each page as we go along.

The point of this site will be to do just about everything you can without consulting the Web server. A growing number of HTML users are able to create sites without back-end programming with the help of JavaScript, client-side images, and similar technologies. Client-side has been the theme throughout this book. Hopefully, these examples will help make that a strong reality for you.

> **Note:** As opposed to the first section of this chapter, the client-side site pushes the envelope of HTML. You'll need the latest version of Netscape Navigator (or a compatible browser) to view these pages—and so will your users.

Example: The Front Door

We've talked about front door pages before: pages designed to introduce users to your Web site, warn them of potentially offensive material, and/or allow them to choose the pages that are best suited to their browser type. In this simple example, you'll create an attractive front door that uses client-pull to draw in Netscape/Internet Explorer users, while giving others a chance to click for the HTML 2.0 compatible version of our site (see Listing 30.5).

> **Note:** For purposes of putting this file on the CD-ROM, I've named it `bg_index.html`. Since it's the first page of this particular site, though, you may want to save it as `index.html` in a different directory from the personal site files you created earlier in this chapter. I recommend that you begin your sites with a document named `index.html` whenever possible.

On the CD

Listing 30.5 *bg_index.html* A Business' Front Door Page

```
<HTML>
<HEAD>
<TITLE>BigCorp - What Type of Browser Are You Using?</TITLE>
<META HTTP-EQUIV="REFRESH" CONTENT = "15; URL=http://www.fakecorp.com/
graf_idx.html">
<IMG SRC="logo.gif">
<H2>Welcome to BigCorp's Web Site!</H2>
```

```
<P>To better serve all different browsers, we've created this site with
both a <A HREF="http://www.fakecorp.com/graf_idx.html">high graphics</A>
choice and a <A HREF="http://www.fakecorp.com/H2_idx.html">HTML 2.0</A>
choice. Please choose the appropriate site for you. After 15 seconds, the
high graphics site (especially appropriate for Netscape and Internet
Explorer users) will load automatically if your browser will support
it.</P>
<H3>Enjoy Your Stay!</H3>
</DIV>
</BODY>
</HTML>
```

This page gives users the choice of either clicking to move directly to their desired site or waiting for the high graphics site to load using client-pull. Also, users with browsers that don't support client-pull will be forced to click one of the choices, since they won't automatically move on. Figure 30.5 shows how this page appears in a browser.

Figure 30.5

Your client-pull front door in Netscape Navigator.

Example: The Graphical Index

The next page will be the "high graphics" index for this site. You'll use client-side image map technology to link users to the various parts of BigCorp's Web presence. In addition, you'll add an Internet Explorer background sound and a background image (see Listing 30.6).

On the CD

Listing 30.6 *graf_idx.html* **The Graphical Index for the Business Site**

```
<HTML>
<HEAD>
<TITLE>BigCorp's Index</TITLE>
</HEAD>
<BODY BACKGROUND="paper.gif">
```

continues

Listing 30.6   Continued

```
<BGSOUND="welcome.wav">
<DIV ALIGN="CENTER">
<H2>Welcome to BigCorp!</H2>
<H5><A HREF="index.html">Index</A> ¦ <A HREF="products.html">Products</A> ¦
<A HREF="service.html">Customer Service</A> ¦ <A HREF="support.html">Tech
Support</A> ¦
<A HREF="about.html"> About BigCorp</A></H5>
<A HREF="help.html"><IMG SRC="main_map.gif" ALT="BigCorp's Map Graphic"
USEMAP="#mainmap"></A>
</DIV>
<IMG SRC="news.gif">
<BLOCKQUOTE>
<P><A HREF="story1.html">BigCorp releases new Pentium Pro Systems.</A>
<B>August 2</B> As the summer boils down to a footrace between popular
computer manufacturers, BigCorp makes the leap to Pentium Pro and multi-
processing Pentium Pro systems for the high-end server and graphics
markets. With clock speeds of up to 300 Mhz, the BigCorp systems should
lead the pack for weeks, at least.</P>
<P><A HREF="story2.html">Better paper towels, less messy residue.</A> <B>
August 3</B> BigCorp, the largest global manufacturer of household paper
products, has announced the next step in paper towels at WipeCon '97.
The new design, based on patented advances in textiles (researched on
BigCorp's orbiting SolarLab deep-space project) should but cloth towels
to bed once and for all. "We're looking to take paper towels into
the shower stall by year's end," said Wilhem Spotz, VP of Clensing
Technology.</P>
</BLOCKQUOTE>
<H5>Please send concerns about this server to <A
HREF="mailto:admin.fakecorp.com"> the WebMaster</A>. For more information
on BigCorp and BigCorp products, call or write:</H5>
<ADDRESS>
BigCorp Customer Service<BR>
0001 Real Tall Building<BR>
Metropolis, USA 00001<BR>
888-BIG-CORP<BR>
</ADDRESS>
<H6>Pages and Content Copyright 1996 BigCorp Multimedia. All rights
reserved. Do not duplicate without permission.</H6>
<MAP NAME="mainmap">
<AREA SHAPE="rect" COORDS="18,12,140,33" HREF="index.html" ALT="Back to
Index">
<AREA SHAPE="rect" COORDS="17,44,245,65" HREF="products.html" ALT="To
Products">
```

```
<AREA SHAPE="rect" COORDS="97,87,327,147" HREF="about.html" ALT="About
BigCorp">
<AREA SHAPE="rect" COORDS="183,159,403,180" HREF="service.html" ALT="To
Customer Service">
<AREA SHAPE="rect" COORDS="265,192,403,213" HREF="support.html" ALT="To
Tech Support">
<AREA SHAPE="rect" COORDS="0,0,424,223" HREF="help.html" ALT="Help with
Map">
</MAP>
</BODY>
</HTML>
```

On this index page, I'm using a client-side image map to allow users to move around on the site, as well as offering some typical home page elements like news, addresses, and **mailto:** links for more information. Using WebMap to determine the client-maps coordinates gave the results in figure 30.6.

Figure 30.6

The map definition file.

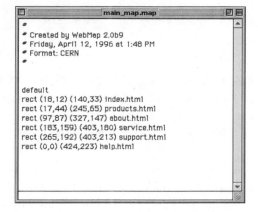

From there, it was as simple as plugging in the coordinates for each shape of the client-map. I turned the client-map background transparent, wrapped it in a regular clickable-image anchor (to allow non-client-side browser to access a help page), and saved. It's ready to go up on my Web site (see fig. 30.7).

Figure 30.7

The finished
index page.

Example: BigCorp's About Page

One of the methods for HTML layout that's gaining a lot of popularity on the Web is using HTML table tags (without borders) to give the user more control over the page. For BigCorp's About page, let's use HTML tables to layout some of the historical information we're going to provide our users (see Listing 30.7).

> **Note:** Again, I've changed the name of this file for saving on the CD-ROM. Changing its name to about.html will allow it to work correctly with the rest of the pages in this site.

Listing 30.7 *bc_about.html* **Using Tables for Page Layout**

```
<HTML>
<HEAD>
<TITLE>About BigCorp</TITLE>
</HEAD>
<BODY BGCOLOR="FFFFFF">
<TABLE BORDER=0 WIDTH="500" CELLPADDING="10" CELLSPACING="5">
<TR>
<TH COLSPAN="3" ALIGN="CENTER"><IMG SRC="ab_logo.gif"></TH>
```

```
</TR>
<TR>
<TD WIDTH="40">
<A HREF="corphist.html">Corporate History Page</A>
</TD>
<TD>
<IMG SRC="mrbig.gif">
</TD>
<TD>
BigCorp started many years ago with a unique vision of the future. Mr.
BigBucks, founder, explained some of those ideas in this story.
</TD>
</TR>
<TR HEIGHT="75"><TD COLSPAN="3" ALIGN="CENTER"><HR></TD></TR>
<TR>
<TD COLSPAN="2">
<A HREF="manfact.html">BigCorp Textile Manufacturing</A>
</TD>
<TD>
Get the inside scoop on our textiles division, plus contacts, phone
numbers and executive biographies.
</TD>
</TR>
<TR HEIGHT="75"><TD COLSPAN="3" ALIGN="CENTER"><HR></TD></TR>
<TR>
<TD COLSPAN="2">
<A HREF="compute.html">BigCorp Computer Manufacturing</A>
</TD>
<TD>
Here's information on the latest plant information and press releases from
BigCorp Computer, including information about retail outlets, service
centers, phone numbers and PR contacts.
</TD>
</TR>
</TABLE>
</BODY>
</HTML>
```

In this way, creative use of tables (especially without borders) can give you amazing control over the layout of your page. The more specific you want to be about where something appears, the more specific you can be with attributes like WIDTH and HEIGHT for rows and columns. Tables are basically a way you can "compartmentalize" each page—giving you rather exacting control over how and where things appear (see fig. 30.8).

Figure 30.8

Using a page-sized table for enhanced layout.

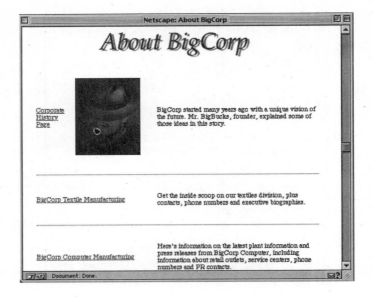

Example: Using Frames

Your next step will be creating a frames interface for the product pages. What we're interested in doing here is creating three basic frames: a logo frame at the top, an icon interface for different products along the left, and a main viewer window to the right. This will allow users to quickly access all of BigCorp's products using a familiar interface.

This sort of interface assumes you have a lot of different pages to get to from this one viewer. I'll create an example of each, but it'll be up to you to fill in with the many pages of information you might want to offer on your company's products or your personal interests.

First, let's create the banner document for the frame interface's top row logo (see Listing 30.8).

Listing 30.8 *prodlogo.html* **Logo and Menu for the Top Frame**

```
<HTML>
<HEAD>
<TITLE>Product Logo</TITLE>
</HEAD>
<BODY BGCOLOR="#FFFFFF">
<DIV ALIGN="CENTER">
<IMG SRC="prodlogo.gif">
<H5><A HREF="index.html">Index</A> ¦
<A HREF="products.html">Products</A> ¦
<A HREF="service.html">Customer Service</A> ¦
<A HREF="support.html">Tech Support</A> ¦
```

```
<A HREF="about.html"> About BigCorp</A></H5>
</DIV>
</BODY>
</HTML>
```

Use Listing 30.9 for the next step of creating the icon interface for the left side of your frame document.

On the CD

Listing 30.9 *prodicon.html* **Icon List for Accessing Pages in** *main_viewer*

```
<HTML>
<HEAD>
<TITLE>Icon List</TITLE>
</HEAD>
<BODY BGCOLOR="#FFFFFF">
<P>
<A HREF="prod_idx.html" TARGET="main_viewer"><IMG SRC="bag.gif" ALT="To
Index" BORDER="0"></A><BR>
Index<BR>
</P>
<P>
<A HREF="books.html" TARGET="main_viewer"><IMG SRC="books.gif"
ALT="Books" BORDER="0"></A><BR>
Books<BR>
</P>
<P>
<A HREF="pe.html" TARGET="main_viewer"><IMG SRC="camera.gif"
ALT="Personal Electronics" BORDER="0"></A><BR>
Personal<BR>
Electronics<BR>
</P>
<P>
<A HREF="hunting.html" TARGET="main_viewer"><IMG SRC="gun.gif"
ALT="Hunting Goods" BORDER="0"></A><BR>
Hunting<BR>
Goods<BR>
</P>
<P>
<A HREF="sporting.html" TARGET="main_viewer"><IMG SRC="sunglass.gif"
ALT="Sporting Goods" BORDER="0"></A><BR>
Sporting<BR>
Goods<BR>
</P>
<P>
<A HREF="computer.html" TARGET="main_viewer"><IMG SRC="computer.gif"
ALT="Computers" BORDER="0"></A><BR>
Computers<BR>
</P>
</BODY>
</HTML>
```

Notice the use of the TARGET attribute for the anchor, so that clicking these icons forces a new page to appear in the main viewer window of your frames interface. Also notice that I've used the Netscape-specific BORDER attribute for IMGs. At least in Netscape (and compatible browsers), this keeps those boxy clickable-image borders from appearing. Luckily, since only Netscape-compatible viewers can see this frames interface in the first place (and we also used a front door for HTML 2.0 users), you're free to experiment a bit here.

Now, let's use Listing 30.10 for the product index page, which will serve as the default page for the main viewer frame.

On the CD

Listing 30.10 *prod_idx.html* **Default Index Page for** *main_viewer*

```
<HTML>
<HEAD>
<TITLE>Product Index</TITLE>
</HEAD>
<BODY BGCOLOR="#FFFFFF">
<H3>BigCorp's Product Index</H3>
<P>Use the icons on the left to choose different product categories, or
select them from the following list:</P>
<UL>
<LI><A HREF="books.html" TARGET="main_viewer">Books</A>
<LI><A HREF="pe.html" TARGET="main_viewer">Personal Electronics</A>
<LI><A HREF="hunting.html" TARGET="main_viewer">Hunting Goods</A>
<LI><A HREF="sporting.html" TARGET="main_viewer">Sporting Goods</A>
<LI><A HREF="computer.html" TARGET="main_viewer">Computers</A>
</UL>
</BODY>
</HTML>
```

Pretty straightforward, huh? This page will be loaded automatically with the frame interface (product.html). It's also linked to the graphic bag.gif in the file prodicon.html so that the user can get back to the index page whenever he or she wants.

Now, you need to create a page that will actually be loaded for this example. Fortunately, you have already done this—quite some time ago. Listing 30.11 is most of an example from using tables with graphics in Chapter 15, "Adding Tables to Your Documents."

On the CD

Listing 30.11 *computer.html* **A Sample Data Page for** *main_viewer*

```
<HTML>
<HEAD>
<TITLE>Computer Products</TITLE>
</HEAD>
</HTML>
```

```
<BODY BGCOLOR="#FFFFFF">
<H2> BigCorp's Computer Systems </H2>
<P>We use only the highest quality components and software for all of our
Wintel computer systems. Plus, if you don't see a configuration you like,
call (or email) and let us know. We'll custom build to please!</P>
<DIV ALIGN="CENTER">
<TABLE ALIGN="CENTER" BORDER="1" FRAME=VOID RULES="NONE" CELLSPACING="3"
CELLPADDING="3">
<CAPTION>BigCorp's Computer Systems and Specifications</CAPTION>
<TR ALIGN="CENTER"><TH>System 486<TH>System 586<TH>System 686
<TR ALIGN=""CENTER"><TD>486DX2-66 CPU<TD>120 MHZ AMD586<TD>200 Mhz
Pentium Pro
<TR><TD>8 MB RAM<TD>16 MB RAM<TD>16 MB RAM
<TR><TD>500 MB HD<TD>1 GB HD<TD>1.4 GB HD
<TR><TD>14.4 Modem<TD>28.8 Modem<TD>28.8 Modem
<TR><TD>desktop case<TD>minitower case<TD>tower case
<TR><TD>DOS/Win 3.1<TD>Windows 95<TD>Windows NT 4.0
</TABLE>
</DIV>
<H2>Product Specifications</H2>
<P>The following table will tell you a little more about our computer
systems. Clicking on the picture of each will tell you even more,
offering a full-size photo of the system and some suggestions on
peripherals.</P>
<HR>
<TABLE BORDER CELLSPACING="2" CELLPADDING="2">
<CAPTION>Our System Configurations</CAPTION>
<TR ALIGN="CENTER"><TH>Photo</TH><TH>Name</TH><TH>RAM</TH><TH>Hard
Drive</TH><TH>Video</TH><TH>Expansion</TH><TH>Case</TH>
<TR ALIGN="CENTER"><TD><IMG SRC="6001.gif"></TD><TD>System 6001-60
</TD><TD>8MB</TD><TD>500 MB</TD><TD>1 MB PCI</TD><TD>4 PCI Slots</TD>
<TD ROWSPAN="2">
Desktop</TD>
<TR ALIGN="CENTER"><TD><IMG SRC="7001.gif"></TD><TD>System 7001-75
</TD><TD>16
MB</TD><TD>1.0 GB</TD><TD>1 MB PCI</TD><TD>5 PCI Slots</TD>
<TR ALIGN="CENTER"><TD><IMG SRC="8001.gif"></TD><TD>System 8001-120
</TD><TD>20MB</TD><TD>1.6 GB</TD><TD>2 MB PCI</TD><TD>5 PCI Slots</TD>
<TD>Tower</TD>
</TABLE>
</BODY>
</HTML>
```

In this example, the page computer.html is linked to the icon computer.gif in the prodicon.html file. When the icon is clicked in the left side of the frames interface, the above page will load in the main viewer.

Finally, you have enough components to demonstrate the product frame interface. Here it is in Listing 30.12.

On the CD

Listing 30.12 *products.html* **Main Frames Interface Page**

```
<HTML>
<HEAD>
<TITLE>BigCorp's Product Viewer</TITLE>
</HEAD>
<FRAMESET ROWS="100,*">
<FRAME SRC="prodlogo.html" MARGINHEIGHT="10">
   <FRAMESET COLS="20%,80%">
   <FRAME SRC="prodicon.html" MARGINHEIGHT="25" MARGINWIDTH="10">
   <FRAME SRC="prod_idx.html" NAME="main_viewer" MARGINHEIGHT="25"
MARGINWIDTH="10">
   </FRAMESET>
</FRAMESET>
</BODY>
</HTML>
```

Murphy's law seems to dictate that this would be the easiest page to create. We've simply used two <FRAMESET> definitions, with the columns definition nested within the rows definition to create a three panel interface. And, with all of this done, it looks something like figure 30.9.

Figure 30.9

The product pages' frame interface.

prodlogo.html

prodicon.html

main_viewer

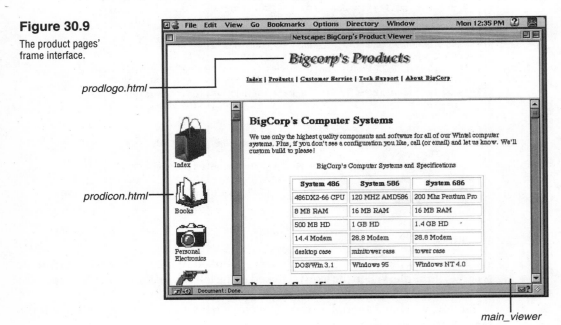

Example: JavaScript and Forms

Continuing with the client-oriented Web site, let's create a customer service form that's good for customers to send in data. Instead of using a CGI script to handle the data, though, you'll do the whole thing in JavaScript. After users have entered their preferences and values, you'll output them to the page for their perusal. If they like it, they can send it to you by mail. Sound good (see Listing 30.13)?

Listing 30.13 *service.html* **Main Service Page, Using JavaScript for Sending Data**

```
<HTML>
<HEAD>
<TITLE>BigCorp Customer Service</TITLE>
<SCRIPT>
<!--
function processForm (doc) {
    if (doc.form1.os[0].checked)
        newline = "\r\n"
    else if (doc.form1.os[1].checked)
        newline = "\n"
    else
        newline = "\r";
result_str = "";
    result_str += doc.form1.name.value + newline;
    result_str += doc.form1.address.value + newline;
    result_str += doc.form1.city.value + newline;
    result_str += doc.form1.state.value + newline;
    result_str += doc.form1.zip.value + newline;
    if (doc.form1.desktop.checked) result_str += "Desktop computers" +
newline;
    if (doc.form1.notebook.checked) result_str += "Notebook computers" +
newline;
    if (doc.form1.peripherals.checked) result_str += "Peripherals" +
newline;
    if (doc.form1.software.checked) result_str += "Software" + newline;
    doc.form2.results.value = result_str;
    return;
    }
// -->
</SCRIPT>
</HEAD>
<BODY>
<DIV ALIGN="CENTER">
<IMG SRC="servlogo.html">
</DIV>
```

continues

501

Listing 30.13 Continued

```
<P>In order that we might better serve you we ask that you simply fill
out this form. When you've submitted the form, the results will appear in
the text area at the bottom of the screen. If everything looks alright,
send it away.</P>
<FORM NAME="form1">
<PRE>
Your Name:      <INPUT TYPE="Text" NAME="name" SIZE="40">
Your Address:   <INPUT TYPE="Text" NAME="address" SIZE="60">
Your City:      <INPUT TYPE="Text" NAME="city" SIZE="20">
State:<INPUT TYPE="Text"
NAME="state" SIZE="2"> Zip:<INPUT TYPE="Text" NAME="zip" SIZE="5">
<HR>
<H4>What products would you like more information about? (Check all that
apply)</H4>
<INPUT TYPE="Checkbox" NAME="desktop"> Desktop computers
<INPUT TYPE="Checkbox" NAME="notebook"> Notebook computers
<INPUT TYPE="Checkbox" NAME="peripherals"> Peripherals
<INPUT TYPE="Checkbox" NAME="software"> Software
<HR>
Please Choose Your Computer's OS:<BR>
<INPUT TYPE="Radio" NAME="os" VALUE="mac" CHECKED> Macintosh
<INPUT TYPE="Radio" NAME="os" NALUE="unix"> Unix
<INPUT TYPE="Radio" NAME="os" VALUE="win"> DOS/Windows/Win95<BR>
<HR>
<INPUT TYPE="Reset" VALUE="Clear Form">
<INPUT TYPE="Button" VALUE="Submit" onClick="processForm (document)">
</PRE>
</FORM>
<HR>
<FORM NAME="form2" METHOD="POST" ACTION="mailto:stauffer@rmii.com"
ENCTYPE="text/ascii">
<H4>Here's what your information will look like. If you'd like to include
a comment, please type it below the other information. Then click below
to mail it to us:</H4>
<TEXTAREA NAME="results" COLS="60" ROWS="10" WRAP="soft"></TEXTAREA>
<INPUT TYPE="Submit" Value="Mail It Off">
</FORM>
</BODY>
</HTML>
```

Basically what this script does is take the information from the first form, translate it into some simple text values, assign those values to the textarea in the second form, and then allow the user to edit the data (see fig. 30.10). The script uses the result from the radio buttons in the first form to determine which newline character to use for the textarea, depending on the user's OS choice. Different OSes require different newline characters to format text correctly in a textarea. This script solves that problem.

Figure 30.10

Client-side form
submissions.

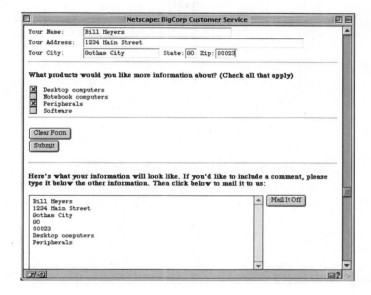

Then, when users click the second Submit button (the "send it in" button), the data is sent via e-mail to the address of your choice. In that way, you've avoided using the Web server and CGI-BIN scripts for any of your form processing.

While this scenario seems like nothing more than beauty and cleverness itself, there is one caveat—what to do with the e-mail when it gets to your e-mail box.

The first problem is the fact that the e-mail message is still encoded in that lovely POST format that forms use to send messages to scripts. Figure 30.11 shows an example of a typical received message.

Figure 30.11

The results of a
mailto: form
POSTing.

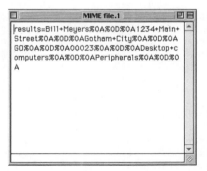

It's not very pretty. The second problem is an extension of the first—you're either going to have to process all of these e-mails by hand or you'll need to write a program on your computer that interacts with your e-mail program in some way. Either way is probably fine for the small-business or home Web designer—at least, you get the form data from users without requiring access to the server.

If you're creating for a large corporate installation, though, your best bet is still to use CGI-BIN scripts. If you don't know C, Perl, or AppleScript (on Mac servers), then have a quick chat with your IS folks.

Example: FTP and HTML

Perhaps it's not the most glamorous of possibilities with HTML, but many sites will find a need to include a repository of files on their pages in order to better serve customers. In this example, you'll create the support page for your site, using definition lists to add your FTP-able files (see Listing 30.14).

On the CD

Listing 30.14 *support.html* **Adding FTP to HTML Documents**

```
<HTML>
<HEAD>
<TITLE>Product Support</TITLE>
</HEAD>
<BODY>
<DIV ALIGN="CENTER">
<IMG SRC="suplogo.gif">
</DIV>
<H2>Support Files and Resources</H2>
<P>The following files are available for download from BigCorp. Included
are fixes, patches and upgrades for various BigCorp software products.
Any comments about this list can be sent to our
<A HREF="mailto:supportweb@fakecorp.com"> Support WebMaster</A>.
Questions about computer product support can be sent to
<A HREF="mailto:questions@fakecorp.com">Support Questions</A>. A
technician will mail you back within a few hours (weekdays).</P>
<H3>Available for Download</H3>
<DL>
<DT> <IMG SRC="file.gif"> <A HREF="ftp://www.fakecorp.com/pub/
12upd496.zip"> Updated for BigCorp Write 1.2</A>
<DD> This update adds support for additional file formats from Microsoft
and Word Perfect. Also fixes version 1.2 crashes when used with serial
printers, supports OLE 2.0 objects and offers new embedded spreadsheet
tools. Updates version 1.2 to version 1.2.4. Please read the enclosed
ReadMe file. Type: PkZip archive.
<DT> <IMG SRC="file.gif"> <A HREF="ftp://www.fakecorp.com/pub/
HTMLad09.zip">HTML Addition for BigCorp Write</A>
<DD> Now available for free (just the cost of the download) is new HTML
functionality for BigCorp Write. Add standard HTML 2.0 tags to your
```

```
documents just as if you were word processing! This beta version (0.9)
has been fairly stable through our internal testing, but we can't guaran-
tee it won't completely destroy your hard drive. Read the enclosed
disclaimer (DISCLAIM.TXT)! Requires BigCorp Write version 1.2 or higher.
For
Windows.
<DT> <IMG SRC="file.gif"> <A HREF="ftp://www.fakecorp.com/pub/
HTMLAddition.sit">HTML
Addition for BigCorp Write for Macintosh</A>
<DD> Same functionality as above, but for BigCorp Write 1.4 and above for
Macintosh. Upgrade is PowerPC accelerated.
<DT> <IMG SRC="folder.gif"> <A HREF="support2.html">Additional Files</A>
<DD> Printer drivers, templates, sample document and additional tools for
file compression; older fixes, patches and upgrades.
</DL>
</BODY>
</HTML>
```

It's pretty straightforward. You can use an FTP-style URL to access files for downloading across the Internet to your users (see fig. 30.12). But, you don't necessarily have to follow the FTP style for folders—especially if you want to offer files with your own descriptions and icons. Notice for the folder at the bottom of the page that you're actually accessing another HTML page where, presumably, you've created another list of files for downloading.

Figure 30.12

The sample support page offers files for download.

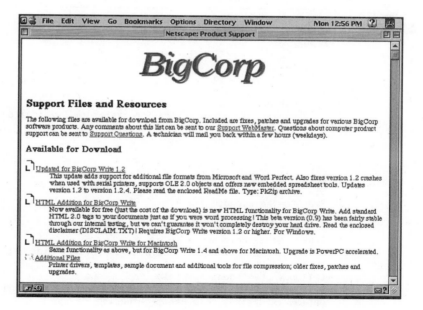

505

Example: The Help Page

Here's a fun one. You may recall that you set up your client-side image map on index.html to point directly to the document help.html, which is supposed to tell your users that they've clicked a client-side map incorrectly (or, perhaps, that they don't have a map-capable browser). But what if you want to offer a number of different Help topics from this one page?

Using forms, frames, and JavaScript, let's create a page that allows the users to select the type of help they'd like to receive. Our default page will discuss the client-side map, so that users who just "appear" at help get the information they need. Otherwise, if they decide to look up help on their own, they can simply use the Select menu in the top frame to choose the help document they'll read—which will then appear in the bottom window.

This can have many applications outside of help files—using scripts to manipulate pages gives you a great way to serve nearly any type of document from within a frames interface. Product spec sheets, public relations material, software documentation, or just about anything else you can come up with.

The first file you'll create is the JavaScript/form interface for the top half of your frames interface (see Listing 30.15).

On the CD

Listing 30.15 *helpform.html* **Scripting for a Forms Interface**

```html
<HTML>
<HEAD>
<TITLE>Help Form</TITLE>
<SCRIPT>
<!--
 function changePage(form) {
      var choice=form.helppage.selectedIndex;
      parent.main_viewer.location.href=form.helppage[choice].value;
      }
// -->
</SCRIPT>
</HEAD>
<BODY>
<DIV ALIGN="CENTER">
<IMG SRC="helplogo.gif"><BR>
<FORM>
Choose the Help Topic You Want to View:
<SELECT NAME="helppage">
<OPTION SELECTED VALUE="maphelp.html"> Client-side Map
<OPTION VALUE="usehelp.html"> Using Our Site
<OPTION VALUE="phonhelp.html"> Contacting BigCorp
<OPTION VALUE="dl_help.html"> Downloading From Our Site
<OPTION VALUE="buy_help.html"> Ordering Products
</SELECT><BR>
```

```
<INPUT TYPE="button" Value="Get Help" onClick="changePage(this.form)">
</FORM>
</DIV>
</BODY>
</HTML>
```

The key to working with frames and JavaScript is the JavaScript object hierarchy `parent.main_viewer`. This is telling the script to look in "the frame called `main_viewer`" of the "parent" document, which, once you're done, will be the frames interface document (`help.html`). All you have to do is assign a value to the frame's `location.href` object variable, and the page is loaded.

Another concept you need to understand here is the "array" in JavaScript. Why? Because it's how JavaScript stores the values for a SELECT form element.

Every time you create a new SELECT OPTION statement, that value is stored in a new variable. But notice that there's nothing to name the variable, since it would simply overwrite the last value that was assigned to `helppage.value`. (That's how you'd do it with some other form elements.)

So your browser creates an "array" of `helppage` values. The first one gets called `helppage[0]` (the one with the value `"maphelp.html"`). The next one gets called `helppage[1]` and so on. The number is the "index" of the OPTION array—it's how you access each individual option.

Another variable is also created, called `helppage.selectedIndex`. It holds a number that tells you which index has been chosen. So, in the previous script, I assign the value in `selectedIndex` to a variable called `choice`, and then I use `choice` to access the value of the OPTION that was chosen by your user. Then the value (in this case, the URL of a help page) gets passed to the frame's `location.href` variable, which causes a new page to be loaded. Cool, huh?

Next, you need to create some filler pages. You'll create a "default" page that talks about the client map, and create one other example to test your frames interface. Use Listing 30.16 for the client map help page.

On the CD

Listing 30.16   *maphelp.html*   The Default Help Document

```
<HTML>
<HEAD>
<TITLE>Client-Map Help</TITLE>
</HEAD>
<BODY>
<DIV ALIGN="CENTER">
<IMG SRC="helplogo.gif">
<H2>BigCorp Web Site Help</H2>
</DIV>
```

continues

Listing 30.16 Continued

```
<P>Please choose the topic you'd like help with from the menu at the top
of this pages. If you've arrived here by clicking on the graphic on our
index page, read on.</P>
<H3>Help with BigCorp Graphical Maps</H3>
<P>BigCorp offers a number of different "graphical maps" for navigating
its site on the World Wide Web. These maps use "client-side" technology,
which means that your Web browser program (the "client") needs to be able
to process the information in the different parts of the graphic, thus
allowing you to go directly to different parts of our Web site.</P>
<P>Since you've arrived here, it seems your browser doesn't support
client-side maps. There are a couple of options. First, we'd definitely
recommend visiting <A HREF="http://www.microsoft.com/">Microsoft Corp.
</A> or <A HREF="http://www.netscape.com/"> Netscape Corp.</A> and
downloading the latest versions of their advanced Web browsers. If this
isn't feasible, or if you're stuck using a text-based system, we recom-
mend you visit our <A HREF="http://www.fakecorp.com/H2_idx.html">HTML 2.0
compliant pages</A>.</P>
<P>If you want to continue to use this enhanced pages, our final recom-
mendation is to use the text links provided on most pages, like those
below (which are functional...use them to leave this page.)</P>
<DIV ALIGN="CENTER">
<H5><A HREF="index.html">Index</A> ¦ <A HREF="products.html">Products</A>
¦
<A HREF="service.html">Customer Service</A> ¦ <A HREF="support.html">Tech
Support</A> ¦ <A HREF="about.html"> About BigCorp</A></H5>
</DIV>
</BODY>
</HTML>
```

Here's another example of a help page that you can use to test the frames interface. Let's create a page that "helps" users by telling them how to order products from BigCorp (see Listing 30.17).

On the CD

Listing 30.17 *buy_help.html* **Another Sample Help Document**

```
<HTML>
<HEAD>
<TITLE>Ordering BigCorp Products</TITLE>
</HEAD>
<BODY>
<DIV ALIGN="CENTER">
<H2>How to Order from BigCorp</H2>
</DIV>
<P>Find something on our Web site you'd like to order? Well, there are a
couple of ways to go about it. Most of the products discussed online are
also available through retail outlets. Or, you can order directly from
us, and we'll send nearly everything out by the next business day.</P>
<UL>
```

```
<LI>To find a retail outlet for BigCorp Products, call 1-800-BIG-CORP and
hit "6" at the main menu.
<LI>To order directly from BigCorp, called 1-800-BIG-CORP for electron-
ics, books and computer goods. Sporting and hunting equipment can be
ordered by calling 1-800-BIG-FISH.
<LI>To order by mail, send a check or money order, including appropriate
handling charges and state sales taxes to: Order Fulfillment, P.O. Box
001, Clearing City, MO 90009.
<LI>For a catalog of our products, send a letter with your name, address
and daytime phone number to: Catalog, P.O. Box 101, Clearing City, MO
90009.
<LI>To order a catalog via the Internet, please send your name, address
and a daytime phone via an email message to
<A HREF="mailto:catalogs@fakecorp.com">catalogs@fakecorp.com</A>.
<LI>For Corporate Sales information, call 1-800-BIG-SALE for information
on creating a corporate account and requesting a personal sales represen-
tative for your company.
</UL>
</BODY>
</HTML>
```

Finally, you need to create the frame interface page. This one should be fairly simple (see Listing 30.18).

On the CD

Listing 30.18   *help.html*   The Help Frames Interface

```
<HTML>
<HEAD>
<TITLE>BigCorp's Web Help</TITLE>
</HEAD>
<FRAMESET ROWS="150, *">
   <FRAME SRC="helpform.html" MARGINHEIGHT="10">
   <FRAME SRC="maphelp.html" NAME="main_viewer" MARGINHEIGHT="5">
</FRAMESET>
</HTML>
```

Gotta love those frame documents.

With all of this said and done, you're ready to test your new interface. When you load help.html, you should see the logo and SELECT menu in the top frame and maphelp.html (the default help page) in the main_viewer frame. Selecting a new help page from the menu and clicking Get Help should change the document in the lower frame (see fig. 30.13).

Figure 30.13

Script-based
frames interface
for documents.

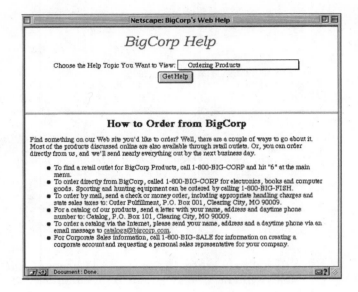

Appendix

Answers to Review Questions

Chapter 1

1. No. It's a text mark-up language.

2. True.

3. SGML (Standard Generalized Mark-up Language.)

4. Explicit formatting means the designer specifies the appearance of text. Implicit formatting leaves appearance up to the Web browser application.

5. False. WordPerfect documents are binary (i.e., non-ASCII) computer files that can't be edited without a special word processing application.

6. No. The HTML Working Group is part of the IETF. The W3C is an organization of Internet companies.

7. To reach the widest possible audience of designers and users.

8. By deciding which elements or commands to use and which to ignore.

Chapter 2

1. The Web protocols allow Web server computers to send many different types of data and information.

2. Hypertext is a system of documentation where certain words in a document are linked to other documents. The Microsoft Windows help system is an example of hypertext.

3. False. Hypermedia links are hypertext links to multimedia files.

4. A site is a collection of Web documents and files. A page is a single Web document.

5. Helper applications are used to display or play non-HTML files and documents, like multimedia files.

6. File extensions help browsers determine the file types of multimedia files.

7. Gopher and FTP.

8. Your e-mail address.

Chapter 3

1. The original graphical browser is NCSA Mosaic. The most popular is Netscape Navigator.

2. Page layout.

3. Lynx is a text-only browser.

4. Server address.

5. `mailto:` is followed by a simple e-mail address instead of a server/path combination.

6. A forward slash (/).

7. Yes (assuming the path and filename were correct).

8. True. All text and graphics on Web pages must be downloaded to the user's computer.

9. (a) binary; (b) ASCII; (c) binary; (d) binary.

Chapter 4

1. Yes. Customer service and technical support.

2. Multimedia makes the Web a unique marketing medium, where customers can interactively experience products and services.

3. The All-Rite travel site could be updated more frequently with special offers than could their brochures, with more appeal than direct mailings.

4. It can sit dormant and unchanged for weeks or months.

5. A Web page or site that acts as a front end for data processing.

6. The next logical medium for publication.

7. HTML 2.0.

8. Tables (also frames and text/graphics alignment).

Chapter 5

1. False.

2. Web server software and a high-speed Internet connection.

3. Kbps is thousands of bits per second. Mbps is millions of bits per second.

4. Call your local phone company.

5. Throughput is the average amount of information per user multiplied by the number of users. ISPs charge for throughput to discourage one site from monopolizing the ISP's Internet connections.

6. Eight characters with a three-character extension (8.3).

7. The hybrid systems uses separate directories for items that appear once (e.g., documents and files specific to a particular Web page), while commonly-accessed files are kept in their own directories (e.g., "logos").

8. A graphics file; most likely a photo of a person. This graphic might be linked to the About the Company page on a Web site.

9. `Put`. Uploading means sending the file.

Chapter 6

1. No. You can use a simple text editor or word processing program.

2. HTML files are saved in the ASCII text file format. The extension should be `.html` or `.htm`.

3. `<HTML>`, `<HEAD>`, and `<BODY>`.

4. `<TITLE>`.

5. Save it with a new file name and HTML extension.

6. Container tags have two parts, the "on" and "off" tags, and containers act on a specific block of text. Empty tags appear once and perform some function on their own.

7. <HR> (also <BR>).

8. The "on" and "off" tags aren't identical except for a forward slash (/).

9. True.

10. <P> is a container that defines a section of text;
 is an empty tag that forces a line return.

Chapter 7

1. Explicit is also known as physical styles; implicit is also known as logical styles.

2. Implicit tags let the browser choose the formatting; explicit tags let the designer choose.

3. Because it gives the browser no choice in how to render the affected text.

4. No, <I> will not work in a text browser. Yes, <EM> will.

5. <VAR>.

6. For internal documentation when your HTML document explains computer-related issues.

7. Yes.

8. The <P> paragraph tag.

9. Yes.

Chapter 8

1. The list type container tag (<OL>) and the list item empty tag (<LI>).

2. A bullet point (and a return).

3. No.

4. Directory list.

5. Yes.

6. It can accept two different list item tags, <DT> and <DD>.

7. No.

8. No.

9. No. The concept comes from computer programming and works with many HTML tags.

10. B.

11. An unordered list (<UL>) nested within an ordered list (<OL>).

Chapter 9

1. The file size of the graphic.

2. True.

3. GIF and JPEG. Yes, but many browsers will require helper applications to view other graphics formats.

4. When compressed, the graphic file loses image quality.

5. Create the graphic. Download public-domain graphics. Use scanned photographs. Use graphics created by a digital camera. Use PhotoCDs.

6. Around 20 kilobytes.

7. Small images that are linked to a larger version of the same image that users can view if interested.

8. The GIF89a format.

9. An attribute.

10. It displays text in browsers that can't view the image file.

11. False.

12. It's the default value.

Chapter 10

1. An attribute.

2. No.

3. A section link. It's going to access another section of the same document.

4. Yes.

5. The <BASE> tag establishes the absolute base for relative URLs in your document. It appears between the <HEAD> tags.

6. False. It requires an absolute URL.

7. No. `mailto:` does not require a double-slash (`//`).

8. <REL> and <REV> (also <HREF>).

9. No.

10. Ask the Web server administrator.

Chapter 11

1. False.

2. Yes, to emphasize the text used for the hypertext link.

3. <U> (underline).

4. No.

5. Yes. It accesses the section `parttwo` in the local document `chapter1.html`.

6. This is an anchor for a clickable graphic thumbnail. It is legal.

7. Yes, but it might not display automatically in the browser window or helper application.

Chapter 12

1. Because these images are "mapped" into different sections that act as hyperlinks.

2. Create the graphic, map it for hot zones, and place the correct information on the Web server.

3. ASCII text.

4. Yes. You need to know if your map definition file should be in CERN or NSCA format.

5. Ask your Web server administrator.

6. Two. 100.

7. True. The map editing program is just designed to create the map definition file, which you could conceivably create in a text editor.

8. The graphic file and the map definition file.

9. No. The shapes are drawn to determine the coordinates of shapes for the map definition file. The map editing program doesn't alter the image file in any way.

10. Any click that doesn't occur in another shape will be evaluated by the server as "close" to the point, and the default will never be accessed.

11. The coordinates of the mouse pointer when clicked. The design adds the ISMAP attribute to the <IMG> tag.

Chapter 13

1. GET and POST. POST is used most often.

2. The URL to a form-processing script.

3. <TEXTAREA> is used for free-form entry. The user enters data with the keyboard.

4. The default text for the textarea.

5. An attribute.

6. Checkboxes work independently of one another; radio buttons allow one selection among a number of choices.

7. Use the attribute CHECKED.

8. With a Submit button (TYPE="SUBMIT"). When the user clicks this button, the data is sent.

9. A pop-up menu.

10. It displays as a scrolling menu.

11. Use the attribute SELECTED.

Chapter 14

1. <P> is designed as a container, not a line-return tag. <P> also adds varying levels of space in different browsers.

2. Yes. Yes.

3. A series of form elements that logically belong together (e.g., name and address).

4. Extra spacing. Multiple <BR> tags don't render consistently in different browsers.

5. Don't use the <BR> tag between them.

6. It doesn't allow the user to enter more than the defined number of characters. It's errorchecking for elements like phone numbers or ZIP codes that should always be a certain number of characters.

7. It allows you to align elements using a monospaced font. You "lose" the use of the browser's paragraph font (all descriptive text between <PRE> tags is rendered in the monospaced font).

8. The <DL> list never uses bullet points or numbers for list items. A <UL> list would display bullets.

9. The <OL> list is used to number form elements.

10. The POST method is more powerful, because it allows for more data to be transferred. The GET method is a bit easier to use.

11. Most scripts can use a standard print command to "standard out" for HTML output. The Web browser acts like a terminal console.

Chapter 15

1. Because most current browsers don't support the full specification.

2. Yes.

3. Inches.

4. CELLPADDING is the distance between the cell walls and the cell's contents. CELLSPACING is the distance between the walls of the table and the individual cells.

5. False. The default (when no value is assigned) is a one pixel border.

6. At the top of the table.

7. Yes.

8. This creates one cell with three lines of text. (Each name appears below the previous name within a stretched cell.)

9. ALIGN.

10. If that particular cell needs special alignment (e.g., dollar amounts).

Chapter 16

1. LEFT and RIGHT.

2. True (aside from LEFT and RIGHT, which align the figure relative to the browser window).

3. Inline.

4. Multipurpose Internet Mail Extensions. The styles used for <INSERT> are not all official MIME types, so we call them MIME-style.

5. It's used when the browser is unable to display the <INSERT> tag's multimedia file.

6. This chapter doesn't include a table of values for NAME and VALUE because different multimedia file formats will use these attributes for different reasons. The best place to find these values is from the company or organization that created the multimedia file format.

7. Yes. <PARAM> is only used when you want to pass a parameter to the multimedia file. If the file doesn't require a special parameter, there's no reason to use the <PARAM> tag.

8. It reserves those functions for HTML 3.0 level style sheets.

9. Light, between tan and gray. HTML 3.0 doesn't let you control font colors, and most browsers default to black text. Dark backgrounds will make pages difficult to read.

Chapter 17

1. A client-side image map doesn't require a special map server program on the Web server.

2. No. The <MAP> tag is used to define the map.

3. Not all browsers support client-side maps, so including support for both types of image map reaches the widest possible audience.

4. True.

5. USEMAP. <MAP>.

6. Rectangle (RECT), circle (CIRCLE), and polygon (POLYGON).

7. The client-side map specification includes support for ALT hypertext links for text-only browsers. The browsers must be updated to recognize this standard, so that the ALT text is rendered.

8. When users with browsers that don't support client-side image maps click an image map, they can be taken to a page that explains this problem and/or gives them an alternative way to access the links on your site.

Chapter 18

1. Shorthand references for HTML tags.

2. Parentheses.

3. False. They are used to represent math formulas.

4. The integration symbol.

5. ẽ.

6. No. <BANNER> is used to fix a portion of the HTML document at the top of the browser window, so that subsequent text scrolls under it.

7. Style sheets are for specific control over the layout and appearance of a Web page. Up until the style sheet specification, the HTML standard gave the browser program more control over page layout than it gave the designer.

8. Cascading Style Sheets standard. It's a specific definition of the different layout and appearance options you have for your Web page. CSS is only one possible definition for HTML style sheets.

9. Classes are defined as extensions to HTML tags in the <STYLE> container (usually in the head of a tag). Classes are implemented using the attribute CLASS= to a given mark-up tag.

10. <SPAN> does nothing on its own; it has to be defined. <DIV> is a similar tag in that it does no specific formatting, but can be used for limited layout functions (like alignment).

11. The background will be a blend from white to blue.

12. It allows you to incorporate a common style sheet for a number of pages.

13. <CENTER>.

Chapter 19

1. <DIV ALIGN="CENTER">.

2. The values for red, green, and blue. This is the hexadecimal numbering system.

3. It sets the color of an active hypertext link.

4. <BLINK>.

5. No. No, <WBR> suggests to Netscape where it's possible to break a word or line;
 forces a break when inserted.

6. False. <BASEFONT> changes all paragraph fonts, but text in header tags (e.g., <H3>) is unaffected.

7. No, a plus or minus sign is not required.

8. False. It accepts no values.

9. Yes.

10. VPSACE and HSPACE.

11. ALIGN creates a floating image when used with the values LEFT or RIGHT.

Chapter 20

1. It actually replaces the <BODY> tag.

2. True.

3. The page has two columns; one column is 25 percent of the screen and uninterrupted, while the second column is 75 percent of the screen and divided into two equal rows.

4. auto.

5. Netscape (and compatible browsers) are designed to ignore text between <NOFRAMES> tags. Browsers that don't recognize frames tags will ignore everything but the markup.

6. Don't start the name with an underscore (_).

7. <FORM> and <BASE>.

8. It forces all links on that page to target a particular frame window without requiring you to enter a TARGET attribute for every anchor.

9. False. Magic targets are special commands that can't be performed any other way.

10. They can't directly access the URL for pages in the frames interface and they can't use the Forward and Back buttons in their browser.

Chapter 21

1. BGSOUND is not an attribute for <BODY>; it's a stand-alone tag.

2. An .au or .wav sound sample or a MIDI format file.

3. Three hexadecimal numbers for red, green, and blue values.

4. As often as desired.

5. It determines how many times the sound will play.

6. It works with <TABLE>, <TR>, and <TD>.

7. <INSERT>.

8. Using the START="MOUSEOVER" attribute to an <IMG DYNSRC> tag allows the video clip to start by pointing the mouse at it.

Chapter 22

1. <APPLET>.

2. Yes.

3. The <PARAM> tag sends any parameters required by the Java program to the applet when it's started.

4. LANGUAGE.

5. A method.

6. It comes from the function call in the body of the document.

7. The end of the comment tag should have // in front of it to keep from confusing some browsers, as in:

```
// -->
```

8. An event handler allows JavaScript to react to an event, which can be defined as any action by the user.

9. False. It could be named nearly anything.

10. this.form.city.value (also document.form.city.value).

11. It's the opposite of focus.

12. *stringname*.length.

Chapter 23

1. `player2.at_bats = 25.`
2. A method.
3. The name assigned to the object by the keyword `new`.
4. False.
5. The second is an assignment. Assignments always evaluate to true.
6. The script simply moves on to the next statement.
7. 1.
8. 6.
9. You can use the plus sign (+) to concatenate strings.
10. *stringname*`.link`.

Chapter 24

1. The use of a binary file format.
2. `x-world/x-vrml, .wrl.`
3. VRML is a different format from HTML and it's very important to get the header and file format correct for VRML worlds.
4. PI and .5PI.
5. Yes. Cube has a default value of one meter for each dimension.
6. Cylinder.
7. False. It will begin at `x=0`.
8. `scaleFactor.`
9. It will be flipped upside-down.
10. True.

Chapter 25

1. The second entry is darker. (As a value approaches 1, it becomes more intense.)
2. Red.

3. REPEAT tiles an entire object with a texture, while CLAMP forces only one copy of the tile graphic on an object. REPEAT is the default, so you only have to type CLAMP when that's the effect you want.

4. It's best to use absolute URLs for VRML worlds in general because many VRML browsers download to file to the user's computer first, making relative URLs ineffective.

5. Separator.

6. There isn't much point in having a Material statement as part of the WWWAnchor node, since an anchor doesn't create a visible object. WWWAnchor nodes should enclose other separator nodes that create visible objects.

7. To indicate the end of a series of point numbers that defines one "side" of a shape.

8. 2.

9. True.

10. Inside of the sphere, at the center (until you move within the VRML browser).

Chapter 26

1. True.

2. Yes.

3. Acrobat.

4. They are generally downloaded and handed over to a helper application.

5. MS Word for Windows 2.0 or above.

6. RTF files maintain a minimal level of formatting (like font sizes and alignment), while ASCII maintains no formatting beyond basic characters, spaces, and returns.

Chapter 27

1. Yes.

2. A word processing program.

3. ASCII text. Yes, any text editor or word processor.

4. True. It creates an Unordered List.

5. Properties, Text. (Then choose the Paragraph tab.)

6. Description Lists.

7. No. Hit Shift+Return for <BR>.

8. Once your HTML documents are on the Web server, their path statements might need to be slightly different than they were on your PC. Browse creates PC-style relative links that may not be appropriate for your site.

9. By default, instead of creating a relative link, Gold copies the graphic to the current directory.

10. No. You need to use the Document Properties dialog box.

Chapter 28

1. No, it's an add-on for Microsoft Word. It can be downloaded free from **http://www.microsoft.com/**.

2. Yes.

3. ASCII text. Yes you can, in any text editor or word processor.

4. True.

5. Select OL from the pull-down menu in the button bar.

6. In 1.0, a tab between the term and definition automatically formats the list. In 2.0, you need to format each term and definition individually.

7. False. When using the HTML template, use the HTML file type for saving, so that Windows correctly recognizes the file and it's given the correct extension.

8. A section link, e.g., <A NAME="*name*">.

9. You enter the bookmark link first, and then create the calling link.

10. The Submit button. SUBMIT and METHOD can be set in the Submit Button Form Field dialog box.

Chapter 29

1. No, you can also use command-key shortcuts for many HTML tags.

2. Use the <P> tag to get back to regular text.

3. Since you need to assign every definition item individually, this saves about half the work.

4. There is no menu command. Press the \<HR> button in the button bar.

5. Yes.

6. PICT files are automatically converted to GIF files.

7. The "magic wand."

8. Use the shape tool to create hotzones and enter corresponding URLs. Select the entire graphic and define a default URL. Return to the editor window, select the graphic, and change the graphic to a map using the Attributes Inspector.

9. Regular text and HTML tags (like we've used throughout the book). If you don't use a special command, PageMill assumes your HTML markup is just text, not actual tags.

10. Through the document button in the Attribute Inspector.

Index

Index

Index

comment tags, 92-94
Common Ground Digital
    Paper, portable
    documents, 425-426
community groups, sites,
    creating, 58
comp (Computing)
    newsgroups, 34
comparison operators,
    JavaScript, 367-368
CompuServe file format, 30
conditions, JavaScript,
    367-368, 372-373
cones, VRML, creating, 392
connections
    Internet, 73-75
        bps (bits per second),
        73-76
        secure connections,
        64-65
    ISDN (Integrated Services
        Digital Network), 74
    modems, speed, 73
    servers, tracking, 72
    T-1 line, 74
container tags, 89
CONTENT attribute, 309
CONTENT_LENGTH variable,
    233
CONTINUE loop statements,
    JavaScript, 370-371
CONTROLS attribute, 337
Coordinate3 node, VRML,
    410-411
coordinates, VRML, 389
copyrights, 64
corporate Web sites, 26-29,
    58
cosine method, JavaScript,
    379
cost considerations, ISPs,
    75-76
cost issues, WWW, 64
counters, adding, forms, 231

covering, VRML primitives,
    407
cubes, VRML, creating,
    394-395
custom controls, graphical
    links, adding, 176
cylinders, VRML, creating,
    392

D

DATA attribute, 257-258
<DD> tag, 120-122, 170
<DDOT> tag, 282-283
declaring functions,
    JavaScript, 350
decrements, JavaScript,
    371-372
default hot zones, 187
default pages, 26
default URLs, 76
defining, hot zones, 188-191
definition lists
    creating, 120-122, 155-156
        Internet Assistant, 451
        Netscape Gold, 439
        PageMill, 466-467
    nesting, 126-128
designing
    clickable image maps,
    194-195
    forms, 215-216
<DFN> tag, 105
digital cameras, 136
<DIR> tag, 119-120
directory by file type sites, 78
directory by function sites, 77
directory lists, creating,
    119-120
disadvantages, WWW, 63-65
distances, VRML, 389
<DIV> tag, 291
<DL> tag, 120-122, 170,
    227-230

document tags, 86-88
document-defined style
    sheets, 284-289
    cascading style sheets,
    285-289
    divisions, 291
    external style sheets,
    289-293
    incorporating, 288-289
    style overrides, 290
    tags, 289-293
documents, see *pages*
domain names, e-mail, 32
<DOT> tag, 282-283
downloading
    graphical sites, 132
    public-domain graphics,
    136
<DT> tag, 120-122, 146, 170
DYNSRC attribute, 337

E

e to power of number method,
    JavaScript, 379
e-mail, 31-33, 160-161
editing
    forms, 222-225
    head elements, Internet
        Assistant, 456
    Netscape Gold, 434-440
.edu (Educational) domains,
    32
<EM> tag, 89, 168
Emacs text editor, 85
embedding graphics, pages,
    144-150
emphasis tags, links, 168
empty tags, 89-90
entering paragraph text,
    pages, 90-94
Envoy, portable documents,
    425-426

Index

HTML, 504-505
hyperlinks, creating, 162
ftp:// protocol (URLs), 47
functions, JavaScript,
    349-352
  calling, 350-351
  declaring, 350
  objects (methods), 364

G

GET method, CGI-BIN scripts,
    233-234
GIF (Graphics Interchange
    Format), 133-134,
    142-144, 256
Gold Editor, see *Netscape
    Gold*
Gopher, 34-35, 161
gopher:// protocol (URLs), 47
.gov (Governmental)
    domains, 32
graphical indexes, 491-493
graphical links, 167
  clickable graphic menu
    bars, creating, 174-176
  creating, 172-176
  custom controls, adding,
    176
graphics, 52-53, 131
  background graphics,
    259-262
  clickable image maps,
    183-184
    creating, 185-187
    designing, 194-195
    hot zones, 187-191
    map definition files,
      186-187
    MapEdit, 188-189
    testing links, 193-194
    URLs, 192-193
  colors, managing, 139

controlling, 251-254
creating, 135-142
  LView Pro, 140-142
  Paint Shop Pro, 136-138
digital cameras, 136
embedding, 144-150
enhanced graphics pages,
  creating, 260-263
GIFs, creating tansparent,
  142-144
inline graphics, 253
inserting
  Internet Assistant,
    455-456
  Netscape Gold, 442-443
  Pagemill, 469
manipulating, 135-142, 470
PhotoCDs, 136
public-domain graphics,
  downloading, 136
scanned photographs, 136
sites, downloads, 132
size, controlling, 139
tags, adding to, 145-146
thumbnail graphics,
  creating, 140
WWW, 131-135
graphics applications, 136
  LView Pro, 140-142
  Paint Shop Pro, 136-138
graphics files, 133-135
  GIF (Graphics Interchange
    Format), 133-134
  JPEG (Joint Photographers
    Expert Group), 134-135
  PNG (Portable Network
    Graphic), 134
  size, 132-135
greater of two numbers
    method, JavaScript, 379
greatest int <= number
    method, JavaScript, 379

H

<H1> tag, 98
<H2> tag, 98
<H3> tag, 98
<H4> tag, 98
<H5> tag, 98
<H6> tag, 98
handlers, events, 355
handling events, JavaScript,
    352-359
<HAT> tag, 282-283
head elements, editing,
    Internet Assistant, 456
<HEAD> tag, 86, 163-164
headers, creating, 97-100
headlines, creating, 97-100
heads, editing, Netscape
    Gold, 443
HEIGHT attribute, 257-258
Hello World Web document,
    creating, 88
Help pages, creating,
    506-509
helper applications, 29
HIDDEN attribute, 206
hiding code, JavaScript, 348
history
  HTML, 13
  VRML, 386-387
  WWW, 23-28
hit counters, adding, 231
hits, servers, 72
hobbies, sites, creating, 58
home pages, creating, 94
horizontal lines
  forms, 217-219
  inserting, PageMill, 467-468
host servers, 32-33
hot zones
  clickable image maps, 183,
    267-268
  client-side image maps,
    shapes, 269-270

Index

Index

Index

Index

O

objects, JavaScript, 363-367
  built-in objects, 374-381
  creating, 364-367
  math object, 378-379
  methods, 364
  string objects, 374-376
off tags (container tags), 89
<OL> tag, 116-118, 227-230
OLE files, 256
on tags (container tags), 89
order forms, creating,
  211-213
ordered lists, creating,
  116-118
.org (Organizational)
  domains, 32
organizations, sites, 18
organizing sites, 77-81
output, scripts, 233-234
<OVER> tag, 280-281
overrides, style, style sheets,
  290

P

<P> tag, 90-94, 220-221
PageMill, 463
  Attribute Inspector,
    475-476
  definition lists, creating,
    466-467
  forms, creating, 473-475
  graphics, adding, 469-470
  horizontal lines, inserting,
    467-468
  HTML, unsupported, 472
  hyperlinks, adding,
    468-469
  keyboard shortcuts, tags,
    464
  lists, creating, 465-466
  pages, creating, 472

pages, 25-26
  About pages, 494-495
  accessing, 49
  binary documents, 52-53
  bookmark links, adding with
    Internet Assistant, 455
  business pages, creating,
    486-487
  clickable image maps,
    adding, 191-194
  client-side image maps,
    adding, 268-271
  control, 421
  creating, 94
    Netscape Gold, 436-437
    PageMill, 472
    reasons, 57-59
  document-defined style
    sheets, 284-289
    cascading style sheets,
      285-289
    divisions, 291
    external style sheets,
      289-293
    style overrides, 290
    tags, 289-293
  document-defined style
    sheets, 288-289
  downloading, 53
  enhanced graphics pages,
    creating, 260-263
  front door pages, 490-491
  graphical indexes, 491-493
  graphics
    background graphics,
      259-262
    controlling, 251-254
    creating, 135-142
    downloading, 132
    embedding, 144-150
    Internet Assistant, 455
    manipulating, 135-142
    Netscape Gold, 442-443

  PageMill, 469
    size, 135
  headers, creating, 97-100
  headlines, creating, 97-100
  heads, editing with
    Netscape Gold, 443
  hyperlinks
    Netscape Gold, 441-442
    PageMill, 468-469
  hypermedia links, 28-31
  hypertext links, adding, 455
  Java applets, adding to,
    344-347
  links, Internet services,
    160-162
  multimedia objects,
    inserting, 255-259
  paragraph text, entering,
    90-94
  personal biography page,
    creating, 484-486
  personal index page,
    creating, 482-483
  portable documents,
    adding to, 423-426
  publishing tools, 85-86
  requirements, 71
  resumes, creating, 488-490
  saving, Internet Assistant,
    452
  scrolling down, 25
  sources, viewing, 93-94
  spaces, creating, 110-112
  tables
    captions, 243-244
    creating, 110-112,
      239-240
    data, 245-250
    rows, 244-250
Paint Shop Pro, graphics,
  creating, 136-138
paragraphs, forms, 220-221
<PARAM> tag, 258-259

PASSWORD attribute, 205
personal biography page,
	creating, 484-486
personal index page,
	creating, 482-483
personal sites, creating, 59
Pete's Easy VRML Tutorial
	site, 418
PhotoCDs, 136
photographs, scanning, 136
PHYSICAL attribute, 203
physical tags, see *explicit
	tags*
Pioneer Joel Web site, 418
PNG (Portable Network
	Graphic) files, 134
point hot zones, 187
poly (polygon) hot zones, 187
POLYGON hot zones,
	client-side image maps,
	270
pop-up menus, forms,
	209-213
portable documents, 421-422
	creating, 426-429
	features, 424-425
	formats, 425-426
	MIME types, 424
	RTF (Rich Text Format),
	427-429
	sites, adding to, 423-426
POST method, CGI-BIN
	scripts, 233-234
PostScript file formats, 30
<PRE> tag, 107-112, 168,
	226-227
preformatted text, 107-112
primitives (VRML), 391-397,
	410-417
	spheres, 392
	appearances, 403-407
	ASCII text, 395-396
	color, adding, 404-405

cones, 392
covering, 407
creating, 410-417
cubes, 394-395
cylinders, 392
flipping, 399-400
moving, 397-400
rooftop primitives, 411-413
rotation property, 398-399
same space, 396-397
scaleFactor property, 399
translation property, 398
programming, HTML, 12
programming tags, 104-105
programs, JavaScript,
	creating, 347-349
properties
	cascading style sheets, 287
	objects, JavaScript,
	363-367
protocols, URLs, 47
public-domain graphics,
	downloading, 136
publisher tags, 105
publishing tools, text editors,
	85-86
publishing tools (Web), 85-86

Q-R

Que Corporation site, 22
QuickTime file formats, 30,
	256

radians, 389
RADIO attribute, 205-206
Real files, 256
RealAudio file format, 30
rec (Recreational)
	newsgroups, 34
rect (rectangle) hot zones,
	187, 270
REFRESH attribute, 309
relative URLs, 156-159

REQUEST_METHOD variable,
	233
requirements, sites, 71
RESET attribute, 206-207
resumes, creating, 488-490
returning values, JavaScript
	events, 353-355
RIGHT value, ALIGN attribute,
	251
rooftop primitive, creating,
	VRML, 411-413
rotation property, VRML,
	398-399
round to nearest int method,
	JavaScript, 379
rows, tables, 244-250
ROWSPAN attribute, 245
RTF (Rich Text Format),
	portable documents,
	427-429

S

<SAMP> tag, 104
saving documents, Internet
	Assistant, 452
scaleFactor property, VRML,
	399
scanning photographs, 136
sci (Scientific) newsgroups,
	34
<SCRIPT> tag, 347-348
scripts, output, 233-234
SCROLLING attribute,
	318-319
scrolling down pages, 25
scrolling menus, creating,
	forms, 209-213
searches, WWW, 59-60
section links, 154-155
secure connections, Internet,
	64-65
security, WWW, 64
select event, JavaScript, 356

Index

Index

Index

Check out Que® Books
on the World Wide Web
http://www.mcp.com/que

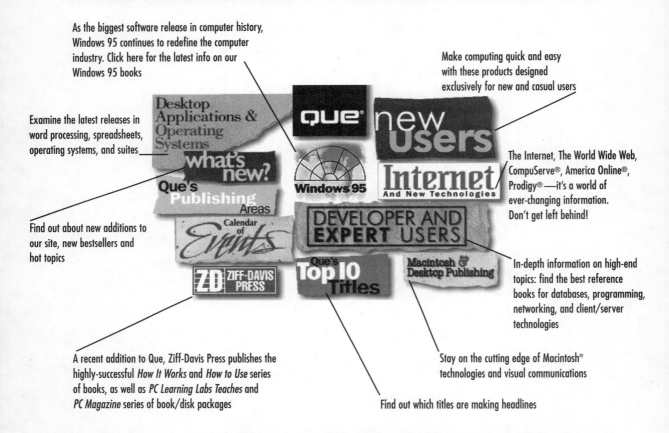

As the biggest software release in computer history, Windows 95 continues to redefine the computer industry. Click here for the latest info on our Windows 95 books

Make computing quick and easy with these products designed exclusively for new and casual users

Examine the latest releases in word processing, spreadsheets, operating systems, and suites

The Internet, The World Wide Web, CompuServe®, America Online®, Prodigy® —it's a world of ever-changing information. Don't get left behind!

Find out about new additions to our site, new bestsellers and hot topics

In-depth information on high-end topics: find the best reference books for databases, programming, networking, and client/server technologies

A recent addition to Que, Ziff-Davis Press publishes the highly-successful *How It Works* and *How to Use* series of books, as well as *PC Learning Labs Teaches* and *PC Magazine* series of book/disk packages

Stay on the cutting edge of Macintosh® technologies and visual communications

Find out which titles are making headlines

With 6 separate publishing groups, Que develops products for many specific market segments and areas of computer technology. Explore our Web Site and you'll find information on best-selling titles, newly published titles, upcoming products, authors, and much more.

- Stay informed on the latest industry trends and products available

- Visit our online bookstore for the latest information and editions

- Download software from Que's library of the best shareware and freeware

Licensing Agreement

By opening this package, you are agreeing to be bound by the following: